THE BRAVE AND THE FAITHFUL

CELEBRATING FIFTEEN YEARS OF MUNSTER RUGBY 2010–2025

IVAN O'RIORDAN

FOREWORD BY PAUL O'CONNELL

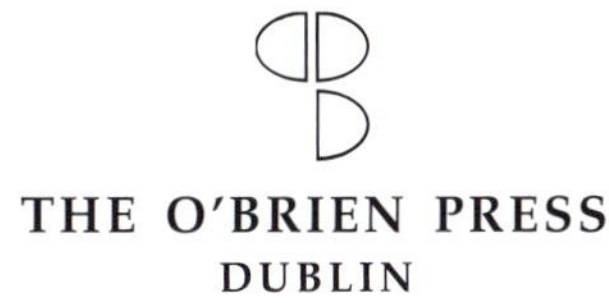

THE O'BRIEN PRESS
DUBLIN

CONTENTS

ACKNOWLEDGEMENTS

This book was made possible by the kindness and generosity of many people. In 2012, Donn O'Sullivan, then editor of the *Limerick Post*, granted me a press pass. This enabled me to get accreditation at Munster away matches at such venues as Stade de France in Paris, Stade Vélodrome in Marseille, Sandy Park in Exeter, Stadium MK in Milton Keynes, Murrayfield in Edinburgh, The Sportsground (now Dexcom Stadium) in Galway and Ravenhill (now Kingspan) Stadium in Belfast. A huge thank-you goes to Donn for this gesture. Thanks also to Dave Kavanagh, Munster Rugby's head of Marketing & Communications, for encouraging me to pursue this project. A mention of thanks also to Sean Geary of Munster Rugby for granting me pitch-side accreditation at Thomond Park from 2022–2023 to 2024–2025, and to Denis Kelleher, former chairman of the Munster Rugby Supporters Club photographers' group, who also enabled me to be pitch-side for a number of games a season. I am also most grateful to the late Pat Geraghty (Munster PRO) for plucking me out of the West Terrace on occasion and offering me a photographer's vest.

Thank you to the Munster squad, coaches and management for giving me time, and especially to team manager Niall O'Donovan for organising the squad to autograph exhibition photos, and to Paul O'Connell for the foreword.

I must mention my friend Ivan Morris, the author of several successful golf books, and Denis Ryan, a fellow member of Limerick Camera Club, for their excellent advice, and my good friends Mick O'Malley, Des O'Sullivan and Paschal O'Flaherty for their encouragement. A huge thank-you to Brian Whelan of Bermingham Cameras Dublin, who kindly lent me camera equipment from time to time.

A number of photographers generously submitted additional photographs for this book: my thanks to INPHO for providing photos taken during the restricted Covid period; to James Crombie/INPHO, for allowing me to use two photos from the URC Championship win in Cape Town; and to Nicol du Toit, a member of Cape Town Photographic Society, for the photo from the 2024–2025 season's match between Stormers and Munster. Denis Kelleher supplied the 2011 Magners League celebration shot. Thanks to Joe Buckley for the photo of me with Paul O'Connell, to John Hickey for editing the collage of Simon Zebo and to Denis Ryan for editing the collage of Mike Haley.

A big thank-you goes to Frank O'Mahony of O'Mahony's, Limerick's leading bookseller, for making The O'Brien Press aware of my photography. I couldn't have done this without the wonderful team at The O'Brien Press and my thanks go to my hardworking editor Paula Elmore (herself a Munster fan), proofreader Eoin O'Brien and Emma Byrne for her design.

In 2012, Paul O'Connell kindly opened an exhibition of my photographs, which raised €6,000 for charities

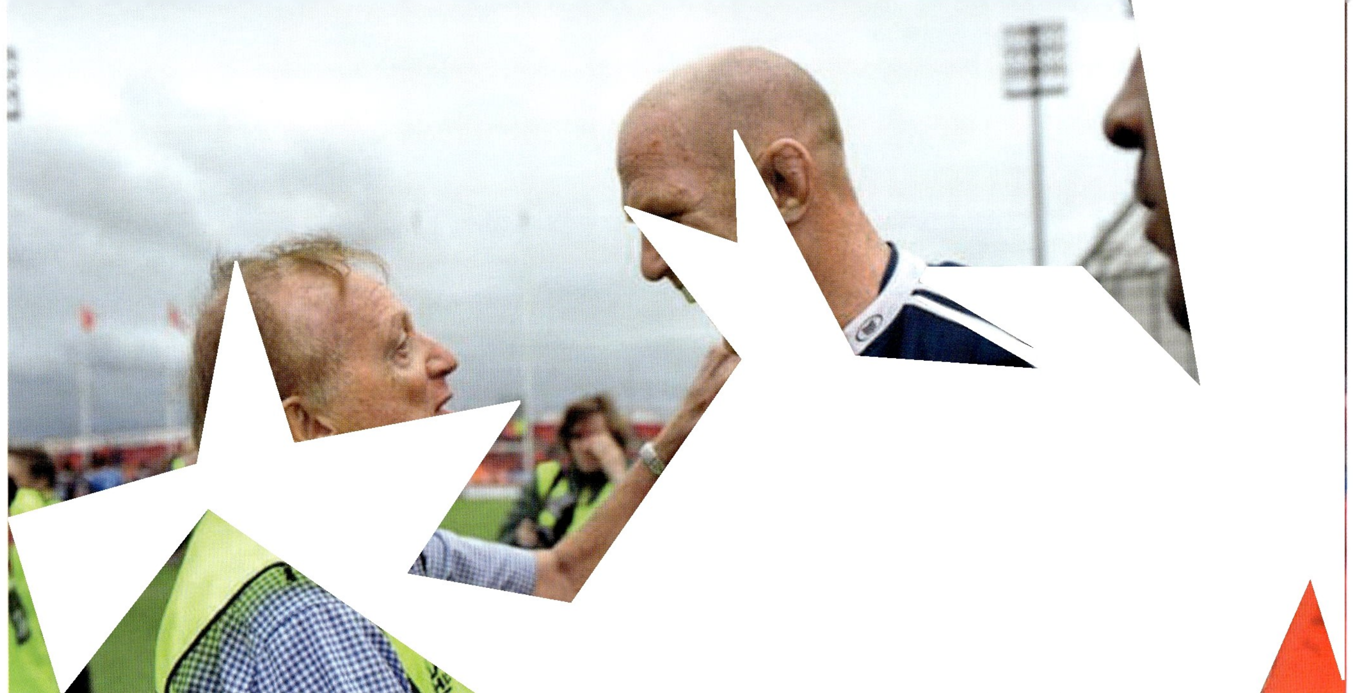

The author with Paul O'Connell on 23 May 2015. Ivan discharged himself from ICU to see the great Paulie play his last game in the red shirt of Munster in Thomond Park.

nominated by Munster Rugby. This figure increased to over €17,000 in subsequent years. Royalties from this book and a photo exhibition in 2025 will be donated to Munster Rugby's nominated charities.

And last, but by no means least, I owe a debt of gratitude to my wife, Annemarie, who uncomplainingly put up with my absences while I was writing the book.

Ivan O'Riordan
2025

Several sponsors kindly donated funds towards the photo exhibition that coincides with the publication of this book: Irish Wire Products Ltd, Limerick; Freefoam Building Products Ltd, Cork; Gerard Boland, Limerick; Brian Whelan, Bermingham Cameras Dublin; and Wolf & Wendy, Wicklow.

AUTHOR'S NOTE

Munster are involved in two rugby championships:

- the **United Rugby Championship** (URC): comprising teams from Ireland, Scotland and Wales, the URC began as the Celtic League (Magners League in 2010–2011), becoming the Pro12 (2011 to 2017) and then the Pro14 (2017 to 2021). Teams from South Africa have been included since the Pro14.
- The **European Rugby Champions Cup** (also known, by reason of sponsorship, as the Investec Champions Cup and previously as the Heineken Cup), the top-tier competition for European clubs, including teams from France and England, as well as the top URC clubs.

FOREWORD

I once heard an interview with Eamonn Cregan, the great limerick hurler and coach of the Offaly team that won the 1996 All-Ireland final. He was asked if he had any regrets from his career and he mentioned something I had never heard a player say before: he said he would have liked to have more photos from his playing days. It immediately made sense to me. Many of my memories from big games are crystalised by video footage or photos taken on the day. I can see Axel Foley lifting the Heineken Cup trophy from the view of the photographer and not the view I had from behind him. I can see Ronan O'Gara dropping the goal against Wales in 2009 to win the Grand Slam as if I am watching on TV and not to the side of him, trying to get out of his way.

I love seeing old photos. The memories of all that went on around that moment come flooding back. It's not something we – or I – do enough of any more: printing photos and putting them in one place to allow ourselves to be taken back to that time. That is why this book by Ivan is such a lovely collector's item.

It was always great seeing Ivan on the sideline of big games, knowing that, in time, I would be handed an envelope with some lovely shots capturing some of the big moments. I especially loved getting photos of us celebrating a moment together. Ivan was and continues to be very generous with his photos, giving them to players and donating them to charity. Indeed, the royalties from this book will be donated to Munster Rugby's nominated charities.

I'm sure you will enjoy Ivan's skill in capturing so many famous moments but also the memories they rekindle.

Paul O'Connell
2025

INTRODUCTION

This is a book of photos more than words: capturing a moment in time is my forte. These photographs trace the heroics of the Men's Munster Rugby team from 2010 to 2025. Win, lose or draw, the team rarely fails to ignite a fire in the hearts of their ardent supporters, of which I count myself a proud member.

While Limerick has always been my spiritual home, Cork is also close to my heart: at the age of ten, I went to live with my grandparents in Cork and attended Presentation Brothers College there. Pres had a wonderful rugby team at the time. When I was in sixth class, in 1957, my two earliest rugby heroes were Jerry Walsh and Tom Kiernan. They played on the Munster Schools winning team, and both went on to play for Ireland and the British & Irish Lions. My friend Donnacha Kelleher and I helped Bill O'Donovan serve tea and sandwiches to the team after matches. After Pres, it was off to boarding school for six years before returning to Cork again to do a B. Comm. Degree at UCC. After six years locked away, to come back to Cork during the Swinging Sixties was utopia.

It was my grandfather Fonsie Roche who honed my great interest in sport. Whether it was watching Cork Athletic FC play at the Mardyke on alternate Sundays, rugby at Musgrave Park or cricket in season, we watched them all and, of course, followed the Pres team. On wet weekends, I'd be glued to the commentary on a Philips radio, which also developed my sporting imagination. As a sports-mad youngster,

I always took a keen interest in the black-and-white sports photos in newspapers and magazines, especially *Charles Buchan's Football Monthly*.

Incredibly (or so it seems to me), it wasn't until I turned sixty that I learnt the skills of photography properly and purchased a 'good' Nikon camera. Over the years I have upgraded my Nikons, but I still only use a 70-200 2.8 VR lens for action. As a keen follower of both rugby and soccer, especially the Men's Munster Rugby team, I began taking photos from the terraces at Thomond Park and the Markets Field. The *Limerick Post* and *Limerick Leader* published some of these shots. Munster Rugby Supporters Club had two slots pitch-side for members to take photos, which enabled each member to be pitch-side for four matches per season.

SUMMARY OF SEASONS FROM 2010 TO 2025

Munster reached the halcyon heights of Heineken Cup wins in 2005–2006 and again in 2007–2008, and their second Celtic League win, in 2008–2009. Expectations were high, and the fifteen years covered in this book began with success. Few, however, predicted the hard road that lay ahead.

In 2011, Munster won the Magners Celtic League final 19-9 at Thomond Park against Leinster, who had won the Heineken Cup against Northampton Saints a week earlier. In the decade following this win, Munster would reach ten semi-finals and three finals but would bring no silverware home.

Under Rob Penney, Munster had a highly creditable

2012–2013 campaign in Europe, reaching the semi-final. The following season, Munster reached the semi-finals in both competitions. When Munster reached the final of the Pro12 in 2015, against Glasgow in Belfast, there was an expectancy of a win in Paul O'Connell's last match, but it wasn't to be. Despite the emotional turmoil of Antony Foley's untimely death in October 2016, Munster won 20 of their next 22 games under Rassie Erasmus, which ended with a semi-final Champions Cup defeat by Saracens at Aviva Stadium and a crushing 46-22 loss to the Scarlets in the Pro12 final at the same stadium four weeks later.

Rassie Erasmus joined Munster in 2016, a clever and charismatic character who was highly popular. His management of the partnership with Antony Foley, who was shifted sideways to accommodate him, was masterful. Erasmus and his assistant Jacques Nienaber made Munster competitive again. Both left prematurely to manage the Springboks.

The big signing for Munster in 2018–2019 was Tadhg Beirne, who had previously played for Leinster and who, with Welsh side Scarlets, had won the Pro12 in 2017. Beirne was named in the 2018–2019 Pro14 Dream Team. Craig Casey, Gavin Coombes and Shane Daly all moved up from the Academy. Among those moving away from the province, Simon Zebo joined Racing 92.

Under Johann van Graan as head coach, Munster reached two Champions Cup semi-finals and three successive Pro14 semi-finals. In the 2021–2022 Champions Cup, Munster's season ended in the quarter-finals, exiting honourably at the Aviva after a thrilling 100-minute draw, before losing a goal-kicking competition against Toulouse.

Graham Rowntree joined Munster in the 2019–2020 season as forwards coach, becoming head coach in 2022 following van Graan's departure. Rowntree was the fifth head coach to attempt to emulate Tony McGahan and Declan Kidney as the only two coaches in the professional era to guide Munster to silverware. After a slow start, Munster began playing a faster game and the handling skills of the forwards improved, with coaches Mike Prendergast and Andi Kyriacou playing a significant part. Under new defence coach Denis Leamy, Munster achieved the best defensive statistics of all the teams in the regular season in the URC, despite a poor start.

Munster had a remarkable five-match away run to the URC victory in 2022–2023. It began in South Africa, where they beat Stormers and drew with Sharks. In Glasgow, Munster met the in-form Warriors, but won a hard-fought victory. Great character was again in evidence in the semi-final against arch-rivals Leinster. Munster engineered a platform for Jack Crowley to drop a match-winning goal in the dying seconds. In the final against the Stormers in Cape Town, Munster overcame the crushing loss of Peter O'Mahony to injury early in the game. A late try from man-of-the-match John Hodnett demonstrated the resolve and will to win that has been part of the DNA of Munster's most successful teams. No wonder the scenes at the final whistle were as raw and emotional as sport can deliver!

Season 2023–2024 was Rowntree's second as head coach. The team performed much more consistently

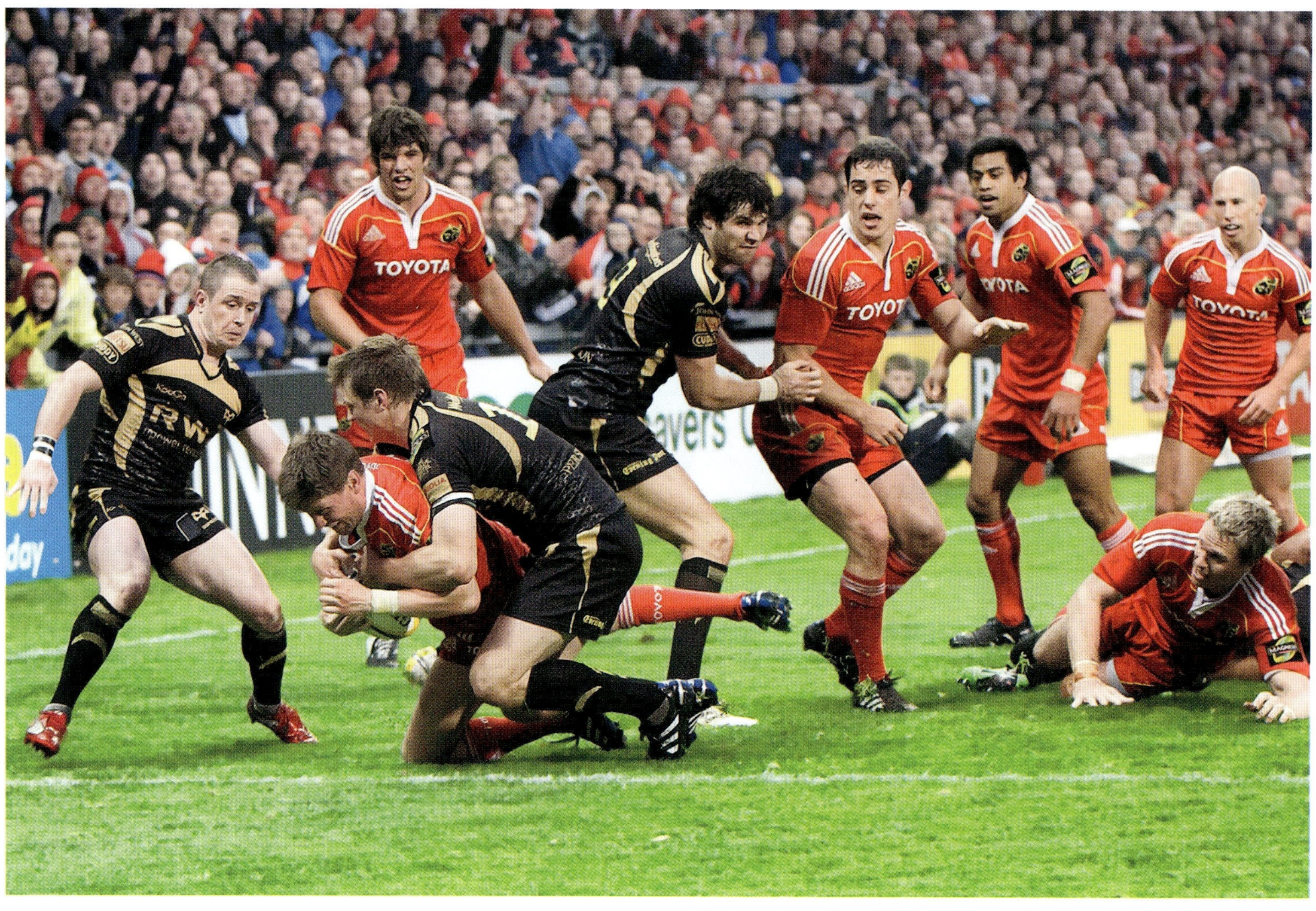

24 April 2010

Ronan O'Gara dives over to score against Ospreys, despite the efforts of Dan Biggar in this Magners Celtic League match in Thomond Park. There are many stars pictured here: (l–r) Shane Williams, ROG, Dan Biggar, Donncha O'Callaghan, Mike Phillips, Tom Gleeson, Lifeimi Mafi, Jean de Villiers and Peter Stringer. Williams played 87 times for Wales; ROG scored over 2,000 points for Munster and made over 200 appearances in addition to 130 caps for Ireland; Donncha O'Callaghan was with Munster for seventeen seasons, earning 268 caps and 94 for Ireland. Biggar was multi-capped for Wales; Mike Phillips won 76 caps for Wales; Mafi played 141 times for Munster and nine times for the All Blacks; de Villiers joined Munster in mid-September 2009 on a one-year contract. He played 23 matches, scoring 43 points. Stringer made 232 appearances for Munster over thirteen years and gained 98 caps for Ireland. Tom Gleeson left Munster at the end of 2011–2012 season to continue his medical studies and is now a doctor practising in Cork. Most of these men also played for the British & Irish Lions. What a collection!

and topped the URC in the pool stages. Munster, however, fell in the semi-final to Glasgow Warriors. They fell to Northampton Saints in the last sixteen in the Champions Cup. It should be mentioned that Munster suffered an inordinate number of injuries, a run of bad luck that continued into 2024–2025. It was an eventful season, both on and off the pitch. Munster performed inconsistently, losing for the first time ever to Zebre Parma, followed by disastrous losses away to the Sharks and Lions in South Africa. Rowntree departed Munster on their return and Mike Prendergast took over as interim head coach. The Bulls became the first South African team to beat Munster at Thomond Park.

Munster clung on in Europe to make the quarter-finals by a stupendous 25-24 away win over Ronan O'Gara's La Rochelle. A scant week later, however, they faced Bordeaux in Stade Chaban-Delmas for the quarter-final and exited the Champions Cup 47-29, with the line-out malfunctioning dismally. A number of factors for the erratic performance include lack of depth in the squad, Rowntree's premature departure and an extensive list of injuries (for the December match against Leinster, twenty of the squad were unavailable due to injury and Jack Crowley was unable to participate due to Irish Rugby protocols). Munster recovered their form for their final three games in the URC, and their season ended most cruelly in a penalty kick-off against Sharks.

On a more positive note, new signings all made positive contributions, including Tom Farrell (named the URC Playmaker for the 2024–2025 season), Diarmuid Kilgallen and Andrew Smith, who all joined from Connacht, the exciting Thaakir Abrahams and front-rower Dian Bleuler.

We said farewell to the retiring Stephen Archer, Dave Kilcoyne and Peter O'Mahony, after illustrious careers, while Conor Murray and Rory Scannell announced their retirements from Munster. Archer achieved a wonderful total of 304 games for Munster. Murray and O'Mahony were invited to play with the Barbarians against the Springboks in June. The match was the first played in South Africa between these two teams, and O'Mahony was given the honour of skippering the Baa-Baas. Team Manager Niall O'Donovan also announced his retirement, having made a huge contribution to Munster as a player, coach and in his latter role since 2012.

The appointment of New Zealander Clayton McMillan as Munster's head coach for the 2025–2026 season created a ripple of excitement. Already familiar with Thomond Park, having coached the All-Blacks XV on their visit in 2024, his achievements include steering the Chiefs to three Super Rugby finals. His reputation is for being tough and uncompromising with his players. Both John Ryan and Alex Nankivell played under him with the Chiefs and spoke highly of him.

Despite the changing of the guard with the retirement of so many legends of the game in 2024–2025, the new crop of players looks promising – Craig Casey, outstanding on and off the pitch, was Ireland captain for the summer 2025 tour, while Tom Ahern, Alex Kendellen and Michael Milne earned their first Ireland caps – and hopes are high once more that greatness lies within Munster's grasp.

2010–2011

Under Tony McGahan, now in his third season as director of rugby, the season began with not-unreasonable expectations. However, it would be the first season Munster failed to qualify for the play-offs of the Heineken Cup. Munster defeated Brive in the quarter-final of the Challenge Cup before losing at home to Harlequins. The Celtic League was another matter: Munster bested Leinster 19-9 in the final.

During the season, Johne Murphy, Sam Tuitupou and Wian du Preez joined Munster while Jeremy Manning moved to Newcastle Falcons and Nick Williams to Aironi in Italy. Jean de Villiers left for Stormers after one year with the province and would go on to represent South Africa in 108 tests, captaining the Springboks 37 times.

CELTIC LEAGUE

Munster finished top of the table with nineteen wins and three defeats in the Magners Celtic League. Leinster were in second place, a total of seven points behind. The semi-final was played in Thomond Park on 14 May 2011, with Munster winning 18-11 against the Ospreys. Danny Barnes scored two tries, the first the result of a neat exchange of passes between Keith Earls, Doug Howlett and Felix Jones. Ronan O'Gara converted one and slotted two penalties out of four. Dan Biggar kept Ospreys in the game with two penalties, and Richard Fussell scored a 78th-minute try.

The Grand Final was played on 28 May 2011 at Thomond Park in front of 26,000 supporters, with Nigel Owens officiating. The opposing team was Leinster, who had just become the European Cup champions. Former All-Black Doug Howlett was put in space by Lifeimi Mafi to enable Howlett to score in the corner for the opening try. In the 66th minute, O'Gara cross-kicked to Earls, who avoided Isa Nacewa's initial tackle to score, despite a despairing tackle from Shane Horgan. The Munster pack, which was excellent all season, drove Leinster back at an alarming rate on more than one occasion and, in the 78th minute, Nigel Owens had no hesitation in awarding a penalty try. Leinster looked tired and managed only three penalty goals from Jonathan Sexton. In the number 7 shirt, David Wallace was awarded man of the match.

This 19-9 victory was Munster's 21st win out of 24 Magners League matches this season and saw them complete an unbeaten thirteen-match run at home over the campaign.

Heineken Cup

On 9 October 2010, Munster played London Irish at the Madejski Stadium, Reading, in front of 20,000 supporters. The visitors' only try came from Sam Tuitupou and Ronan O'Gara converted four penalties as Munster went down 23-17.

Next saw Toulon at Thomond Park on 16 October. With 26,000 supporters in the stadium, Munster had a storming win: Denis Leamy, Tom Buckley, Doug Howlett (with two), Mick O'Driscoll and James Coughlan all scored tries in the 45-18 victory. Ospreys came to Limerick in the next match, on 12 December, again in front of a full house. Doug Howlett, David Wallace and Johne Murphy scored tries, with ROG adding the extras, in a closely fought 22-16 win. It was then off to Swansea for the return match on 18 December. Tony Buckley and Keith Earls scored tries and Ronan O'Gara converted one and scored a penalty. It wasn't enough, however, to stop Ospreys winning 19-15 in another close match.

Toulon were at home to Munster on 16 January 2011. Dave Wallace was Munster's only try-scorer, converted by Ronan O'Gara, who added three penalties. Toulon's 32-16 victory meant that Munster could not progress further in the competition, whatever the result in the final pool match against London Irish, which Munster won 28-14. In that match, on 22 January, all of Munster's tries came in the second half, from Damien Varley six minutes after the restart, and from Niall Ronan, Earls and Darragh Hurley after the seventieth minute.

Amlin Challenge Cup

After elimination from the Heineken Cup, Munster competed in the European Amlin Challenge Cup for the first time. In the quarter-final played on 9 April 2011, Munster faced Brive at the Stade Amédée-Domenech. Doug Howlett and Keith Earls scored two tries each, with one more from Peter Stringer, in a 42-37 away victory. Ronan O'Gara added considerably to the tally with four out of five conversions and three out of three penalties.

Harlequins came to Thomond Park on 30 April 2011 for the semi-final in front of 25,000 faithful fans. Felix Jones and Doug Howlett scored tries and Ronan O'Gara converted one. However, it wasn't enough: Quins won 20-12.

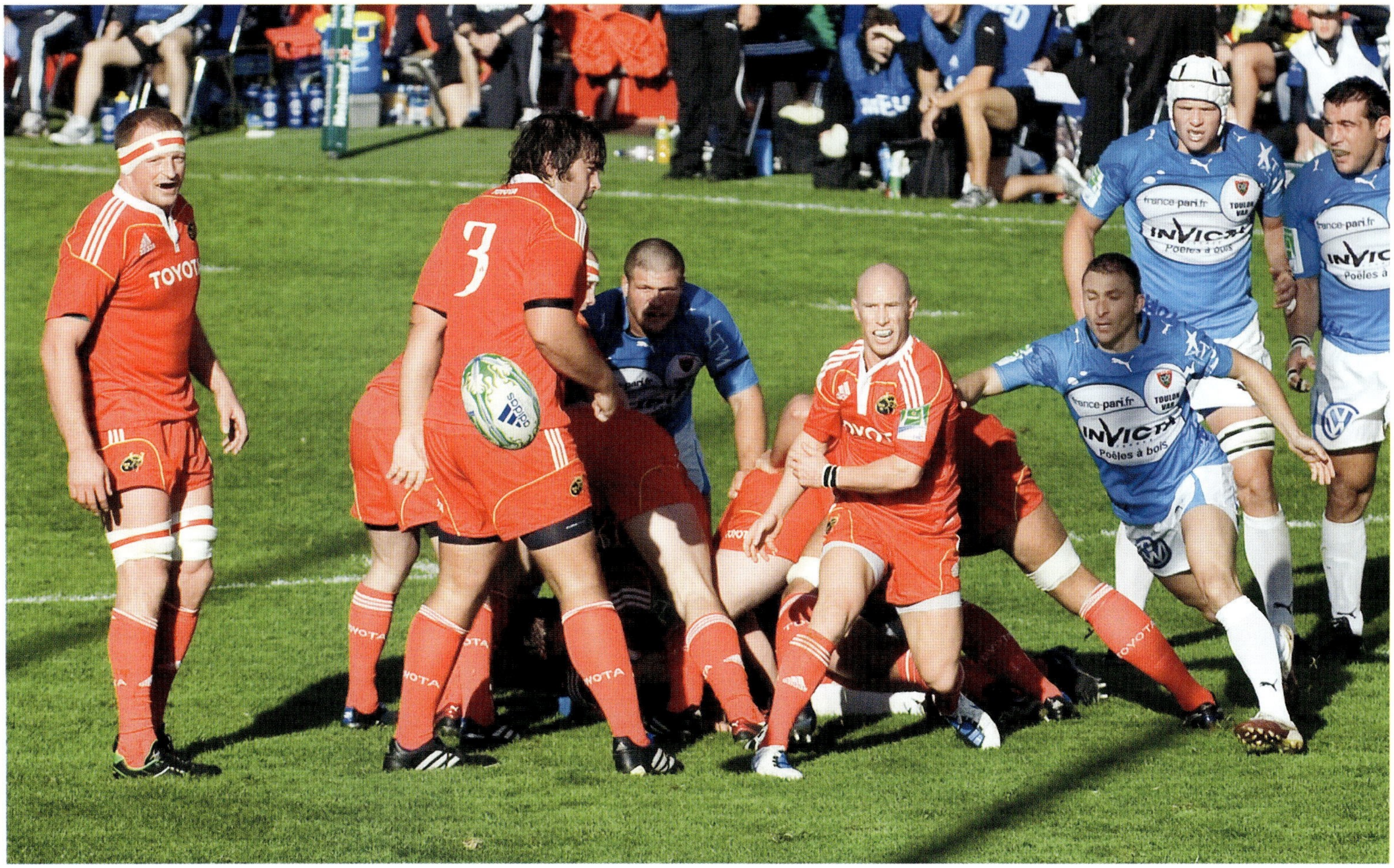

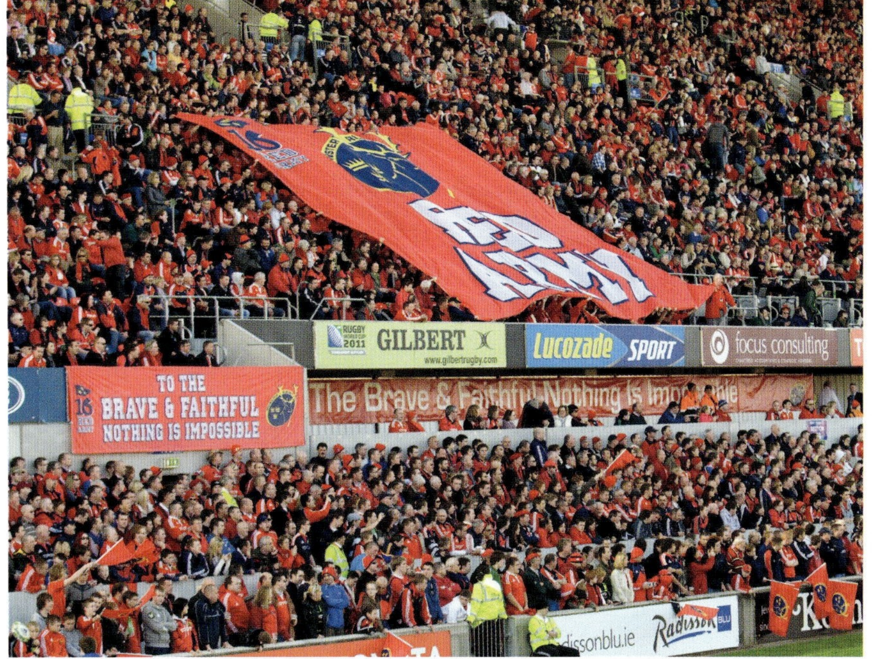

16 October 2010

Peter Stringer, renowned for having the fastest pass in Europe, in action against Toulon in the Heineken Cup. Munster won the game 45-18 in front of a packed home crowd.

1 January 2011

Opposite top: Jerry Flannery celebrates Barry Murphy's 78th-minute try against Ulster.
Opposite Bottom: Denis Leamy (with the ball) supported by Peter Stringer (far left) against Ulster. Munster went on to win 35-10.

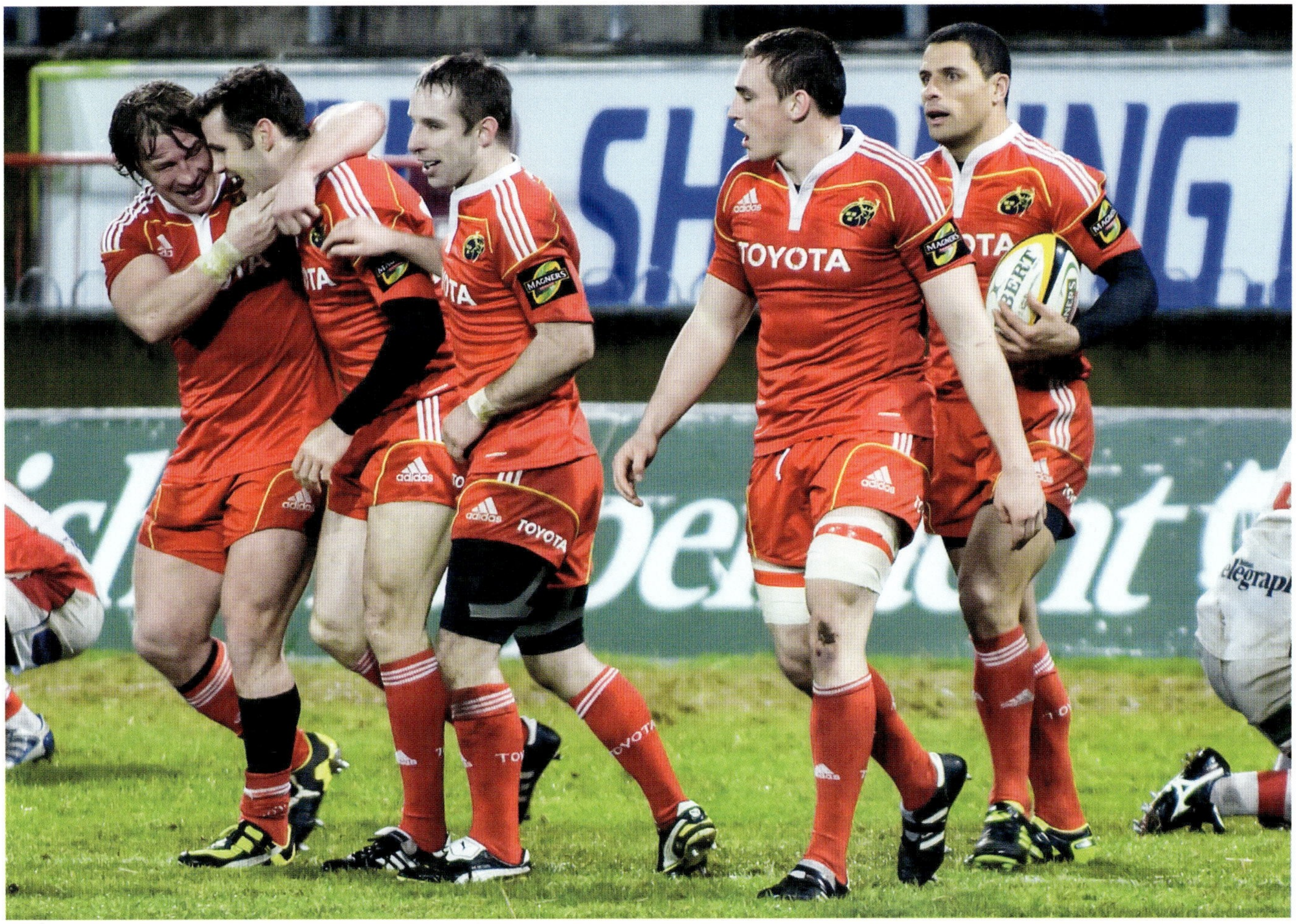

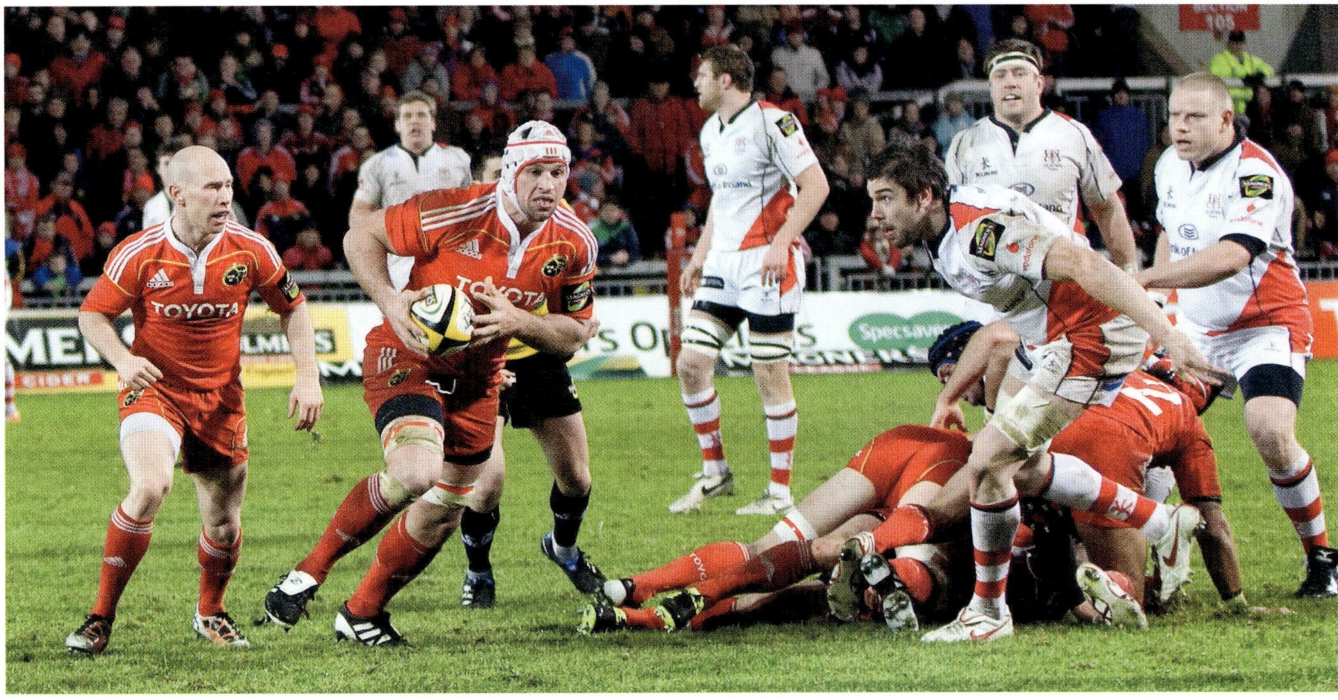

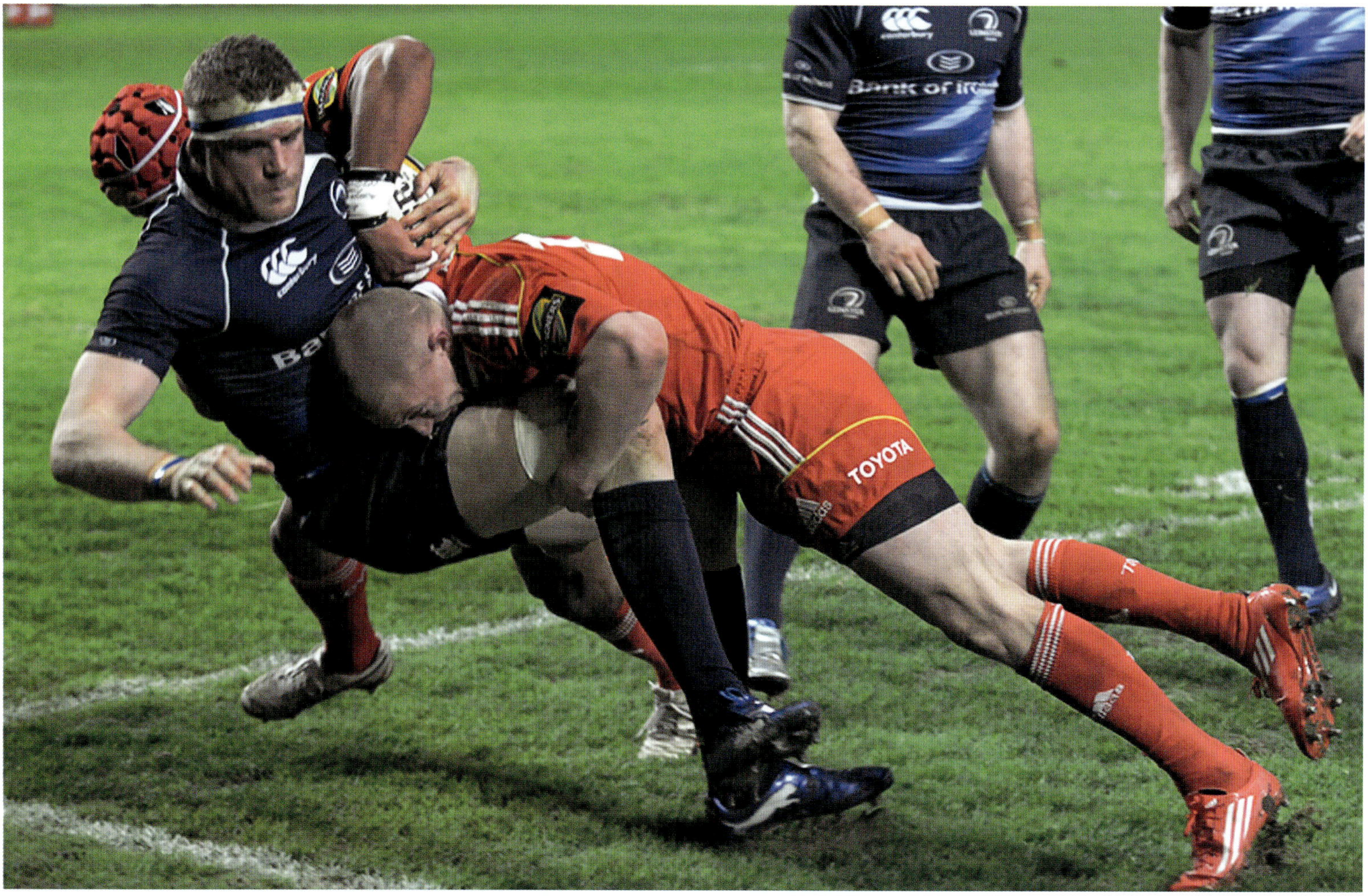

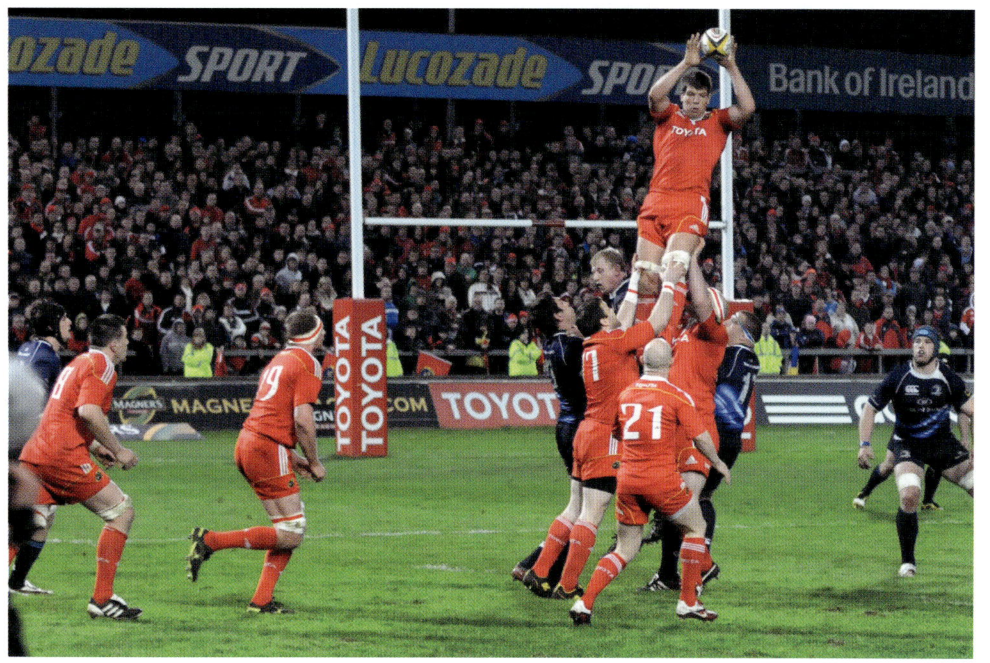

2 April 2011

Top: A crashing tackle by Keith Earls and Sam Tuitupou (wearing skull cap) sends Leinster's Jamie Heaslip into touch. Munster squeak past Leinster, 24-23, with the boot of Ronan O'Gara supplying 21 points.

Bottom: Donncha O'Callaghan claims the line-out against Leinster.

Paul O'Connell, back from injury, is brought on in the second half of the Amlin Challenge Cup semi-final against Harlequins. Quins' first-half display proved decisive, however, and they won 20-12.

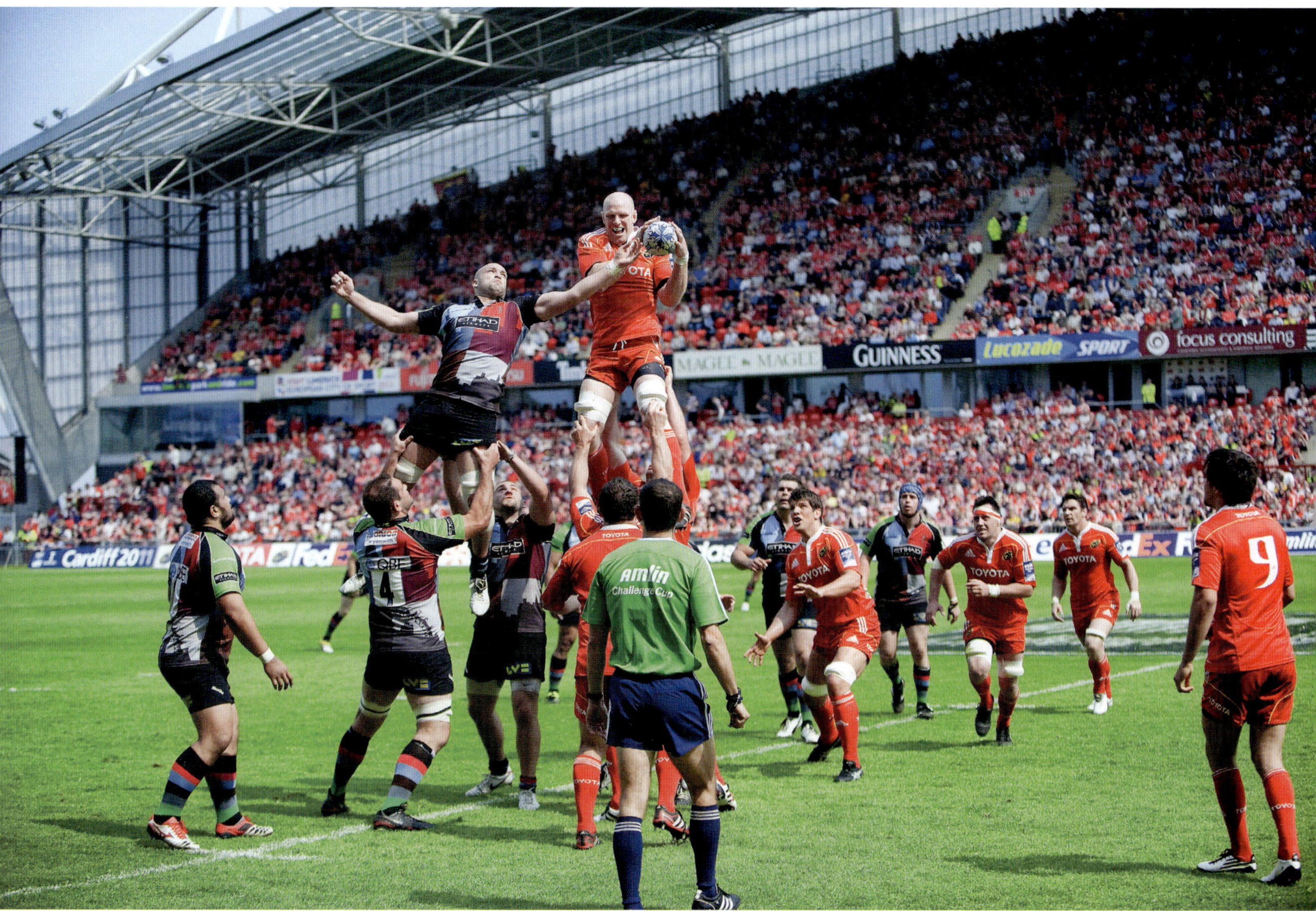

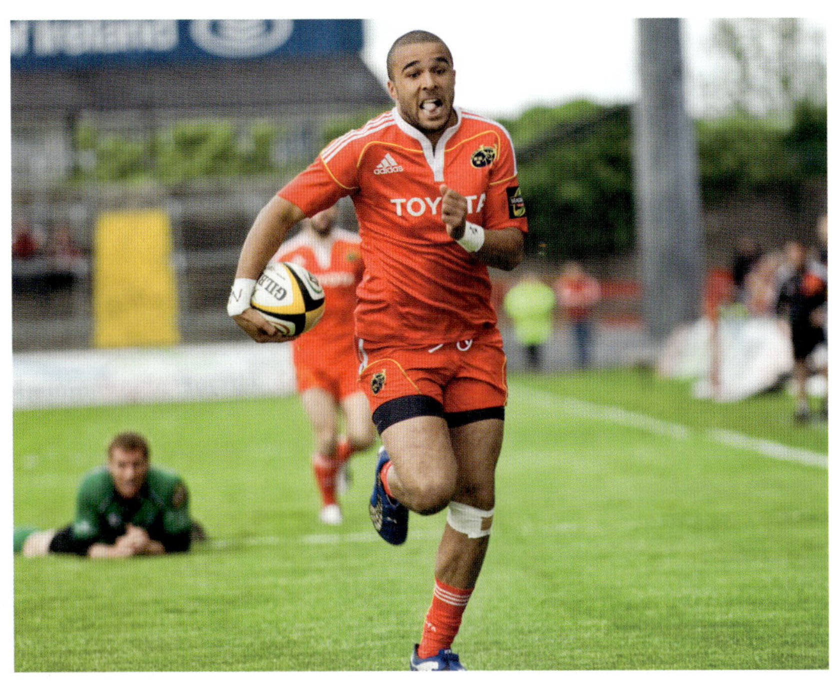

6 May 2011

Simon Zebo sprints for the line against Connacht in a Magners League fixture, a match that Munster win 22-6.

14 May 2011

Below: John 'The Bull' Hayes charges for the ball in Munster's Magners League semi-final against Ospreys in Thomond Park. Munster win 18-11.
Opposite top: Felix Jones showing pace against Ospreys in the Magners League semi-final.
Opposite bottom: James Coughlan – Munster's Player of the Year in 2011 – in action against Ospreys.

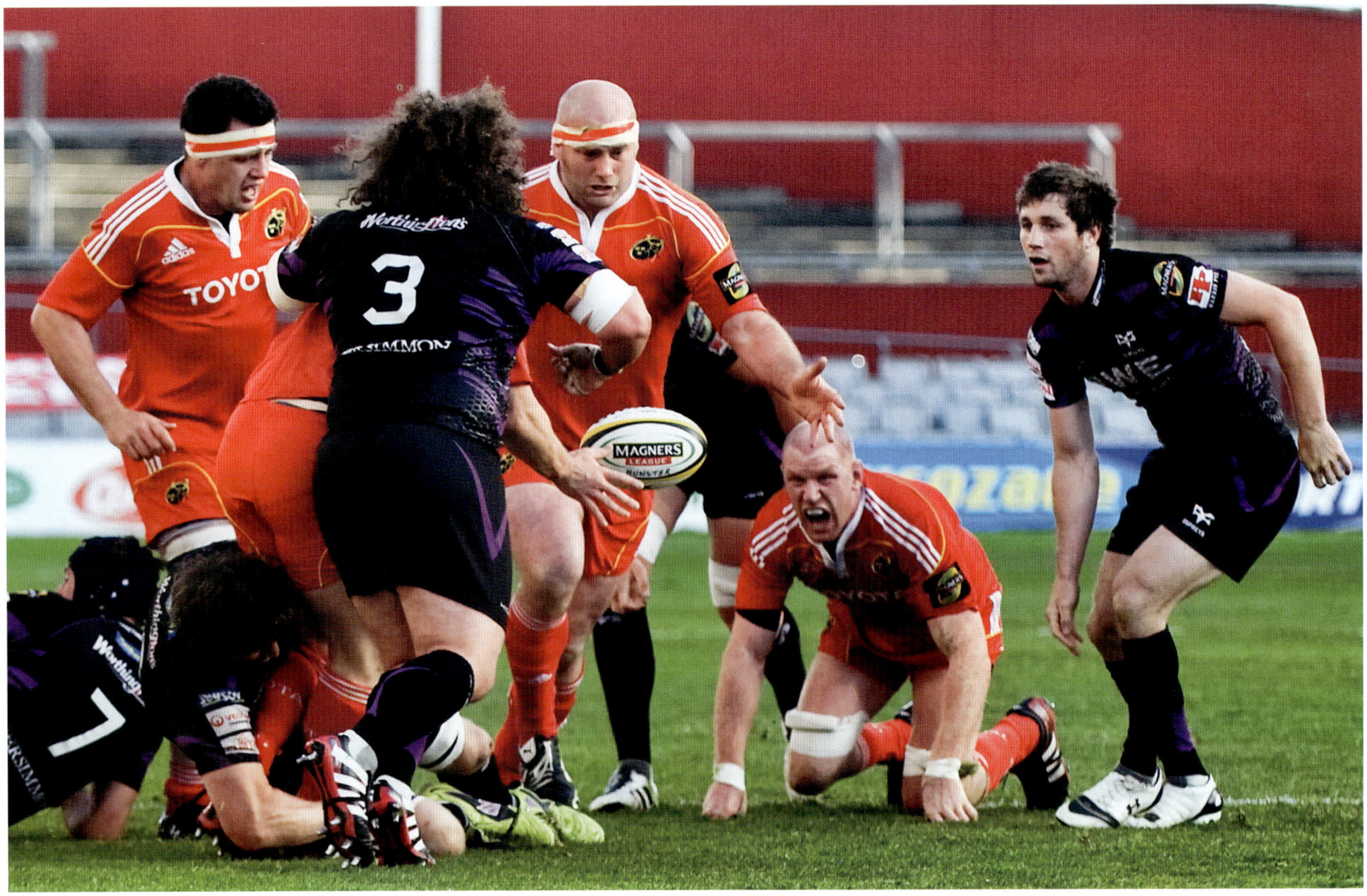

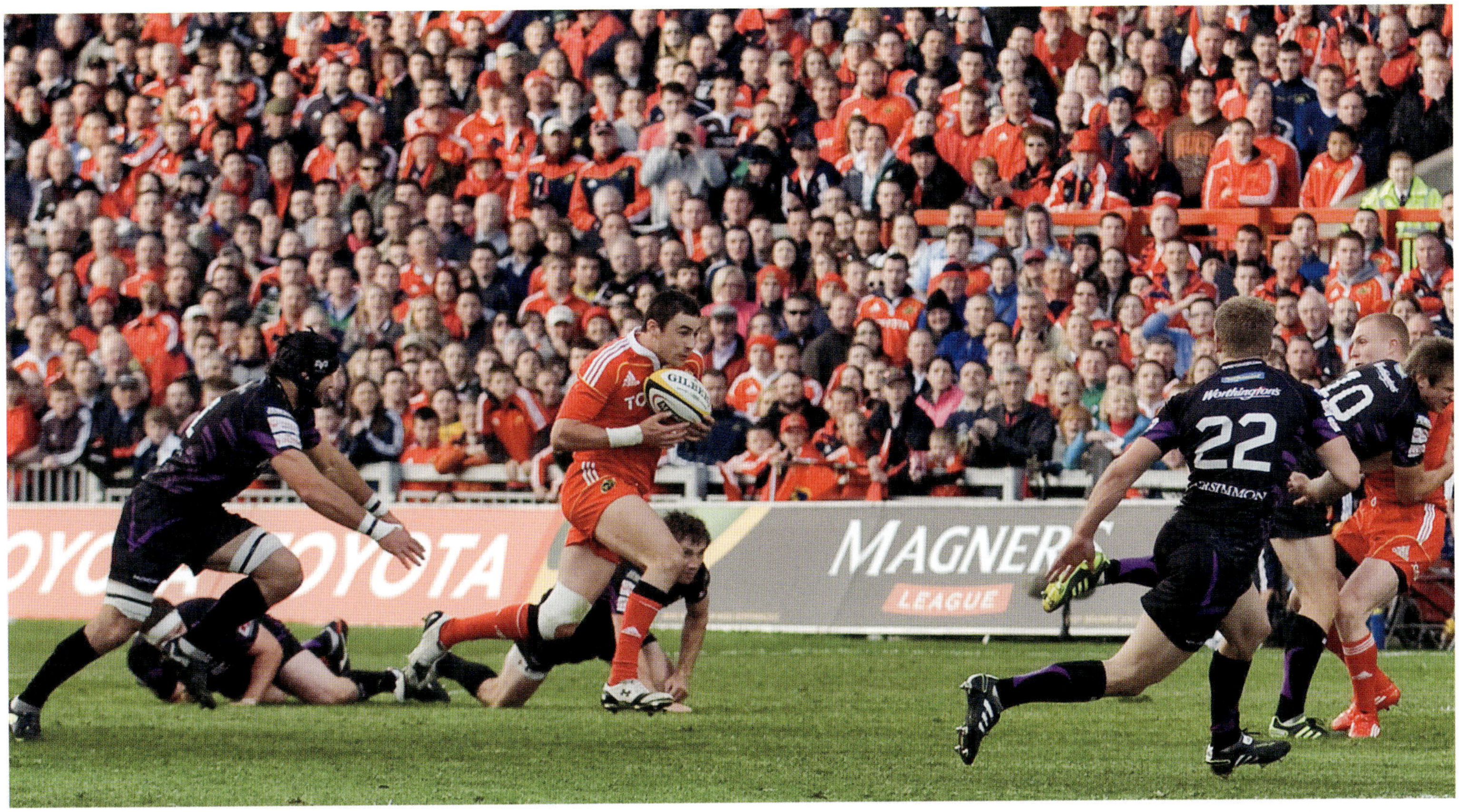
TOYOTA
LEAGUE
Worthington's
22

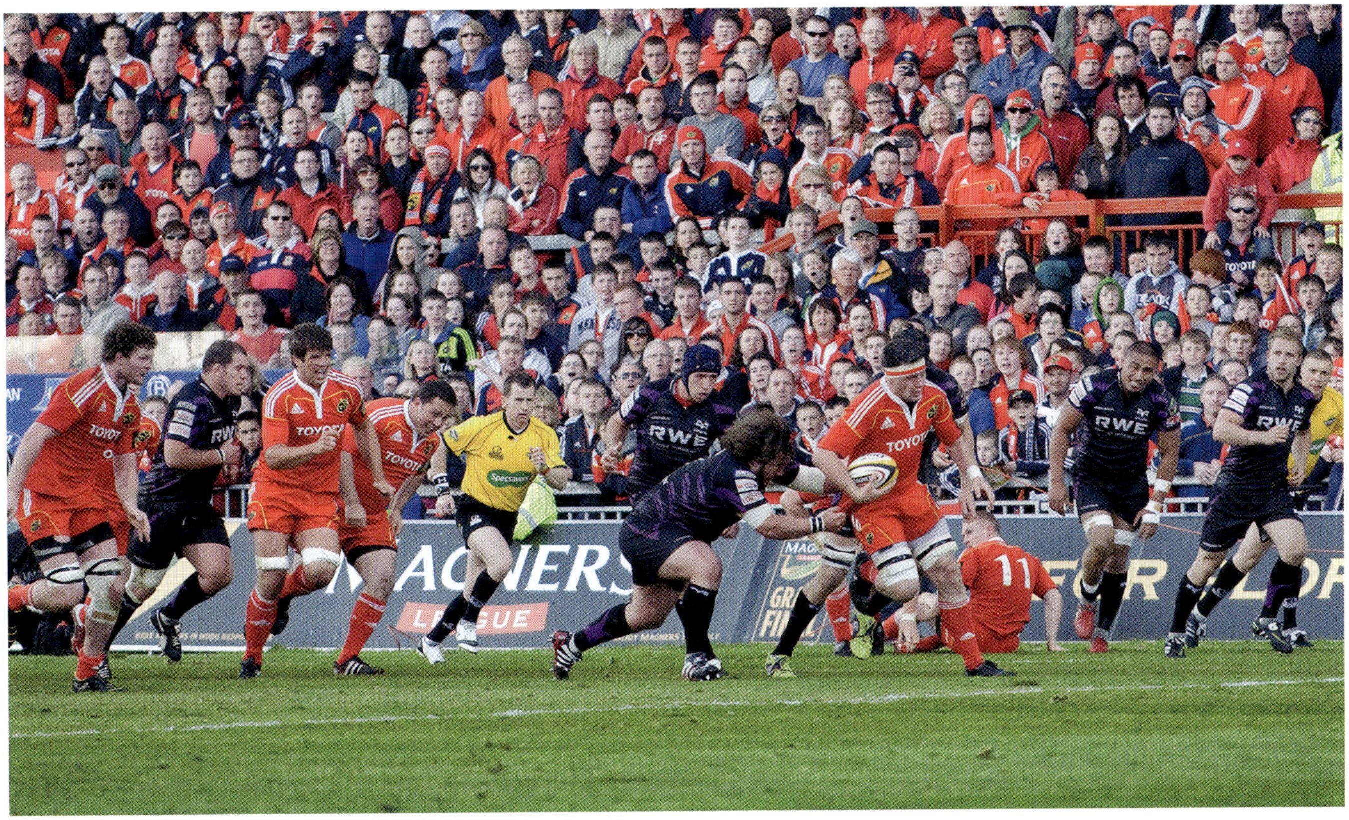
RWE
RWE
RWE

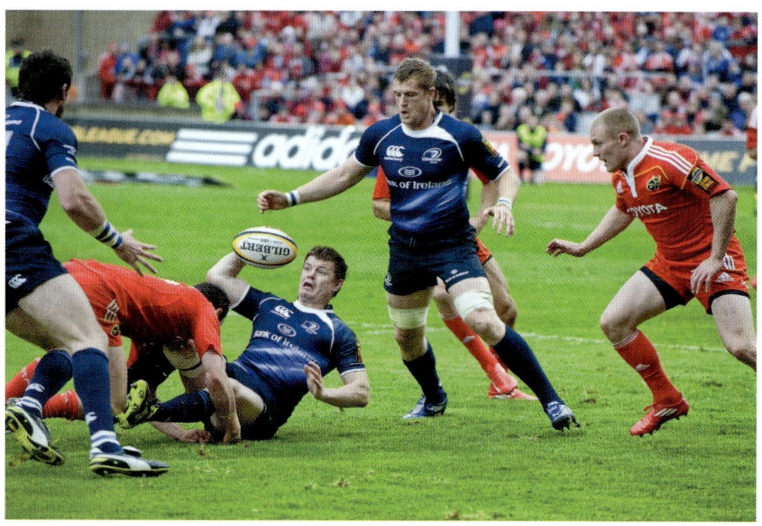

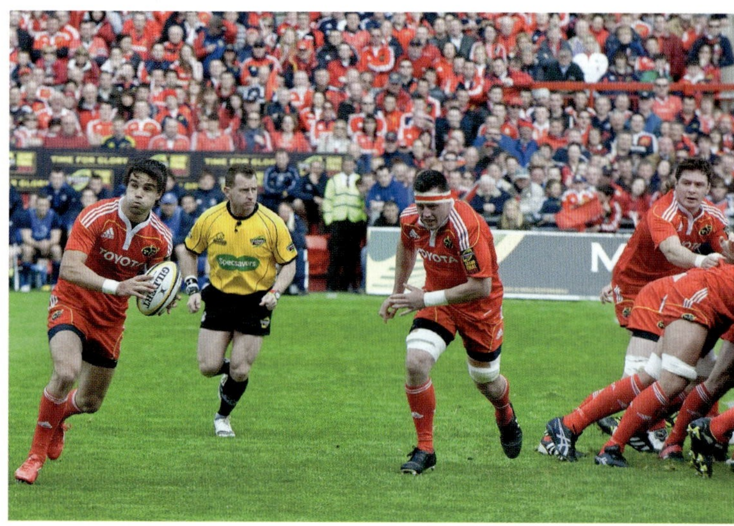

28 May 2011

Above left: In the final of the Magners Celtic League, Leinster's Brian O'Driscoll is tackled by Felix Jones with Keith Earls (far right) ready to pounce. Munster win 19-9.

Above right: Referee Nigel Owens still has an eye on the scrum while a fresh-faced Conor Murray is already a move ahead.

Left: Donnacha Ryan comfortably wins a line-out against Leinster.

Opposite top: Paul O'Connell 'bloodied' in the match against Leinster.

Opposite bottom: Munster are crowned Magners League champions 2010–2011.

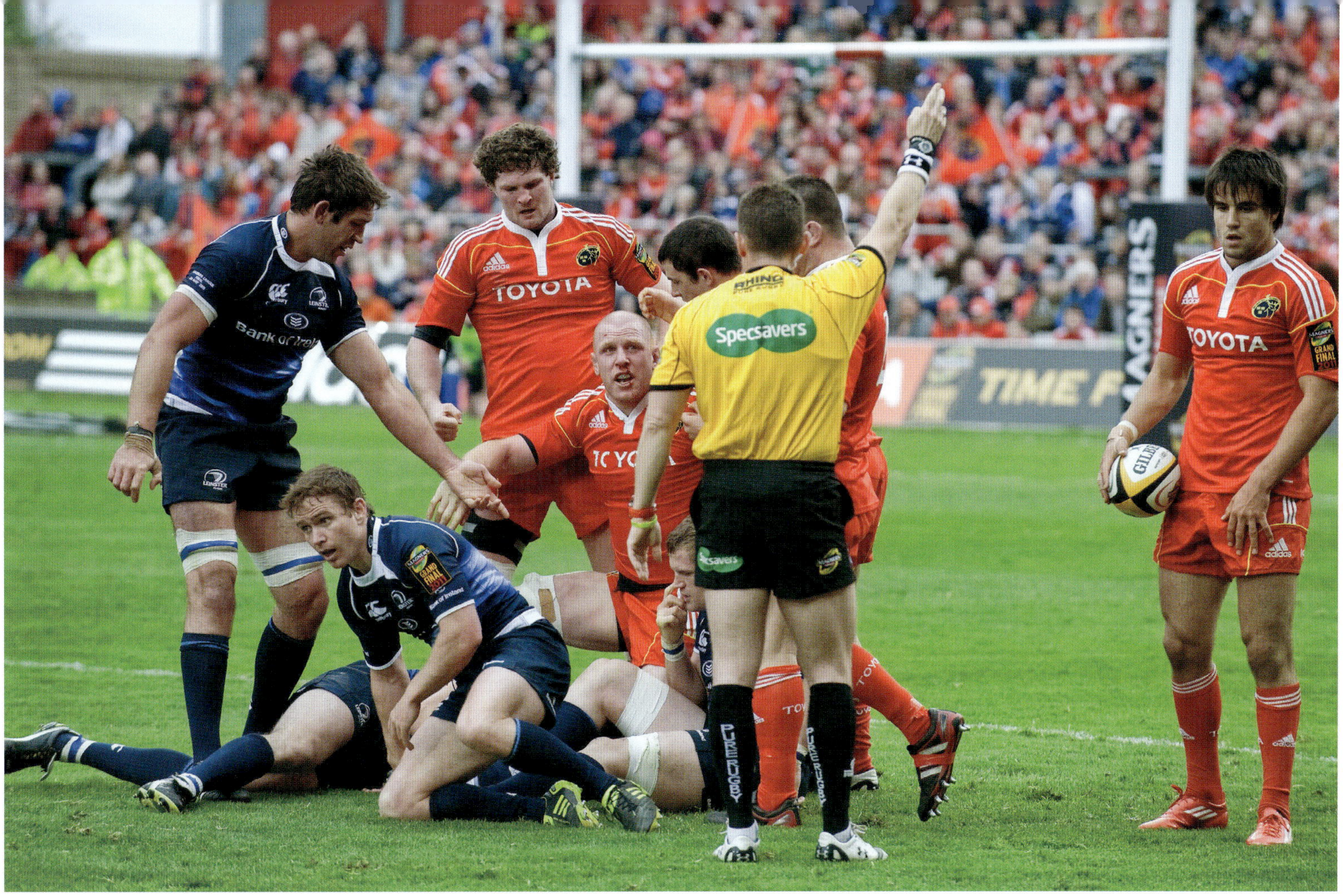
TOYOTA
Specsavers
TIME F

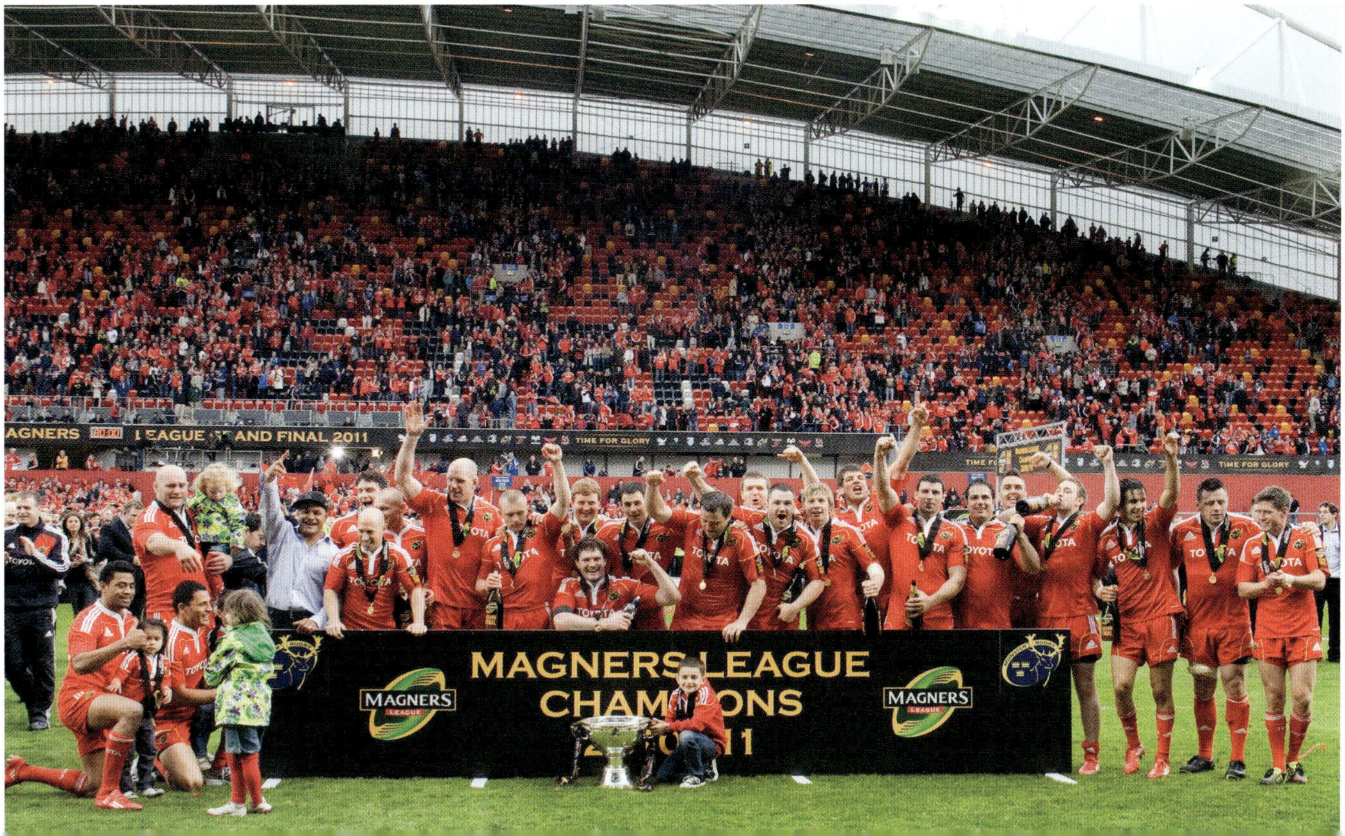
MAGNERS
TIME FOR GLORY
MAGNERS

2011–2012

Pro12   **Pool wins: 14; Pool losses: 7; Drew: 1; Eliminated: semi-final**
Heineken Cup   **Pool wins: 6; Pool losses: 0; Eliminated: quarter-final**

This would be Tony McGahan's final season as Munster head coach. New Zealander Rob Penney was confirmed as his replacement. Italian side Aironi, having debuted only the previous season, would come last in the Pro12 for the second year in a row. They would lose their status as a regional side at the end of this season, to be replaced by Zebre.

Pro12

Munster's Pro12 season began promisingly, with a 20-12 win over Newport Gwent Dragons, played on 3 September 2011 at Musgrave Park in Cork, and a superb 23-12 away victory against Glasgow Warriors on 9 September. Next to fall to the Munster sword were Scarlets, 35-12, in Musgrave Park on 17 September. The good form continued with another away victory on 23 September, against Cardiff Blues: 18-13.

The first loss of the season occurred away to Edinburgh on 30 September when the Scots won 29-14, followed by another loss, in Thomond Park on 8 October, Ospreys winning 17-13. Munster beat Aironi 18-6 on 28 October at Musgrave Park, all of Munster's points coming from Ronan O'Gara. On 4 November, Munster travelled to Aviva Stadium where Leinster won by 24-19 in front of 48,000 spectators. Munster coughed up seven penalties, all slotted between the posts by Johnny Sexton.

Munster hosted Edinburgh at Thomond Park on 26 November and won 34-17, with tries from Danny Barnes, Simon Zebo, Luke O'Dea and a penalty try. Away to Ospreys on 3 December, Munster lost 19-13. Next, Connacht came to Thomond Park on 26 December, where 21,000 supporters saw a victory for the home team, 24-9. In Belfast on 30 December, Munster lost 33-17 to Ulster. Next up was Treviso in Thomond Park on 7 January 2012, which Munster won comprehensively by 29-11. The following week, Munster played Treviso at the Stadio Comunale di Monigo and had an excellent away win, 35-14. Man of the match James Coughlan scored Munster's third try.

In a close encounter played on 24 February at Thomond Park, Munster scraped home by 16-13 against Cardiff Blues. On 3 March, Newport Gwent Dragons hosted Munster at Rodney Parade. Bucking their record there, Munster were victorious by 24-14.

Struggling Italian side Aironi were surprising victors against Munster on 11 March, winning 21-17 at Stadio Zaffanella. Munster then got back to winning ways at Galway Sportsgrounds on 24 March, beating hosts Connacht 20-16. Arch-rivals Leinster travelled to Thomond Park on 31 March. A full house of 26,500 fans watched a try-less match: Munster's tally all came from ROG's boot, with Leinster earning twelve of their points from his opposite number, Johnny Sexton. Ian Madigan sealed the 18-9 win for the visitors with a drop goal in the 74th minute.

Undeterred, Munster had an excellent home victory at Musgrave Park against Glasgow Warriors on 14 April, winning 35-29. Luke O'Dea, Peter O'Mahony and Conor Murray all scored tries. A match against Scarlets followed on 21 April, a 20-20 draw. Ulster were the next visitors to Thomond Park for the quarter-final and a good performance saw Munster win 36-8.

Munster had an away semi-final at the Liberty Stadium on 11 May. Ospreys were too strong on the day and won 45-10, ending Munster's campaign.

HEINEKEN CUP

Munster were drawn in Pool 1 together with Northampton Saints, Scarlets and Castres. In the first match, played on 12 November 2011 at Thomond Park, Munster won narrowly, 23-21, against Northampton Saints, thanks to a legendary 83rd-minute drop goal by Ronan O'Gara.

Away to Castres on 19 November in the second pool game, ROG did it again, securing a 27-24 win with another late drop goal. Following that victory, Munster played Scarlets away, winning 17-14 and beating them again at home the following week, 19-13. The away game was played on 10 December and the return on 18 December.

Munster then played Castres at Thomond Park on 14 January 2012 and won 26-10, ensuring Munster's qualification for the quarter-finals. The final pool game was away to Northampton Saints in a match played at Stadium MK in Milton Keynes. Munster were outstanding that day, winning 51-36. The match featured a hat-trick of tries scored by Simon Zebo. It was the first season that Munster won all their pool games in the Heineken Cup.

However, when Ulster came to Thomond Park for the quarter-final on 8 April, the visitors powered to a 19-0 lead, with Munster pulling the score back to 19-10 just before half-time. In spite of being down to fourteen men in the second half, Ulster held firm to win 22-16. This was only Munster's second loss at home in the Heineken Cup.

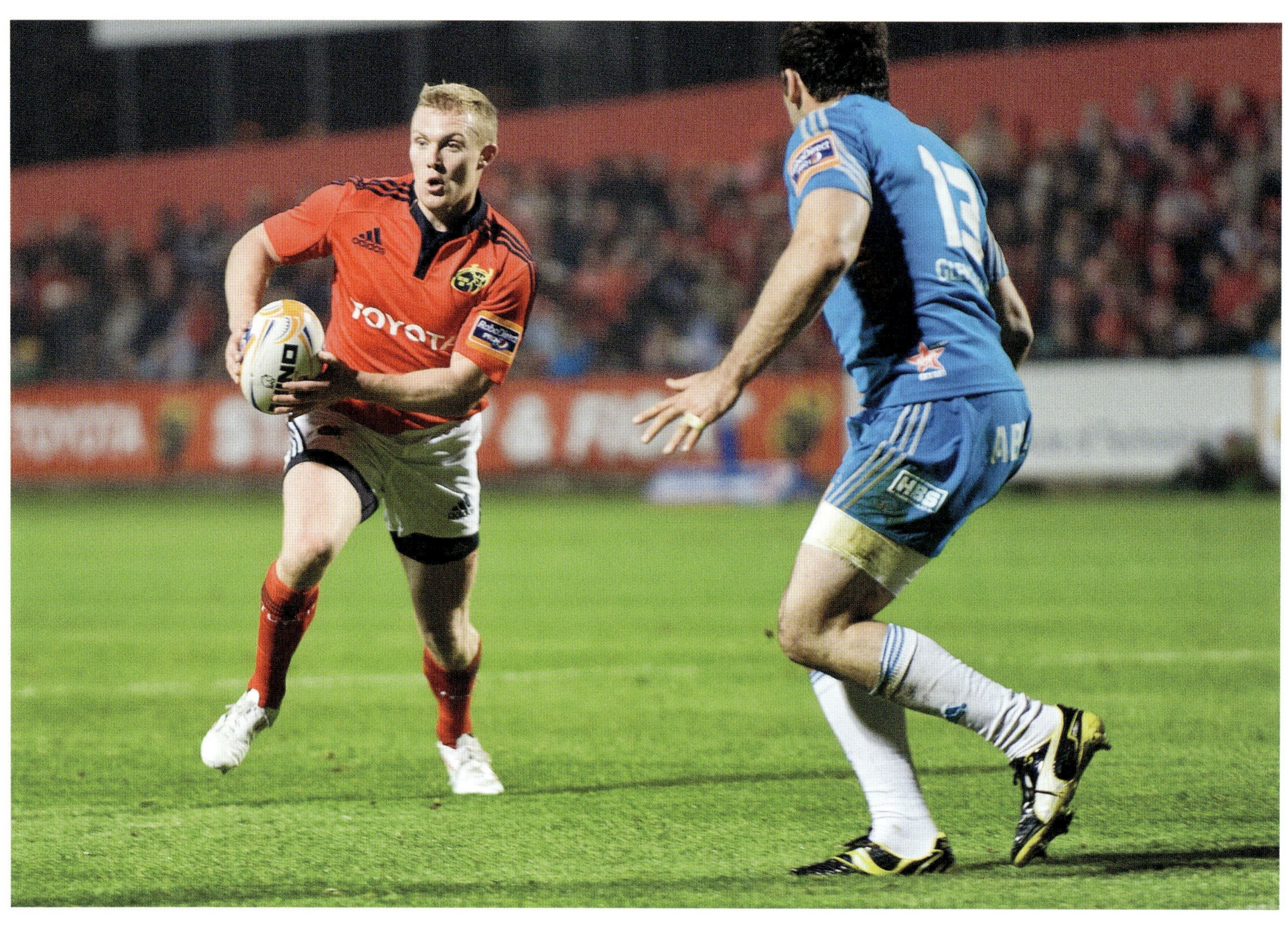

28 October 2011

Keith Earls prepares to dodge Aironi's Andrea Masi in the 18-6 home win at Thomond Park.

An unstoppable Doug Howlett about to score against Northampton Saints. This would prove to be a thrilling encounter at Thomond Park, with the sides swapping the lead. Munster were one point behind as the clock ticked into red, but a phenomenal 40 phases led to ROG's 35-metre drop goal. Munster won 23-21.

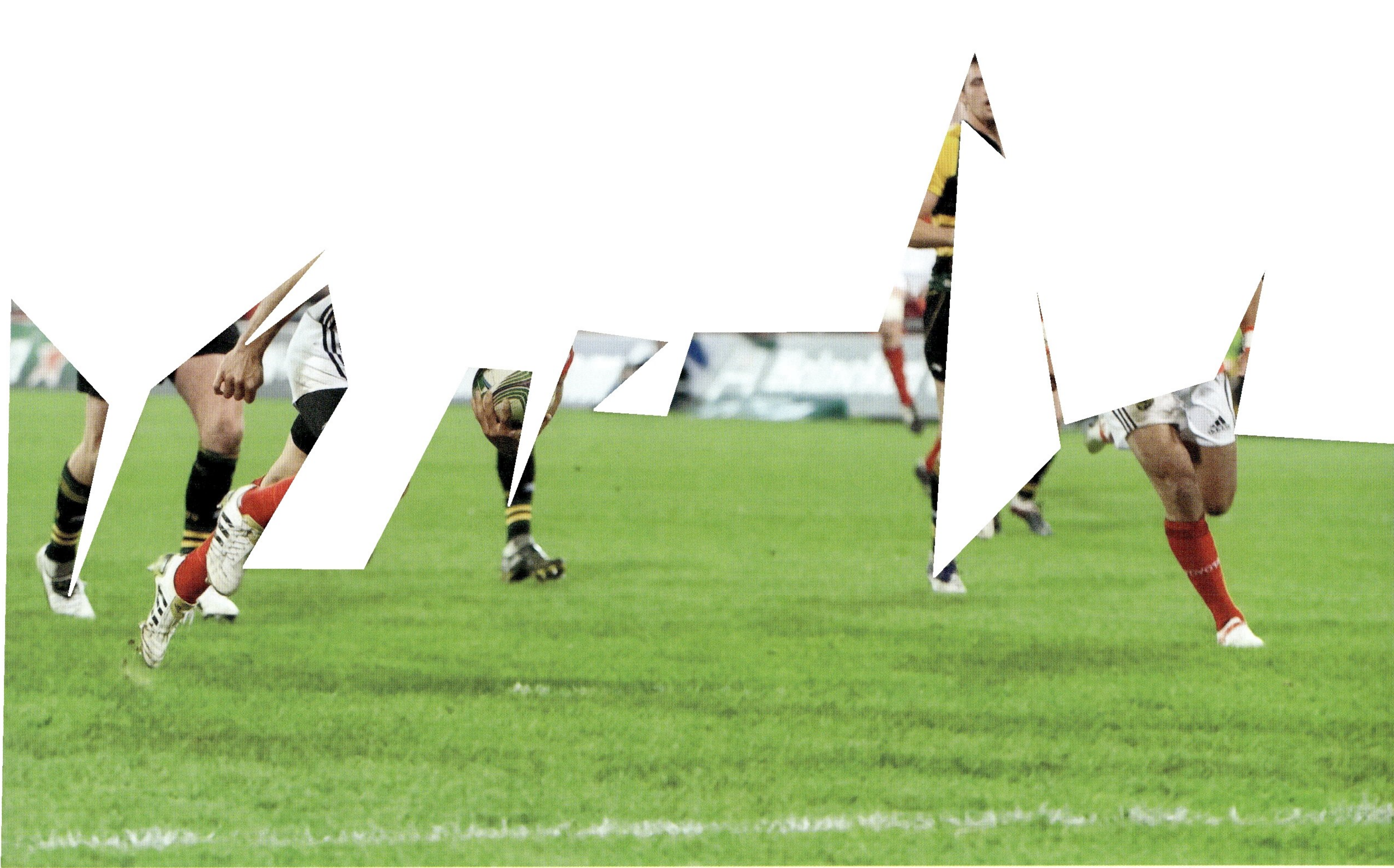

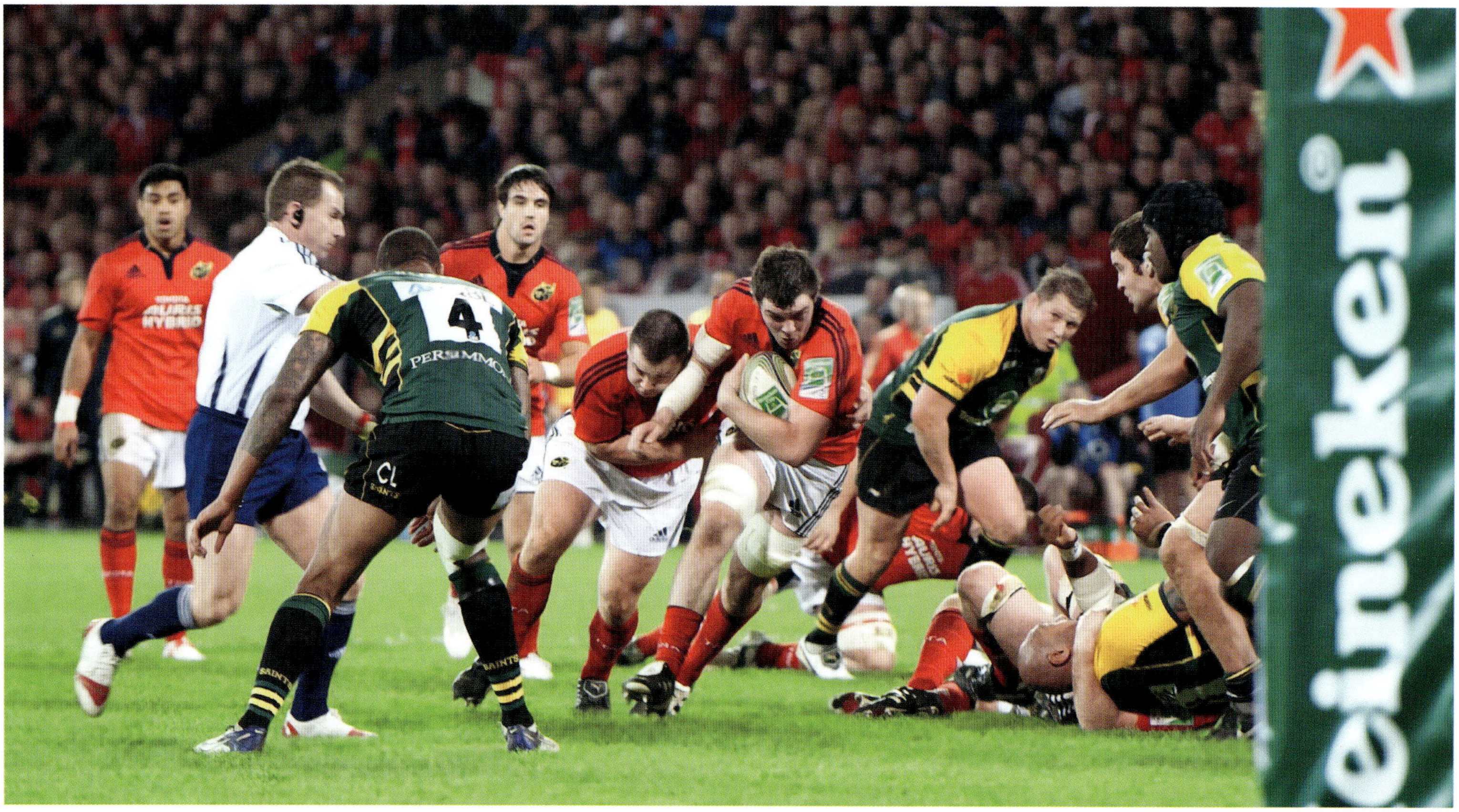

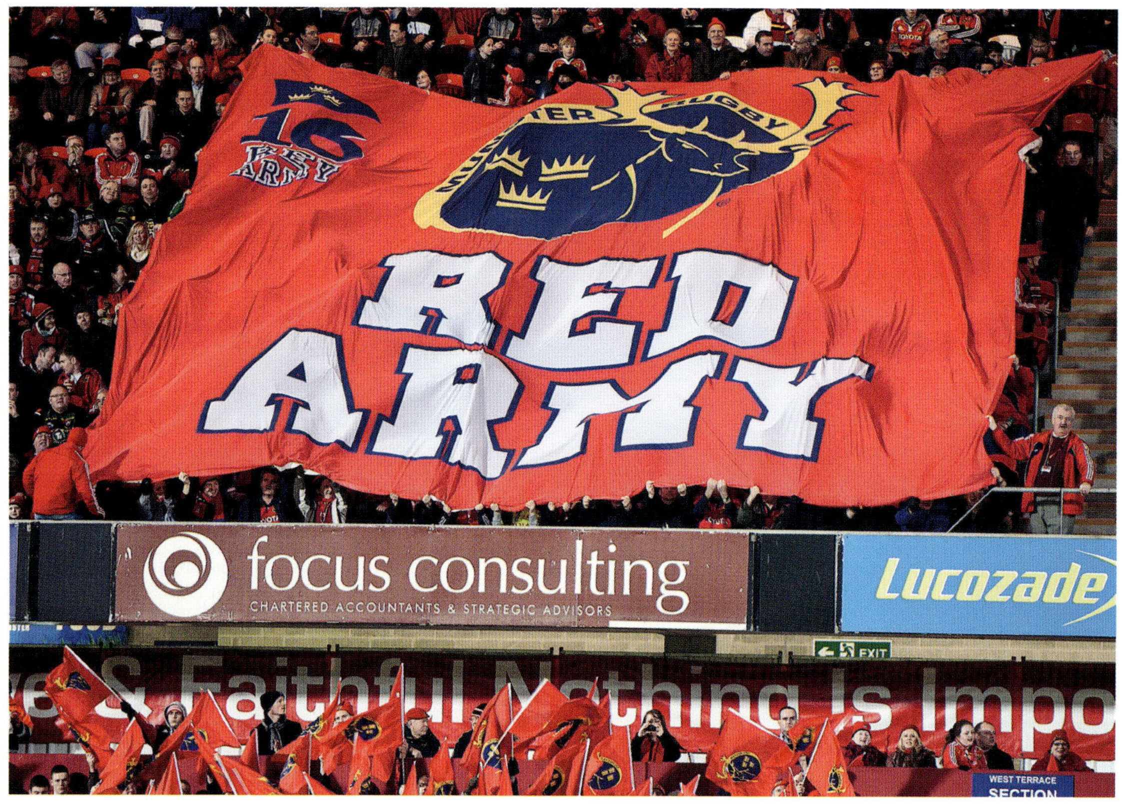

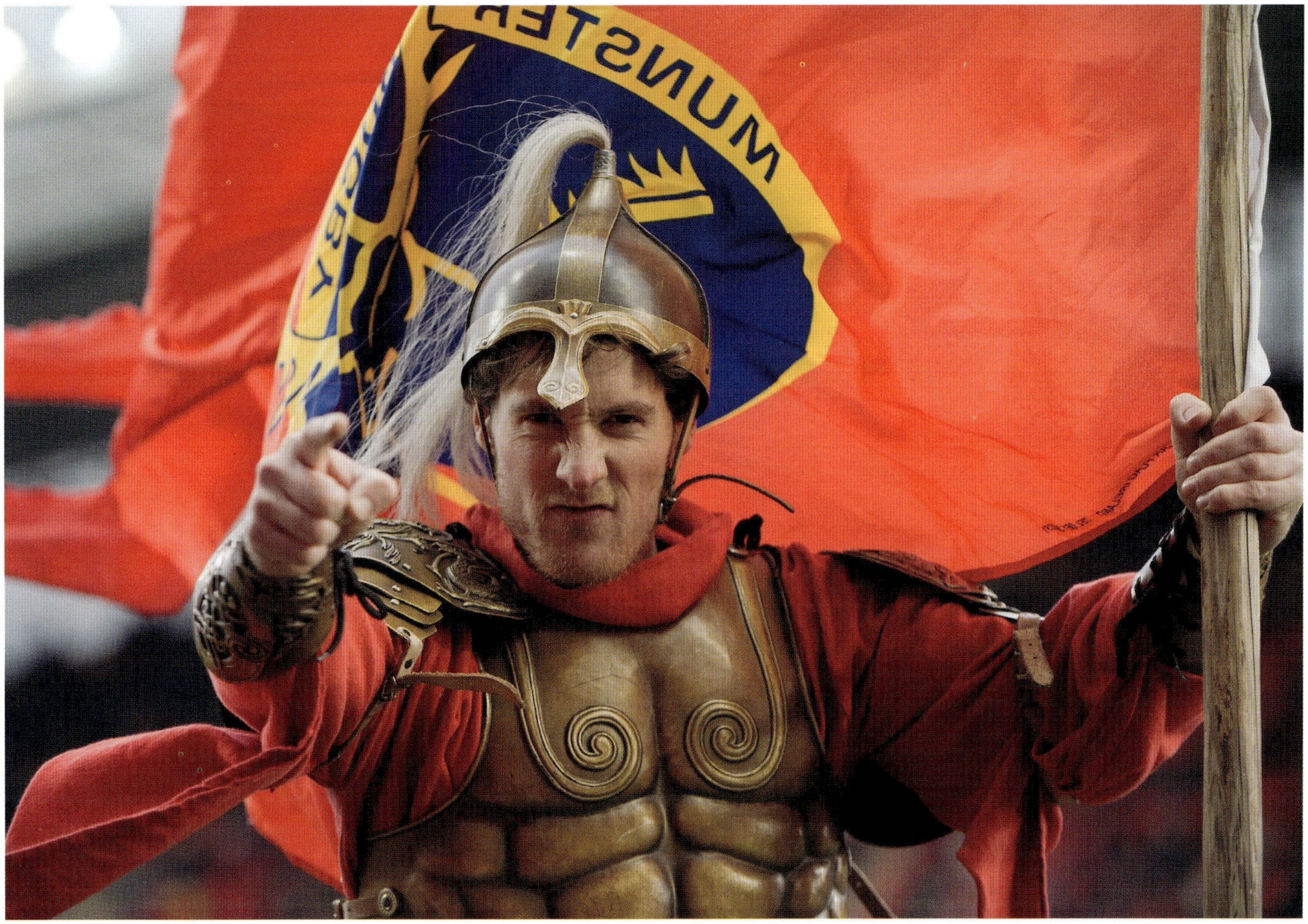

12 November 2011

Opposite top: Peter O'Mahony bursts for the line against Saints.

Opposite bottom: The Red Army – the 'sixteenth man' – make themselves heard.

Above: An ardent fan showing his colours at this historic match.

December 2011

Right: Shaun Payne with his wife, Michelle, and their children at the Thomond Park Christmas party. Shaun was Munster's full back in their first Heineken Cup victory, in 2006, and Munster team manager from 2007 to 2012. Michelle later became Marketing Manager at Thomond Park. Sadly, she died of cancer in May 2025.

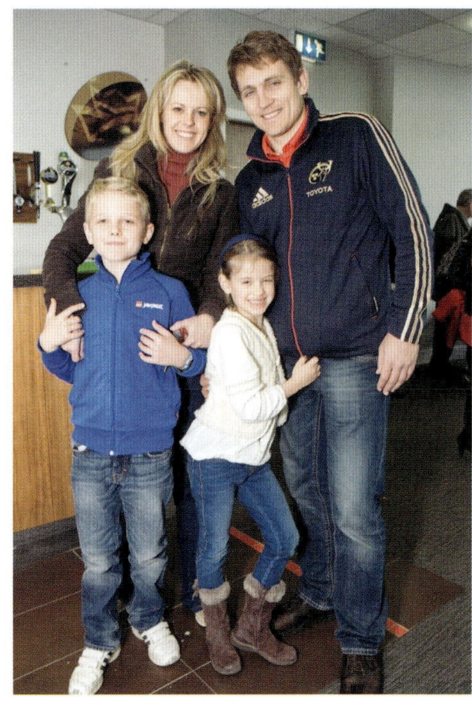

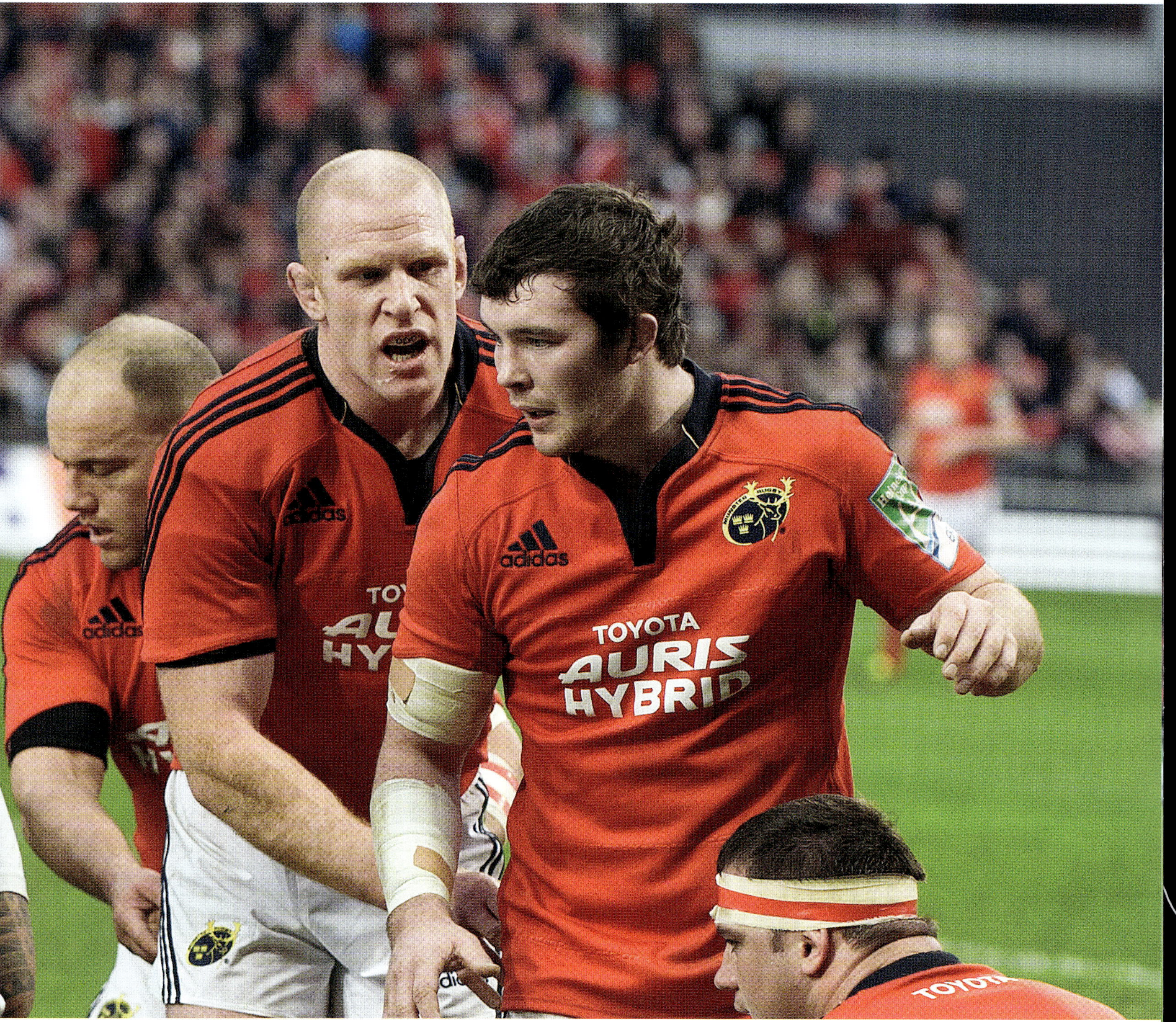

14 January 2012

Above: (l–r) BJ Botha, Paul O'Connell, Peter O'Mahony and Wian du Preeze prepare for a line-out against Castres.

Right: Star man Paul Warwick was an unsung hero with Munster, playing in the shadow of Ronan O'Gara as an out-half, centre or full back.

Below: Ronan O'Gara goes down the line against Castres. Munster win comfortably 26-10 and secure a quarter-final slot in the Heineken Cup.

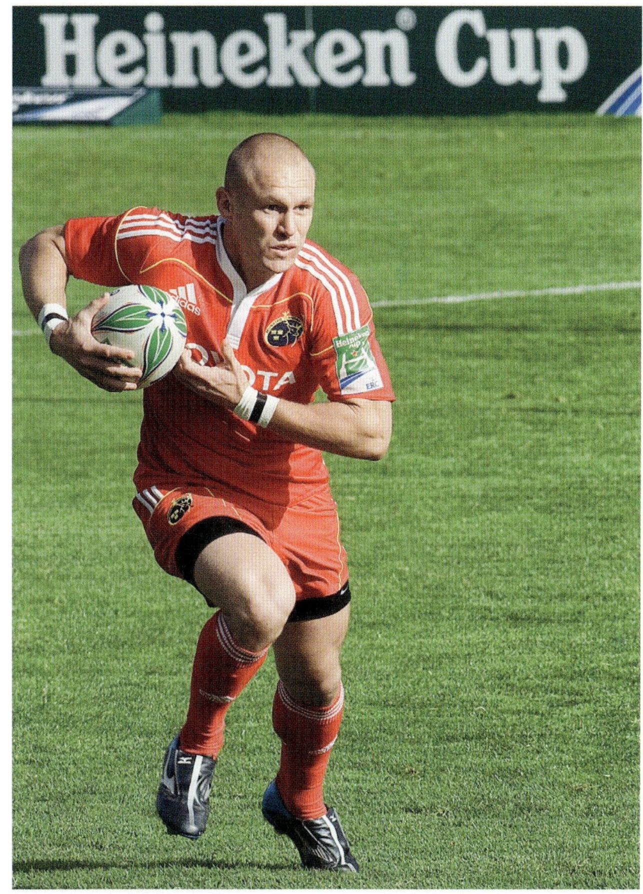

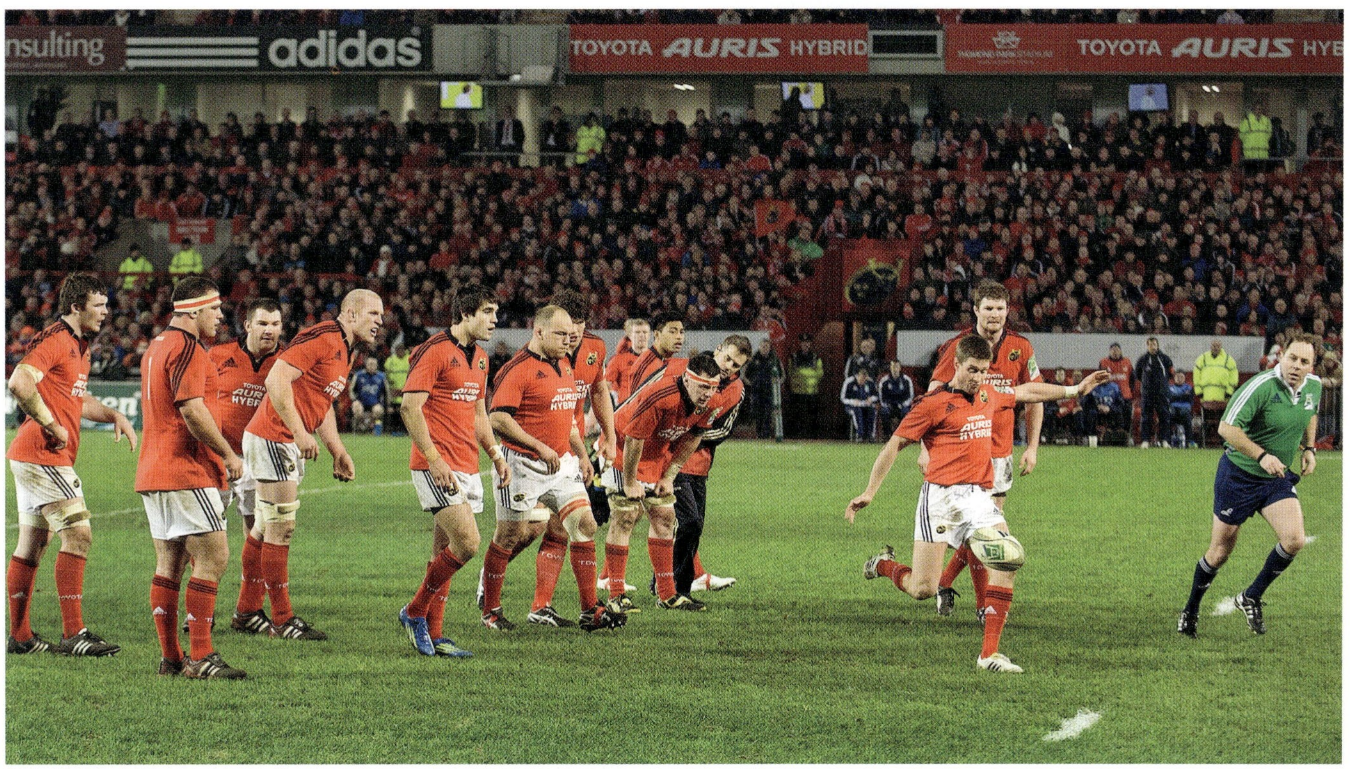

Simon Zebo scores his third try against Northampton Saints. After an intercept from inside his own half, Zebo romped over, unopposed. Munster secured a resounding 51–36 away win.

(Photo edited by John Hickey)

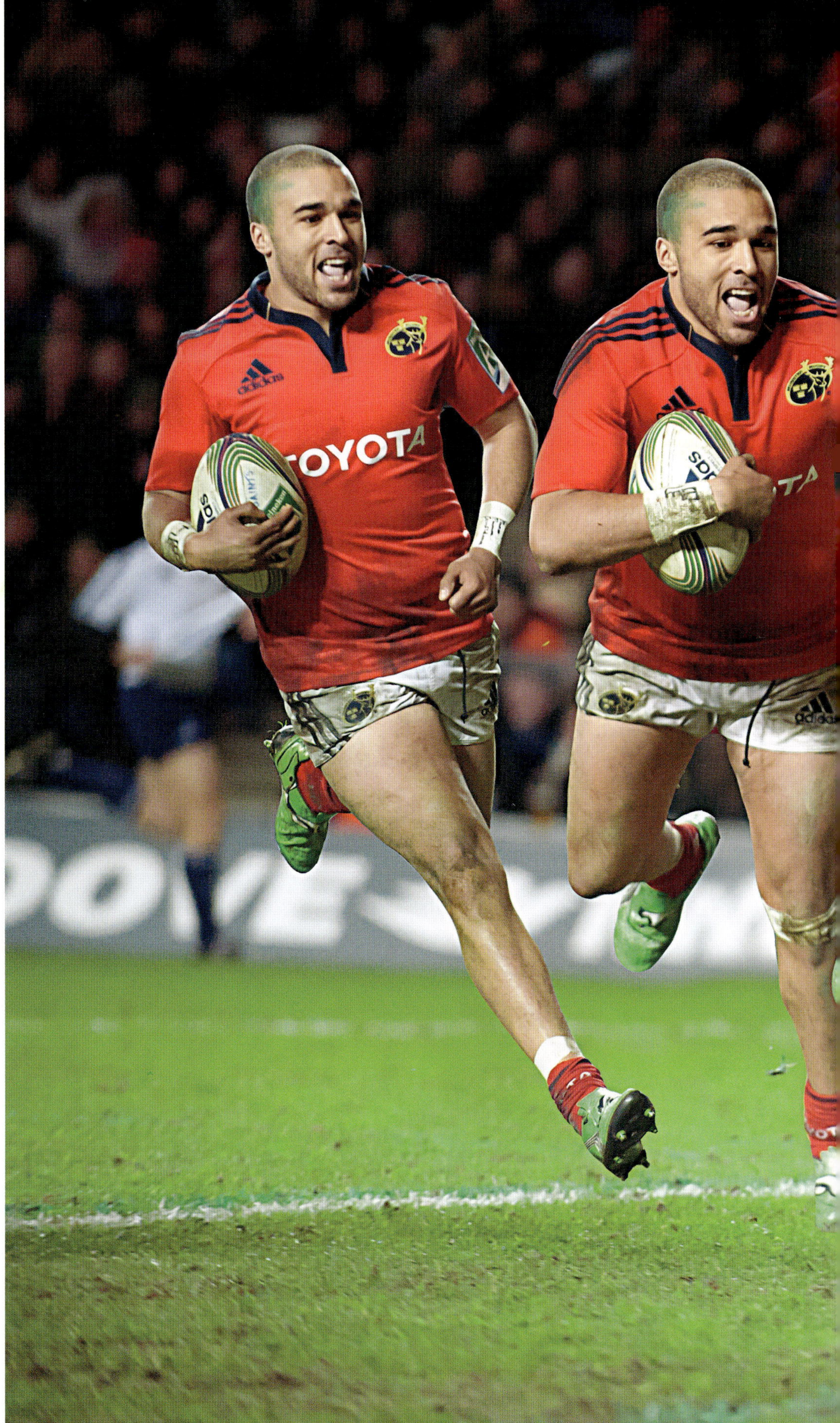

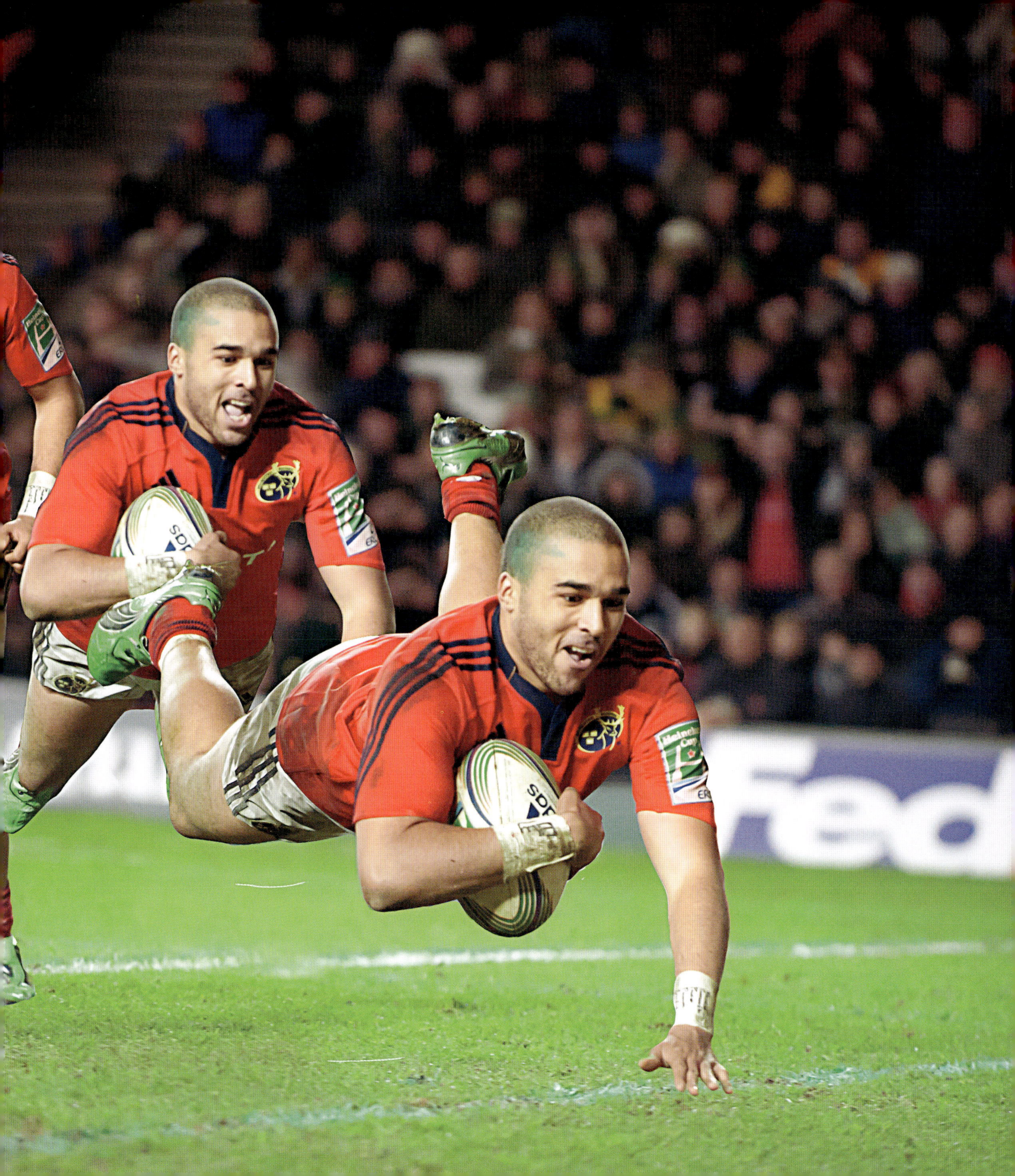

2012-2013

Pro12   Pool wins: 11; Pool losses: 10; Drew: 1; Did not progress further
Heineken Cup   Pool wins: 4; Losses : 2; Eliminated: semi-final

Some of the greatest stars ever to play for Munster retired this season, including Jerry Flannery, John Hayes, Marcus Horan, Darragh Hurley, Denis Leamy, Mick O'Driscoll, Ronan O'Gara and David Wallace. Lifeimi Mafi moved to Perpignan, Thomas O'Leary to London Irish and Denis Fogarty to Aurillac. New arrivals this season included Sean Dougall from Rotherham Titans, James Downey from Northampton Saints, Casey Laulala from Cardiff Blues and CJ Stander from Bulls. JJ Hanrahan, Luke O'Dea, Dave O'Callaghan and Cathal Sheridan were all promoted from the Academy. New head coach Rob Penney appointed Doug Howlett as the squad captain.

Pro12

The season started on 1 September 2012 with a 23-18 win against Edinburgh in Murrayfield. A week later, on 7 September, Munster coasted to a 19-6 home win against Treviso, with fourteen points from the boot of Ian Keatley. However, away to Ulster the following week at Ravenhill, Munster went down by a single point, 20-19. At home against Newport Gwent Dragons on 22 September, Munster had a comprehensive win by 33-13. Tries came from Ian Keatley, Niall Ronan, Conor Murray, Simon Zebo and Tommy O'Donnell.

Next up, Munster were away to Ospreys on 29 September, where they suffered a 30-15 defeat. Leinster proved too strong for Munster in front of a packed Aviva on 6 October, winning by 30-21 in a riveting contest. Zebre were the next visitors to Thomond Park, on 26 October. JJ Hanrahan, in his first start for Munster, scored a brace of tries, helping Munster to a decisive 29-3 win.

A good away win, 24-18, against Cardiff Blues on 2 November, was followed by a loss to Scarlets at Musgrave Park by 13-6 on 25 November. Munster got back on the winning trail against Connacht at the Galway Sportsgrounds, winning 16-12 on 22 December in appalling conditions. Munster defeated Ulster at Thomond Park on 29 December, 24-10.

Cardiff Blues came to Musgrave Park on 5 January 2013, but a poor performance from the home team saw them go down 17-6. Next were Edinburgh, again in Musgrave Park, on 9 February. CJ Stander and Mike Sherry each provided two tries, while Ian Keatley accounted for 20 points, giving Munster a comfortable 30-3 win. Away to an on-form Scarlets on 16 February, Munster lost 18-10. Next, they travelled to Treviso on 24 February, losing 34-10.

Back in Thomond Park on 2 March, a better performance from Munster against Ospreys ended in a 13-13 draw. Next up were Connacht at Musgrave Park on 23 March. Paul O'Connell, back to senior level for the first time since surgery, scored the first try, followed by two from Damien Varley. The 22-0 win, however, failed to produce a much-needed bonus point.

Munster's away form suffered again when Glasgow Warriors had a resounding 51-25 win at Scotstoun on 29 March. Doug Howlett suffered a shoulder injury and was forced to retire. Back at home on 13 April, Munster faced a determined Leinster. Despite leading 16-12 at half-time, Munster were unable to turn the screw. Brian O'Driscoll scored the match-winning try and Munster lost 22-16. Another loss followed, away to Newport Gwent Dragons on 19 April, on a final score of 30-24, in Marcus Horan's 225th – and last – appearance for the province. Away to Zebre on 3 May, Munster won 27-25, with tries from Johne Murphy, Paddy Butler and BJ Botha, Ian Keatley converting all three and adding two penalties. Munster missed out on the play-offs, finishing sixth in the league.

HEINEKEN CUP

Munster were drawn with Edinburgh, Saracens and Racing Métro in Pool 1. In the opening game, Munster lost to Racing 22-17 at Stade de France in Paris in front of 21,000 supporters on 13 October 2012.

The first home game on 21 October against Edinburgh was a happier outcome with the hosts winning 33-0. From 6-0 at half-time, second-half tries from Conor Murray, Peter O'Mahony, Sean Dougall and Damien Varley, with Ian Keatley converting two, put a sheen on the scoreboard. Back-to-back games against Saracens followed, with Munster winning 15-9 at home on 8 December. Eight days later, they faced a determined Saracens at Vicarage Road for an epic battle. Doug Howlett scored the visitors' only try, while Ronan O'Gara supplied the rest of the points. Saracens similarly scored only one try, but four penalties from the boot of Owen Farrell gave them a 19-13 victory.

Munster followed with an away win against Edinburgh 26-17 on 13 January. A week later, Racing fell 29-6 at Thomond Park, thus securing the second-best runner-up spot for Munster, who advanced to the knock-out stage. The quarter-final was played away from home against Harlequins, which Munster won 18-12, with Paul O'Connell captaining the team in place of the injured Doug Howlett. In the semi-final, Munster lost 16-10 away to Clermont. This was Ronan O'Gara's last match for Munster; he announced his retirement from rugby some weeks later. In his 240 games for the province, he scored a record 2,625 points.

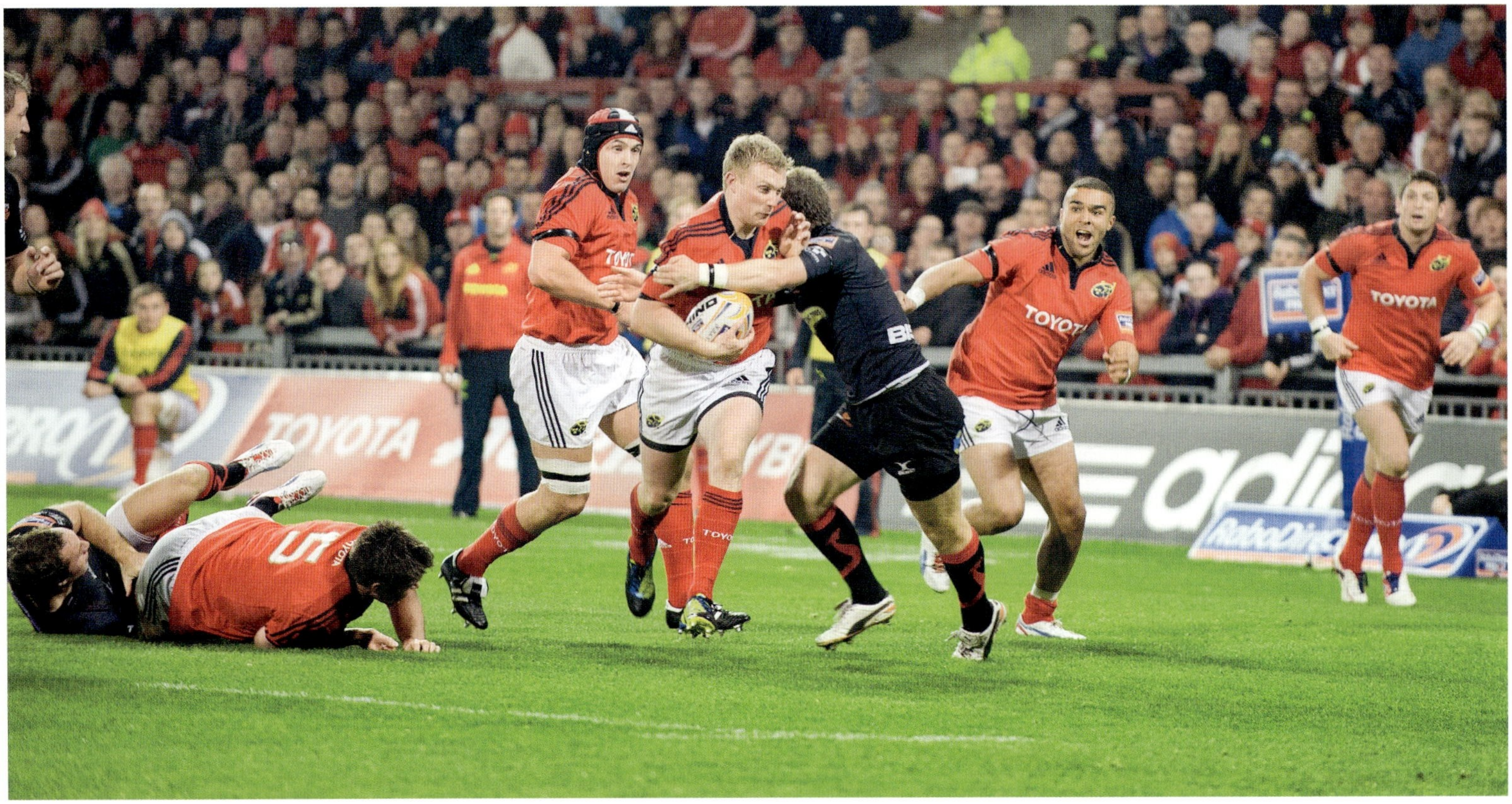

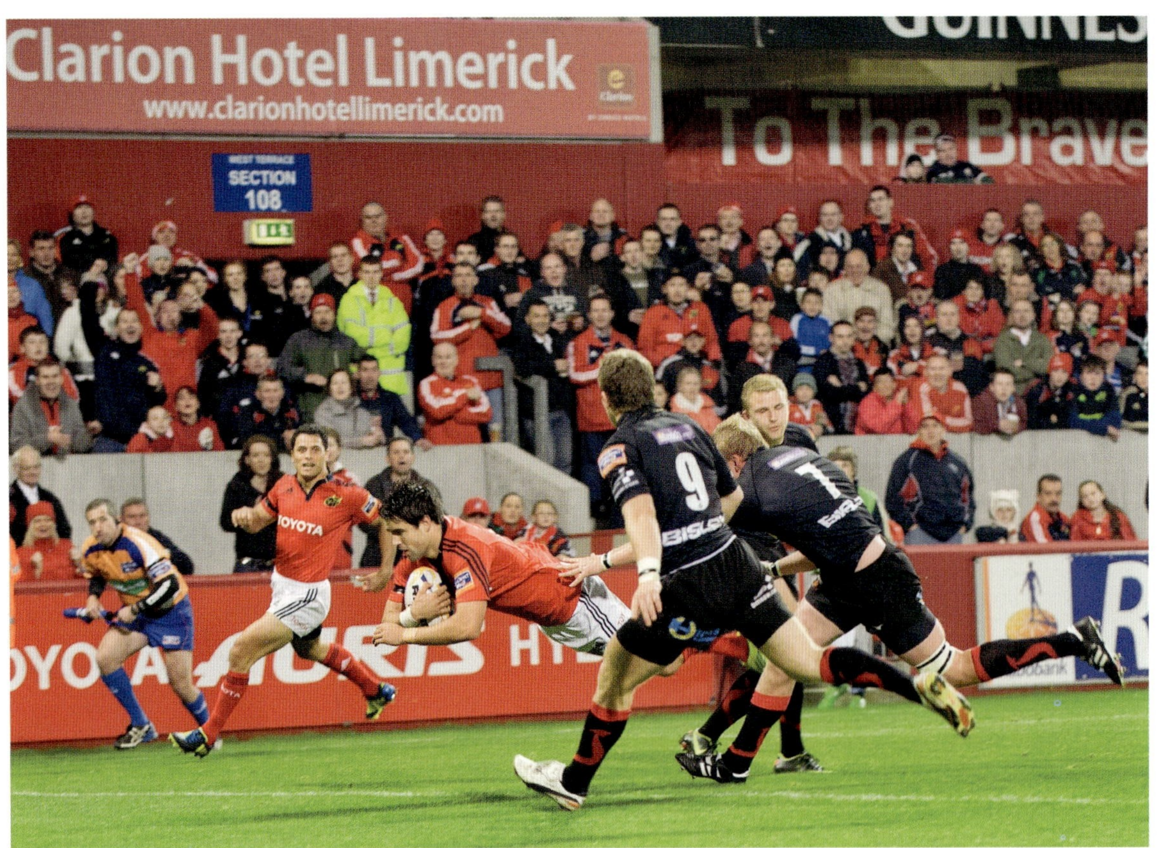

22 September 2012

Top: (l–r) Billy Holland (number 5) is felled while Niall Ronan watches as Keith Earls looks for Simon Zebo, with James Downey in support against Newport Gwent Dragons.

Left: A try for Conor Murray against the Dragons helps Munster to a 33-13 win.

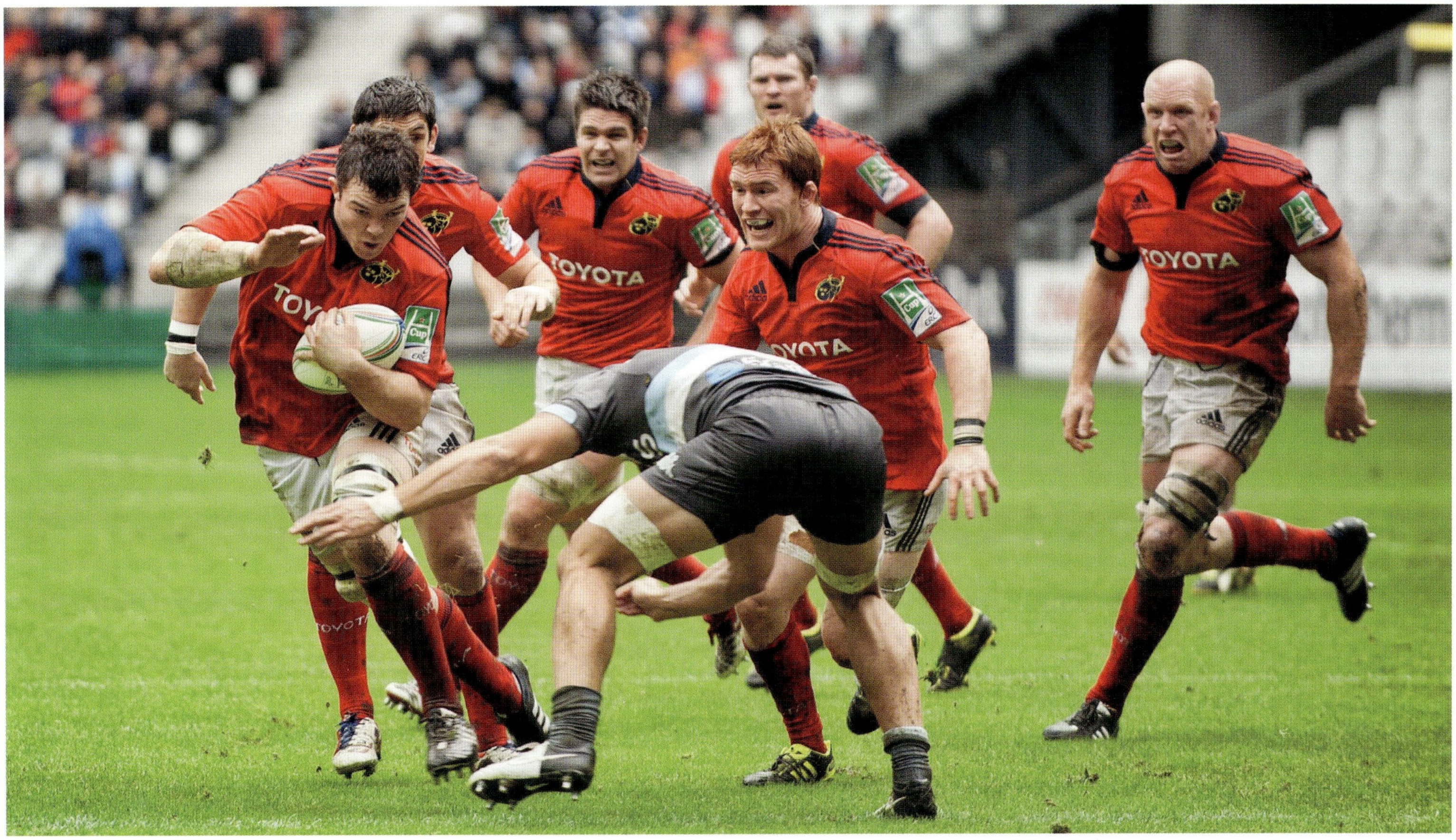

Top: Peter O'Mahony nimbly sidesteps his Racing Métro 92 opponent, followed by teammates (l–r) James Downey, Billy Holland, Sean Dougall, Donnacha Ryan and Paul O'Connell in the Heineken Cup match held in the Stade de France in Paris.

Below: Sean Dougall secures his try against Racing. Munster forced their opponents to pull out all the stops in Racing's 22-17 win.

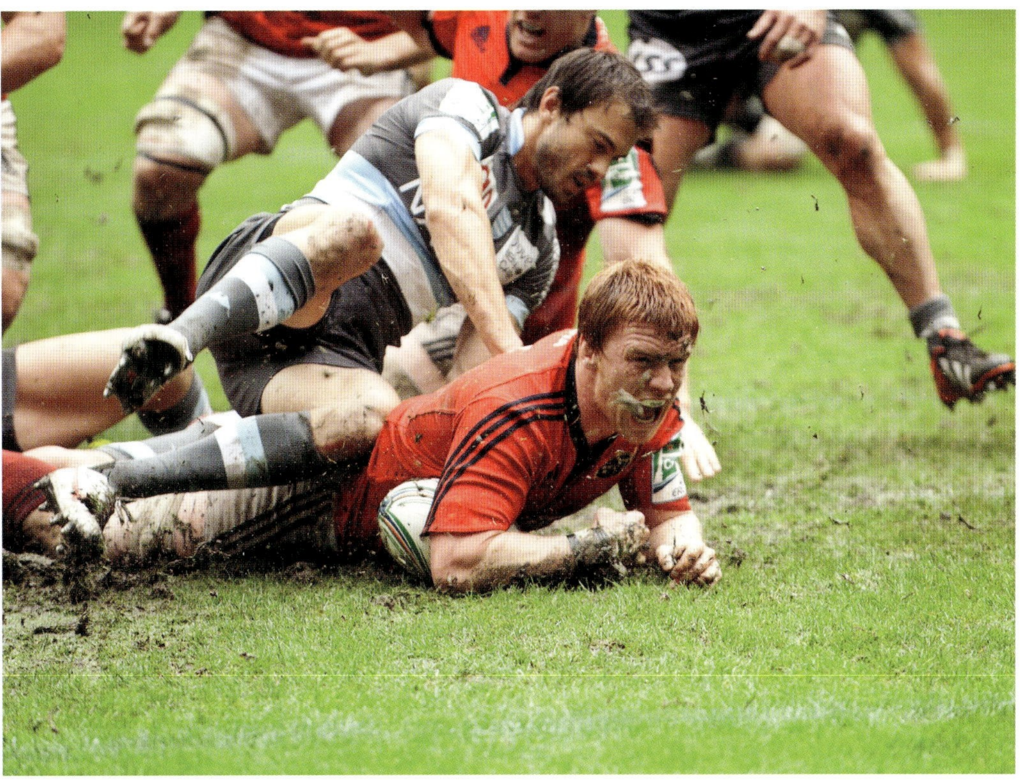

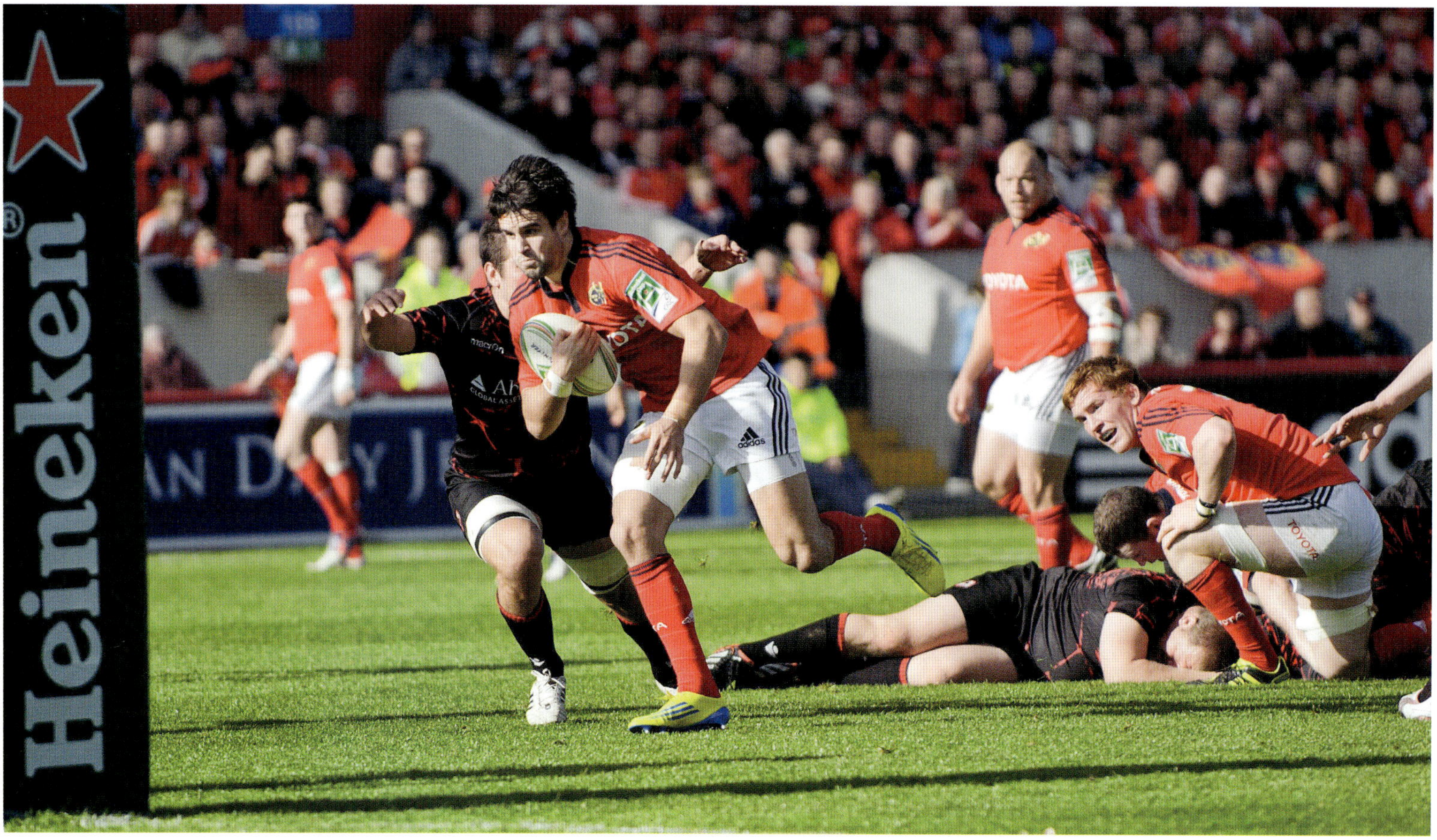

21 October 2012

Top: Conor Murray sprints for the line against Edinburgh. Munster claim a bonus point in the 33-0 win.

Below: Paul O'Connell hands off his opponent.

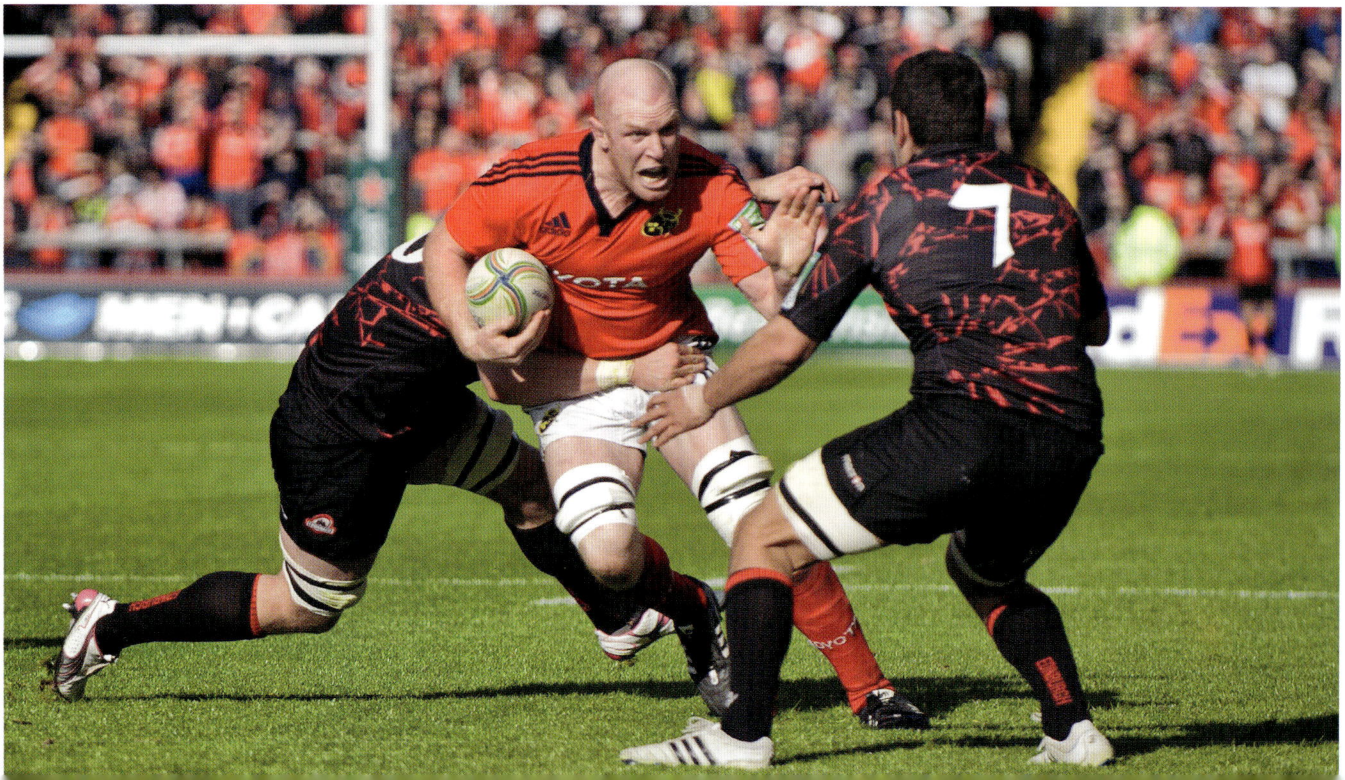

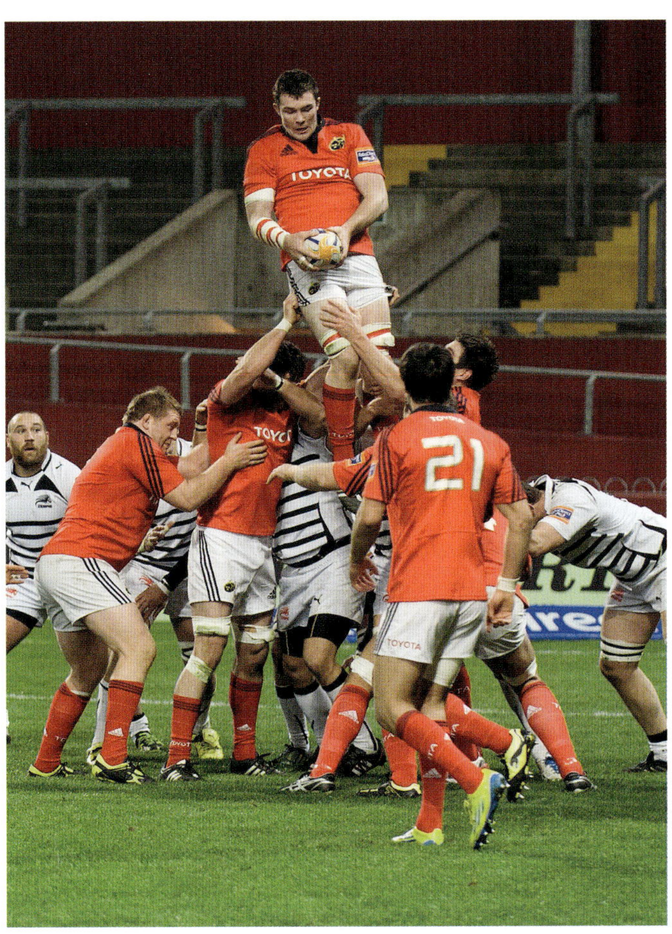

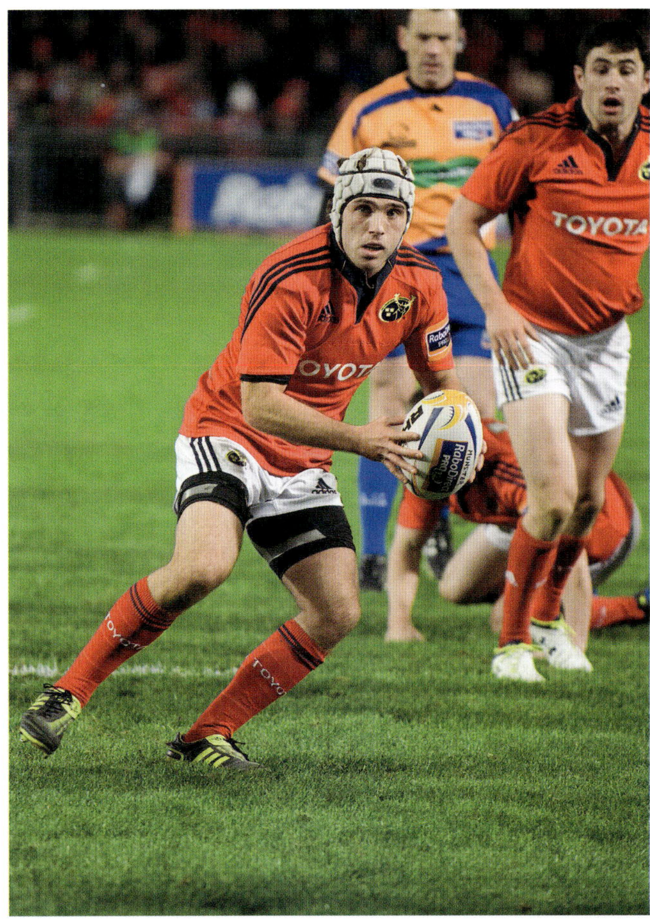

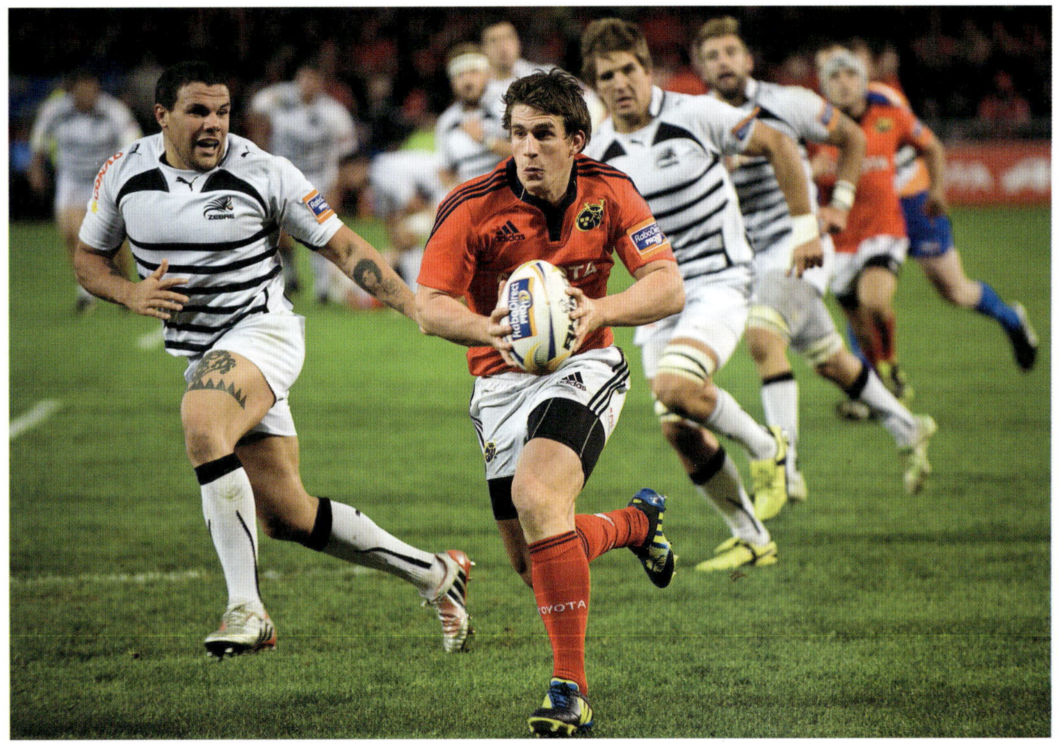

26 October 2012

Top left: Peter O'Mahony secures the line-out ball against Zebre.

Top right: Duncan Williams makes a break.

Right: Ian Keatley in full flight against Zebre. He contributed ten points to the final score. Munster's four tries – a brace from JJ Hanrahan and one each from Felix Jones and Luke O'Dea – secure the win, 29-3.

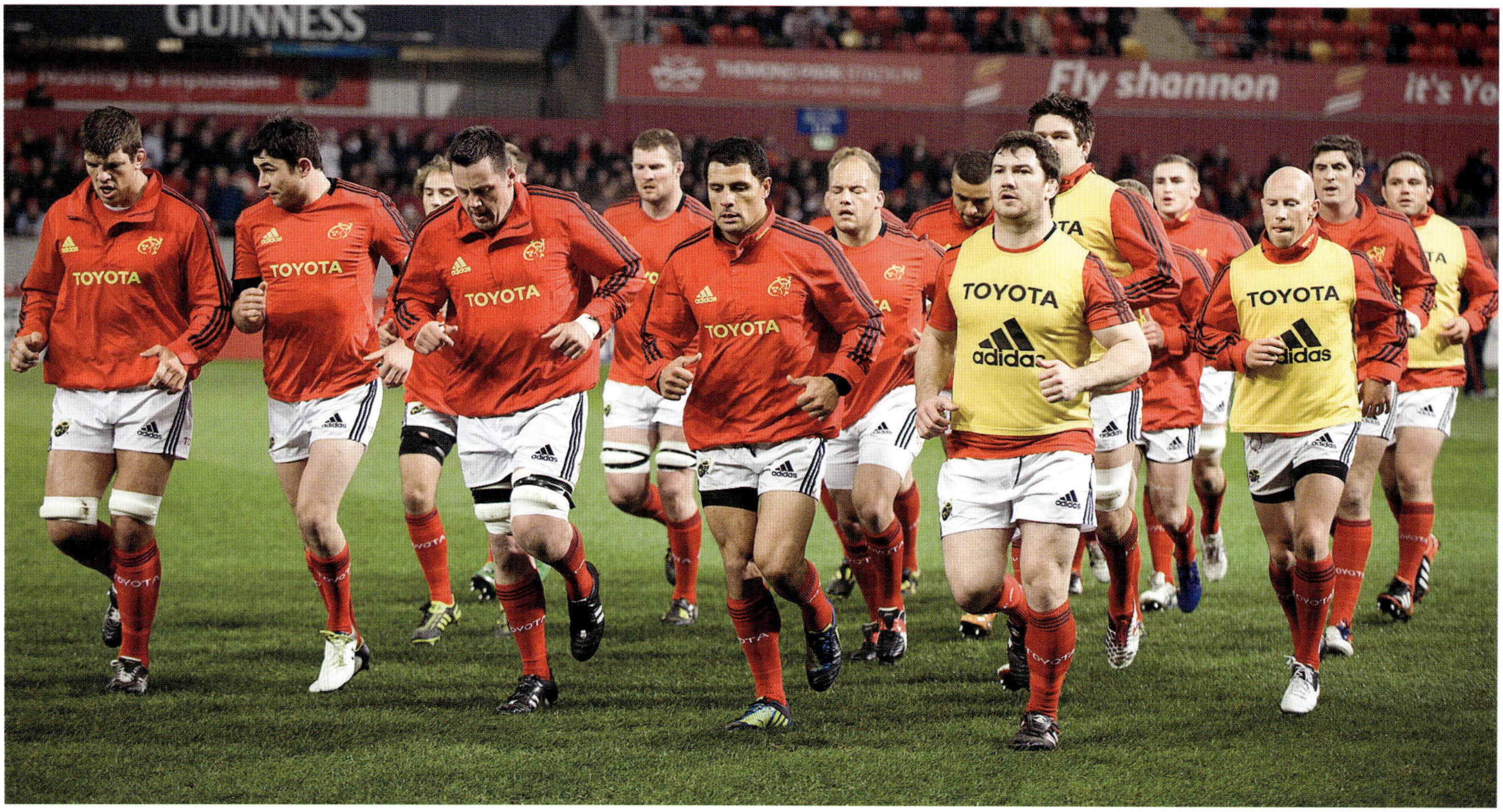

 THE BRAVE AND THE FAITHFUL

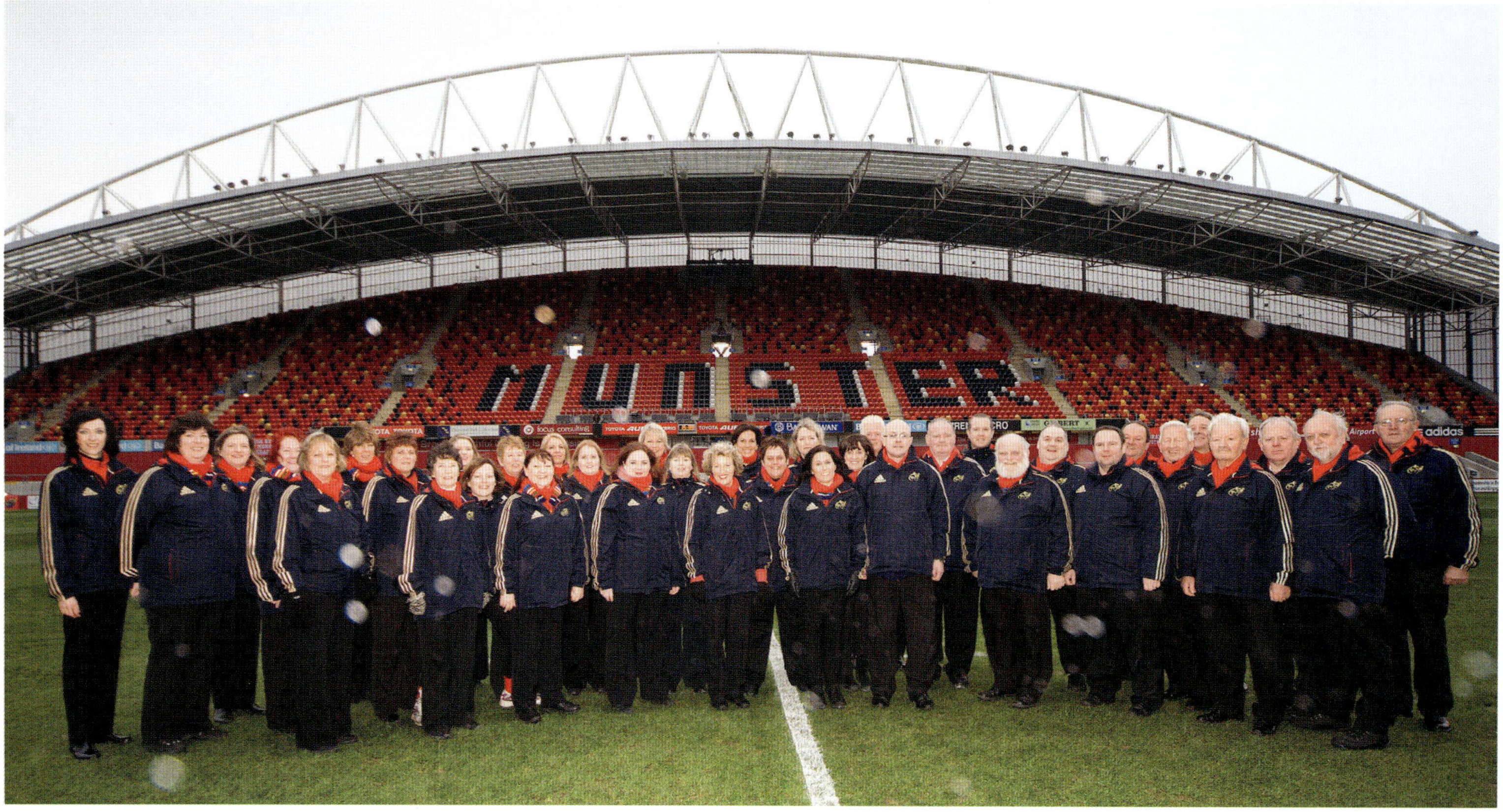

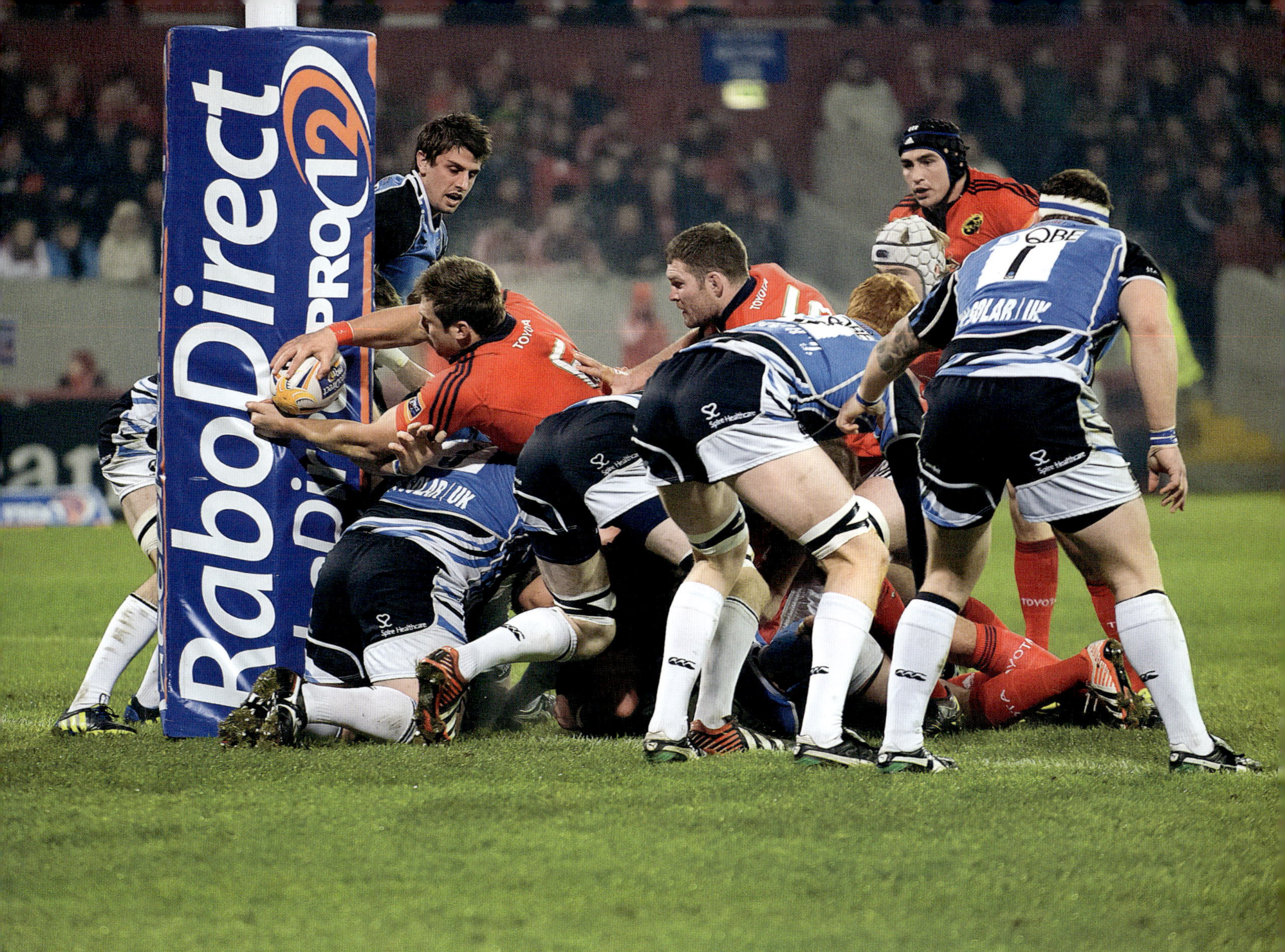

1 December 2012

Opposite top: Ready for the off: the team warms up before the Pro12 fixture against Glasgow Warriors in Thomond Park.

Opposite below: The Munster choir add greatly to the atmosphere before matches.

Above: After just eight minutes, CJ Stander scores his first of two tries against Glasgow Warriors, earning him a man-of-the-match award. Tommy O'Donnell scored Munster's second try, which, along with a penalty try plus four conversions and a penalty from Ronan O'Gara, give Munster a comfortable 31-3 victory.

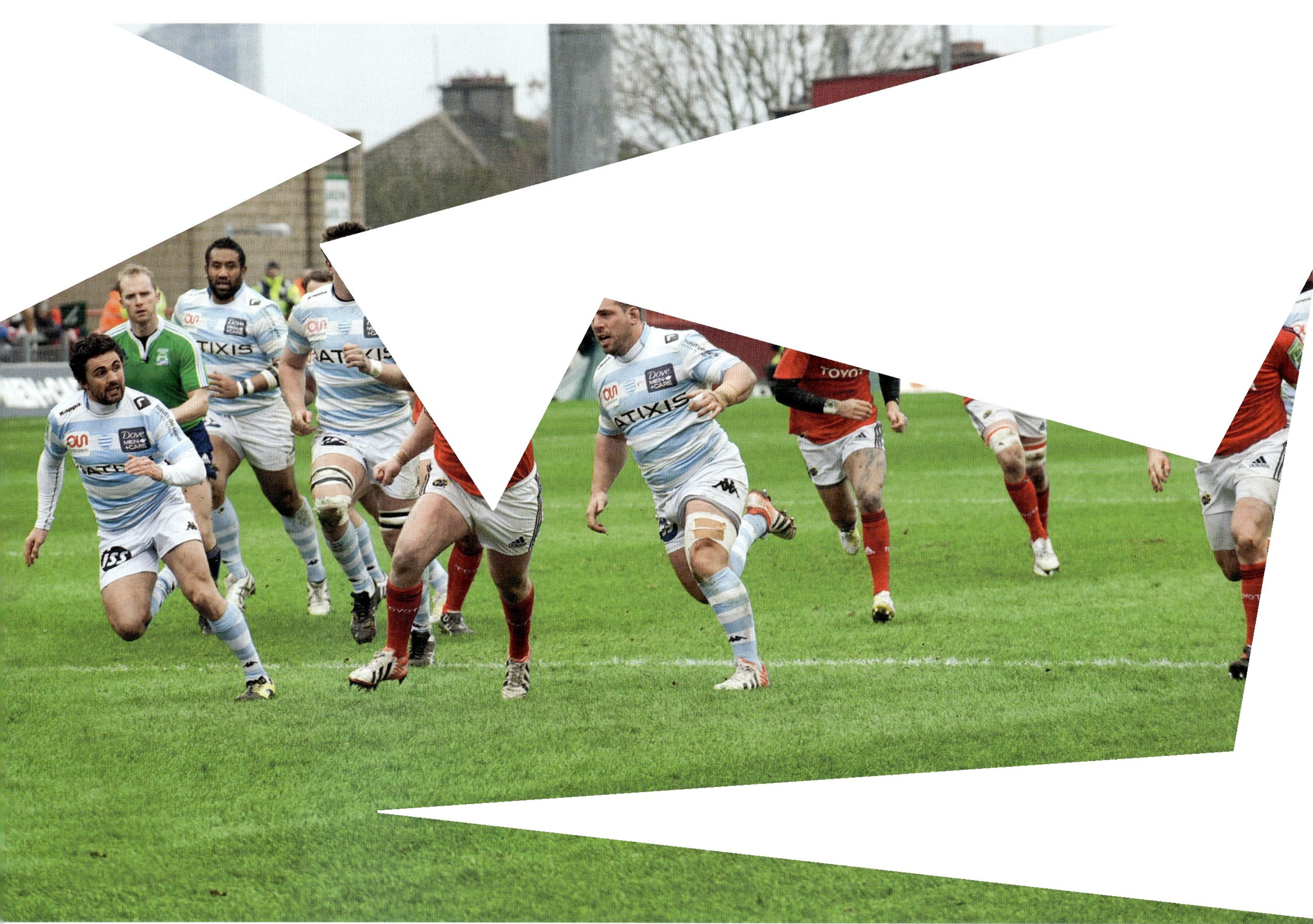

20 January 2013

Watched by referee Wayne Barnes, Dave Kilcoyne makes a break against Racing Métro 92. In support are Munster teammates (l-r) Donncha O'Callaghan, Conor Murray, James Coughlan and BJ Botha. Captained by Doug Howlett, Munster win 29-6, with tries from Murray, Simon Zebo (three) and Mike Sherry.

Below: Ian Keatley scores a try against Leinster, closely watched by (l–r) Leinster's Isaac Boss and Rob Kearney (number 15), teammates Donncha O'Callaghan and Peter O'Mahony, and Leinster's Mike Ross and Dave Kearney. Leinster capitalised on Munster's high penalty count, Ian Madigan scoring nine points in the first twenty minutes. Leinster win 22-16.

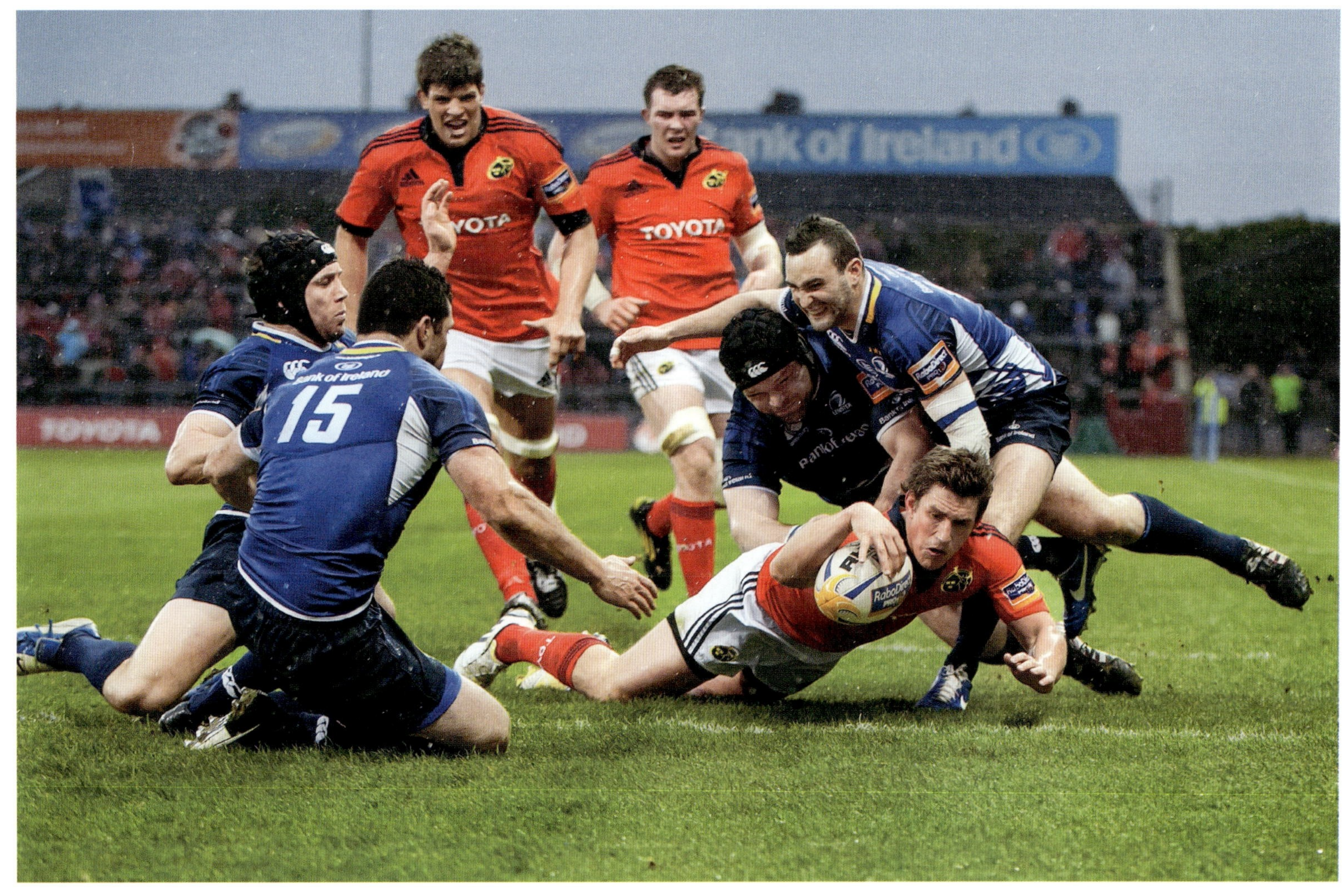

2013–2014

Pro12 **Pool wins: 16; Pool losses: 6; Eliminated: semi-final**
Heineken Cup **Pool wins: 5; Pool losses: 1; Eliminated: semi-final**

This season saw Marcus Horan retire and the great Peter Stringer move to Bath. James Coughlan won the IRUPA Unsung Hero of the Year award. Munster's Young Player of the Year was JJ Hanrahan, who won three man-of-the-match awards. Peter O'Mahony, CJ Stander and Ian Keatley all received the accolade twice. Donncha O'Callaghan became Munster's most capped player, winning his 241st cap against Zebre, while Paul O'Connell won his 75th Heineken Cup cap. Simon Zebo was top try-scorer, with seven. Rob Penney and backs coach Simon Mannix left at the end of the season. Forwards coach and former captain Anthony Foley was confirmed as the next Munster coach.

Pro12

The season started with Munster defeating Edinburgh 34-23 on 7 September at Musgrave Park. Next was an away match against Zebre on 13 September, another try-fest and a bonus-point 43-21 win for Munster. On 20 September, Munster were in Italy again, to play Benetton Treviso. A strong second half from the hosts saw Munster go down 29-19. Newport Gwent Dragons came to Musgrave Park on 28 September, and the hosts returned to winning ways with a 23-9 victory.

At Thomond Park on 5 October, Munster were victorious over old foes Leinster, winning 19-15. Munster were away to Glasgow Warriors on 25 October, and won 13-6. JJ Hanrahan was the star, scoring all of Munster's points with a converted try and two penalties. Munster battled the Ospreys at Thomond Park on 2 November, grinding out a 12-6 win.

Next came an excellent away win, 31-10, against Cardiff Blues on 23 November, with tries from Felix Jones, Damien Varley, James Cronin and Andrew Conway, all of which Hanrahan converted, adding a penalty for good measure.

At Rodney Parade on 29 November, Munster beat Newport Gwent Dragons 18-14, all the visitors' points from the boot of Ian Keatley. On 21 December at Musgrave Park, it took an 80th-minute try from Ronan O'Mahony to seal a 16-10 win over Scarlets. Munster ended the year with a 22-16 win over Connacht at

Thomond Park on 27 December. Hanrahan scored all Munster's points with a try, conversion and five out of five penalties.

A trip to Ravenhill on 3 January 2014 saw Ulster win 29-19. Back at home on 8 February, Munster trounced Cardiff Blues 54-13, followed by a 36-8 victory over Zebre at Musgrave Park on 15 February. Next to fall were Ospreys, in a 25-11 away win for Munster. In Liberty Stadium on 1 March, Scarlets ended Munster's streak, with an 18-13 win for the hosts. Benetton Treviso went down 14-3 at Thomond Park on 22 March.

At Aviva Stadium on 29 March, Leinster won a closely contested game by 22-18. Back in Limerick, Glasgow Warriors gave the hosts a 22-5 hiding on 12 April, CJ Stander Munster's only scorer. Munster beat Connacht at Galway Sportsgrounds 32-23 on 19 April, and ran riot away to Edinburgh on 3 May with a seven-try haul, winning 55-12. The tries were from Conway, Denis Hurley, Varley, two penalty tries, Duncan Williams and Tommy O'Donnell, with three conversions from Hanrahan and two from Conor Murray, and two penalties from Hanrahan.

Ulster were victorious at Thomond Park on 10 May, winning a close game by 19-17. This meant Munster had to travel to Scotstoun on 16 May for the semi-final, where Glasgow Warriors edged the match by a single point, to win 16-15.

HEINEKEN CUP

The first round started with a 29-23 away loss to Edinburgh on 12 October 2013. Gloucester visited Thomond Park on 19 October where the home team won 26-10, a scoreline that flattered the hosts. At home on 8 December, Munster had a bonus-point victory over Perpignan, 36-8. The reverse fixture at Stade Aimé Giral on 14 December saw the province scrape home by the narrowest of margins, 18-17, with an 80th-minute try from JJ Hanrahan.

On 11 January 2014, tries from Keith Earls and Peter O'Mahony, with two conversions and two penalties by Ian Keatley, secured an excellent 20-7 victory over Gloucester at Kingsholm. Munster avenged themselves against Edinburgh on 19 January, winning 38-6. James Coughlan, Johne Murphy, Murray, O'Mahony, Zebo and Jones scored the tries in the bonus-point victory, with Keatley converting four. This earned Munster a home quarter-final against Toulouse on 5 April. On a special day in front of 26,000 supporters, Munster had an outstanding win, 47-23. Earls, Dave Kilcoyne, Stander, Casey Laulala, Zebo and Paul O'Connell scored tries. Keatley also had a good day at the office with four conversions and three out of four penalties.

The semi-final against Toulon was played at Stade Vélodrome in Marseille on 27 April. Jonny Wilkinson was Munster's nemesis, scoring seven out of eight penalty attempts and a drop goal. The final score was 24-16 to the hosts, who would go on to beat Saracens in the final.

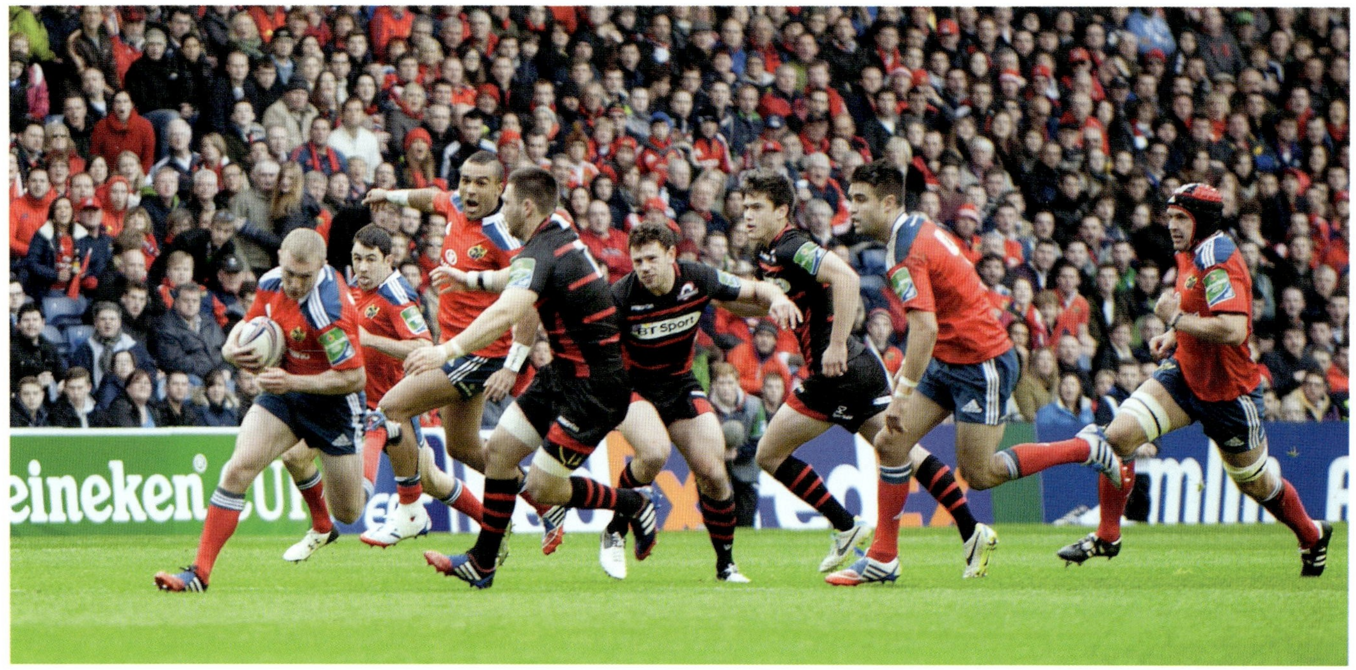

12 October 2013

Keith Earls breaks against Edinburgh, with teammates (l–r) Felix Jones, Simon Zebo, Conor Murray and Niall Ronan in support. Captained by Paul O'Connell, Munster, playing away, rack up a high penalty count. Edinburgh win 29-23.

19 October 2013

Flight of Earls. Munster put the previous week's defeat in Scotland behind them to beat Gloucester at Thomond Park by 26-10, Ian Keatley accounting for sixteen of the points (two conversions and four penalties).

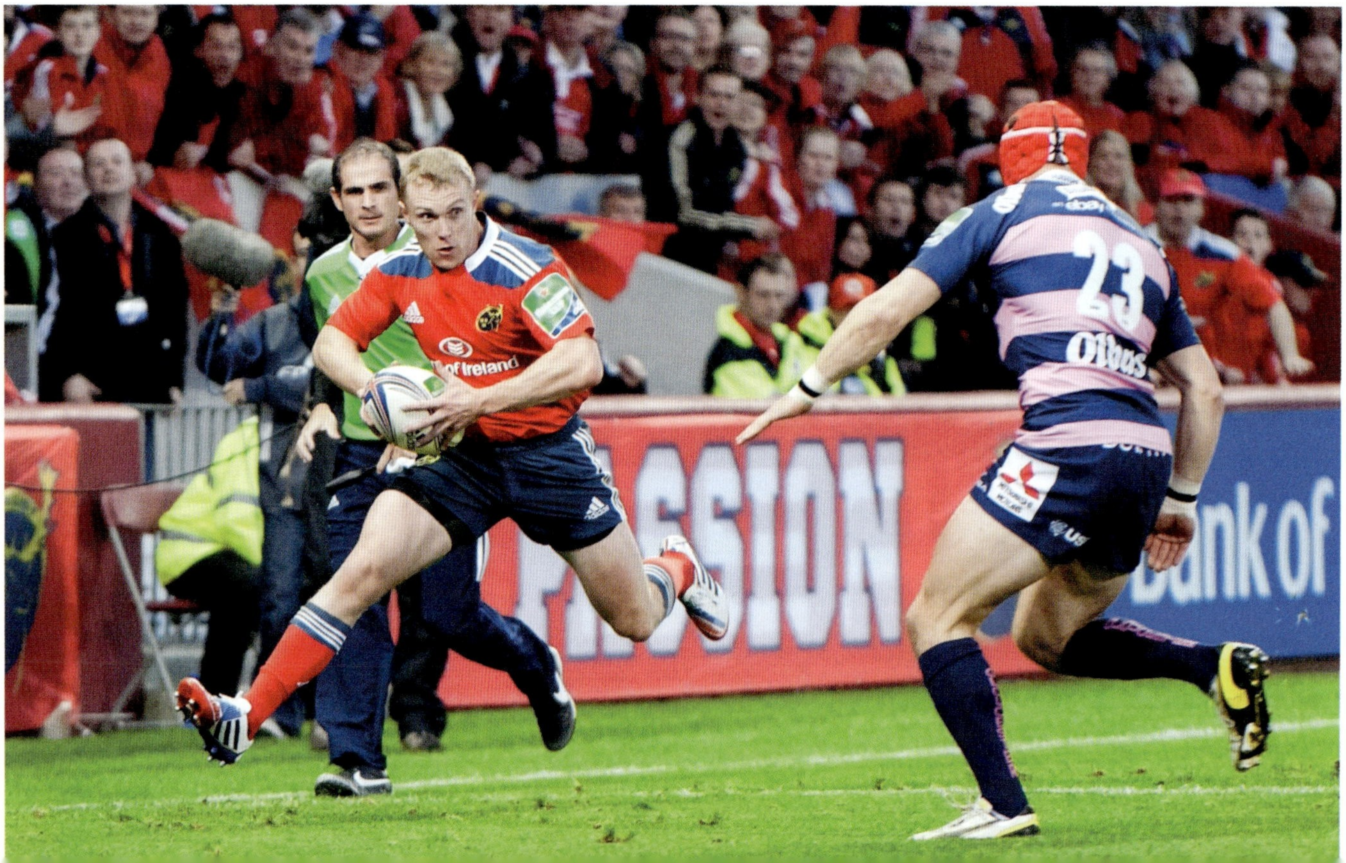

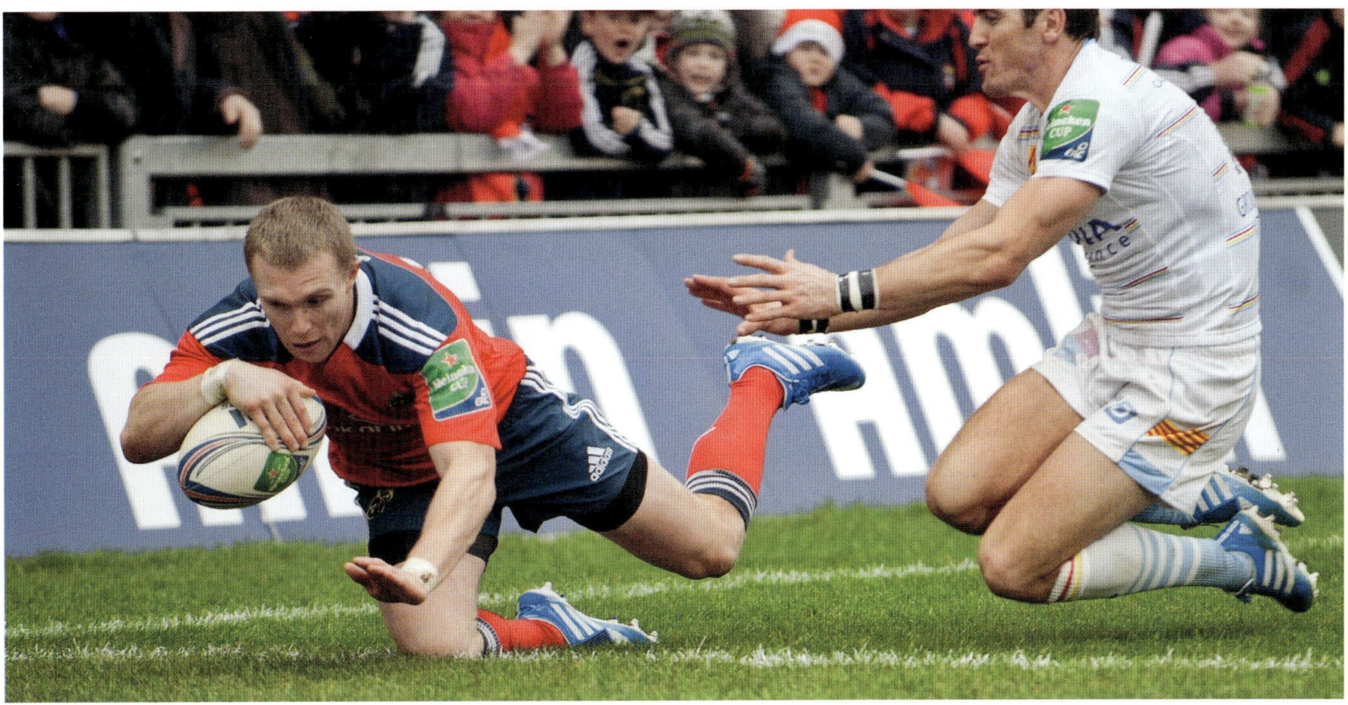

Top: Keith Earls makes a solo run to score in the 34th minute. By half-time, Munster were 22-0 up against Perpignan, eventually winning by a comfortable 36-8.

Bottom: Billy Holland charges into a Perpignan tackle.

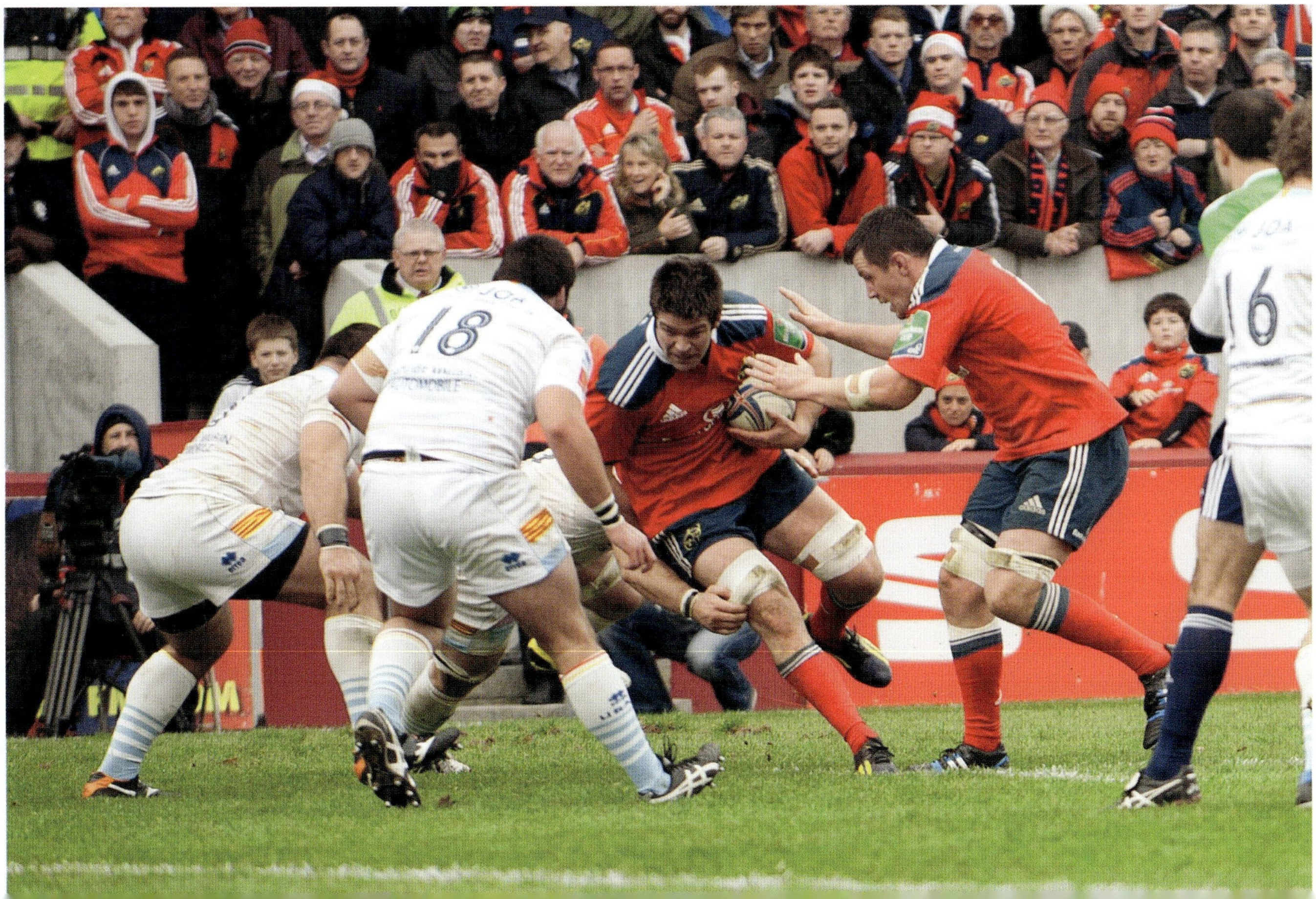

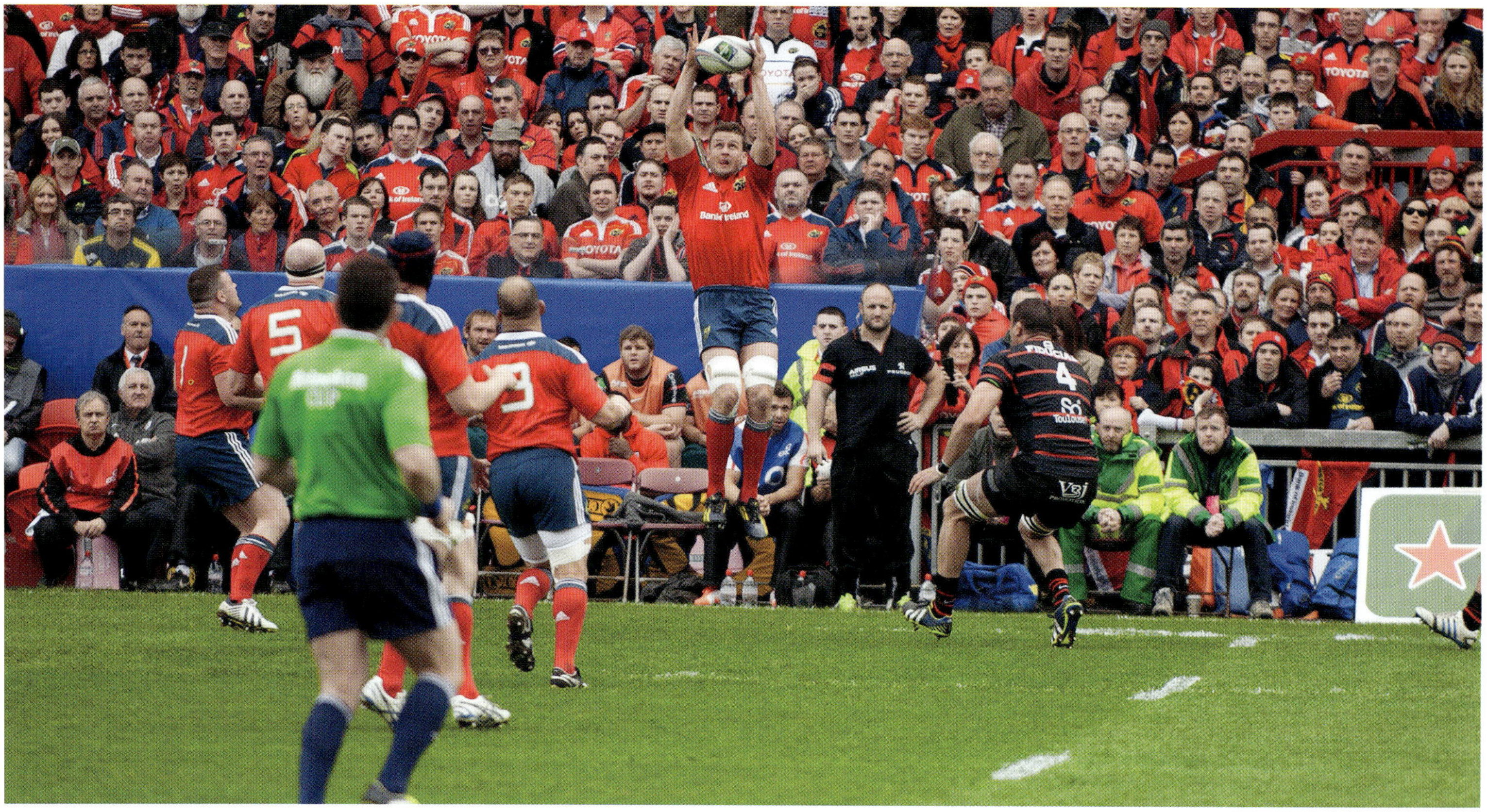

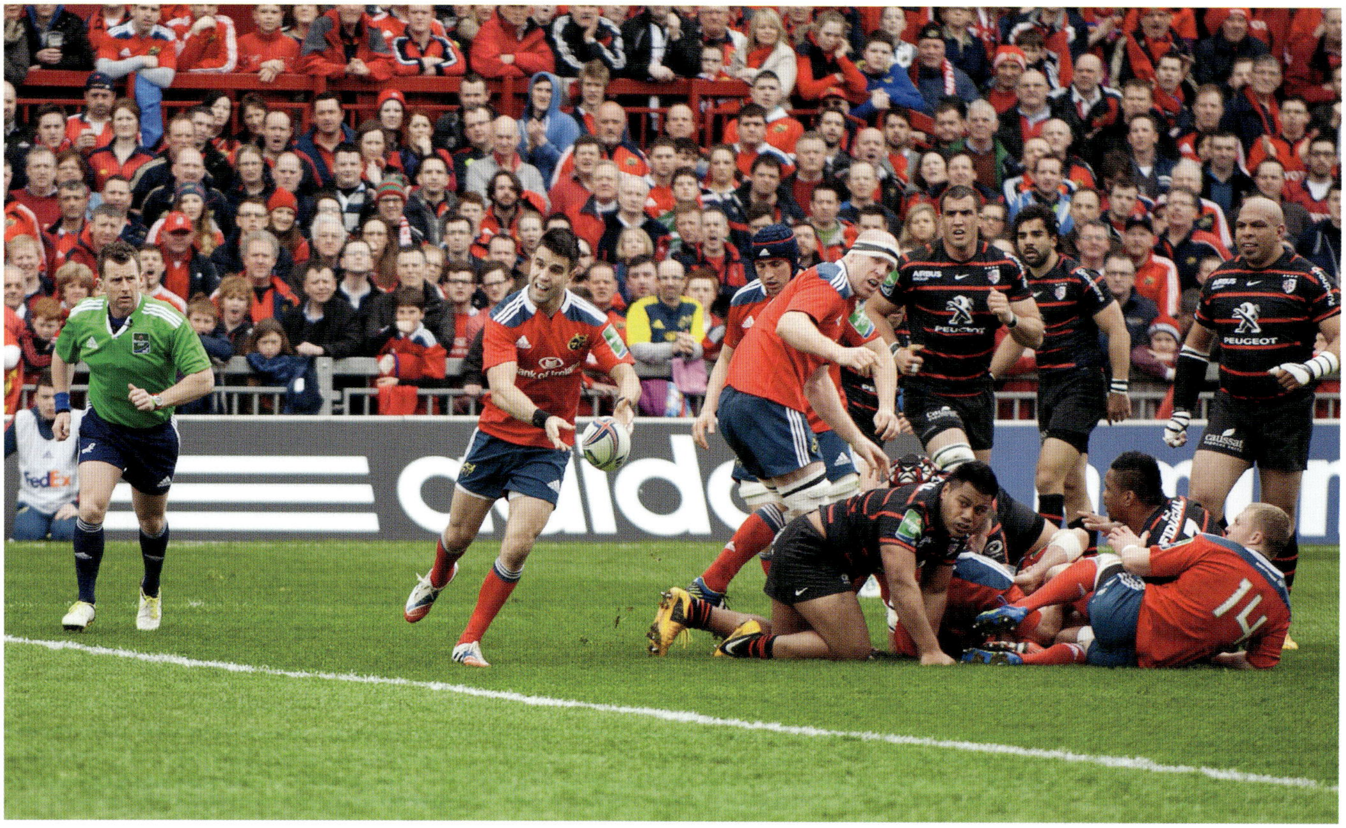

5 April 2014

Opposite top:
Dave Foley collects against Toulouse in the Heineken Cup quarter-final in Thomond Park.

Opposite bottom:
Conor Murray in top form against Toulouse, watched closely by referee Nigel Owens.

Right: Paul O'Connell catches an uncontested line-out ball. An outstanding performance by Munster saw them romp home 47-23 winners.

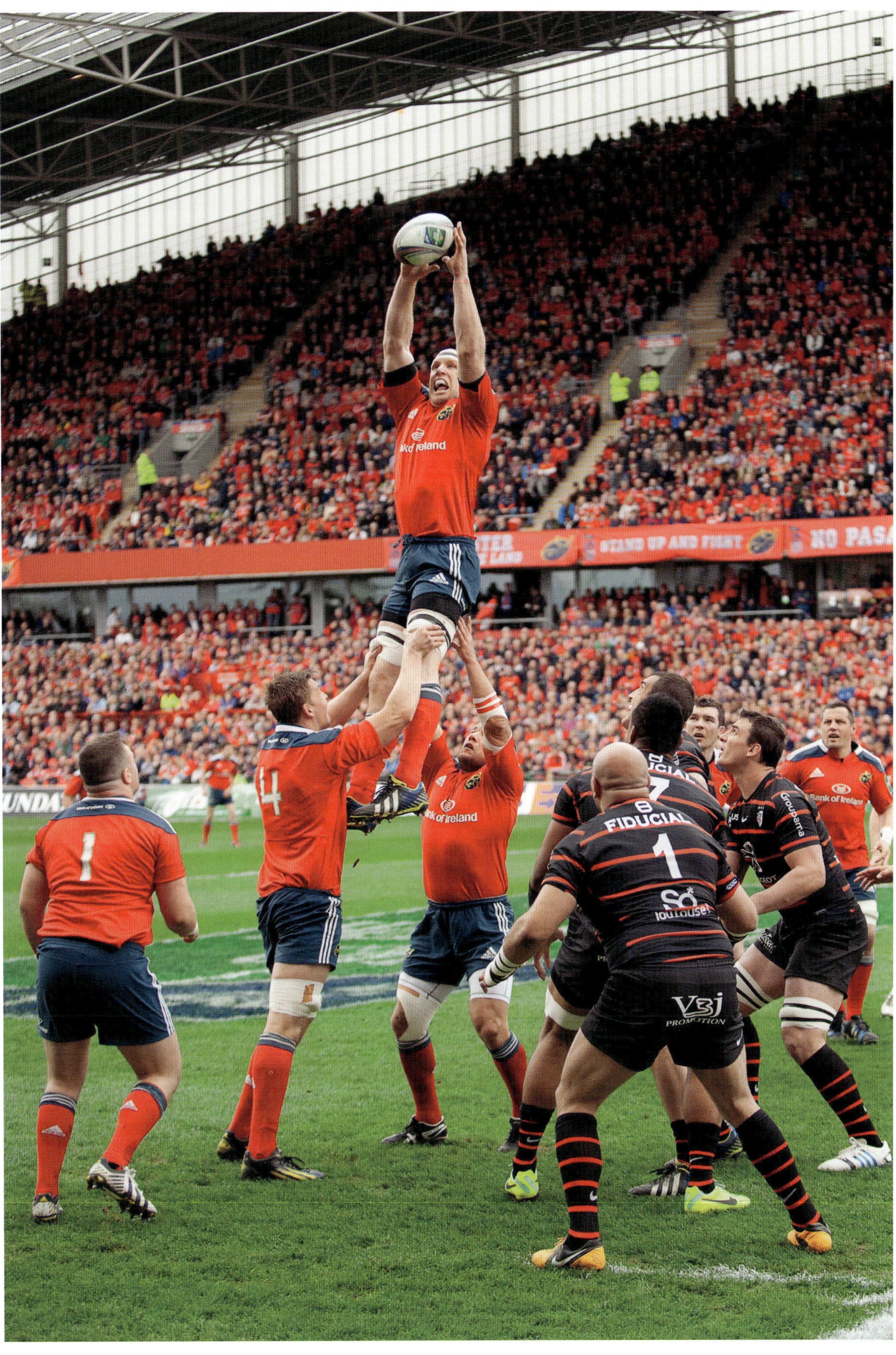

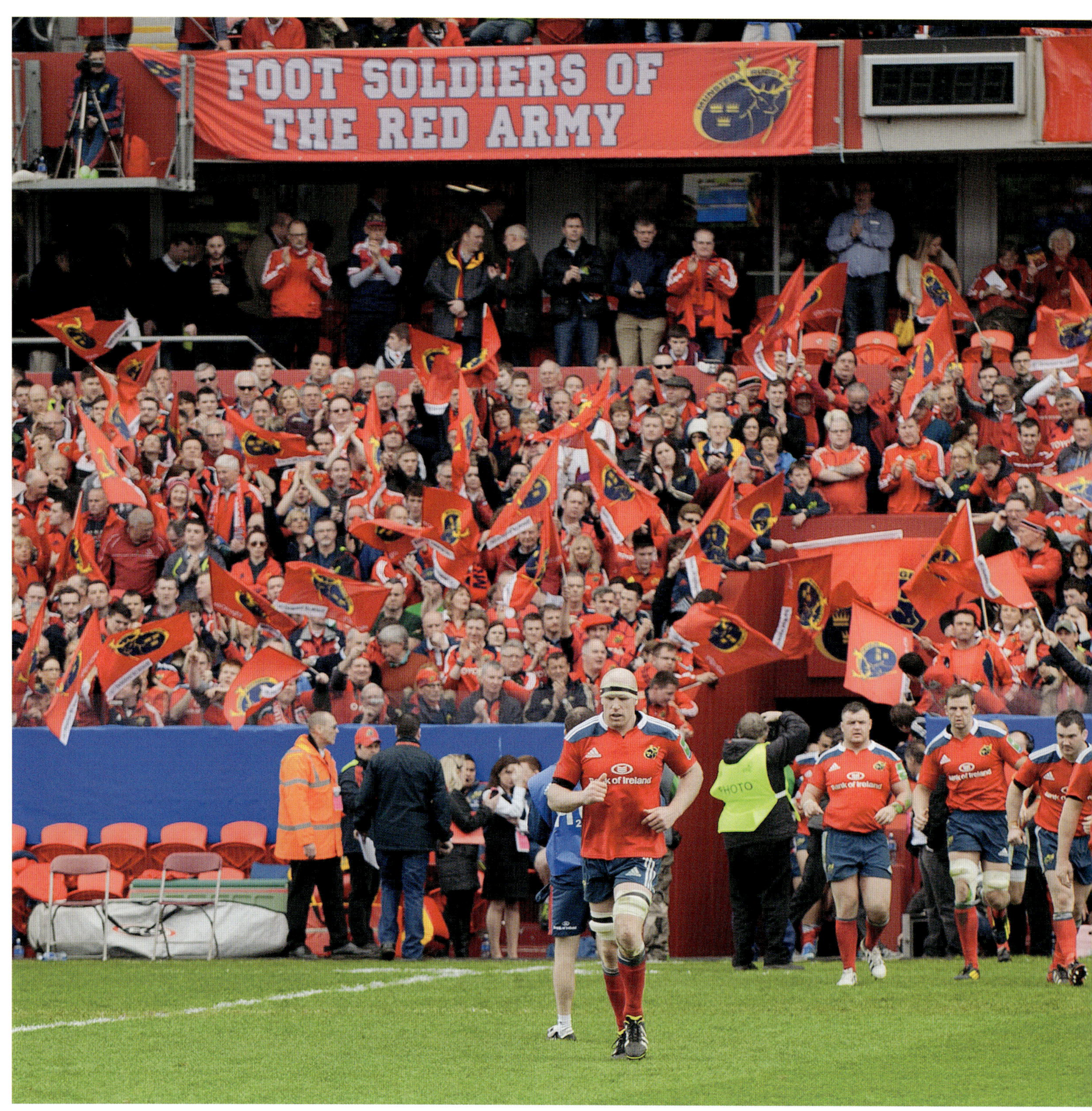

FOOT SOLDIERS OF
THE RED ARMY

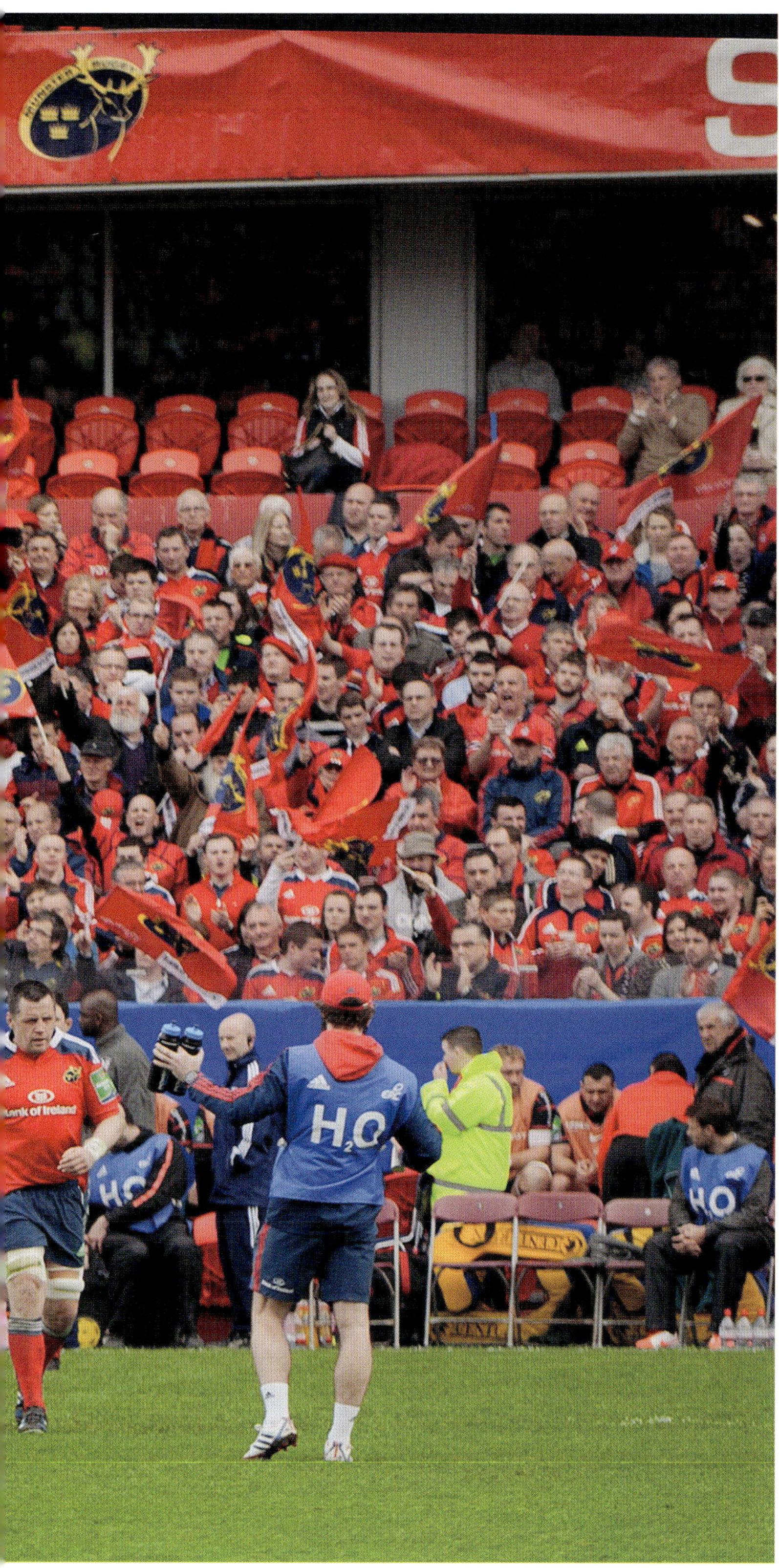

5 April 2014

Paul O'Connell leads out for the second half, with a sea of red in the stands behind him. Peter O'Mahony was captain on the day, but was injured in the first quarter.

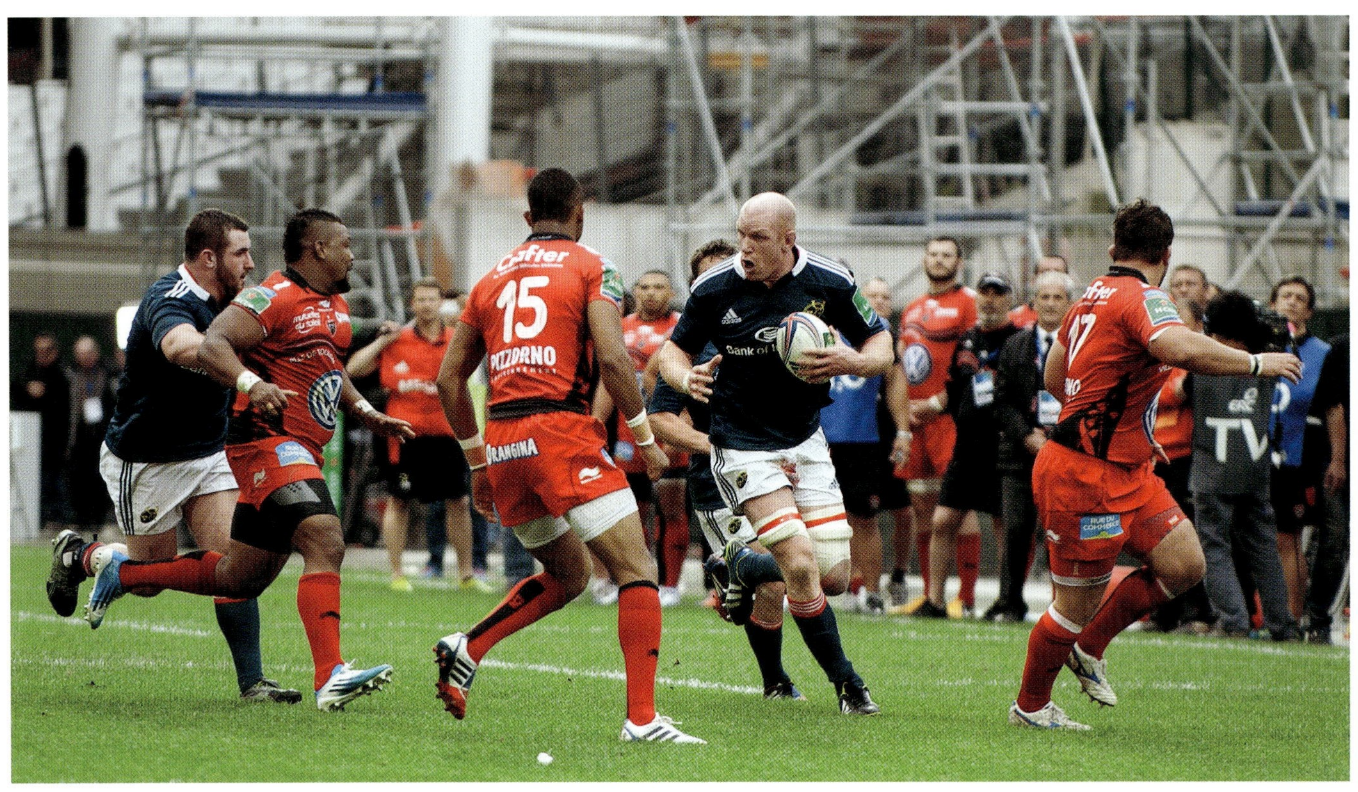

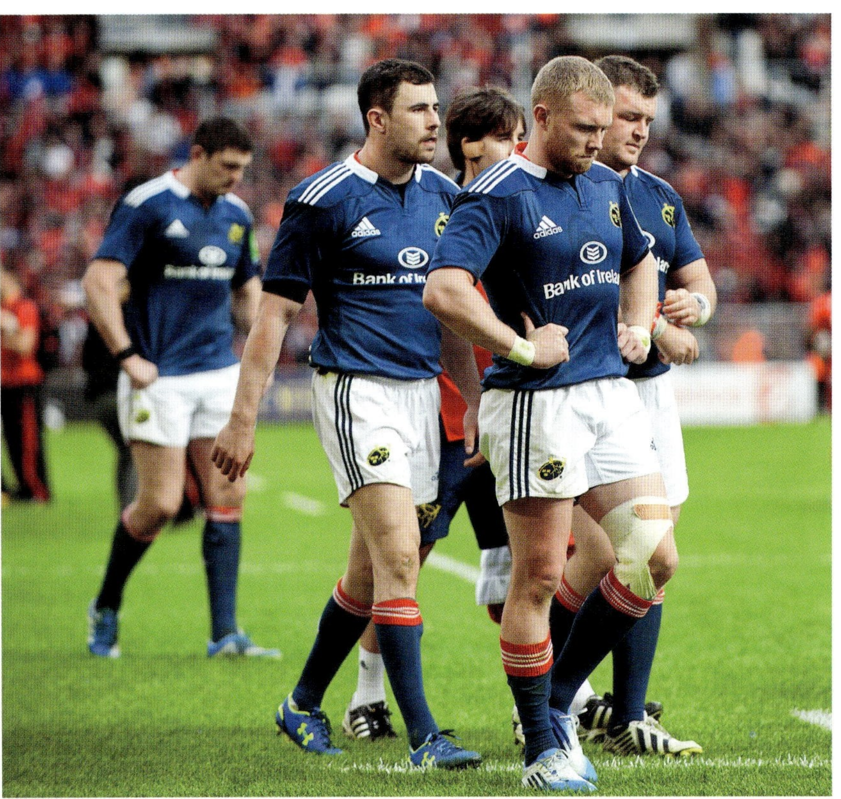

Above: Munster in blue against Toulon in red for the Heineken Cup semi-final at Stade Vélodrome in Marseille: Paul O'Connell eyes up the great Mathieu Bastareaud of Toulon (first player in red on left) and Delon Armitage (number 15). Munster's discipline in the first half cost them dearly and Toulon won 24-16.

Left: Pain in defeat. (L–r): Felix Jones, Keith Earls and Dave Kilcoyne.

Opposite top: Munster's Paul O'Connell makes a break in Munster's 55-12 win against hosts Edinburgh.

Opposite bottom: Donncha O'Callaghan wins a line-out against Glasgow Warriors in the Pro12 semi-final at Scotstoun.

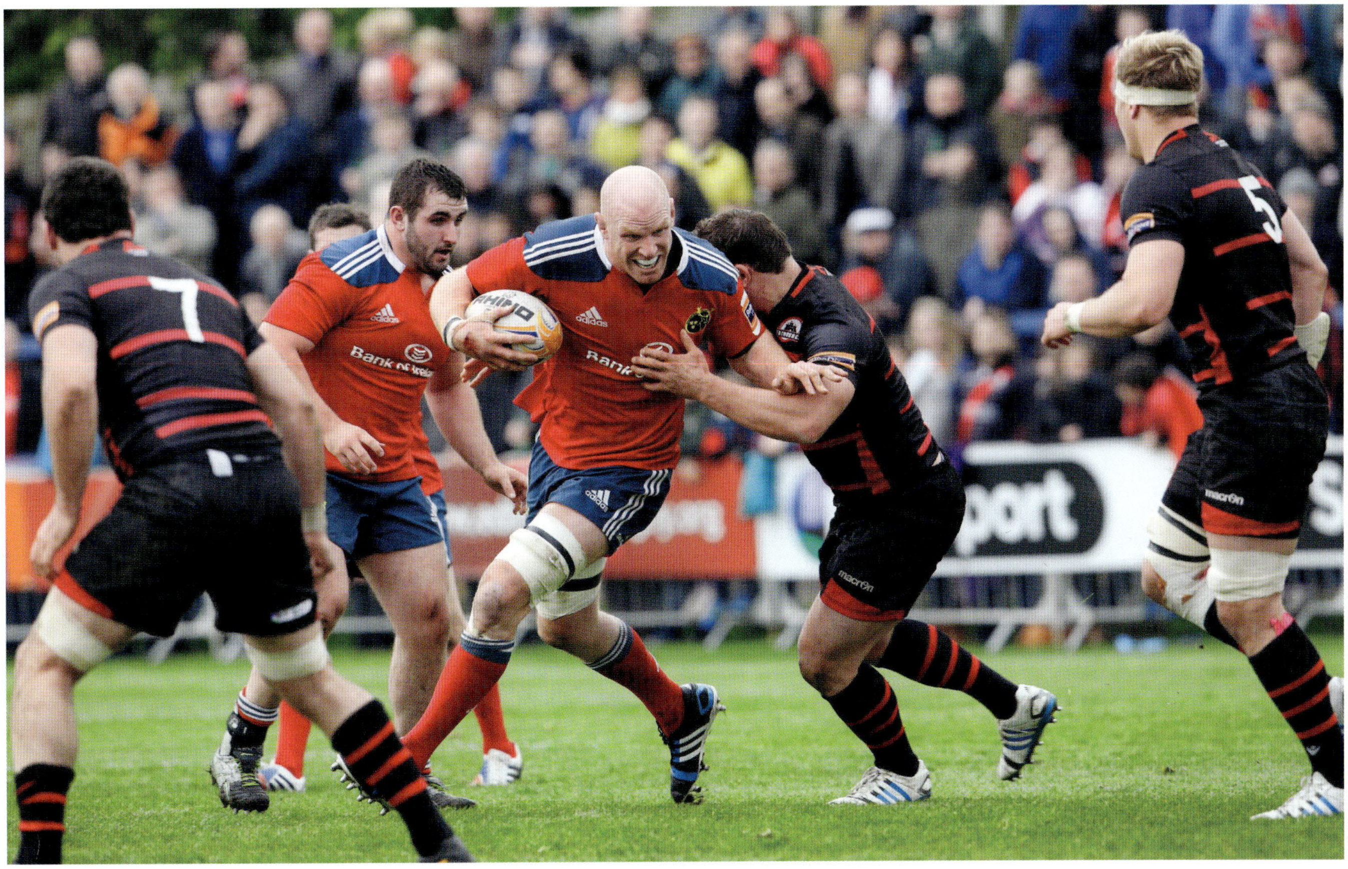
7
5
Bank of Ireland
adidas
macron
port

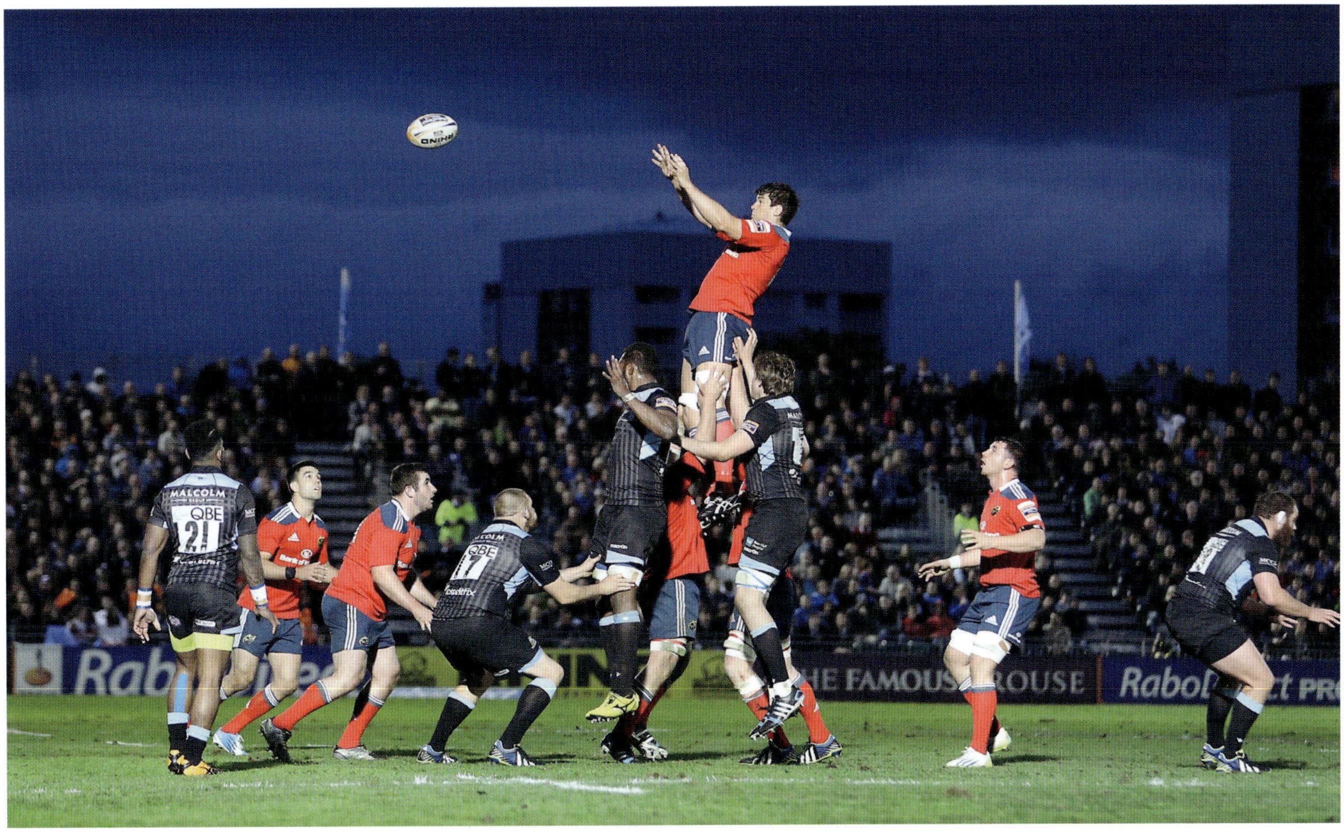
MALCOLM
QBE
21
HE FAMOUS
ROUSE

2014–2015

Pro12   Pool wins: 15; Pool losses: 5; Drew: 2; Eliminated: final
Heineken Cup   Pool wins: 3; Pool losses: 3; Did not progress further

Anthony Foley began his first season as Munster head coach. It would be Paul O'Connell's final season playing for Munster after an illustrious career. New signings included Robin Copeland from Cardiff Blues, Tyler Bleyendaal from Crusaders, Andrew Smith from Brumbies and Eusebio Guiñazú from Bath. Shane Buckley and Jonathan Holland were promoted from the academy. Niall Ronan retired through injury, while James Coughlan and Casey Laulala moved, to Pau and Racing Métro respectively.

Pro12

Under new head coach Anthony Foley, Munster's first Pro12 game, against Edinburgh at Thomond Park on 5 September, was a surprise 14-13 win for the visitors. An away fixture against Benetton Treviso on 12 September happily resulted in a 21-10 win for Munster. Zebre came to Thomond Park on 19 September; Munster crushed the visitors 31-5, including a hat trick of tries by Simon Zebo. Next at Thomond Park were Ospreys on 27 September, who beat the hosts 19-14. A successful visit to Aviva Stadium on 4 October saw Munster win 34-23. Next were Scarlets at Thomond Park on 10 October, which Munster won 17-6.

Munster travelled to play Cardiff Blues on 1 November, winning 28-24. A further visit to Wales on 21 November saw a bonus-point 38-12 win over Newport Gwent Dragons. In a tense encounter in Thomond Park on 28 November, Munster emerged victorious against Ulster, winning 21-20. Another close match in Scotstoun on 20 December was edged by Glasgow Warriors 21-18.

Leinster came to Thomond Park on 26 December. In front of a full house, Munster had a comprehensive 28-13 win. The try-scorers were CJ Stander, Andrew Conway and Dave O'Callaghan. Ian Keatley converted two and kicked three penalties.

Munster headed to Galway Sportsgrounds on 1 January 2015 but lost to Connacht for the first time since 2008. The final score was 24-16. In Italy on 10 January against Zebre, Munster cruised to a 31-7 bonus-point victory. Cardiff Blues came to Irish Independent Park on 14 February and were comprehensively beaten 33-16. Tries came from Denis Hurley, Jack O'Donoghue and Ronan O'Mahony. JJ Hanrahan converted all three and added four penalties. A 25-25 draw at Parc y Scarlets followed on 21 February, with Munster coughing up six penalties. Glasgow Warriors were next, at Irish Independent Park on 28 February. Munster scored four tries, through Jack O'Donoghue, Eusebio Guiñazú, Keith Earls and Stander, to win 22-10. At Liberty Stadium on 7 March, Ospreys proved too strong for Munster, winning 26-12.

Munster got back on the winning trail against Connacht on 28 March at Thomond Park, with a 42-20 win, with tries from Billy Holland, Duncan Casey, Simon Zebo, Andrew Smith, Hurley and Earls, all converted by Keatley and Hanrahan. Munster had another try-fest, against Edinburgh in Murrayfield on 11 April, winning 34-3. The try-scorers were Casey, Stander, Conor Murray, Zebo and Earls, with Keatley adding three conversions and a penalty. Benetton Treviso were next, at Irish Independent Park on 25 April. Munster had an excellent win, 30-19. At Kingspan Stadium on 9 May, Ulster and Munster played out a 23-23 draw.

A thumping 50-27 victory over Newport Gwent Dragons at Irish Independent Park on 16 May assured Munster of a home semi-final. The try-scorers were Smith, Stander, Murray (three), Paul O'Connell, Earls and Ronan O'Mahony, with Keatley converting five.

In the semi-final on 23 May, Munster and Ospreys met in a close contest. Josh Matavesi looked to have won it for Ospreys with a last-minute try, but referee Nigel Owens ruled it out for a knock-on. Munster progressed to the final by 21-18. The final against Glasgow Warriors was played at neutral venue Kingspan Stadium on 30 May 2015. Alas, Warriors were too strong, winning their first Pro12 title 31-13 in what would be Paul O'Connell's final game for Munster.

HEINEKEN CUP

Munster's first match was against Sale Sharks on 18 October at AJ Bell Stadium. In spite of tries from Dave Kilcoyne, Conway and Murray, with Keatley converting all three and adding a penalty, it still took a drop goal in the 80th minute from Keatley to seal the 27-26 win.

Munster then defeated Saracens 14-3 at Thomond Park on 24 October. A physical Clermont Auvergne came to Thomond Park on 6 December and beat the hosts 16-9. The reverse match played in France on 14 December saw Clermont win again, 26-19. Duncan Casey scored the sole Munster try and Keatley's accuracy with the boot at least gave the visitors a losing bonus point.

Next was an away match for Munster, played at Allianz Park on 17 January 2015 against Saracens, which Munster lost 33-10. Although Munster hammered Sale Sharks at Thomond Park on 25 January by 65-10, Munster failed to advance in the competition. Tries came from Zebo (two), Earls, a penalty try, Pat Howard, Conway, Tommy O'Donnell and Duncan Williams. Keatley converted four of five and Hanrahan three of four. Keatley also kicked two penalties.

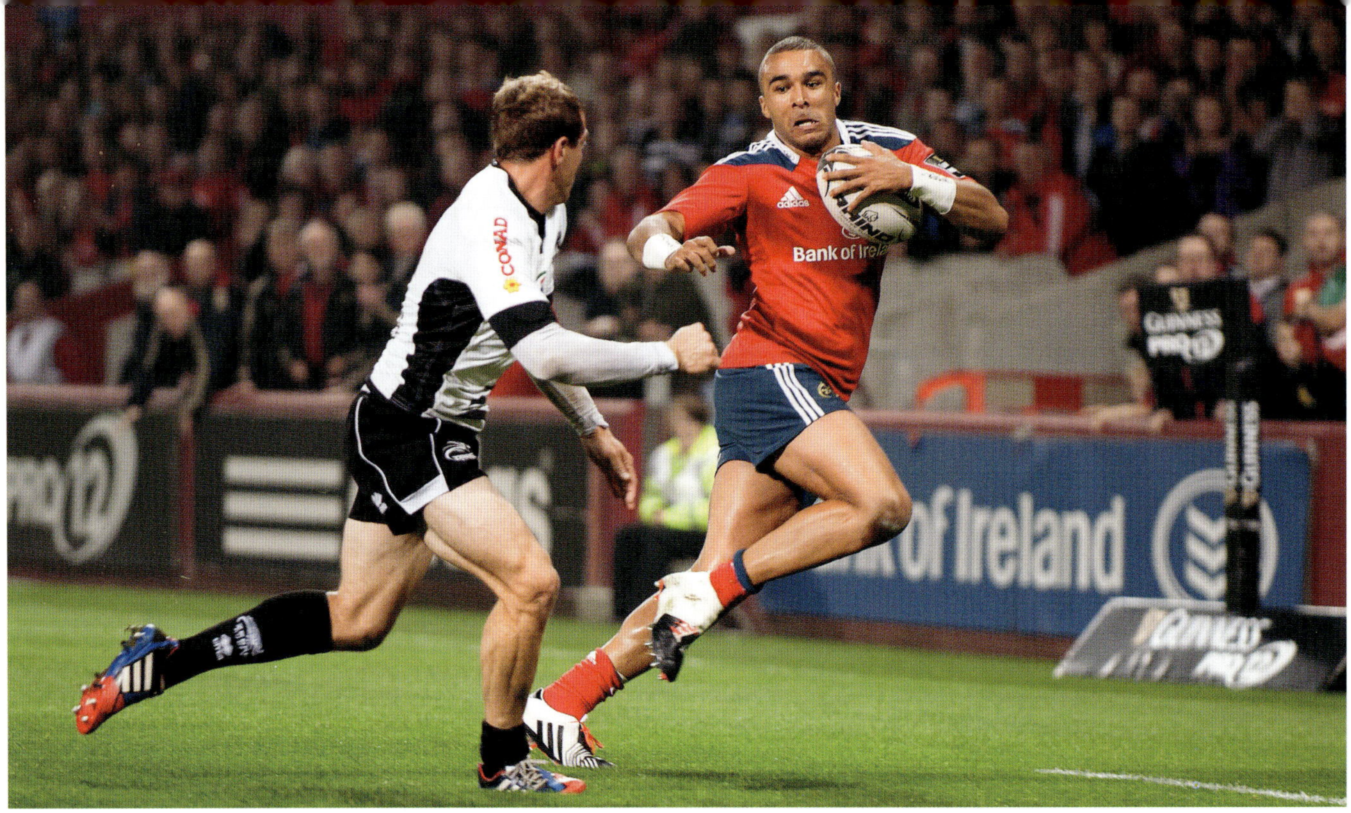

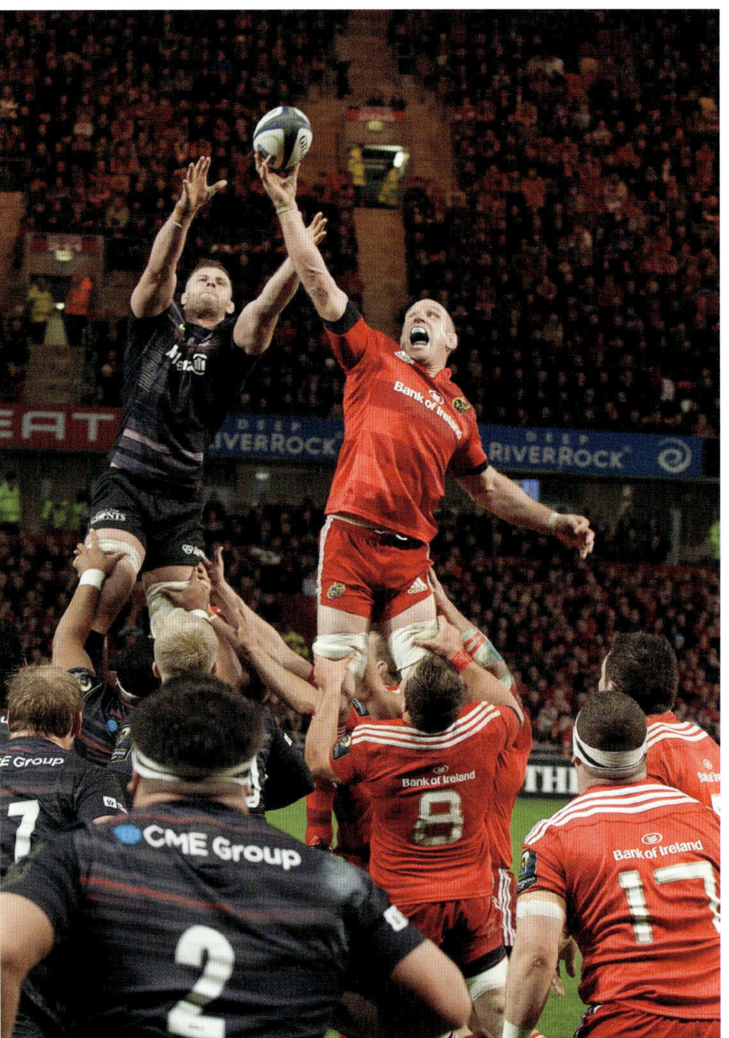

Above: Simon Zebo at his best. Under head coach Anthony Foley, Munster win convincingly against Zebre 31-5, scoring five tries, including a hat trick from Zebo.

Left: Paul O'Connell steals the Saracens line-out in a home 14-3 win for Munster in the Champions Cup.

Opposite top: Ian Keatley kicks for goal, watched by Jerry Flannery.

Opposite bottom: Watched by teammate Donncha O'Callaghan, Robin Copeland leaves Ulster defenders behind. Munster cling on for a thrilling 21-20 win.

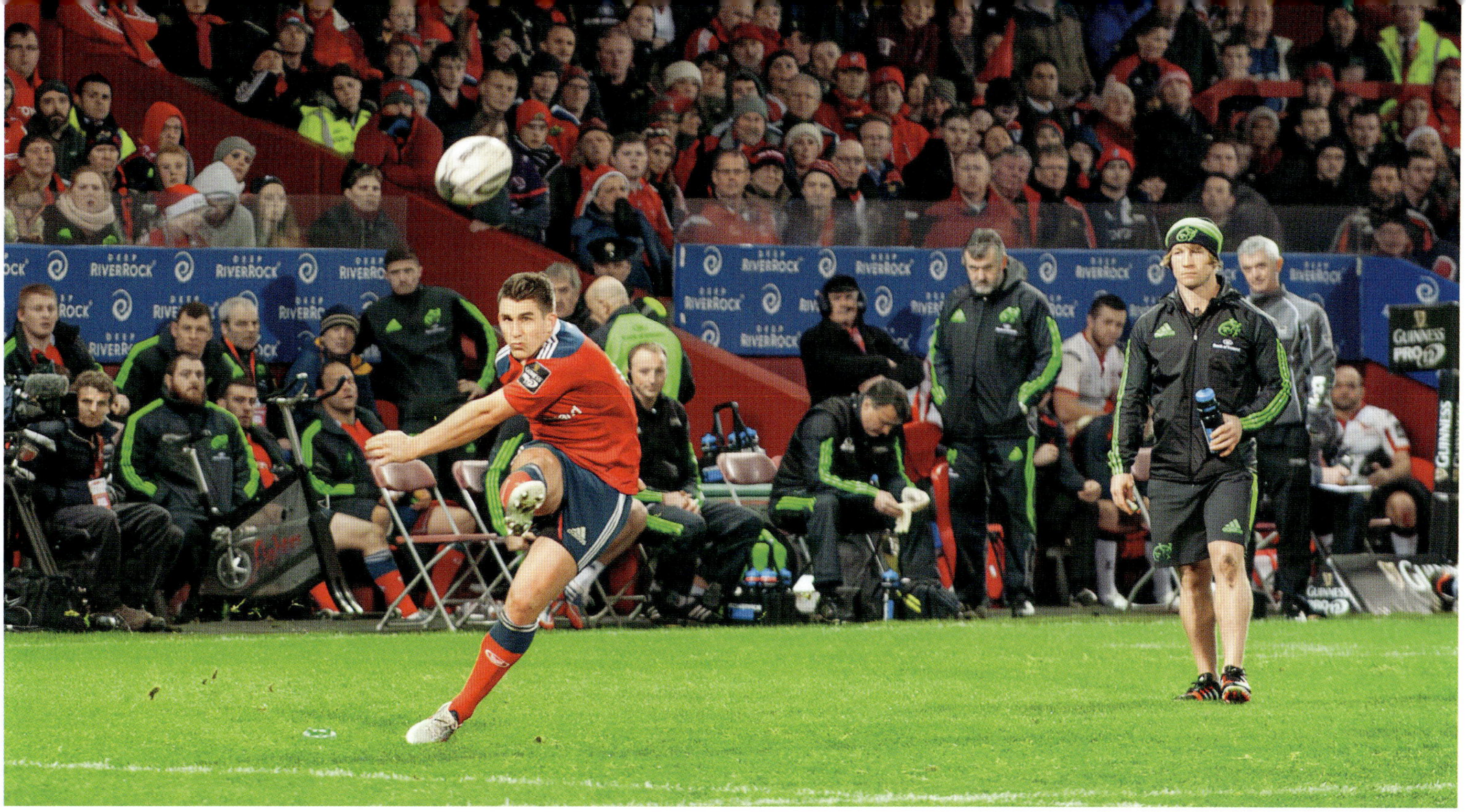

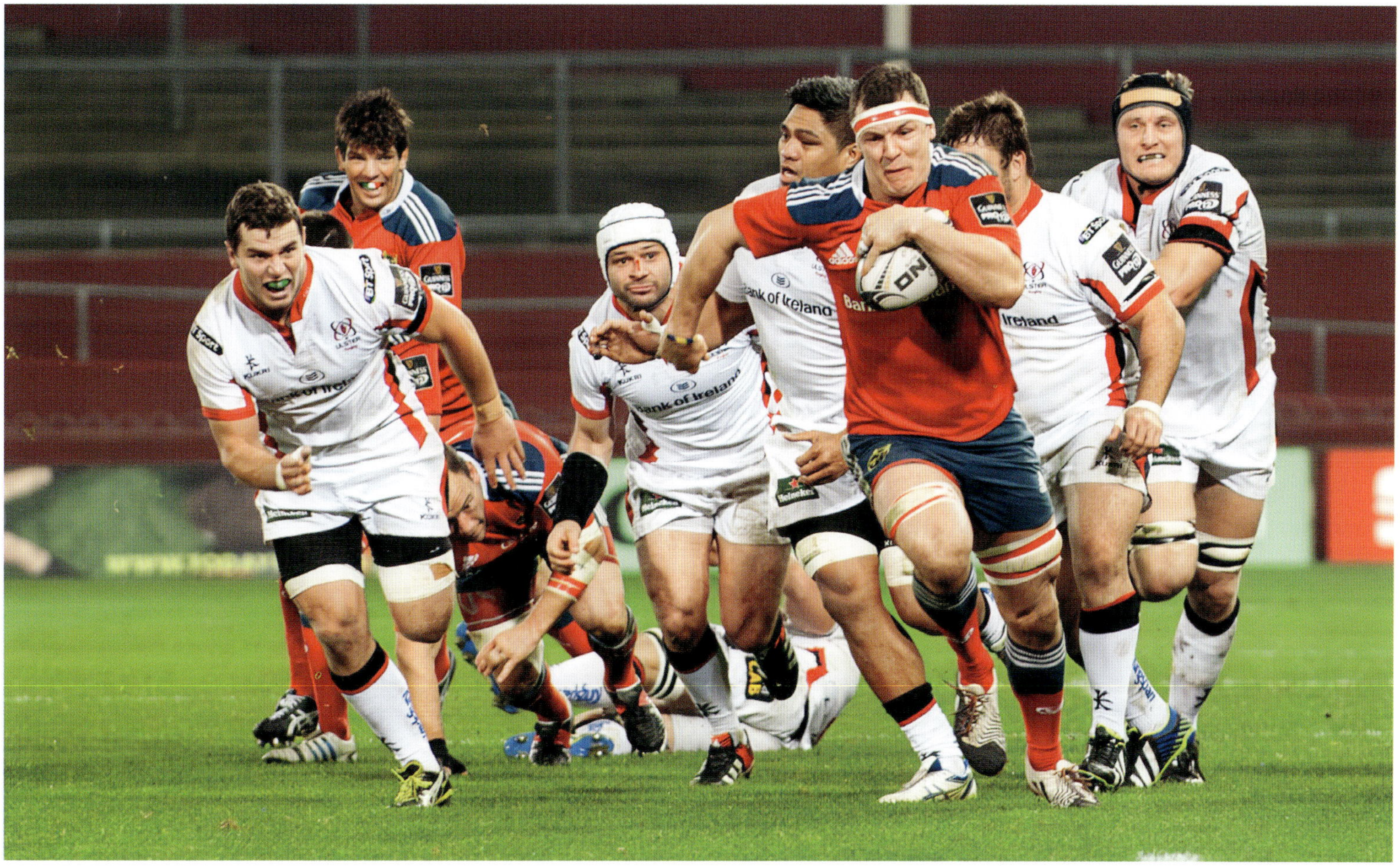

Dubbed the 'War God' and 'King Peter' by his fans, Peter O'Mahony wins the line-out against Clermont Auvergne. Clermont scored the only two tries of the game, leaving Munster with the unenviable statistic of losing at home to a French team for the first time in the European Champions Cup. The final score was 16–9.

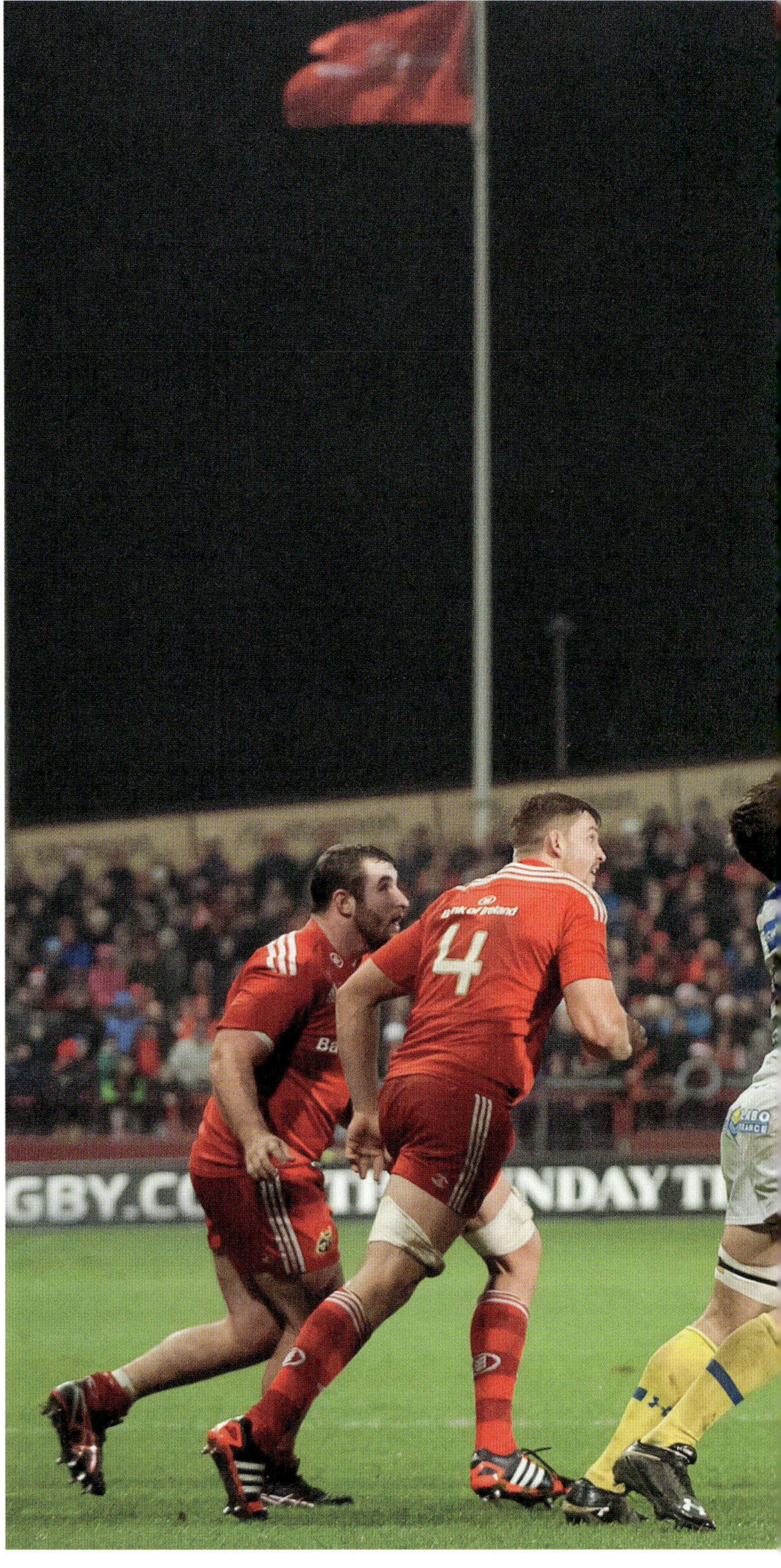

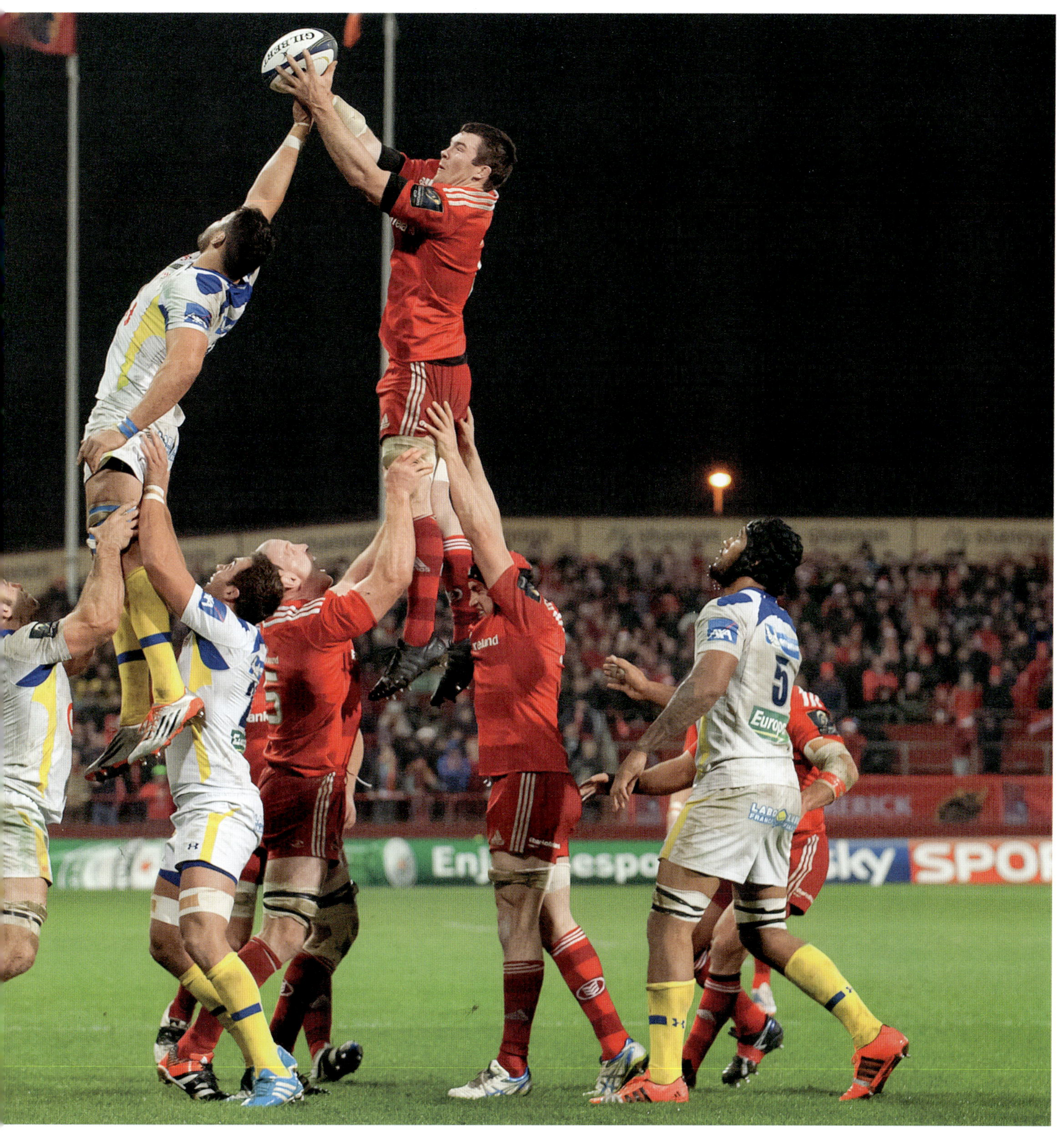

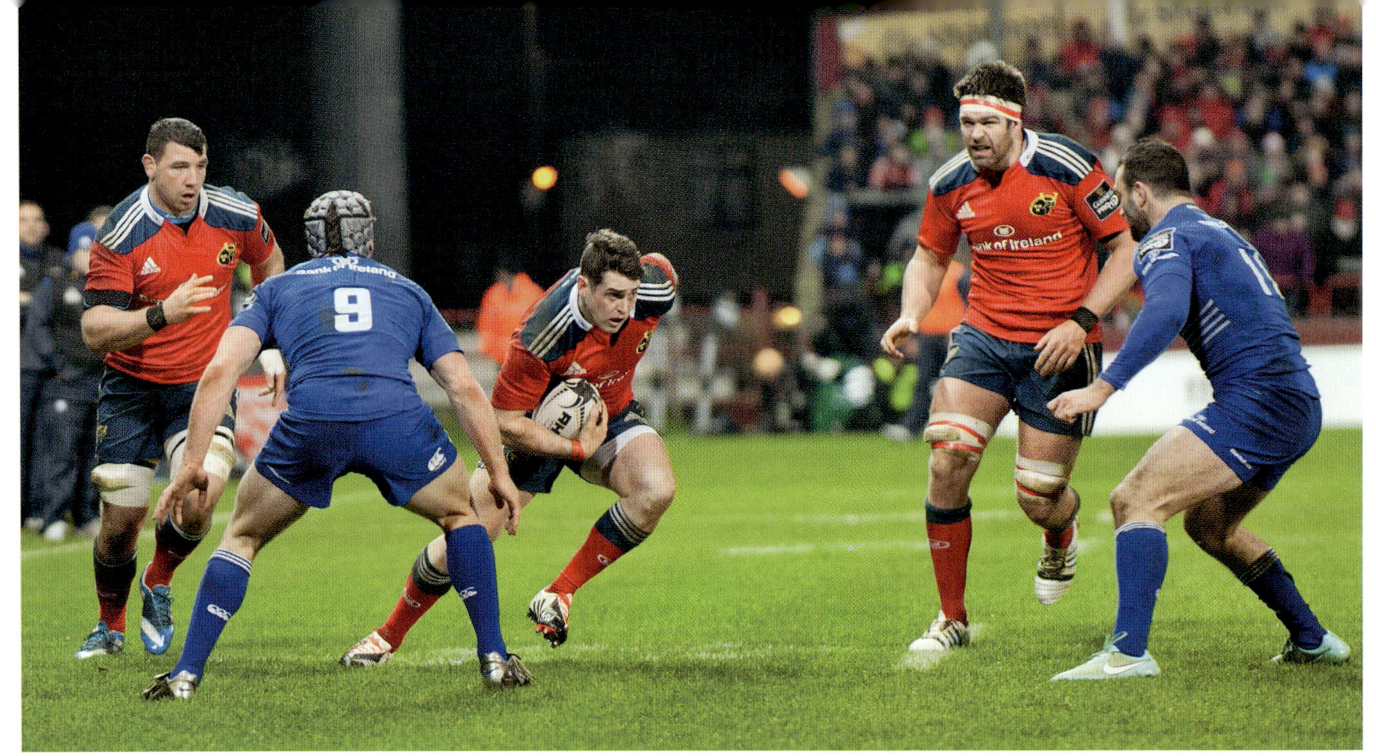

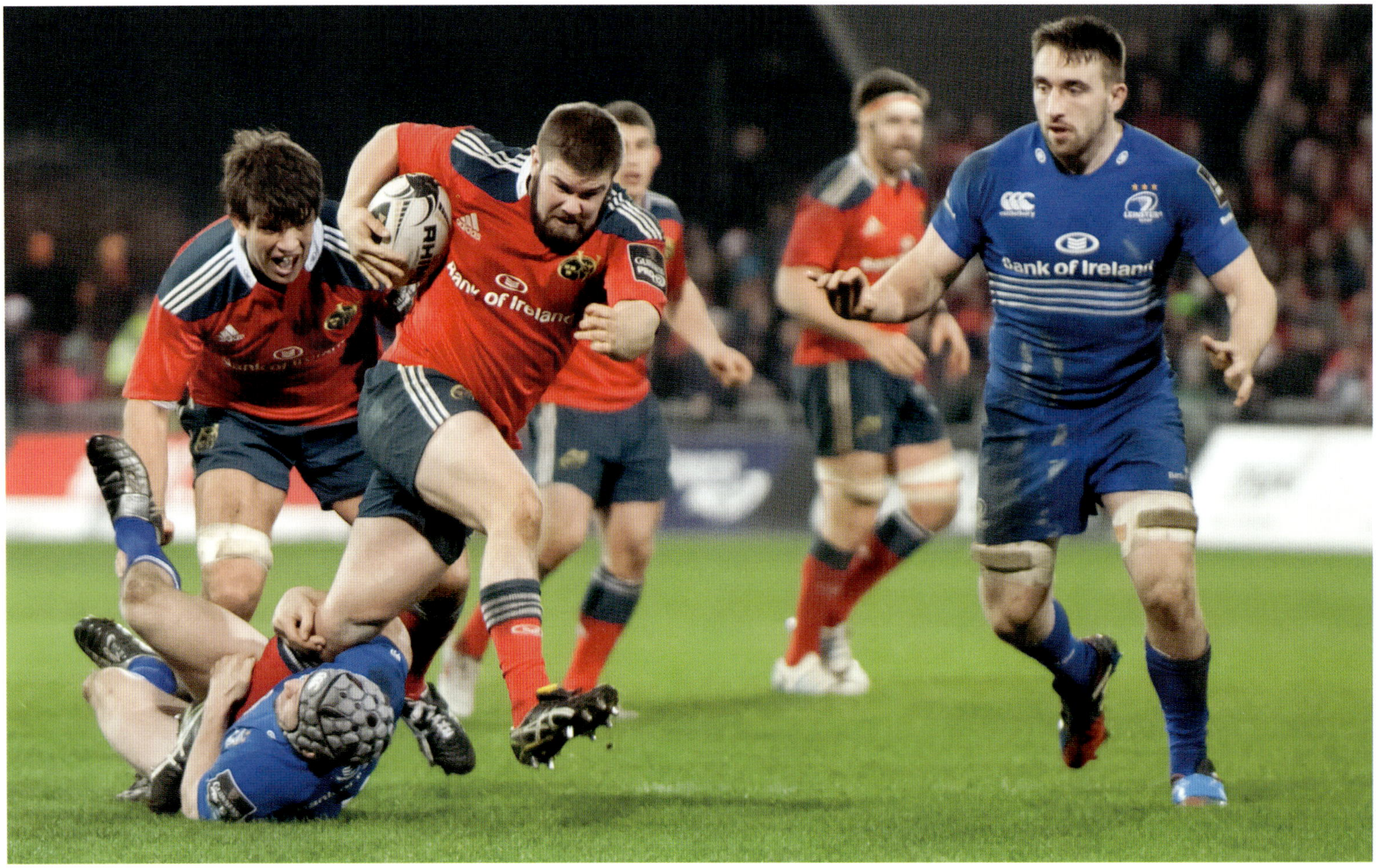

Opposite top: An on-form Ian Keatley helped Munster to a 28-13 win against arch-rivals Leinster, with tries from CJ Stander, Andrew Conway and Dave O'Callaghan. Here, Ronan O'Mahony breaks, supported by Paddy Butler (far left) and Billy Holland as Isaac Boss (number 9) and Dave Kearney defend for Leinster.

Opposite bottom: Duncan Casey makes a strong run with Donncha O'Callaghan in support, while Leinster's Jack Conan sizes up the situation.

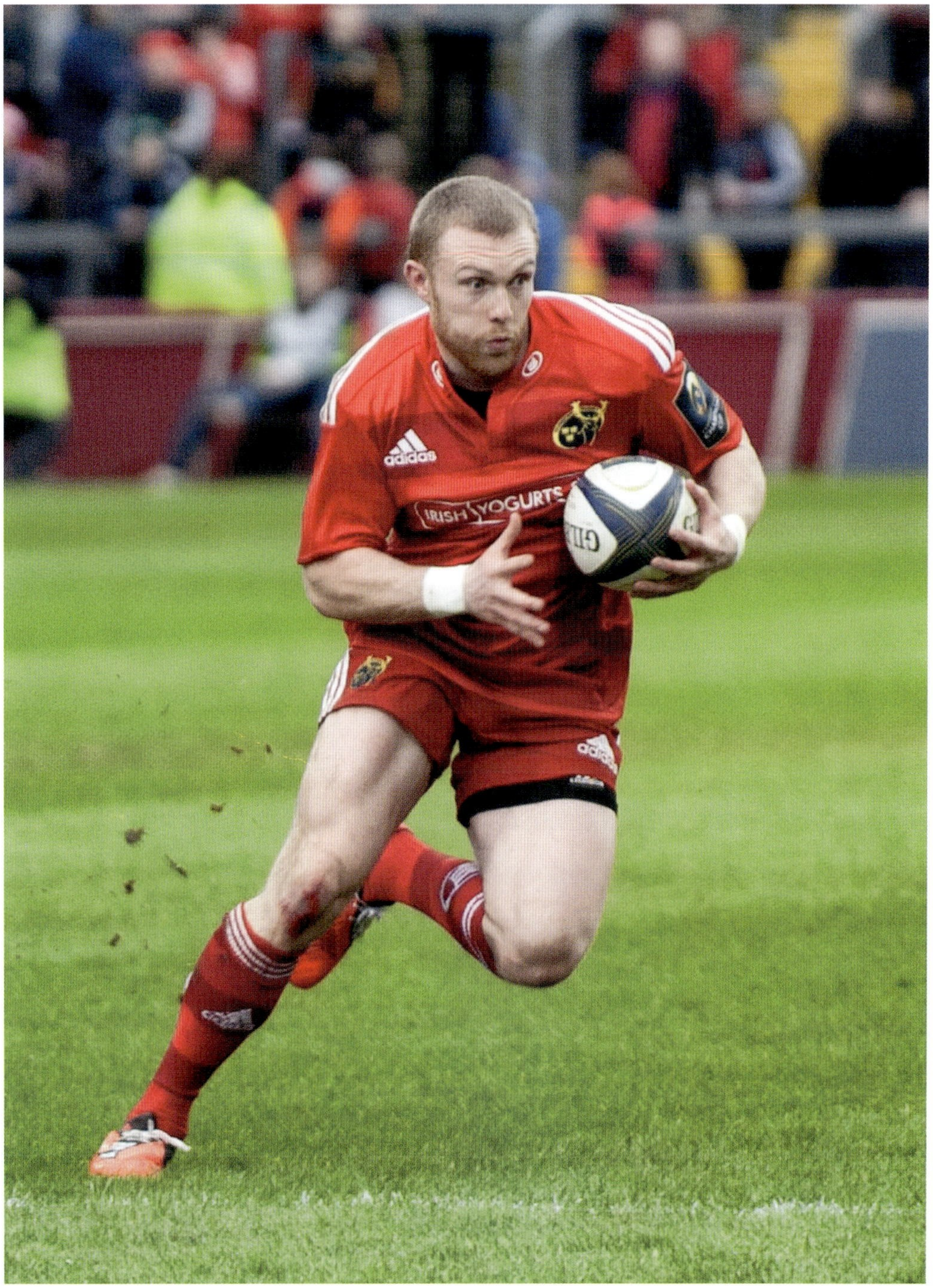

25 January 2015

Right: Keith Earls in classic 'dancing feet' mode against Sale Sharks. Munster celebrate their 100th win in Europe with nine tries, and the final score is 65-10. However, it is too little, too late and their Champions Cup campaign comes to an end.

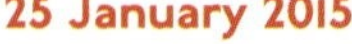

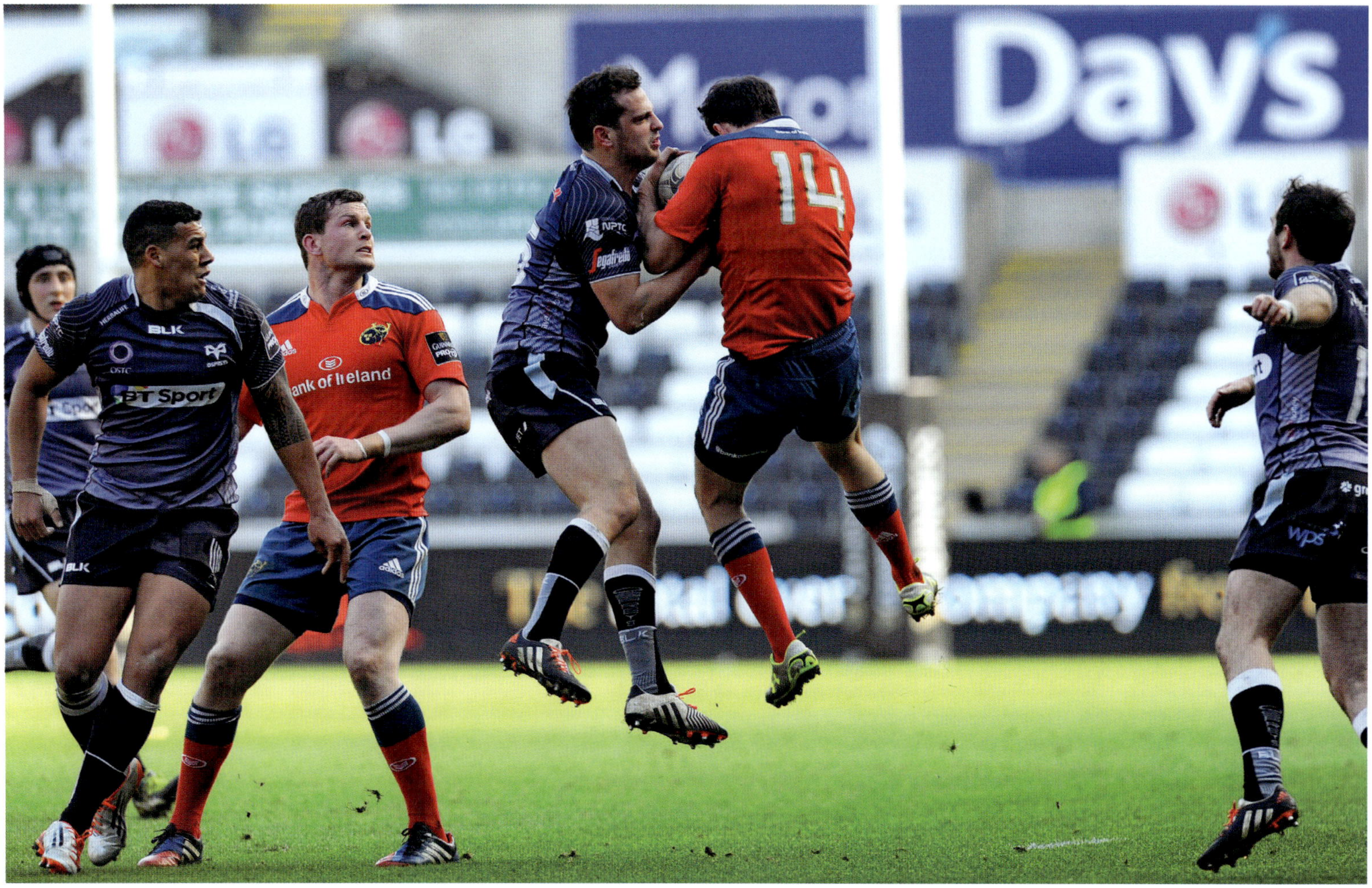

Top: Ospreys' Dan Evans and Munster's Felix Jones challenge for the high ball in a 26–12 away defeat for Munster.

Bottom: Donnacha Ryan in action in Munster's 34–3 win against hosts Edinburgh in Murrayfield.

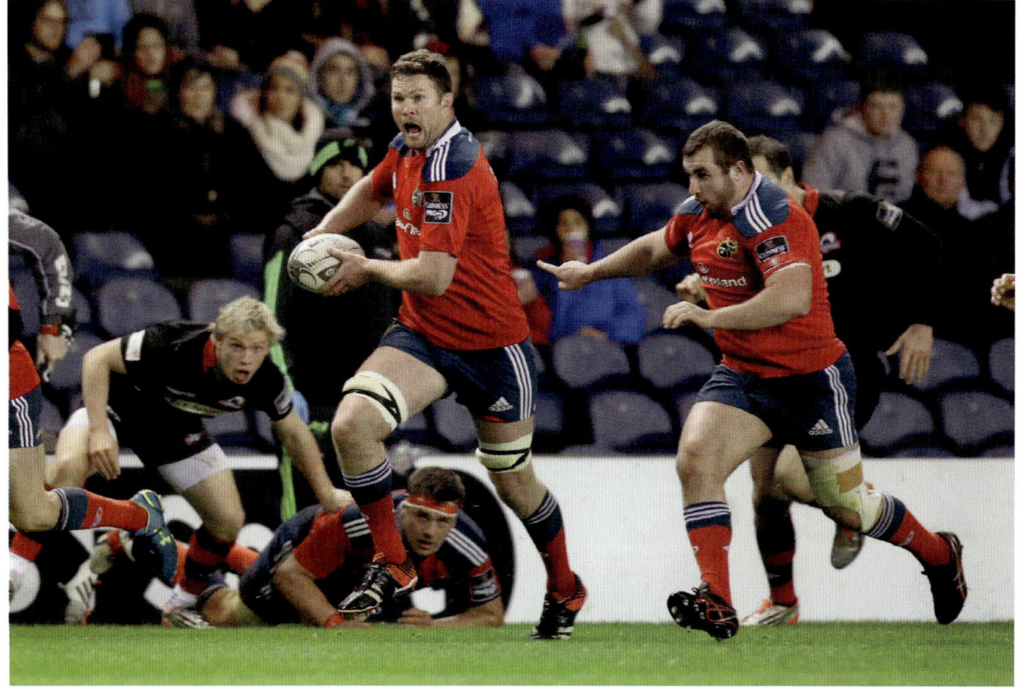

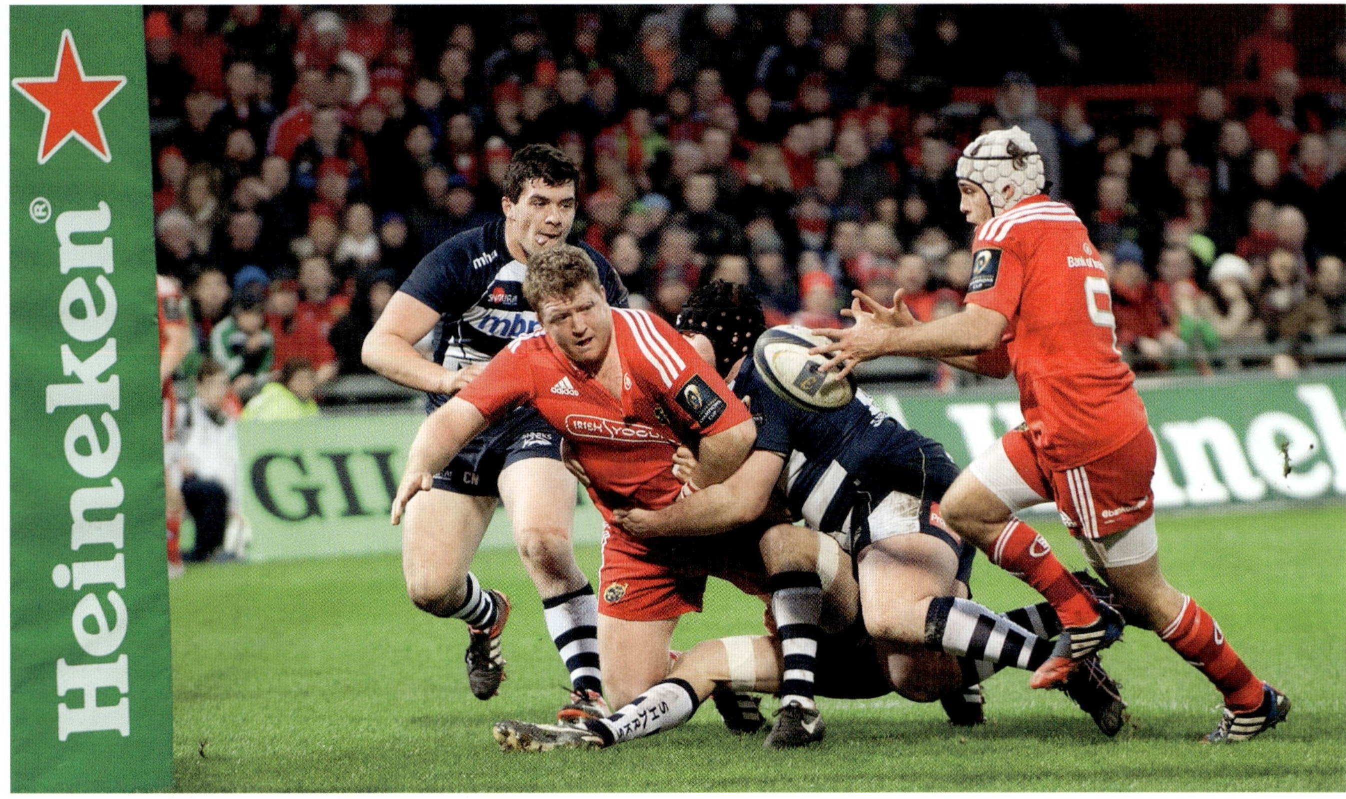

23 May 2015

Top: Stephen Archer (left) sets up Duncan Williams. In a pulsating Pro12 semi-final against Ospreys, Munster steal the win 21–18. This was Paul O'Connell's last home game in the Munster jersey.

Bottom: Stephen Archer leaves Ospreys standing, watched by teammate Ian Keatley. In the final on 30 May, Munster face Glasgow Warriors in Belfast, but lose 13–31.

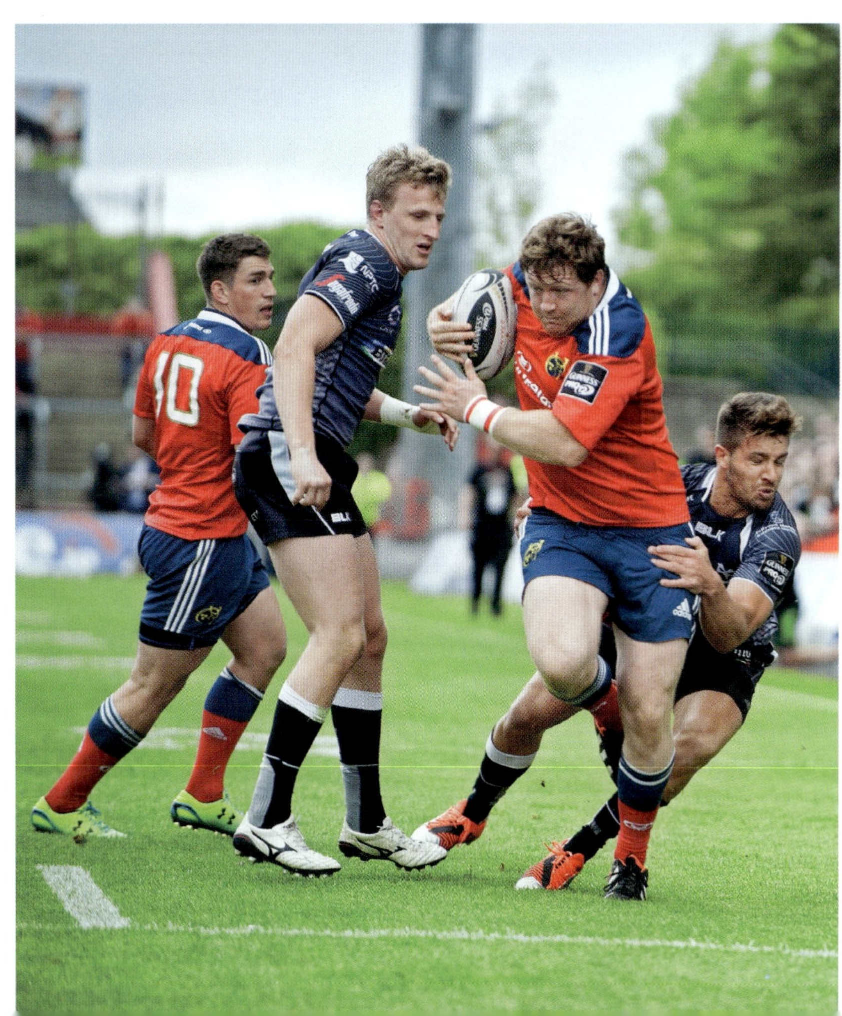

2015–2016

Anthony Foley began his second season as Munster head coach. Andy Farrell joined the province in January in an advisory capacity (before taking the reins as Ireland head coach in the summer of 2016). In April, it was confirmed that former Springbok Rassie Erasmus would join Munster as director of rugby, a newly created position, on a three-year contract, beginning on 1 July. Peter O'Mahony was captain for the season.

PRO12

The season started on 5 September with an 18-13 win over Benetton Treviso at Irish Independent Park. CJ Stander was captain for the night and scored two tries in a man-of-the-match performance. Munster visited Liberty Stadium in Swansea on 13 September and gained a hard-earned victory against Ospreys, winning 20-18. Stephen Fitzgerald and Stander were the try-scorers, with Tyler Bleyendaal and Ian Keatley converting. Bleyendaal also converted two penalties. In Thomond Park on 2 October, Munster scraped home against Glasgow Warriors, 23-21, thanks to a Keatley penalty three minutes from time. Away against Scarlets on 23 October, an 80th-minute try gave the home team the win, 25-22.

A thrilling contest on 30 October in Thomond Park saw Munster score five tries against Ulster, to win 32-28. Andrew Conway, Robin Copeland, Gerhard van den Heever, Denis Hurley and Simon Zebo were the try-scorers. In Murrayfield on 7 November, Munster beat Edinburgh in another closely contested match, winning 16-14. Connacht visited Thomond Park on 28 November and ended Munster's home winning streak, with a 18-12 victory. Travelling to Rodney Parade on 6 December, Munster lost to Newport Gwent Dragons by 22-6, with Rory Scannell scoring Munster's only points, all in the first half.

Leinster came to Thomond Park on 27 December and won emphatically, 24-7, in front of 25,600 spectators. Munster's fortunes returned on 2 January when they defeated Ulster in the Kingspan Stadium, 9-7. Keatley's two penalties and a drop goal ensured the victory. Zebre hosted Munster on 30 January. Mark Chisholm scored a try, which Keatley converted, adding two penalties and a drop goal, for the visitors to win 16-12.

Ospreys defeated Munster 21-17 at Irish Independent Park on 14 February. The misery continued on 19 February when Glasgow Warriors edged Munster by 27-24 at Rugby Park. Dave Kilcoyne scored two tries, Mike Sherry added a third and Keatley converted all three. In Stadio Comunale di Monigo on 28 February, tries from van den Heever and Francis Saili and two late penalties by Keatley saw Munster beat hosts Benetton Treviso by 16-13.

Munster had a bonus-point 26-5 win over Newport Gwent Dragons at Thomond Park on 5 March. Tries came from Dave Kilcoyne (two), Rory Scannell and James Cronin. On 18 March, a gritty Cardiff Blues took the lead in Cardiff Arms Park after 34 minutes and defeated the visitors 37-28.

Next, Munster trounced Zebre 47-0 at Thomond Park on 25 March. Two of the seven tries came from Zebo, bringing his total to 43 in 97 games, surpassing Anthony Horgan's previous record of 41 tries for Munster. There were tries also from Ronan O'Mahony, Stander and Murray, plus two penalty tries. Johnny Holland converted five of five and Murray one of two. Leinster defeated Munster 16-13 at Aviva Stadium on 2 April. Connacht again proved too strong for Munster on 16 April at the Galway Sportsgrounds, Pat Lam's side winning 35-14 (in fact, Connacht would go on to win the Pro12). Munster had a solid win over Edinburgh in Irish Independent Park on 29 April, taking the game by 27-19. The try-scorers were Scannell, Zebo, Conway and Saili. Holland converted two and added a penalty. Despite defeating Scarlets at Thomond Park on 7 May, 31-15, Munster could only manage to finish sixth in the Pro12.

EUROPEAN CHAMPIONS CUP

Drawn against Stade Français, Leicester Tigers and Benetton Treviso, Munster opened their European Cup campaign against Treviso at a wet and windy Thomond Park on 14 November. Try-scorers for the hosts were BJ Botha, Stander, Duncan Casey and Zebo. Keatley converted three and kicked two penalties for the 32-7 win. The next fixture, against Stade, was postponed following the November Paris attacks.

On 12 December, Munster lost to Leicester Tigers at Thomond Park by 31-19. In the return game on 20 December, Leicester again beat Munster, this time by 17-6, the visitors crucially failing to secure a losing bonus point. On 9 January, Munster were eliminated from the European Cup after a 27-7 defeat to Stade Français at Stade Jean-Bouin. In spite of playing 40 minutes with fourteen men, Stade Français outscored Munster 17-7 during that period. A week later, on 16 January, Munster defeated Stade Français 26-13 at Thomond Park, avoiding a fourth straight defeat in the competition. Sherry, Earls, Zebo and Stander scored tries, with Keatley converting three.

Munster finished their European Champions Cup campaign with a bonus-point win away to Benetton Treviso on 24 January. The final score was 28-5, with tries from Ronan O'Mahony (two), Kilcoyne and Murray, Keatley converting all four.

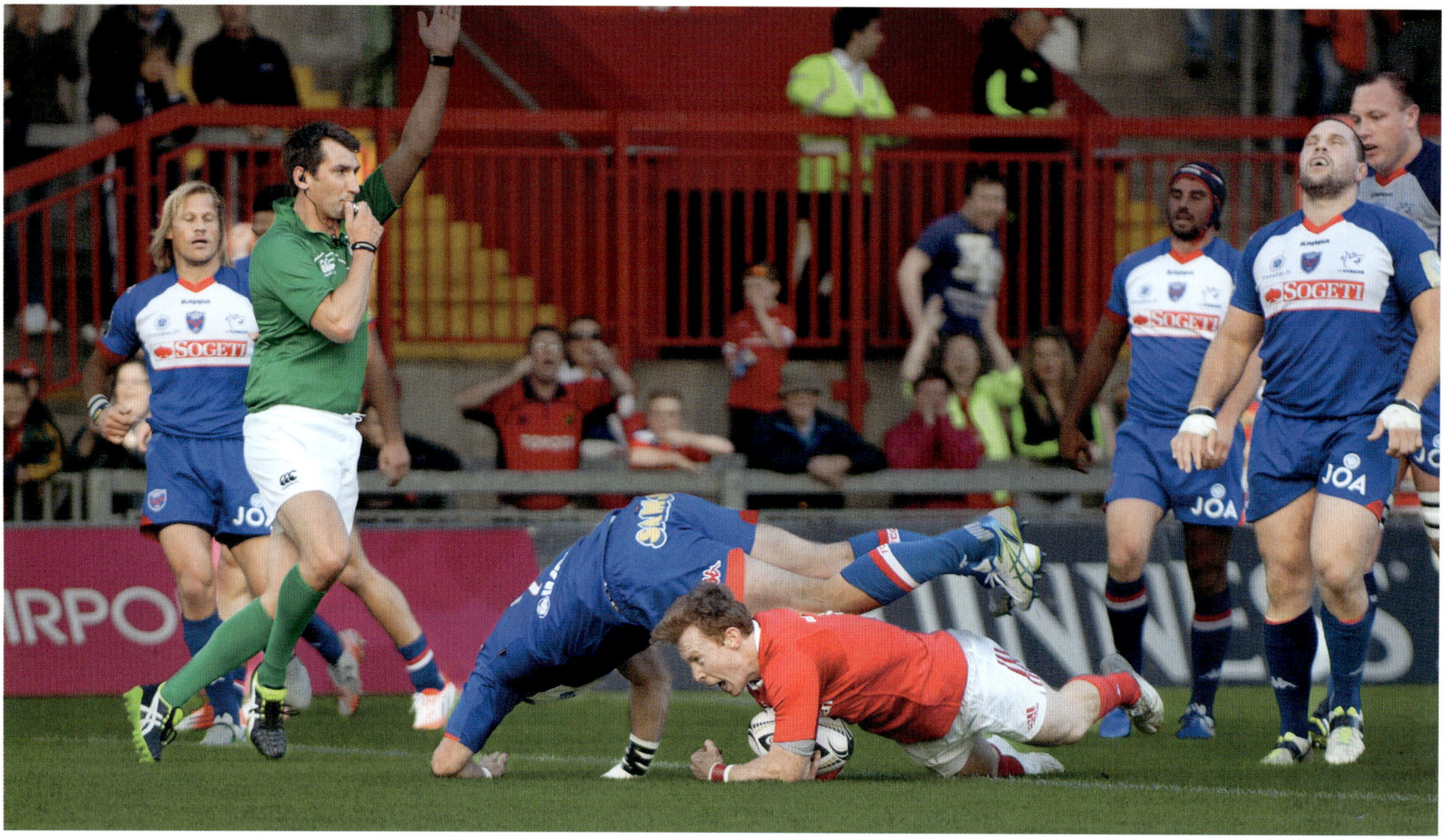

14 August 2015

Top: Captain Cathal Sheridan scores a fine try against Grenoble in a pre-season friendly. In an entertaining try-fest, Munster unfortunately lose 29-38.

2 October 2015

Below left: The Munster dressing room before the fixture with Glasgow Warriors.

Below right: Felix Jones prepares to pass.

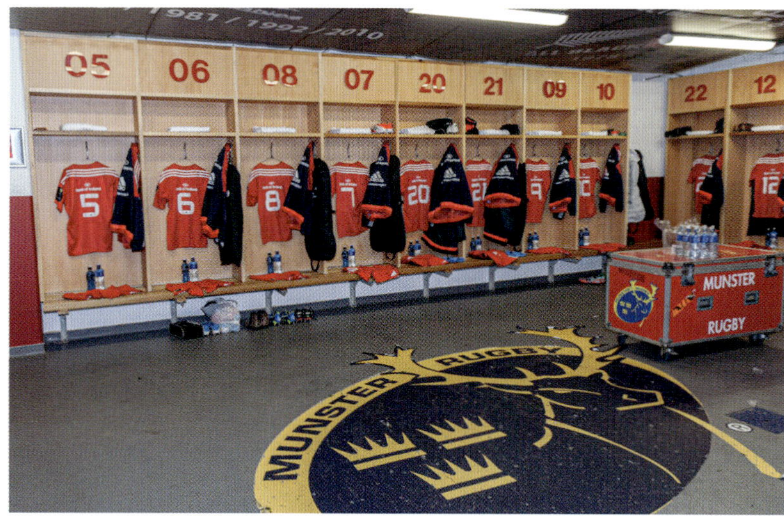

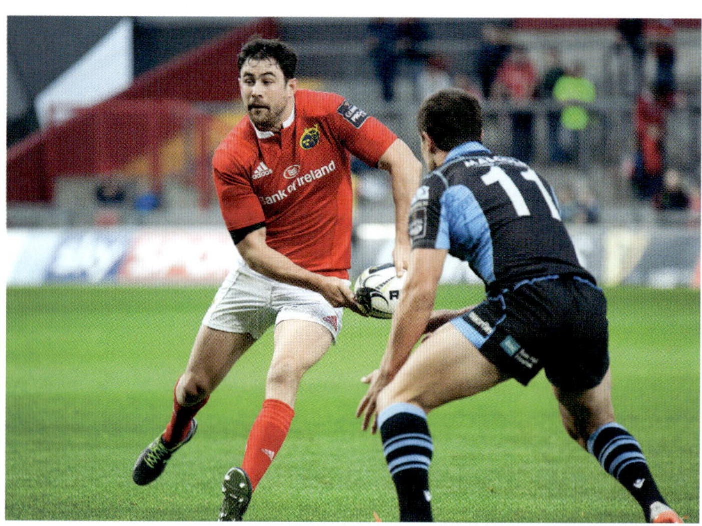

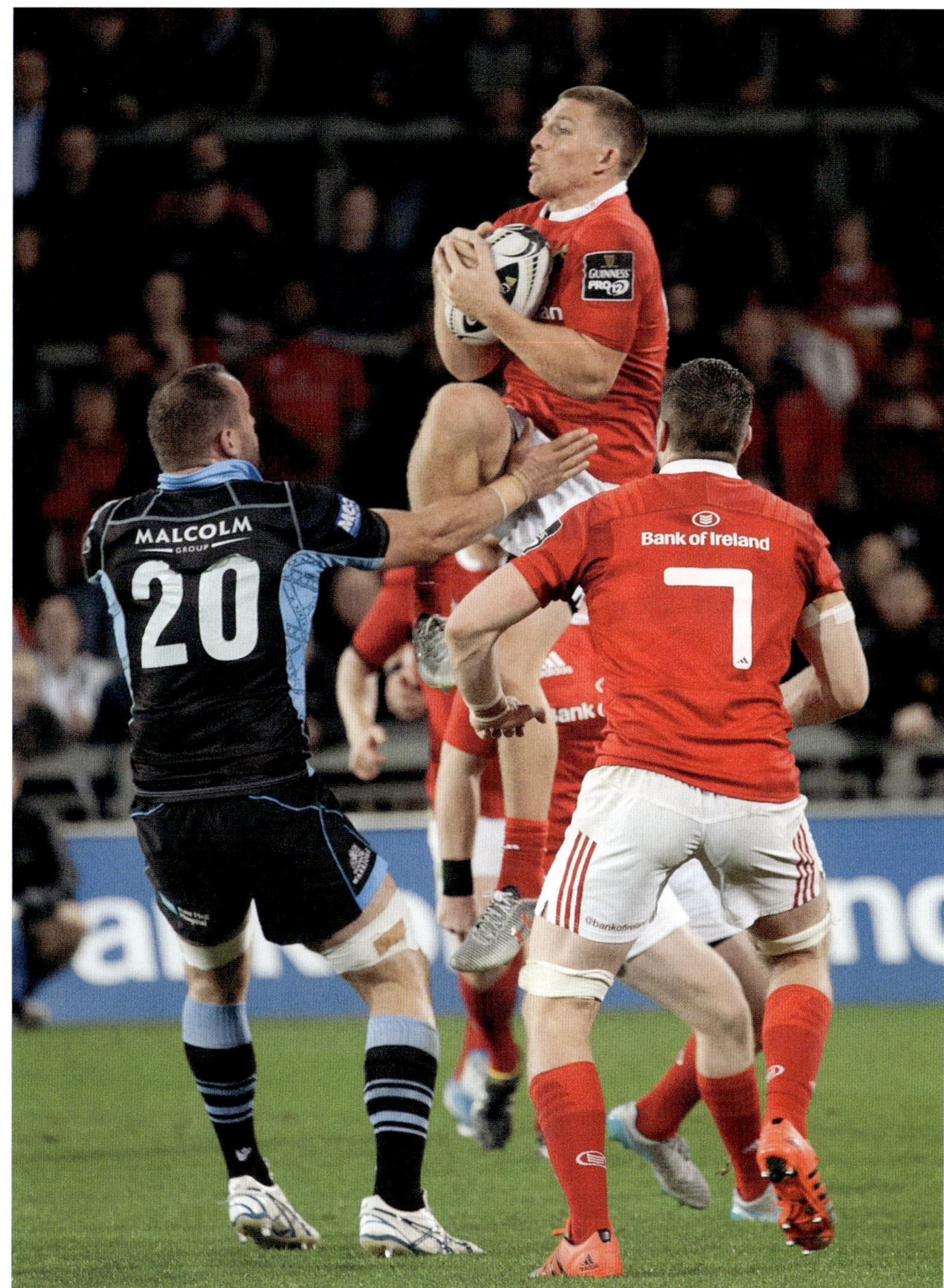

2 October 2015

Andrew Conway gathers in the air against Glasgow Warriors. Munster win 23-21, with Ian Keatley converting both tries and slotting three penalties between the posts.

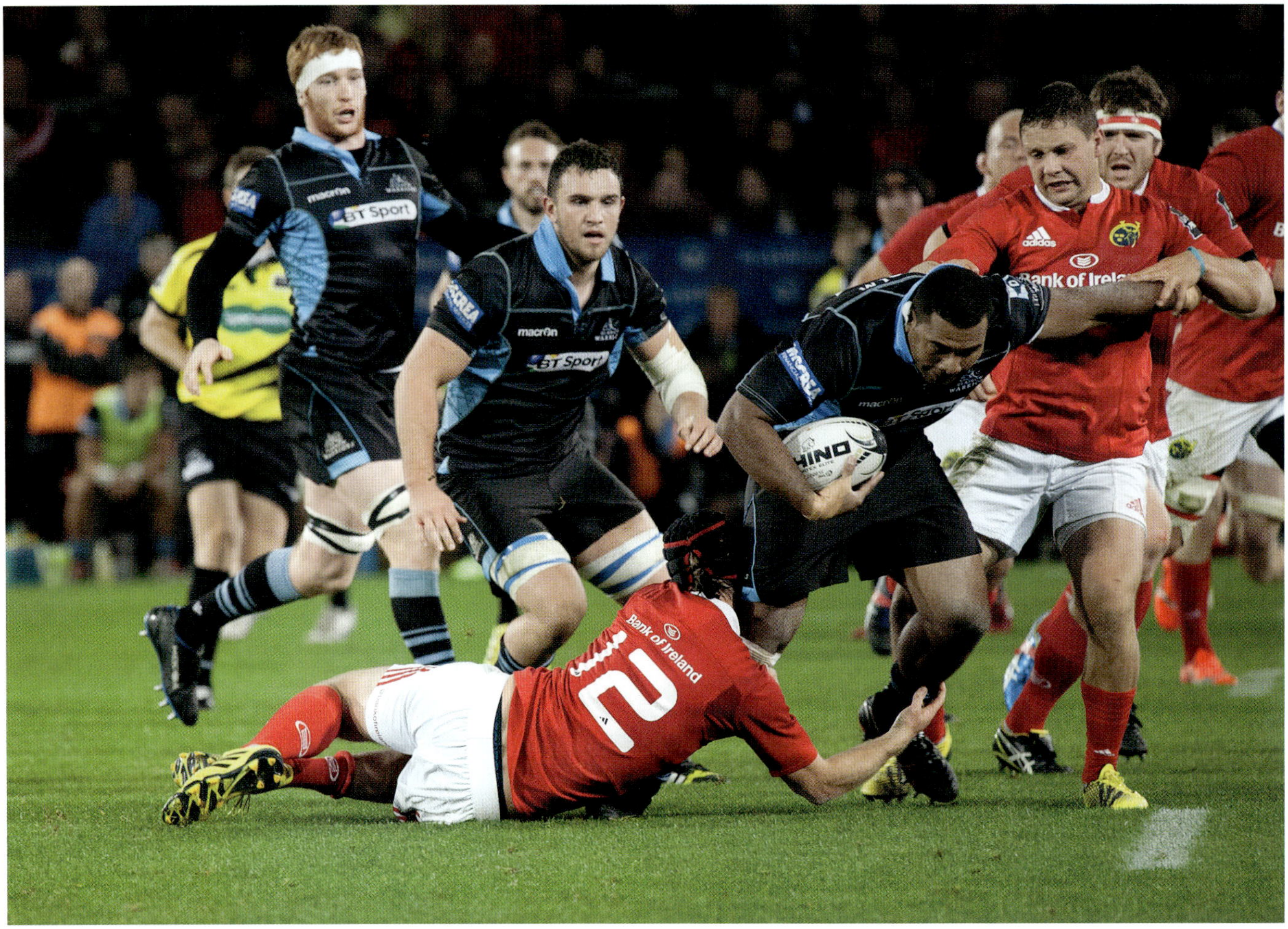

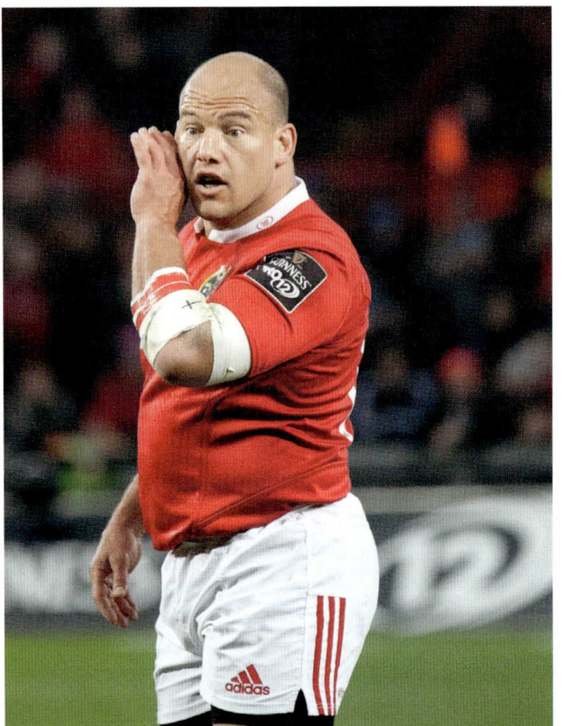

2 October 2015

Above: Tyler Bleyendaal makes a superb tackle against Glasgow Warriors.

Left: BJ Botha gives instructions.

12 December 2015

Opposite top: CJ Stander is about to be tackled by Leicester Tigers' Dan Cole. Leicester handed Munster their fourth European defeat, winning 31-19.

27 December 2015

Opposite bottom: CJ Stander hands off Devin Toner in the annual post-Christmas derby against Leinster, which the men in blue win convincingly, 24-7.

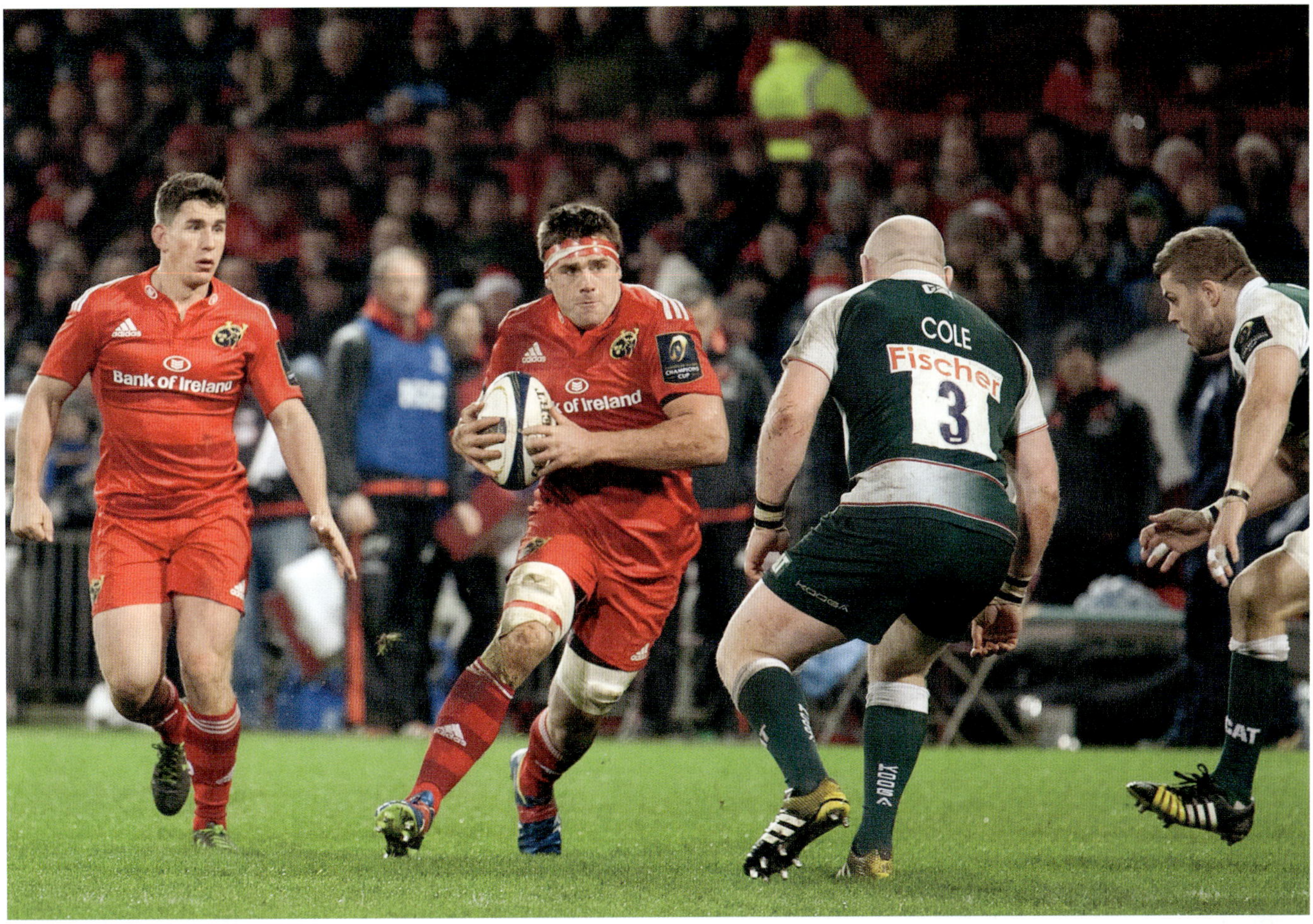

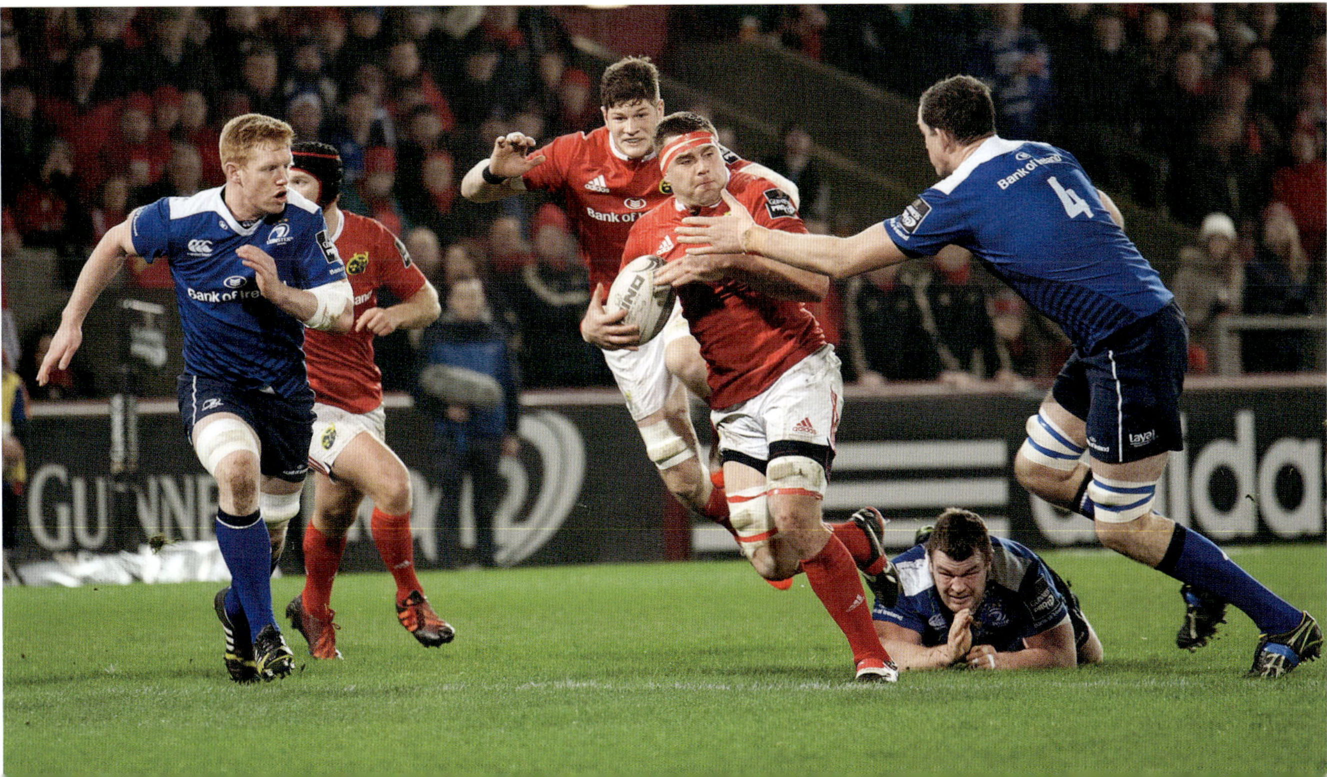

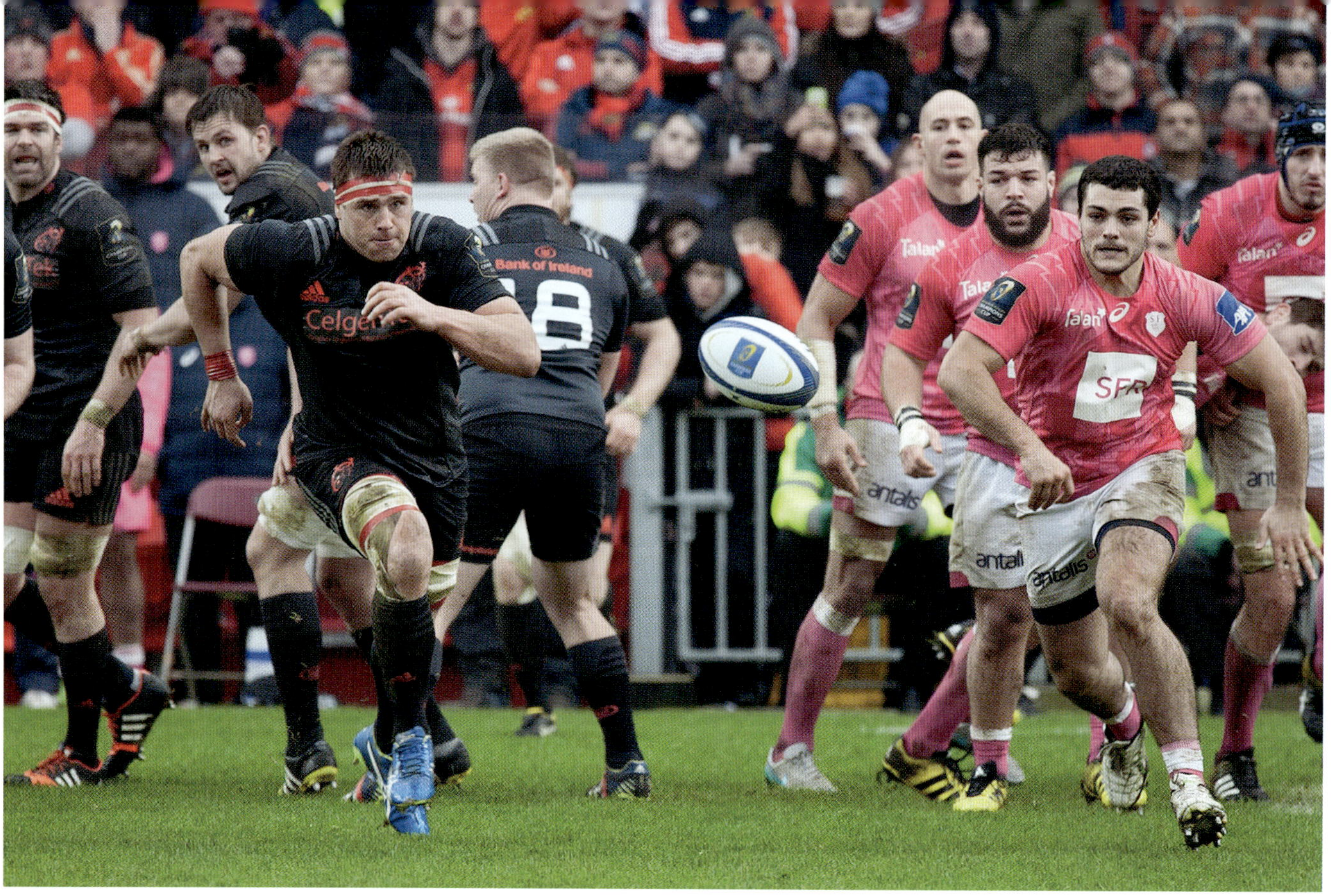

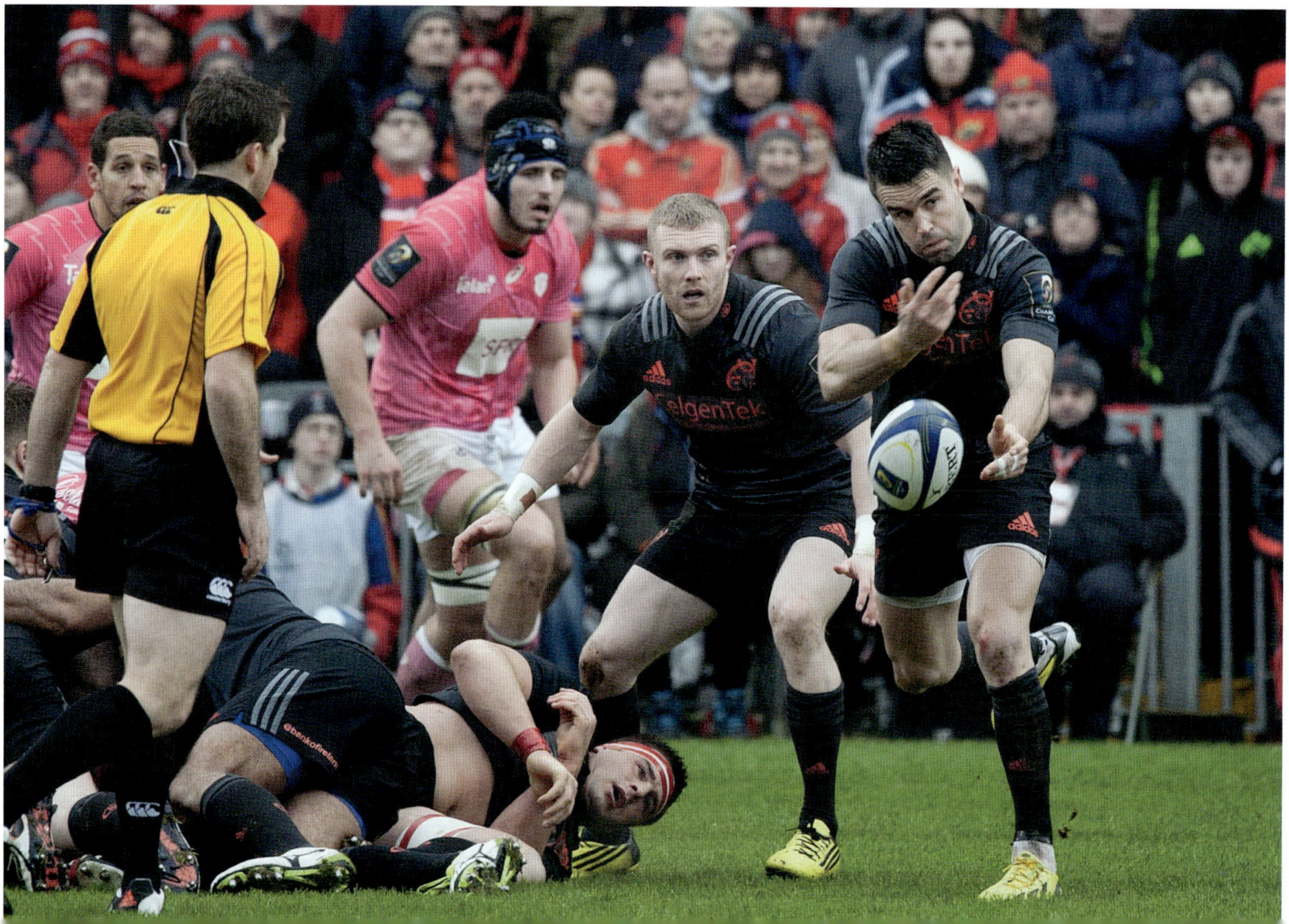

Opposite top: A determined CJ Stander in the fixture against Stade Français. He was awarded man of the match in Munster's 26–13 win.

Opposite bottom: Conor Murray offloads, closely watched by Keith Earls.

29 April 2016

Andrew Conway touches down to score Munster's third try of the day, helping the home team to a 27–19 victory against Edinburgh in Irish Independent Park.

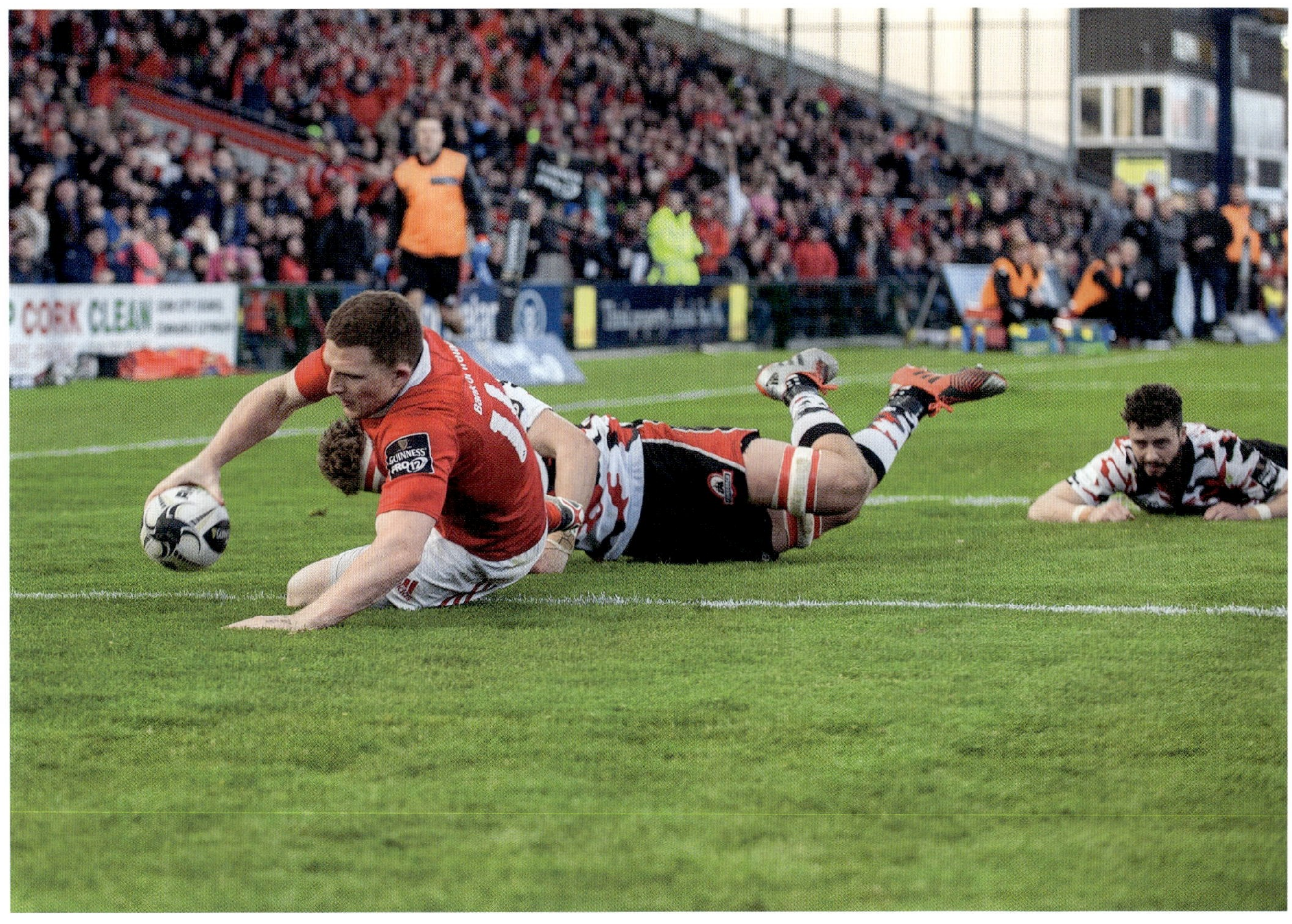

2016–2017

PRO12   **POOL WINS: 19; POOL LOSSES: 3; ELIMINATED: FINAL**
EUROPEAN CHAMPIONS CUP   POOL WINS: 5; POOL LOSSES: 1; ELIMINATED: SEMI-FINAL

This season saw Rassie Erasmus come on board as director of rugby, with Jacques Nienaber as defence coach. The new training base at University of Limerick also opened. New arrivals included Sammy Arnold, Thomas du Toit, Jean Kleyn, Rhys Marshall and Jaco Taute. Donnacha Ryan would leave at season's end to join Racing 92. Shockingly, in October 2016, head coach Anthony Foley died suddenly (see page 70). On 4 May 2017, Tyler Bleyendaal, in his second playing season with the province, was named as the Munster Player of the Year.

PRO12

The season began with an excellent away victory against Scarlets on 3 September by 23-13. Next, Munster played Cardiff Blues at Irish Independent Park on 9 September in a tense match, losing 24-23. Away to Newport Gwent Dragons on 17 September, Munster won 20-16. Two home wins at Thomond Park followed: Edinburgh fell 28-14 on 24 September and Zebre on 1 October, 49-5. The try-scorers against Zebre were Darren Sweetnam, Conor Murray, CJ Stander, Simon Zebo, penalty try and Stephen Archer, with Tyler Bleyendaal converting four and Ian Keatley, who came on early in the second half, converting three.

Leinster had a decisive win by 25-14 at Aviva Stadium on 8 October. Another away game, against Ulster on 28 October, saw an excellent win for Munster, 15-14, with tries by Rory Scannell and Jaco Taute, with Scannell adding the extra points. Munster dismantled the Ospreys 33-0 at Irish Independent Park on 4 November. Tries came from Dave Kilcoyne (two), Darren Sweetnam, Peter O'Mahony and Robin Copeland, with Bleyendaal converting 4 out of 5.

Benetton Treviso met a top-form Munster in Thomond Park on 26 November, the home side winning 46-3. Next, Glasgow Warriors hosted Munster at Scotstoun Stadium on 2 December, where Munster ground out a 16-15 win. A comprehensive 29-17 win over Leinster at Thomond Park followed, in front of 26,200 spectators on 26 December. Connacht hosted Munster on 31 December, which the visitors won 16-9, their good form continuing.

Munster travelled to Edinburgh next on 3 February 2017 and eked out a close win, 10-9. Newport Gwent

Dragons then played Munster at Irish Independent Park on 10 February, with the hosts winning 45-17. Next to fall were Ospreys in Swansea on 18 February, the visitors winning 25-23. The try-scorers were Jack O'Donoghue, Francis Saili and Dave Kilcoyne, with two converted by Bleyendaal who also slotted two penalties.

Munster's nine-game winning run ended at Thomond Park on 24 February against Scarlets. Tries from Jaco Taute, Darren Sweetnam and Conor Oliver, all converted by Bleyendaal, put the hosts 21-0 up at half-time, but they failed to score in the second half. Scarlets won 30-21. Munster got back to winning ways with a 23-13 away win against Cardiff Blues on 4 March. Zebre were no match for Munster at Stadio Sergio Lanfranchi on 25 March, the visitors having an outstanding 50-14 win. The victories continued on 8 April when Glasgow Warriors were beaten by 10-7 at Irish Independent Park. James Cronin touched down in the fourth minute, which Bleyendaal converted, and Rory Scannell added a penalty.

Munster faced Ulster at Thomond Park on 15 April and scraped home by 22-20, with tries from Angus Lloyd, Keith Earls and Dave O'Callaghan, Keatley and Bleyendaal adding the extras. Benetton Treviso hosted Munster on 29 April, with the visitors winning 34-14. Connacht were roundly beaten 50-14 at Thomond Park on 6 May. This led to Munster reaching the semi-final play-off. Munster also had, by far, the tightest defence in the Pro12. The semi-final was played at Thomond Park on 20 May against Ospreys. Munster recorded a 23-3 win with man-of-the-match Saili, Zebo and Andrew Conway scoring tries. Bleyendaal converted one and added two penalties. The final was played on 27 May at Aviva Stadium in front of over 44,000 spectators. A flat performance, however, resulted in a 46-22 loss to Scarlets.

European Champions Cup

On 22 October 2016, Munster honoured the late Anthony Foley with a superb 38-17 victory over Glasgow Warriors. Tries came from Bleyendaal, Taute, Zebo, a penalty try and Rory Scannell. Bleyendaal converted all four. He and Keatley added a penalty each. Munster overwhelmed Leicester Tigers 38-0 on 10 December at Thomond Park but the tables were turned at Welford Road on 17 December, Leicester winning 18-16. On 7 January 2017, in a rescheduled round 1 away fixture for Munster, the visitors beat Racing 32-7. Simon Zebo's opening try was Munster's 400th in European competition. On 14 January, Saili scored the winning try in Munster's 14-12 away victory against Glasgow Warriors. Their place in the quarter-final secured, Munster went on to gain a home quarter-final by defeating Racing 92 by 20-10, on 21 January 2017 at Thomond Park.

On 1 April, Munster reached their first Champions Cup semi-final in three years with a 41-16 win over Toulouse. John Ryan scored a fourth-minute try, followed by Stander, Sweetnam and Conway. Bleyendaal converted three and scored five penalties. On 22 April, however, Saracens put an end to Munster's dream. In the semi-final at Aviva Stadium, watched by 51,000 spectators, Saracens controlled the game against an out-of-sorts Munster team, winning 26-10.

Anthony Foley (30 October 1973 – 16 October 2016)

On 16 October 2016, head coach Anthony Foley died while in Paris with Munster. The team was preparing to face Racing 92 in their opening game of the European Cup. Axel died in his sleep. Due to his sad and sudden passing, the fixture was rescheduled. Munster supporters in Paris for the match were shocked and lost for words. How could a man so close to them and so young – only 42 – die so suddenly? Supporters gathered outside the entrance to the Stade Olympique Yves-du-Manoir, Racing's home ground, and sang songs such as 'The Fields of Athenry'.

During a playing career spanning fourteen years, Axel won 62 caps with Ireland and was on the Triple Crown-winning team of 2004. His skill and determination enabled his beloved Munster to reach an elite level of achievement in rugby, with Heineken Cup wins in 2005–2006 and 2007–2008.

In Munster's first game after his untimely death, a minute's silence was observed at Thomond Park before the match, during which a special tribute took place in the West Stand with 'AXEL' spelled out, with the number 8 on either side. The Munster number 8 jersey was retired for the game, CJ Stander wearing number 24 for the occasion. The Munster Rugby Supporter's Club Choir performed 'There Is an Isle' and soprano Sinead O'Brien joined the choir to perform 'Stand Up and Fight'. The commemorative programme raised over €39,000, which was donated to various causes.

To honour Axel's memory and contribution to European rugby, the EPCR announced that the 2016–2017 European Player of the Year would receive the Anthony Foley Memorial Trophy. President Michael D. Higgins and Taoiseach Enda Kenny paid tribute to Foley and the Irish flag flew at half mast at government buildings in Munster.

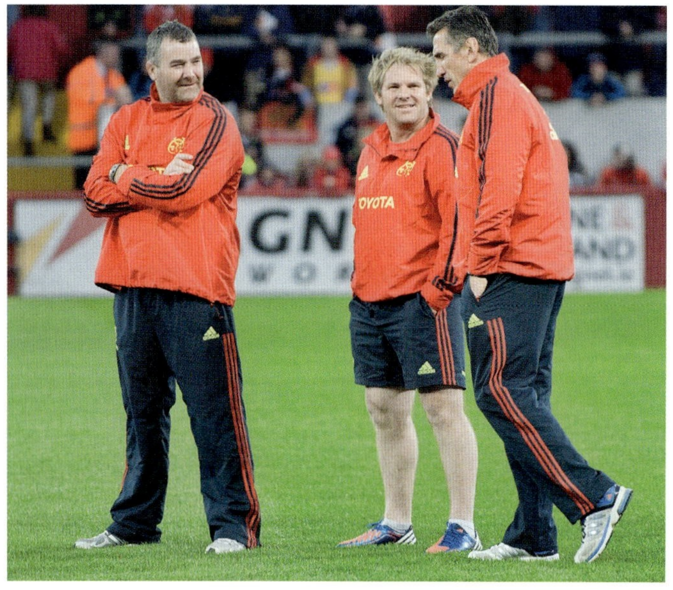

Anthony Foley's funeral took place in Killaloe, County Clare, on Friday, 21 October, and the next day, Munster had a Heineken Cup match at Thomond Park against Glasgow Warriors. Munster were outstanding that day in front of 26,000 supporters. Passions ran high, both with the supporters and on the pitch. Munster went on to win 22 of their following 26 games. They topped their European pool despite being bottom seeds, beating Racing at home and away. Although they lost the Champions Cup semi-final to Saracens and the Pro12 final to Scarlets, that season saw Munster concede five fewer tries than any other team.

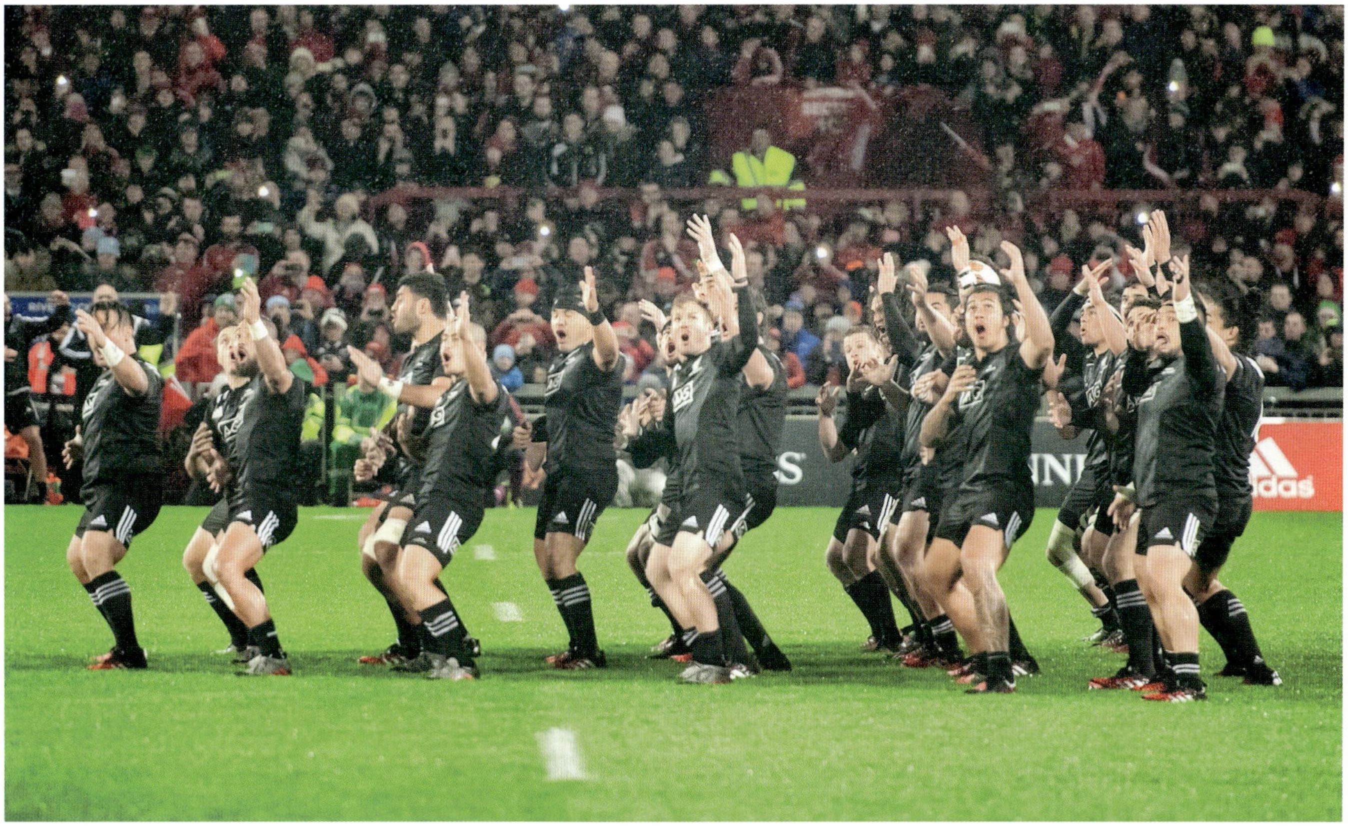

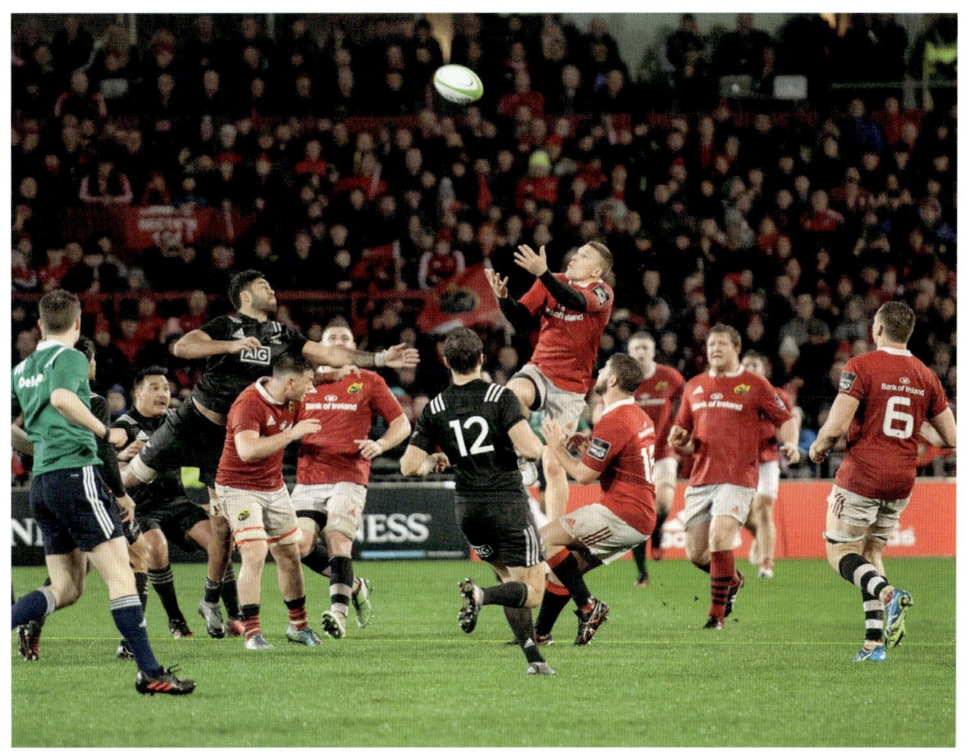

11 November 2016

Above: The Māori All-Blacks perform the haka on a rainy night in Thomond Park. The visitors paid tribute to the late Anthony Foley by laying a jersey with the initials AF on the pitch before the haka.

Right: Andrew Conway gathers a high ball. Munster win the entertaining try-fest 27-14.

23 September 2012

Opposite: (l–r) Axel, Simon Mannix and Rob Penney prior to the match against Newport Gwent Dragons at Thomond Park.

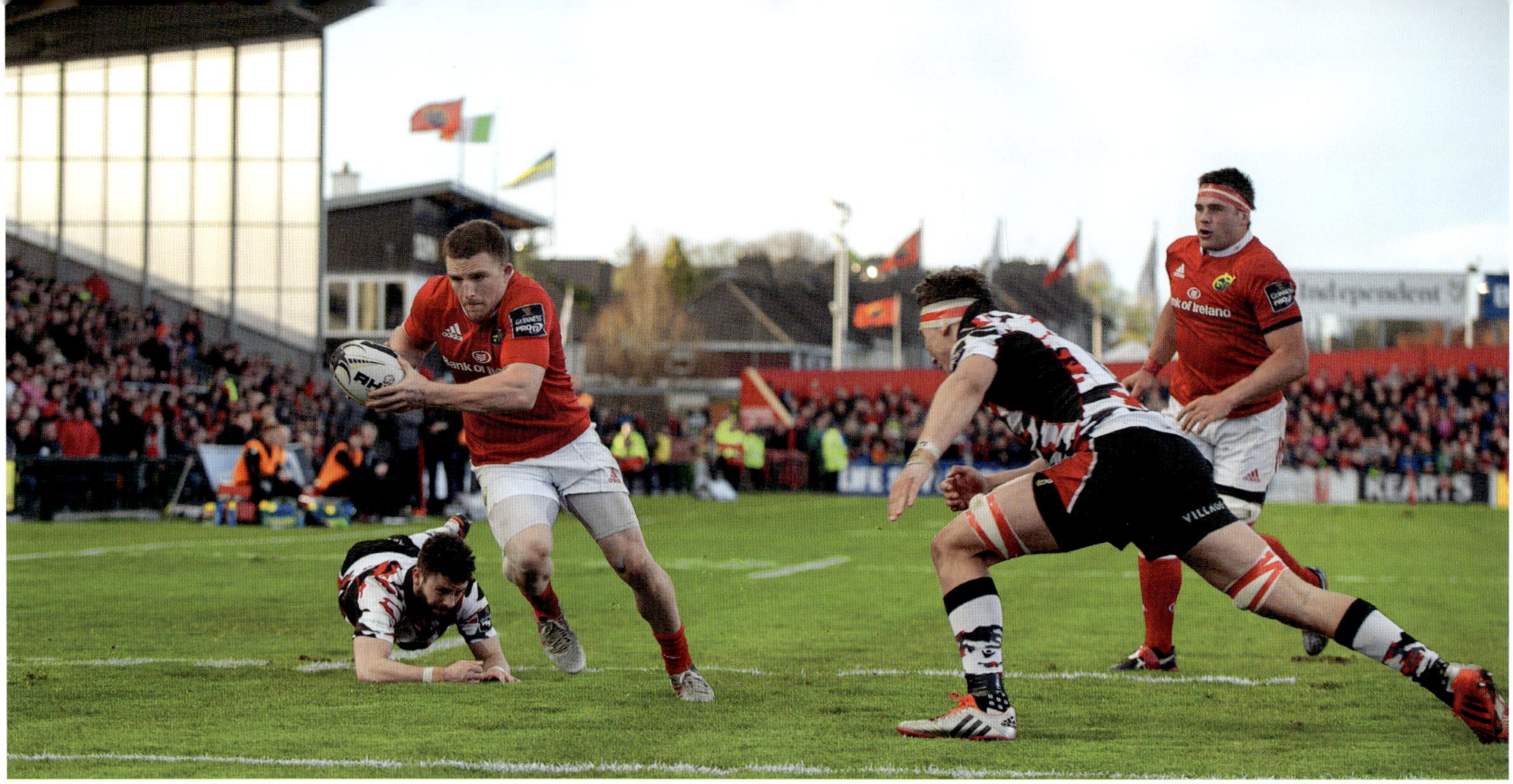

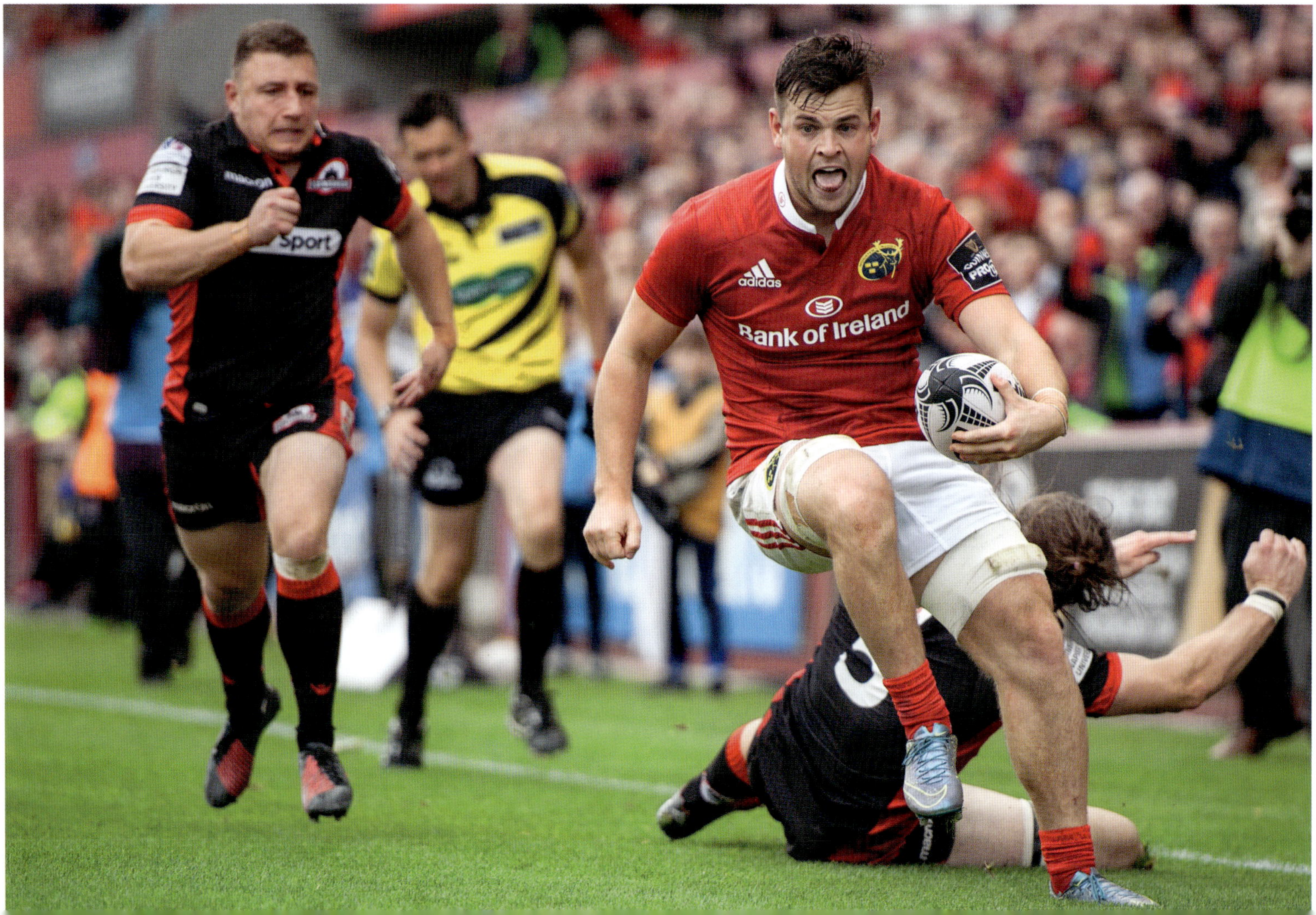
adidas
Bank of Ireland
Sport

Opposite top: Andrew Conway about to score at Irish Independent Park against Cardiff Blues. Munster lose by a point, 24–23.

Opposite bottom: Conor Oliver, who came on after twelve minutes for the injured Jack O'Donoghue, shows his pace against Edinburgh. Munster earn a bonus point in the 28–14 home win.

Right: CJ Stander in action as Munster cruise to victory over Zebre at Thomond Park, winning 49–5.

Bottom: Conor Murray at full stretch against Ulster in Kingspan Stadium. Munster win 15–14.

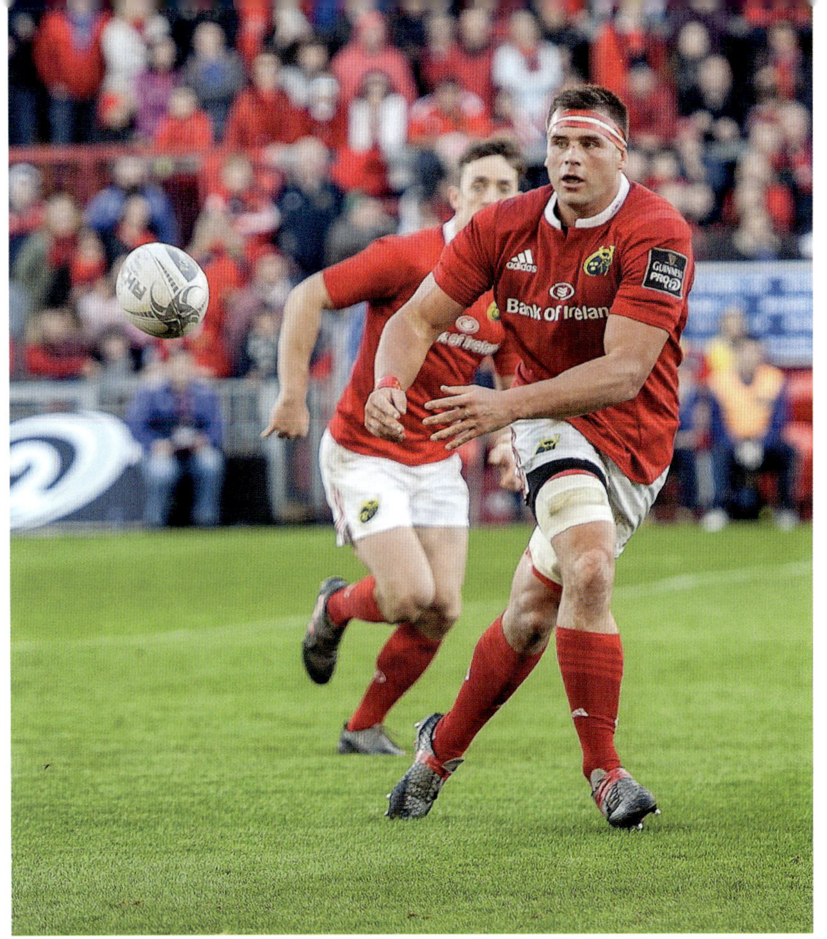

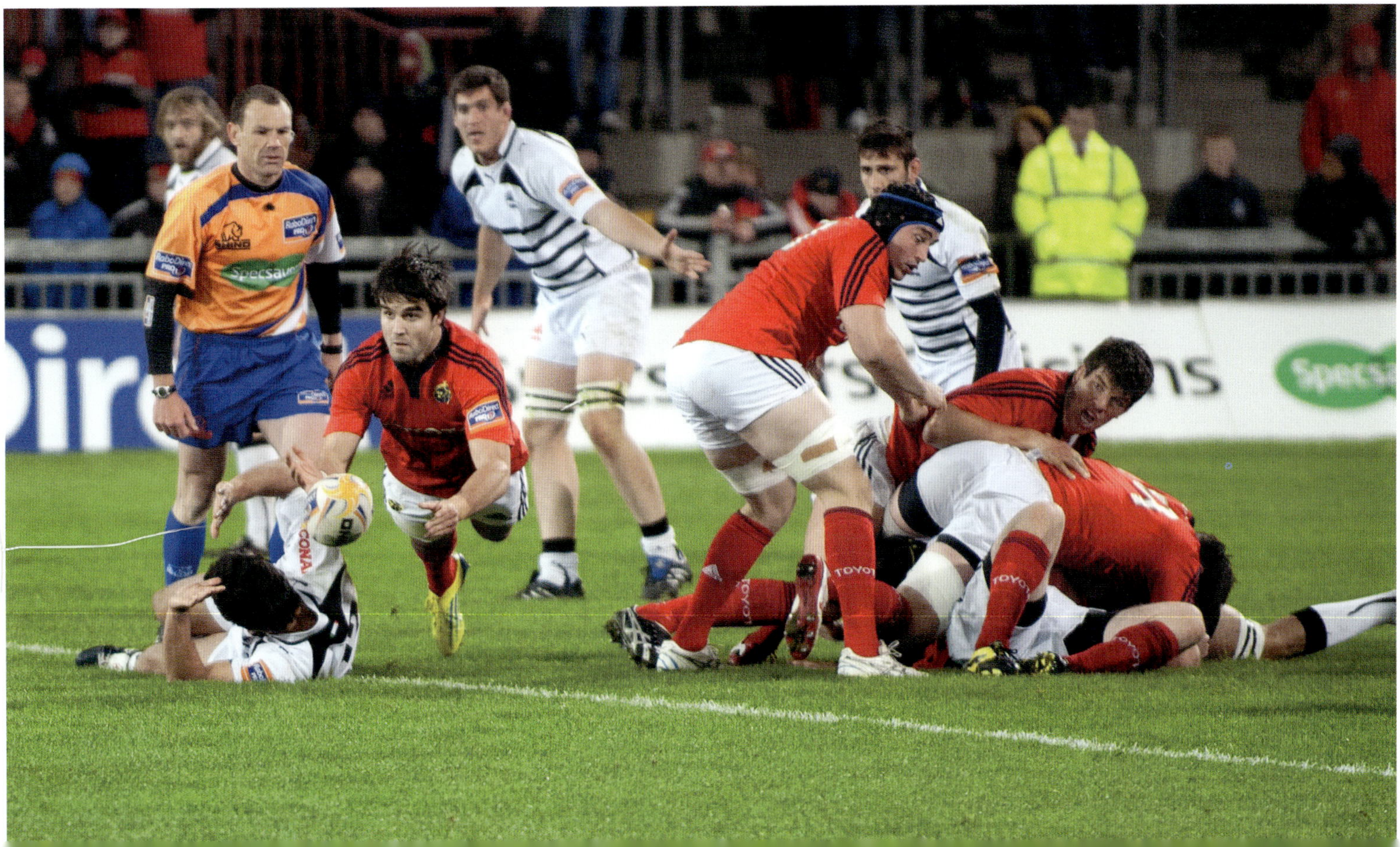

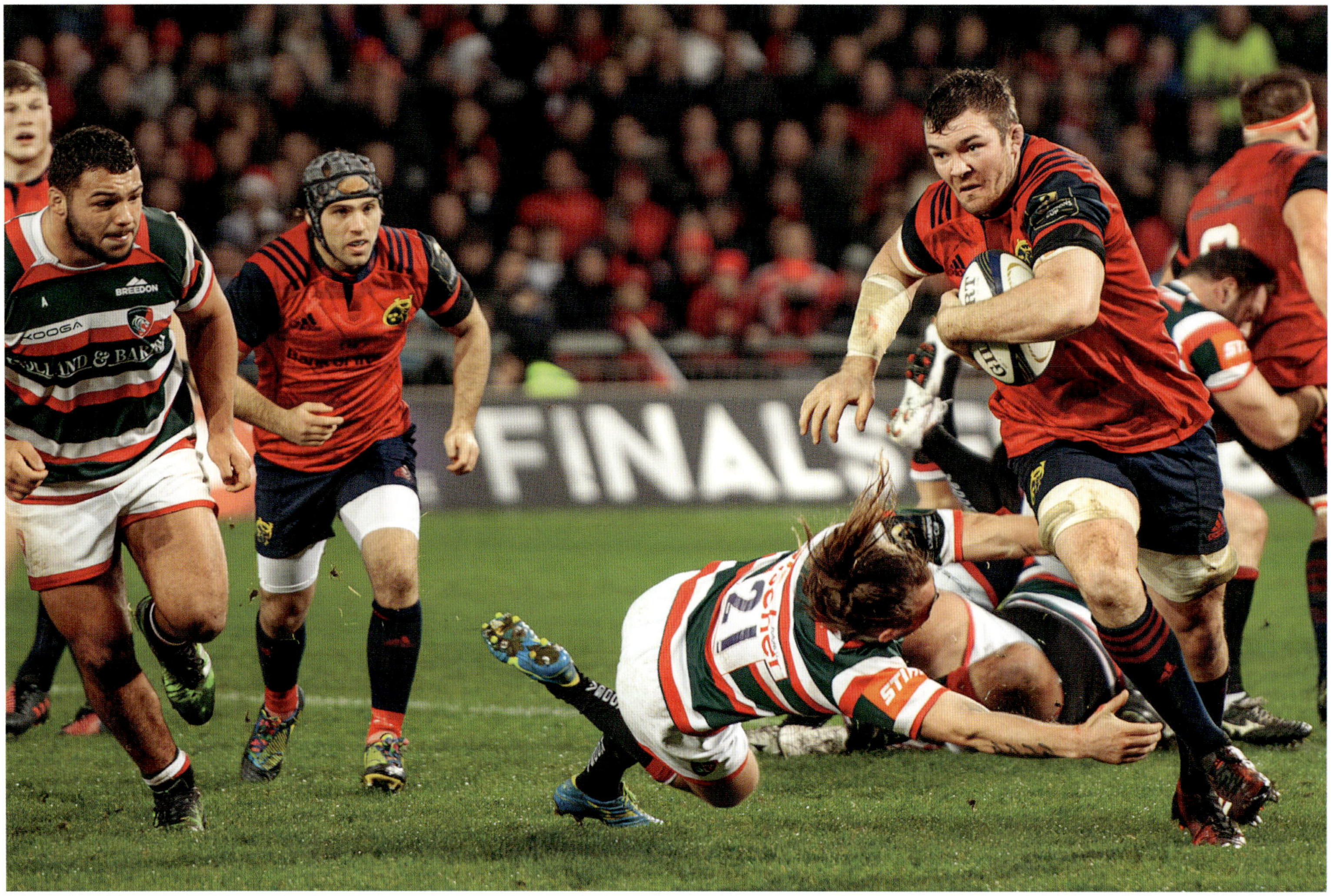

10 December 2016

Top: Peter O'Mahony makes a strong break against Leicester Tigers.
Right: Assistant coach Jacques Nienaber watches intently as his team
clinically keep the Tigers at bay in their 38-0 win.

26 December 2016

Opposite top: CJ Stander in the thick of the action against Leinster at
Thomond Park. Munster win 29-17.

21 January 2017

Opposite bottom: CJ Stander makes a sprint worthy of an Olympic
100-metre runner against Racing 92 (whose assistant coach was
former Munster great, Ronan O'Gara). The 22-10 win secures a home
Champions Cup quarter-final for Munster. Also pictured are (l–r) Jaco
Taute and Tommy O'Donnelly

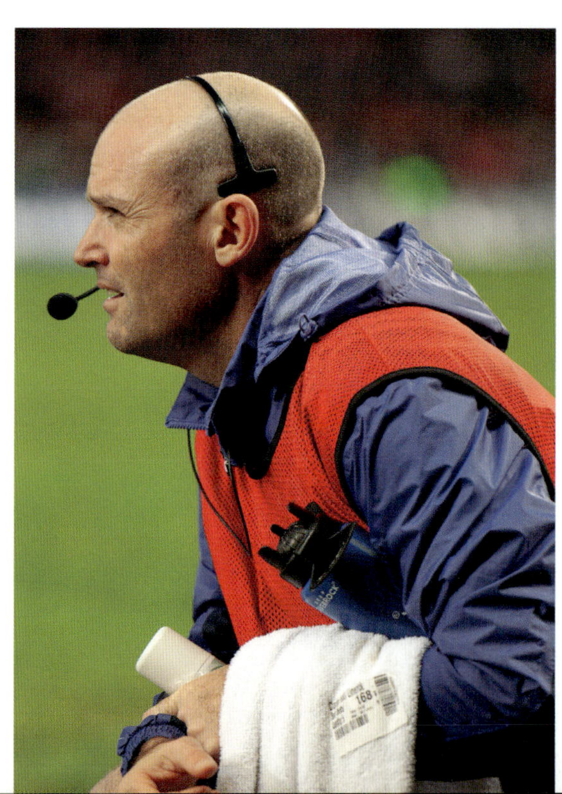

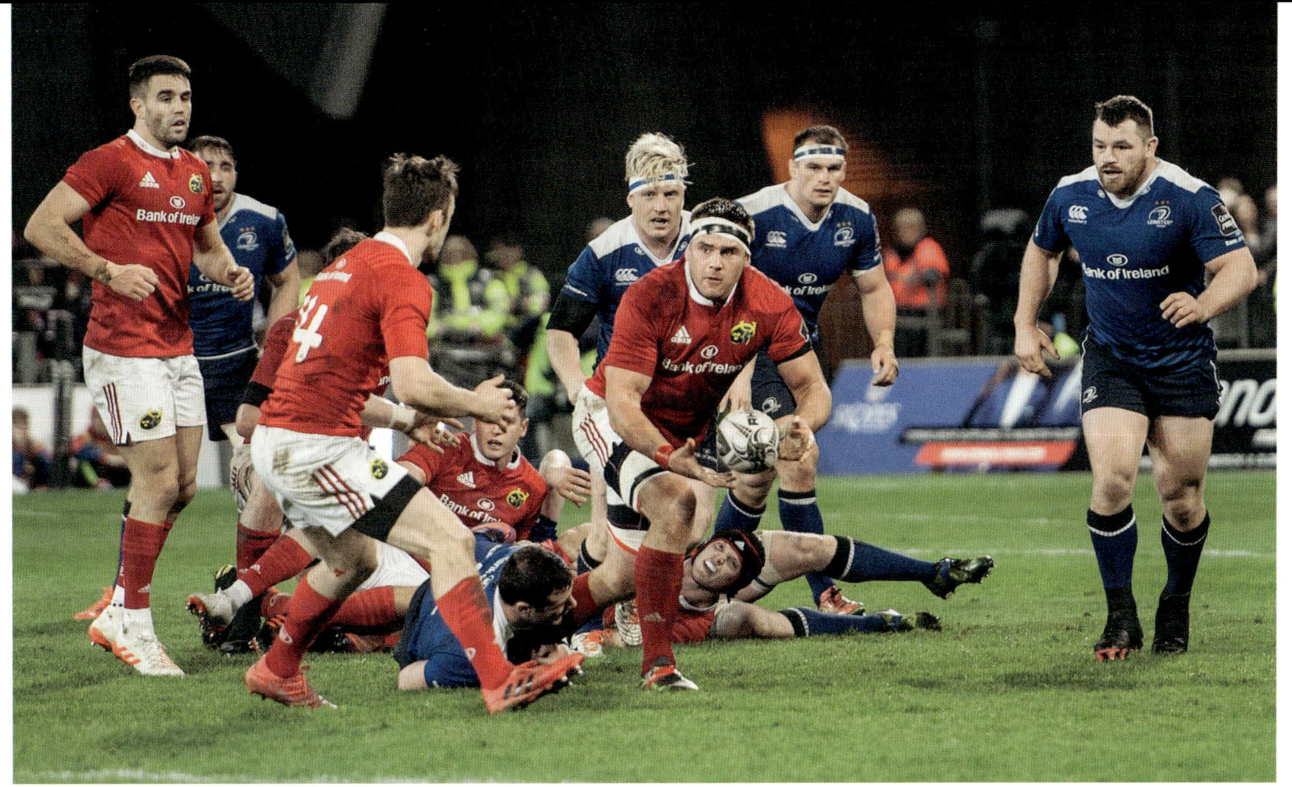

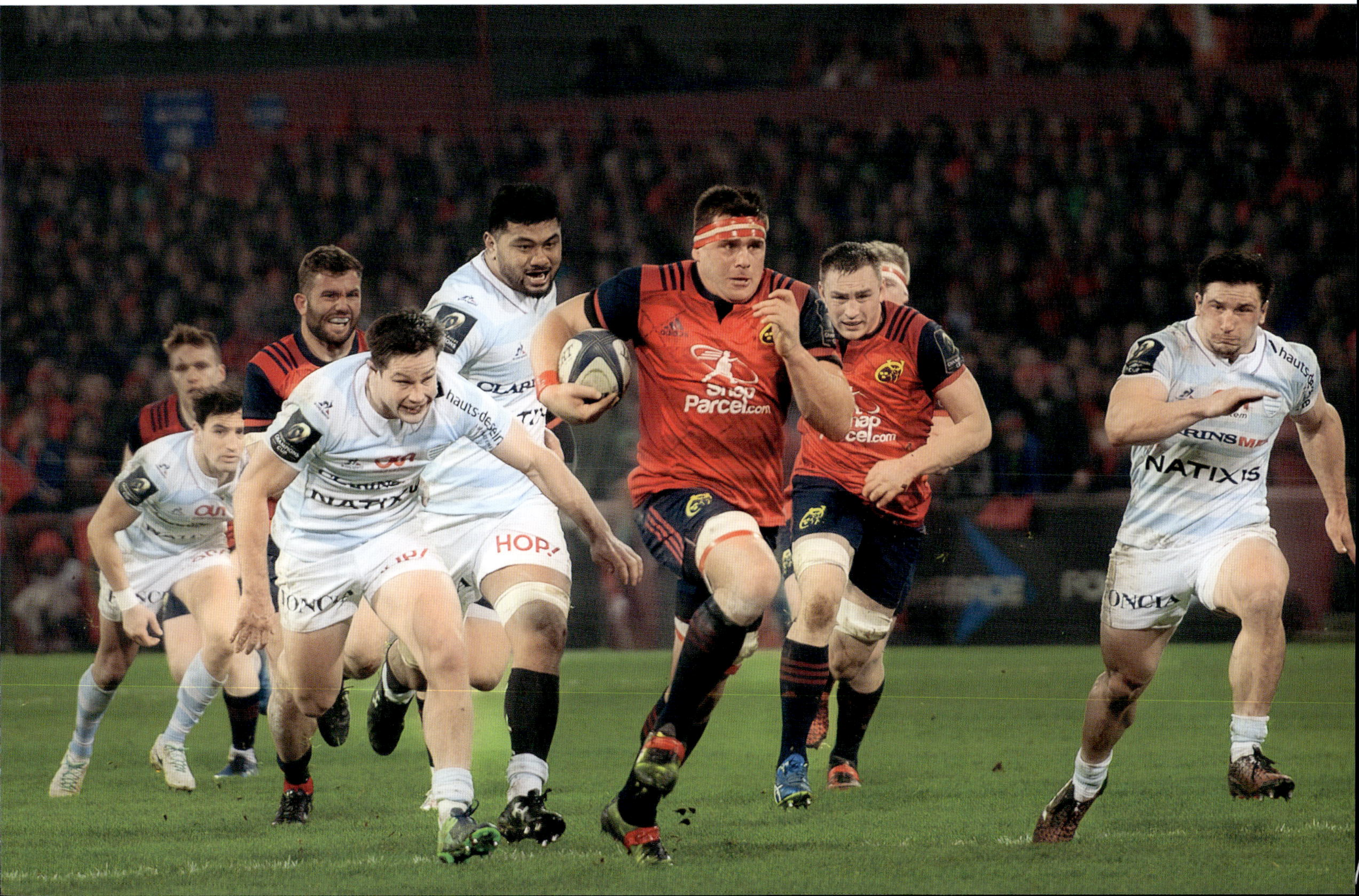

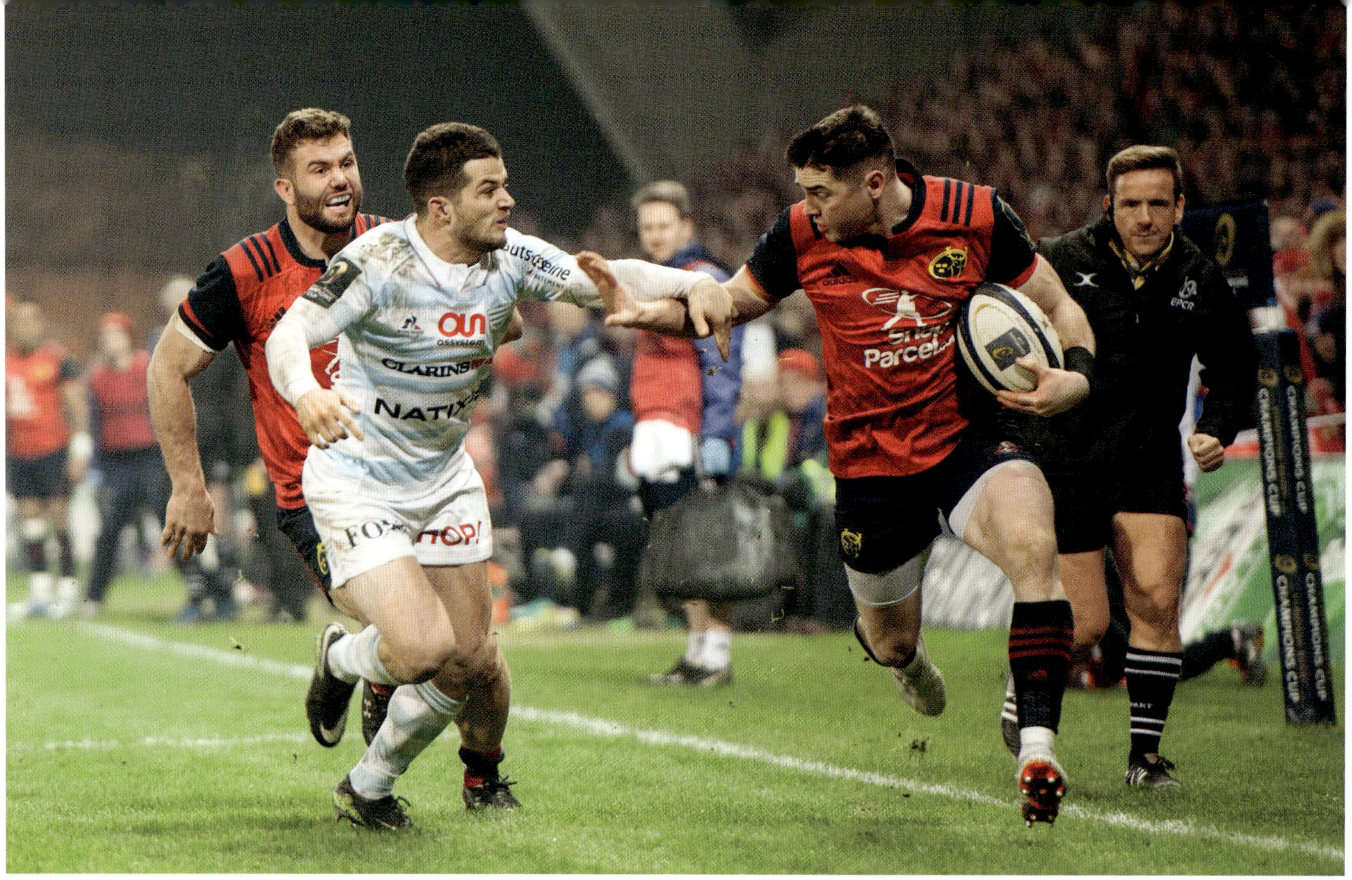

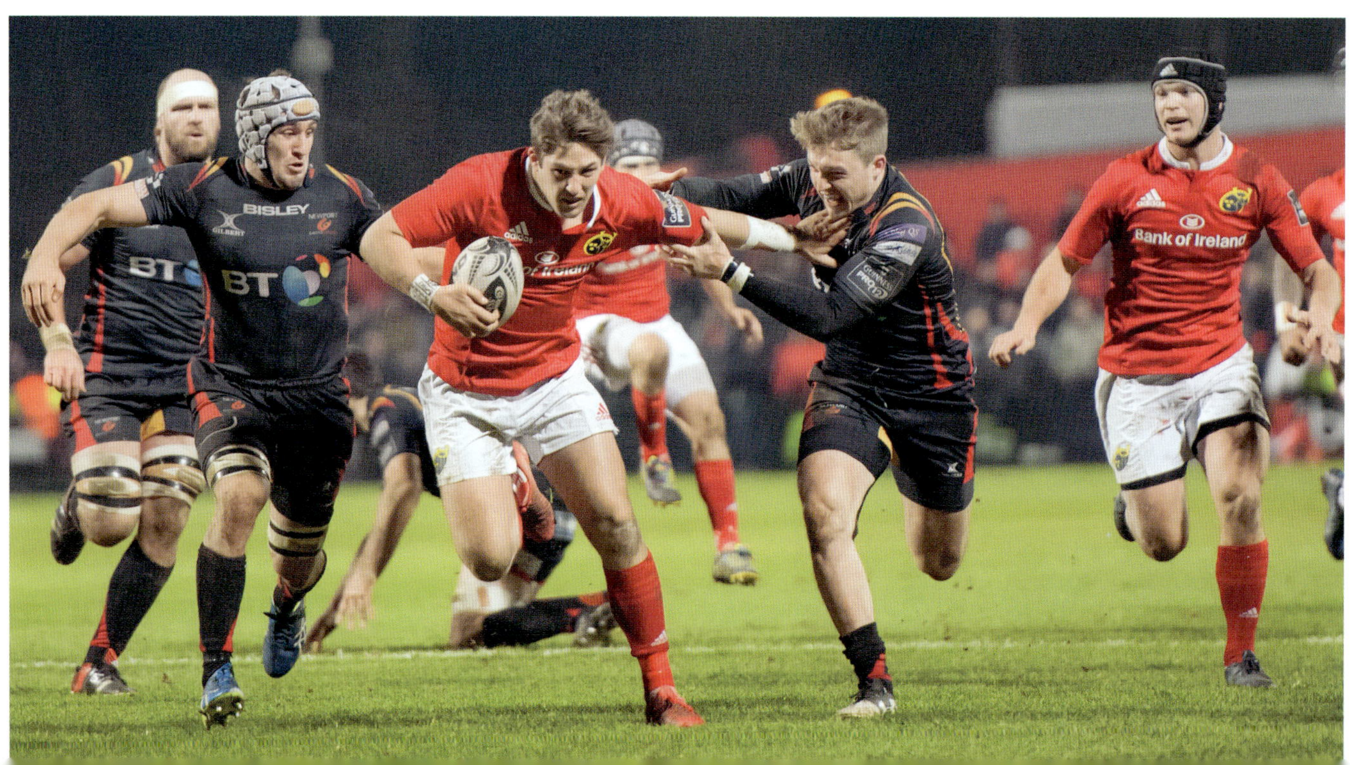

21 January 2017

Above: Ronan O'Mahony about to score against Racing 92 in Munster's 22-10 home victory.

10 February 2017

Below: Dan Goggin charges with ball in hand against Newport Gwent Dragons. Despite conceding a try when down to fourteen men for ten minutes in the second half, Munster increase their half-time lead of 30-10 to win 45-17.

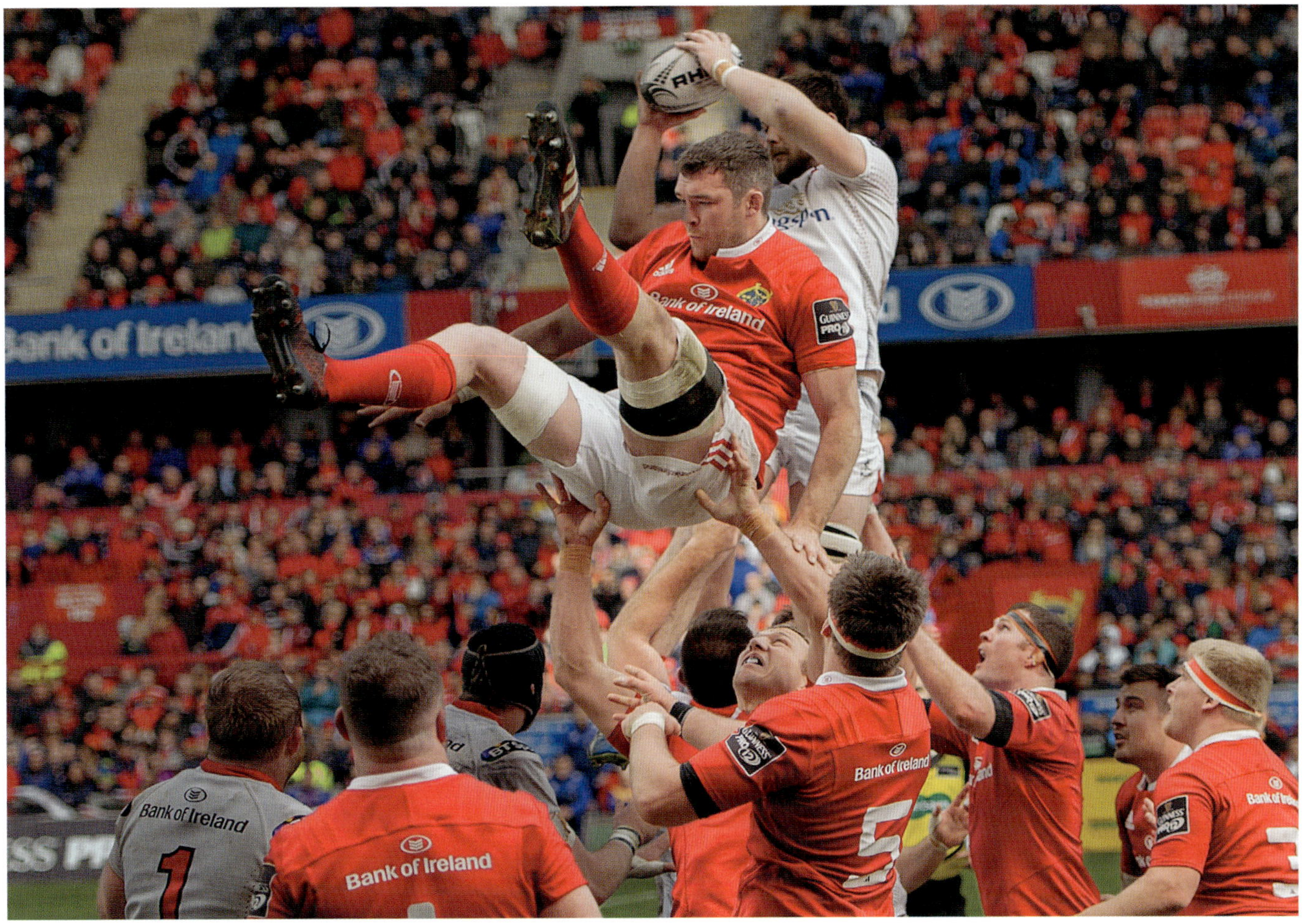

15 April 2017

Above: Captain Peter O'Mahony competes against Ulster's Iain Henderson in a line-out. Munster eke out the win, 22–20, in a tightly fought battle, to secure a place in the Pro12 semi-finals.

6 May 2017

Right: Keith Earls in action against Connacht, a game Munster win convincingly, 50–14.

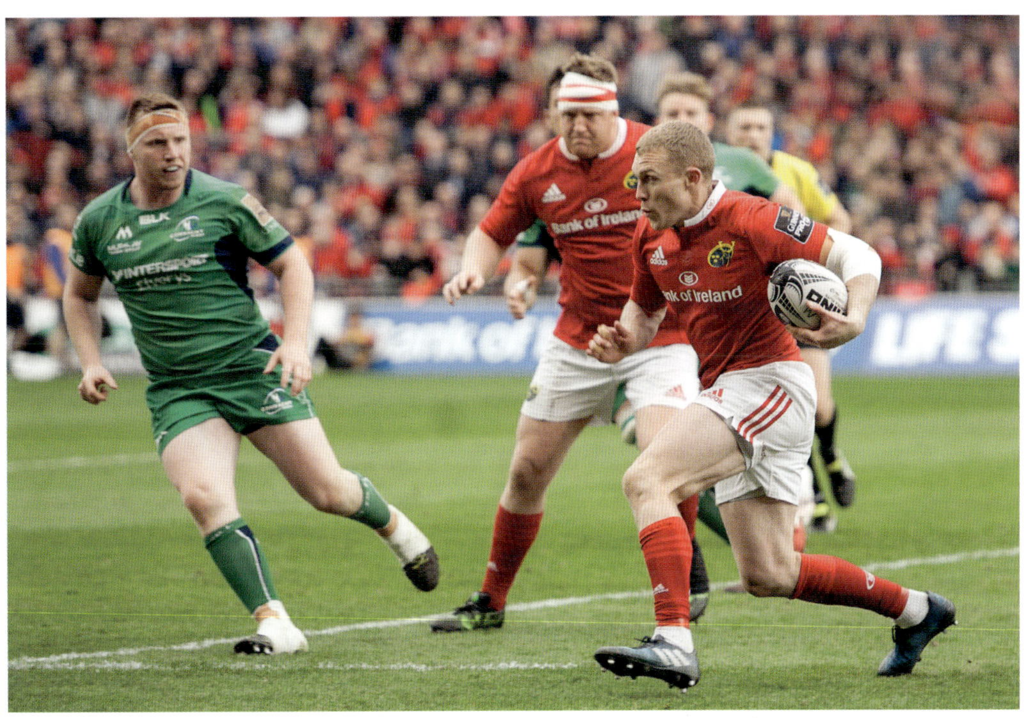

2017-2018

PRO14   POOL WINS: 13; POOL LOSSES: 7; DRAWS: 1; ELIMINATED: SEMI-FINAL
EUROPEAN CHAMPIONS CUP   POOL WINS: 4; POOL LOSSES: 1; DRAWS: 1; ELIMINATED: SEMI-FINAL

Springboks forwards coach Johann van Graan came to Munster in November as new head coach, joined in December by Lions defence coach JP Ferreira. Rassie Erasmus and Jacques Nienaber both left in December. Coaches Jerry Flannery and Felix Jones extended their contracts by a further two years, and team manager Niall O'Donovan by another three. A pre-season match saw former greats Donncha O'Callaghan and Peter Stringer playing for Worcester Warriors against Munster, which Munster won 35-26. New signings for the province included Chris Farrell, Gerbrandt Grobler, Chris Cloete and Jeremy Loughman, with JJ Hanrahan returning from Northampton Saints. Conor Oliver, Bill Johnston, Dan Goggin and Stephen Fitzgerald were promoted from the academy. Dave Foley left for pastures new, as did Donnacha Ryan, Francis Saili and Duncan Casey. Simon Zebo would leave for Racing 92 at the end of this season.

PRO14

The Rabo league was expanded to fourteen teams with the addition of Cheetahs and Southern Kings from South Africa. The structure was changed to feature two conferences, A and B. Munster were in conference A with Cardiff Blues, Ospreys, Glasgow Warriors, Connacht, Cheetahs and Zebra Parma.

Munster finished in second place in conference A. In the pool games they beat Benetton, Cheetahs (twice: at home and away), Ospreys (twice: at home and away), Cardiff Blues, Dragons, Zebre (twice: at home and away), Connacht, Glasgow Warriors, Scarlets, Southern Kings, and Edinburgh. The season saw a series of away losses for Munster: to Glasgow Warriors, Leinster, Connacht, Ulster, Cardiff Blues and Edinburgh. They lost at home to Leinster, and drew with Ulster at Thomond Park.

In the semi-final qualifier against Edinburgh on 5 May 2018, Munster won 20-16. Rhys Marshall and Keith Earls scored tries; Hanrahan converted both and added two penalties. In the semi-final away against newly crowned Champions Cup winners Leinster on 19 May, Munster lost agonisingly 16-15, which ended their season.

European Champions Cup

The Heineken Cup draw saw Munster play Leicester Tigers for a third time in a row and Racing 92 for the second season. French team Castres Olympique completed the draw.

Munster's first game was on 15 October away against Castres, and ended in a 17-17 draw. Simon Zebo and Dave Kilcoyne scored tries and Tyler Bleyendaal added the extra points. This was followed by a 14-7 home win against Racing 92 on 21 October. Conor Murray and Andrew Conway scored tries, both converted by Ian Keatley.

A double-header against Leicester Tigers followed in December, with Munster emphatic 33-10 winners at home on 9 December and 25-16 away on 17 December. It was Munster's first win at Welford Road in eleven years and the first time that Tigers lost a double-header in this competition. Marshall, Zebo, Peter O'Mahony and Cloete scored tries; Keatley converted two and added three penalties in the home game. CJ Stander scored a try away, converted by Keatley, who added six penalties.

Munster played Racing 92 at Paris La Défense Arena on 14 January 2018. Racing 92 won 34-30. Tries by Jean Kleyn, Earls and Chris Farrell, all converted by Keatley, who added two penalties and Murray a third, provided the small consolation of a losing bonus point.

Castres were the next visitors to Thomond Park, where, in front of 23,000 supporters on 21 January 2018, Munster had a decisive 48-3 win. Tries came from Earls, Marshall, a penalty try, Zebo, Alex Wootton and James Cronin. Keatley converted three and was successful with two out of two penalty attempts. JJ Hanrahan converted the last two tries.

A thrilling quarter-final was played against Toulon at Thomond Park in front of 26,000 supporters, refereed by Nigel Owens, on 31 March. With fifteen minutes remaining, Toulon moved to a six-point lead. In the 74th minute, François Trinh-Duc kicked for touch. Conway kept his feet pitch-side, reaching over the touchline for the ball, and was on his way. He swerved inside the chasing Trinh-Duc at pace, Jean Kleyn standing like a statue with both hands up so as not to obstruct any defender; Conway evaded Raphaël Lakafia and then brilliantly stepped inside Malakai Fekitoa to dive over the tryline from 45 metres out and send Thomond Park into eardrum-bursting raptures. This 74th-minute moment of magic is still regarded as probably the best individual try scored at Thomond Park. Keatley sealed the deal with the conversion and the 20-19 win sent Munster into the European semi-finals.

The semi-final was played against Racing 92 at Stade Chaban-Delmas with over 24,500 in attendance. It took until the 62nd minute for Zebo to cross for a try. Heroically, two further tries were scored in the last five minutes – Marshall scoring in the 75th minute and Conway in the 80th – but it was too late: in a one-score victory, Racing took the game by 27-22.

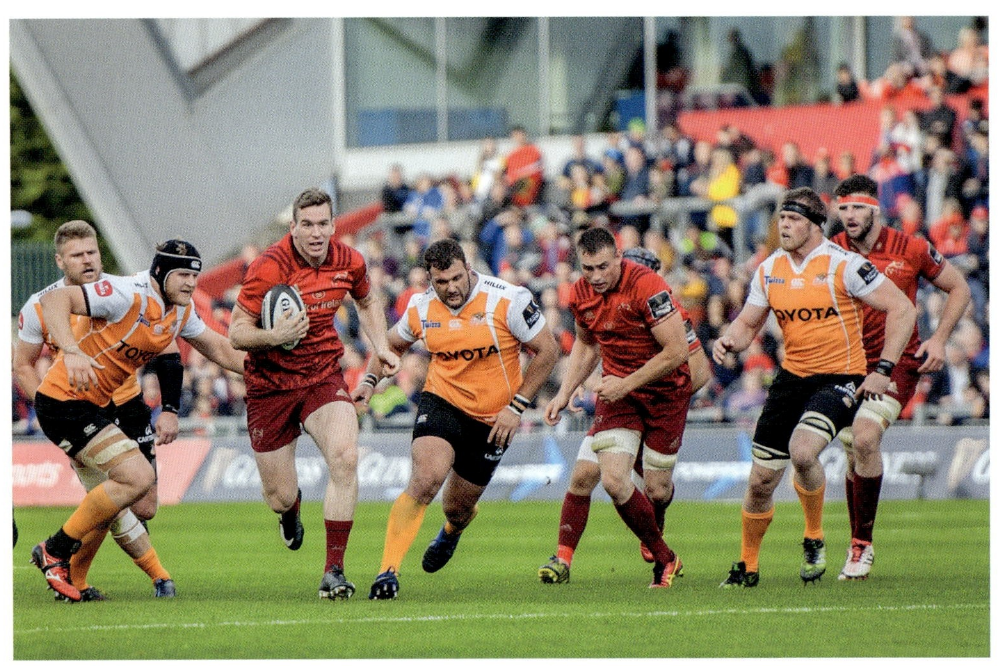

9 September 2017

Left: Chris Farrell pursued by the Cheetahs pack in the course of Munster's emphatic eight-try 51–18 victory.

Below: Alex Wootton scoring one of his four tries against Cheetahs in a man-of-the-match performance.

9 December 2017

Opposite: Billy Holland competes in the line-out in Munster's 33–10 bonus-point victory over Leicester Tigers.

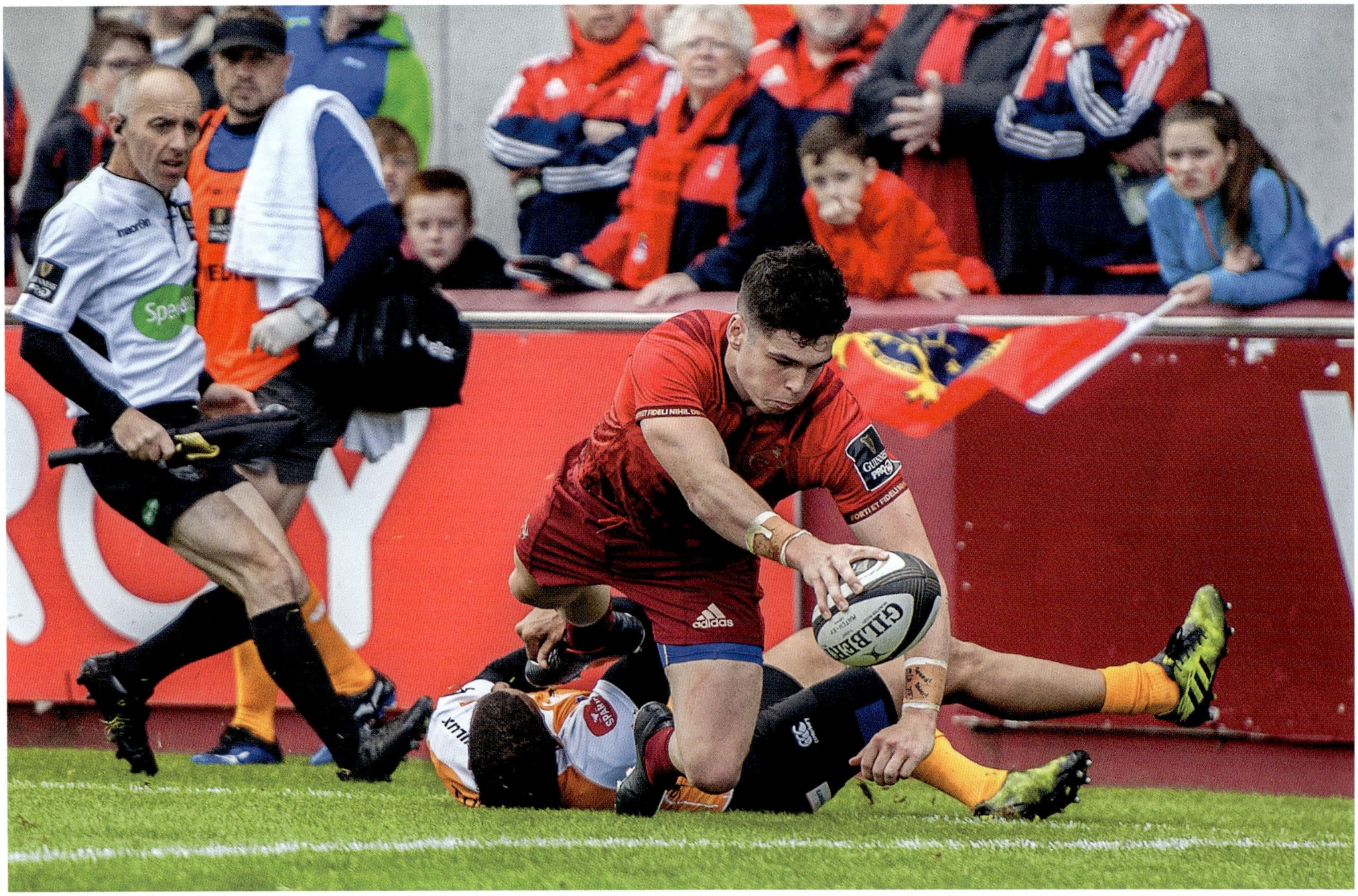

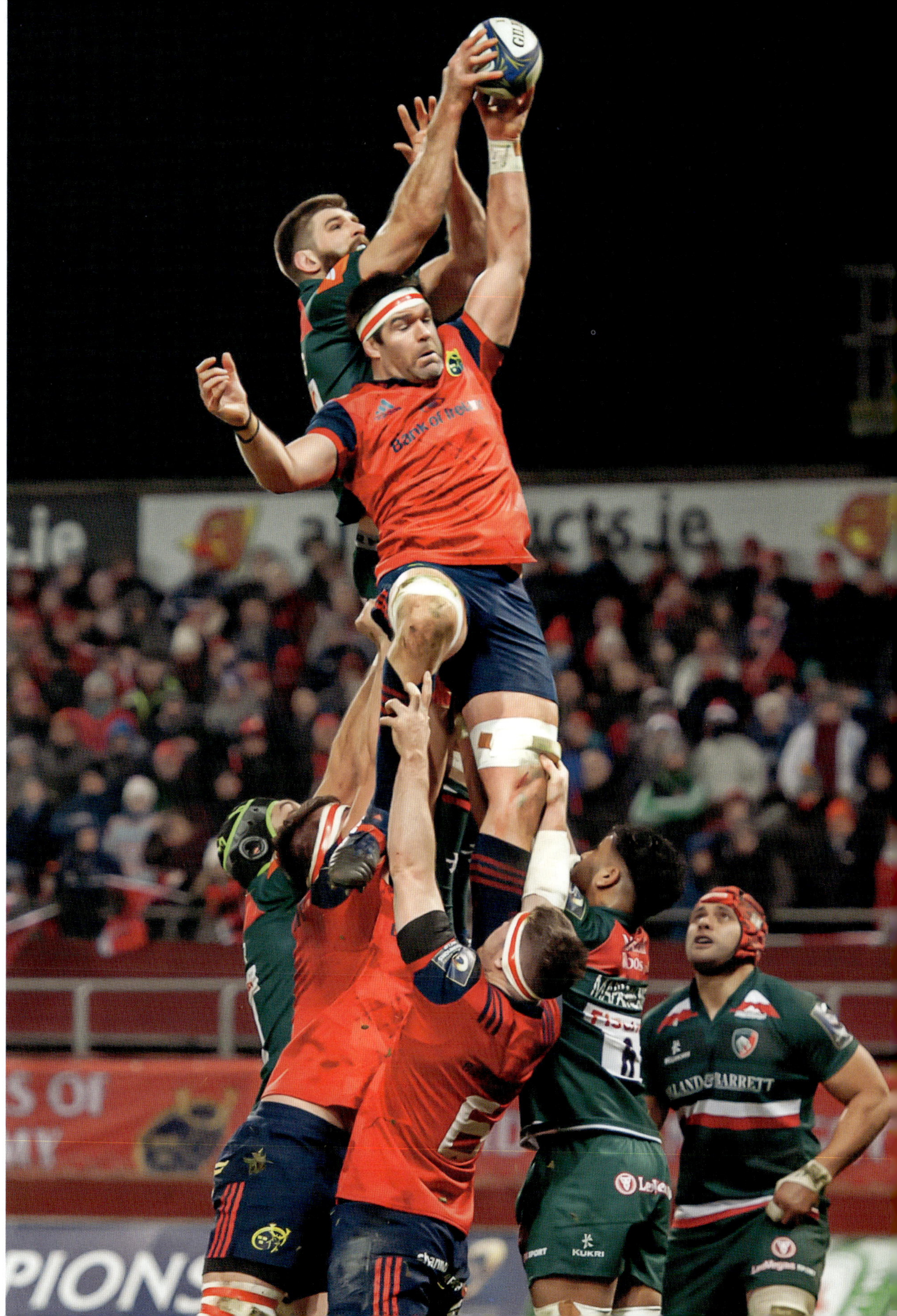

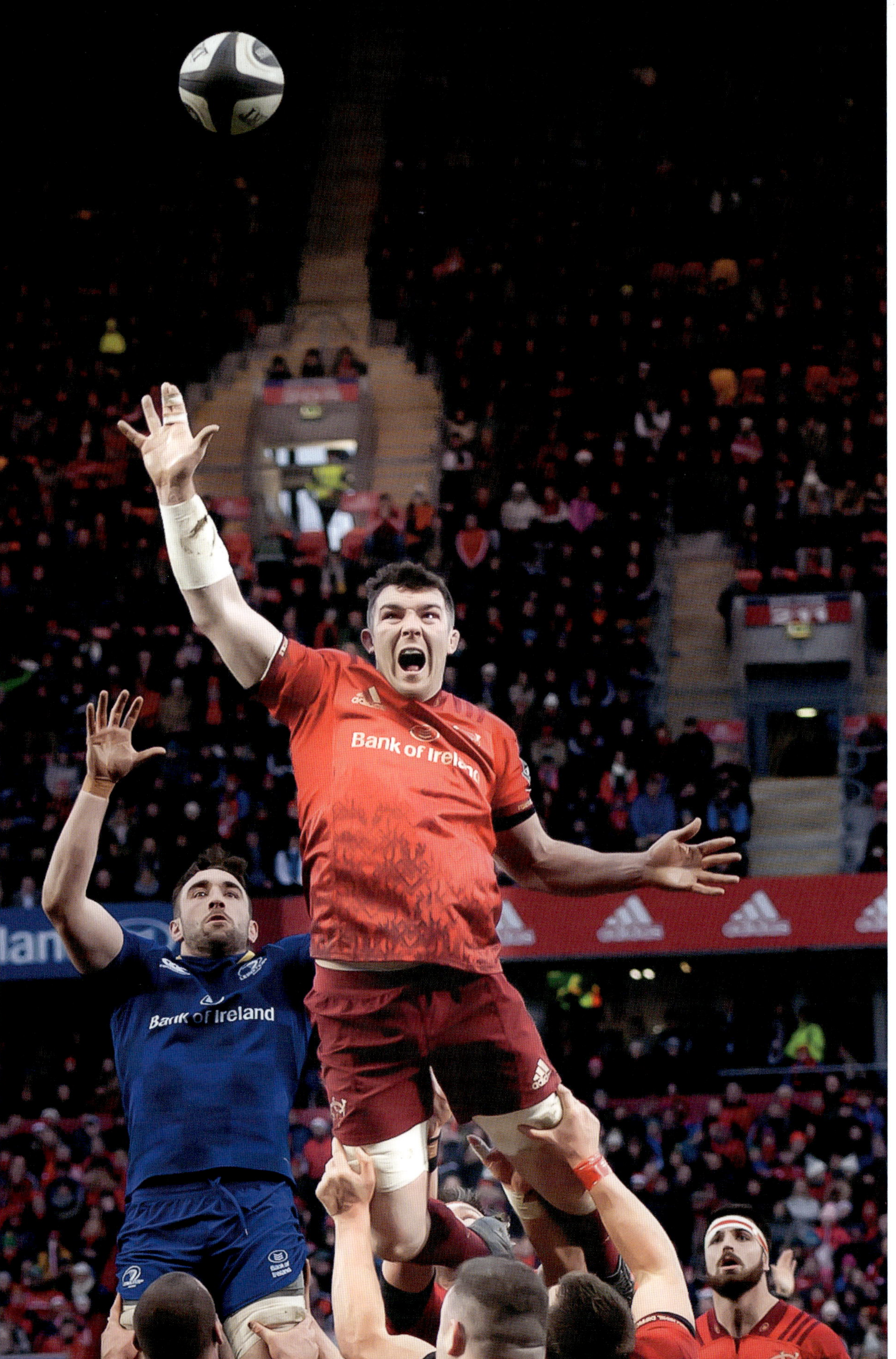

26 December 2017

Left: Peter O'Mahony takes on Jack Conan of Leinster, who go on to win the game 34–24.

10 February 2018

Opposite top: Sammy Arnold gets his man, with (l–r) Alex Wootton and JJ Hanrahan in support. Munster win comfortably against Zebre in Thomond Park, 33–5.

23 February 2018

Opposite bottom: Calvin Nash is denied a try by being bundled into touch by Glasgow Warriors in this top-of-the-table clash. Munster secure a 21–10 win in Thomond Park.

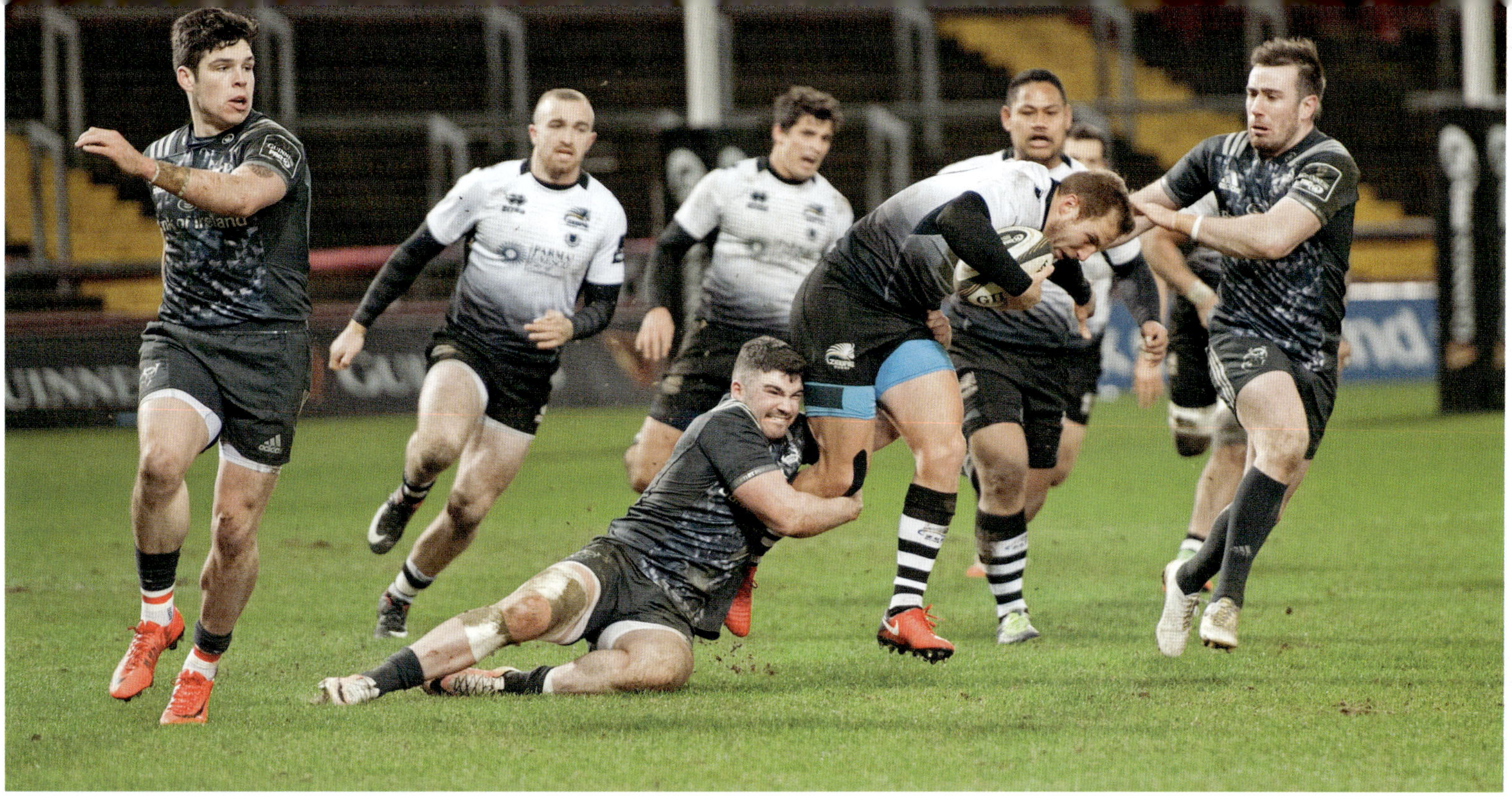

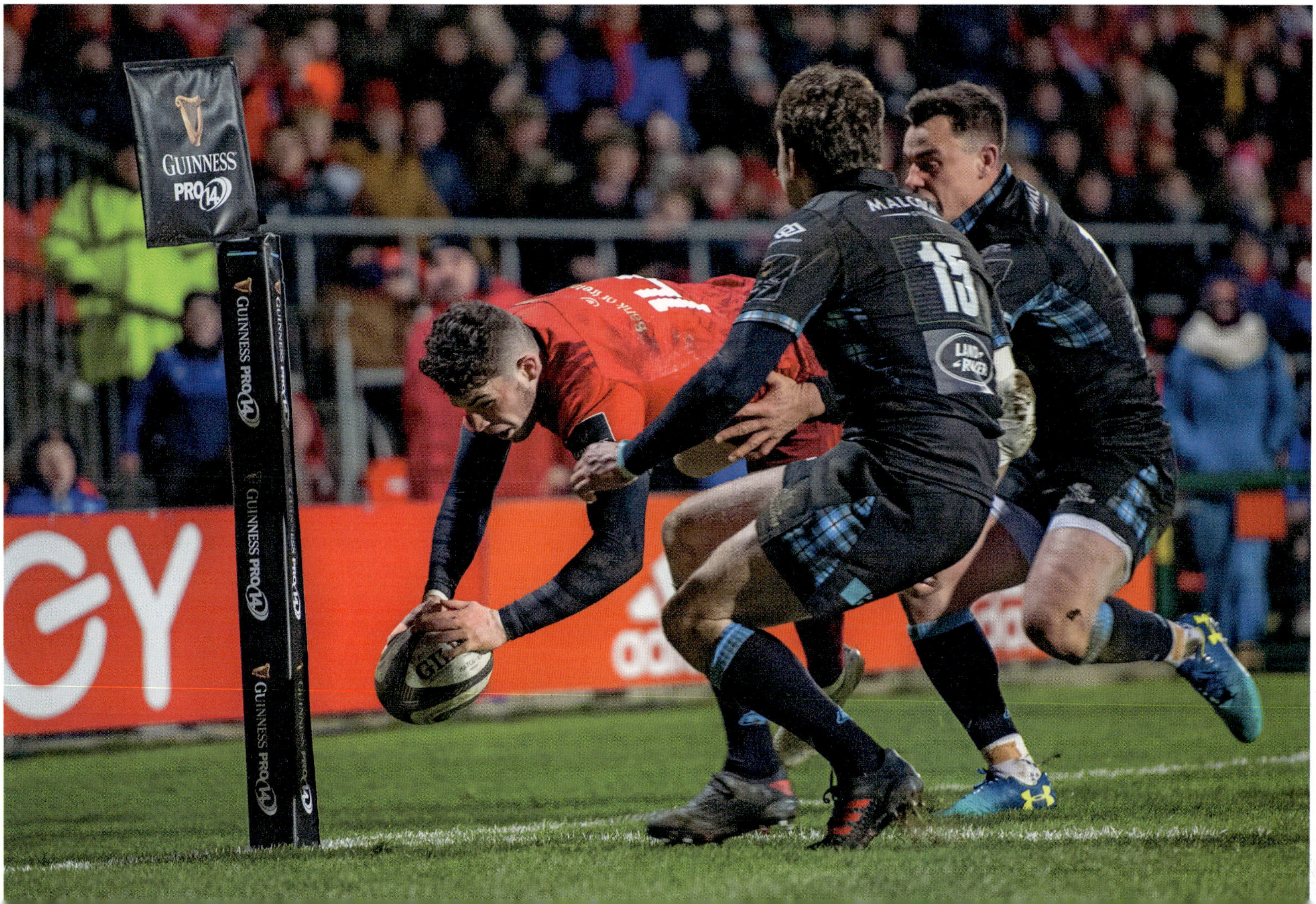

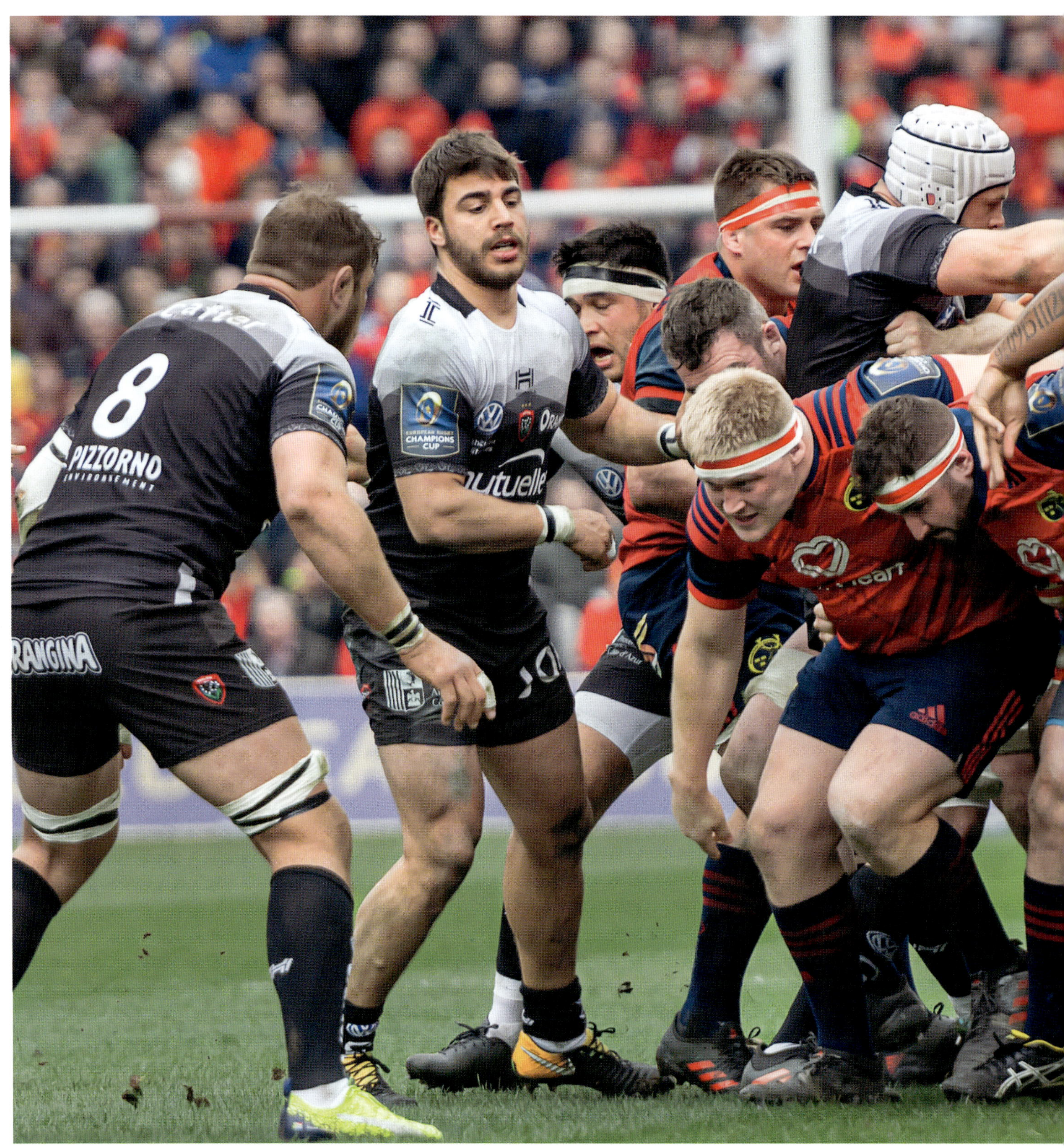

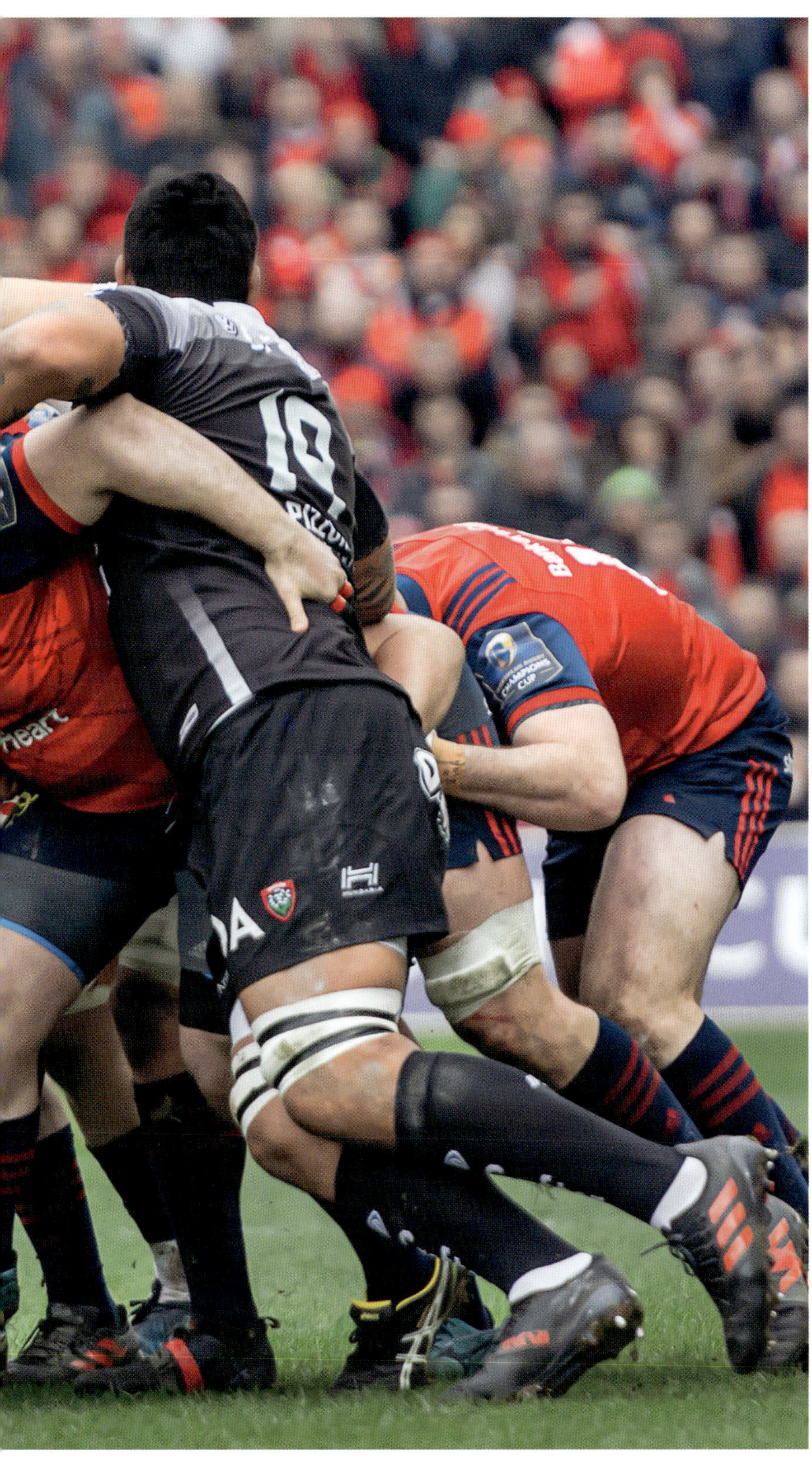

Maul! John Ryan & Co. show Toulon they mean business. The 20-19 win gives Munster a place in the semi-final of the European Champions Cup.

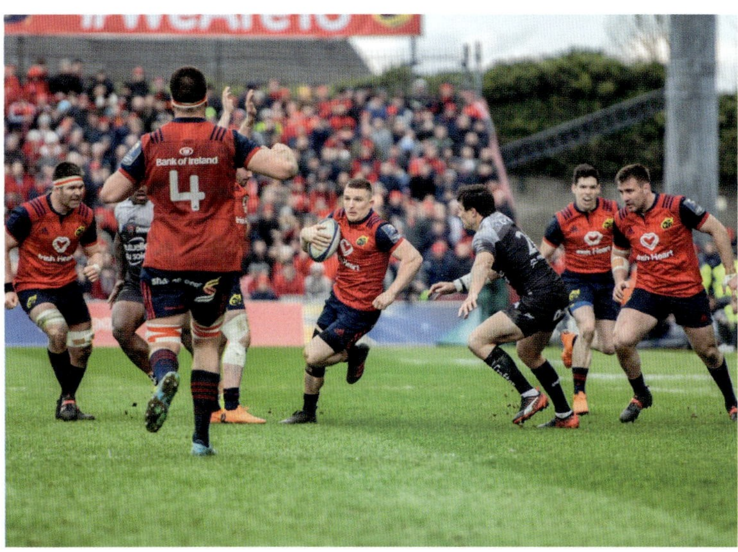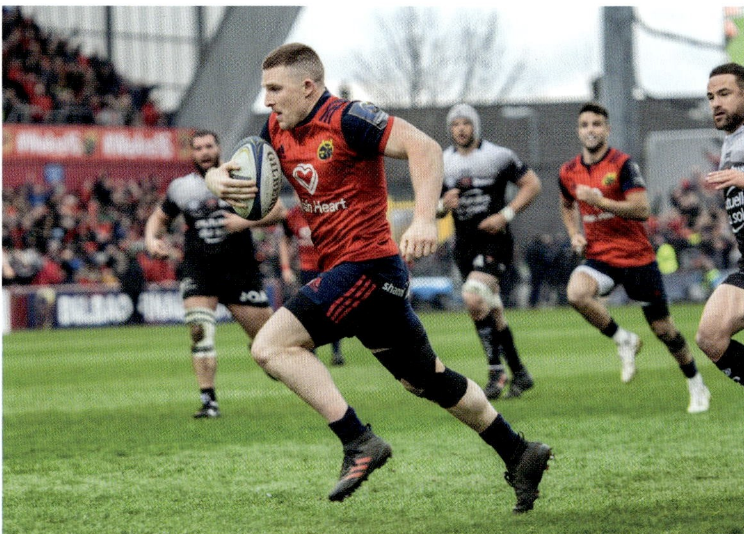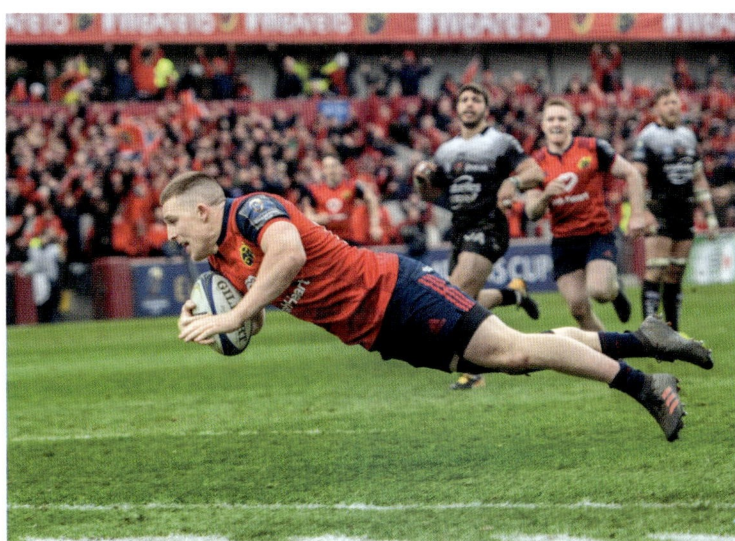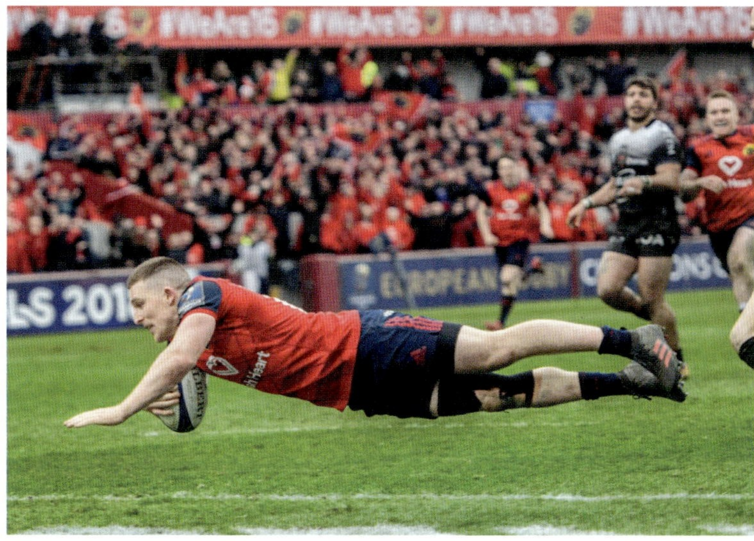

31 March 2018

Andrew Conway's wonder try against Toulon at Thomond Park. His phenomenal solo 45-metre sprint in the 74th minute put Munster a point behind Toulon. Ian Keatley's conversion sealed the win.

Opposite bottom: celebrations from the team.

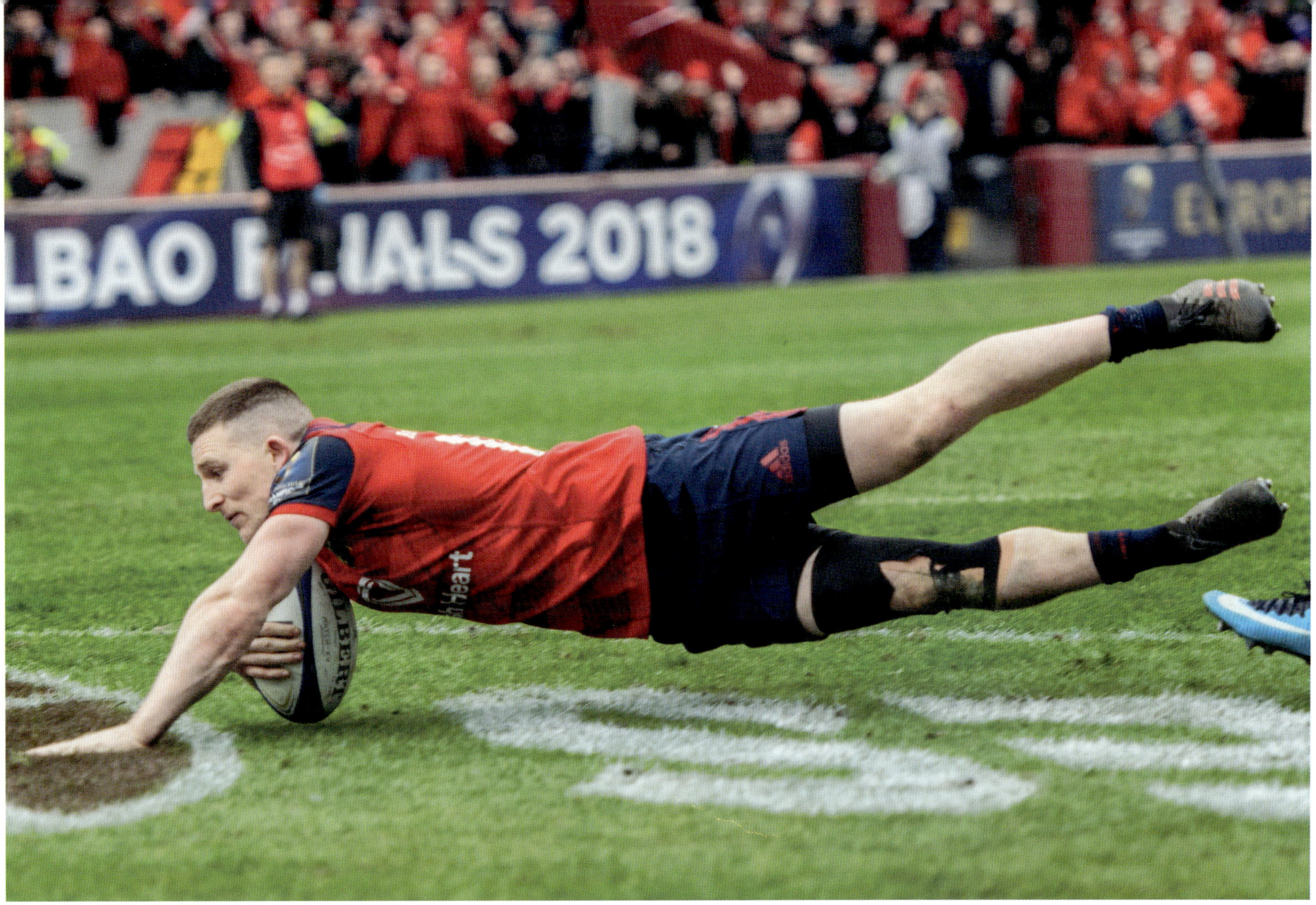

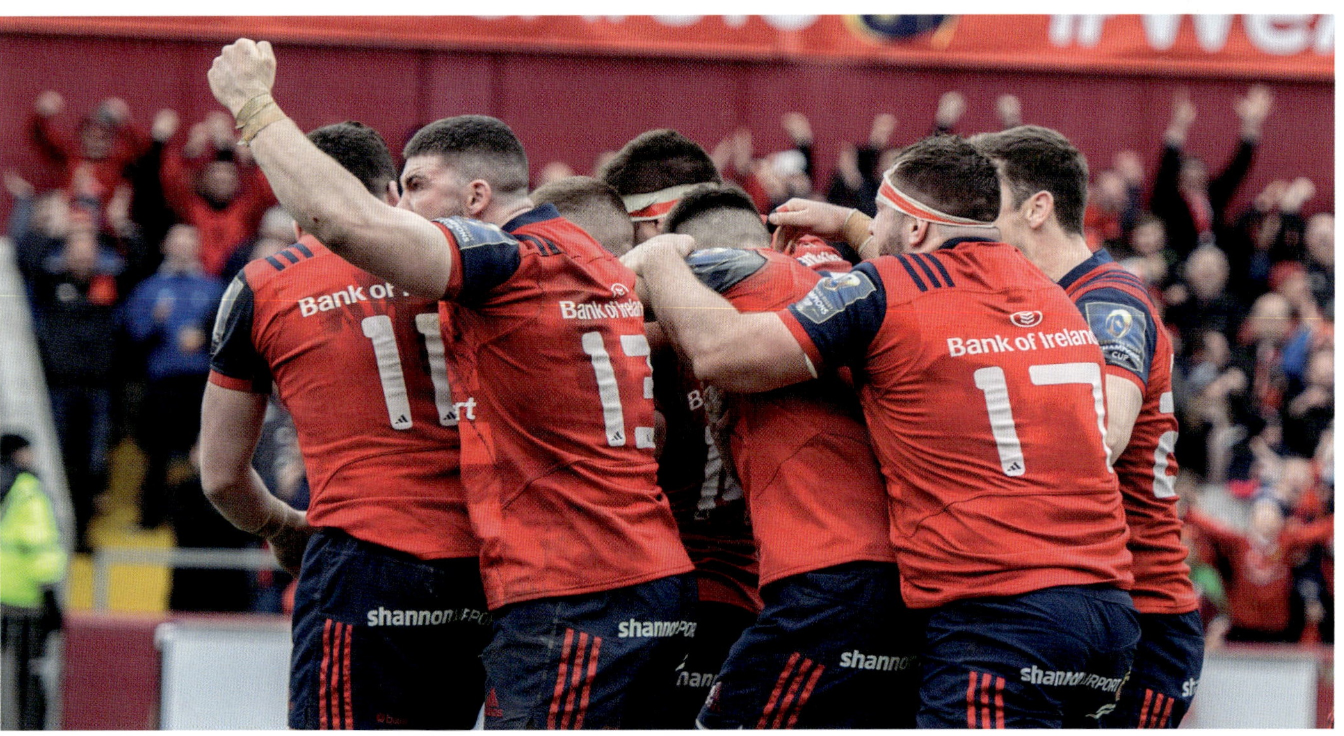

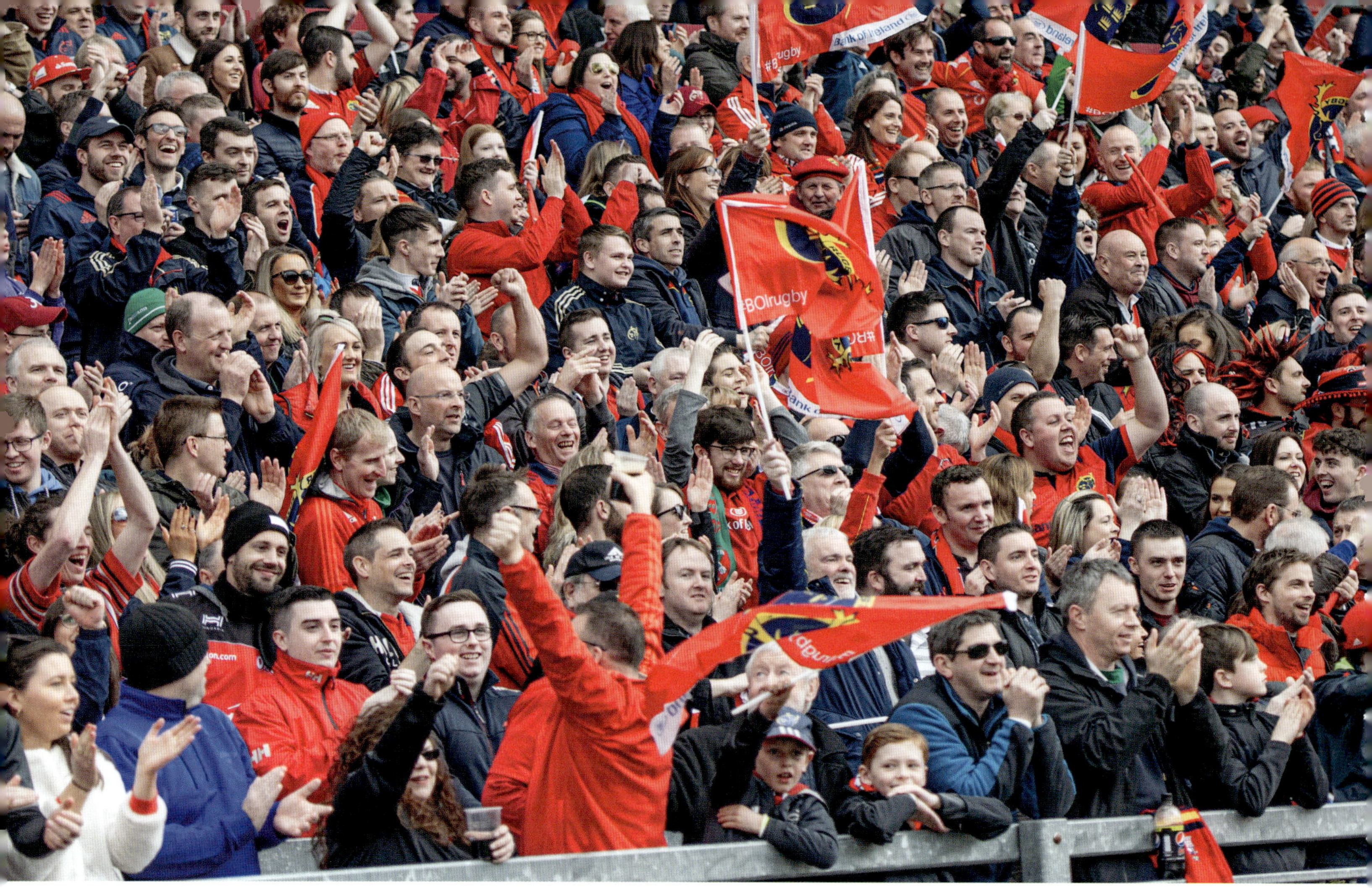

Above: Jubiliation after the win over Toulon.

Right: A very happy Johann van Graan (left) and CJ Stander.

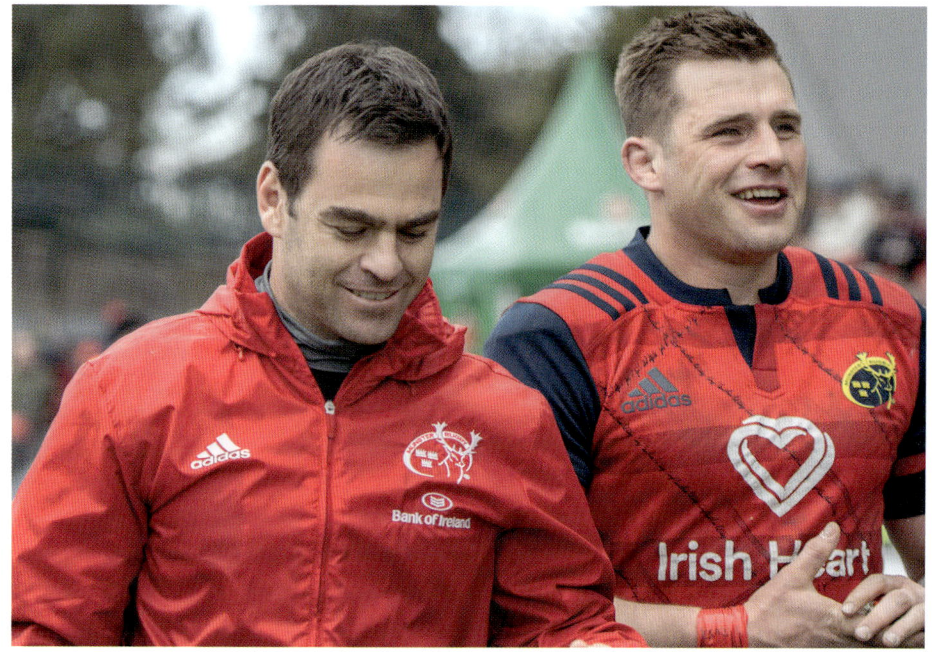

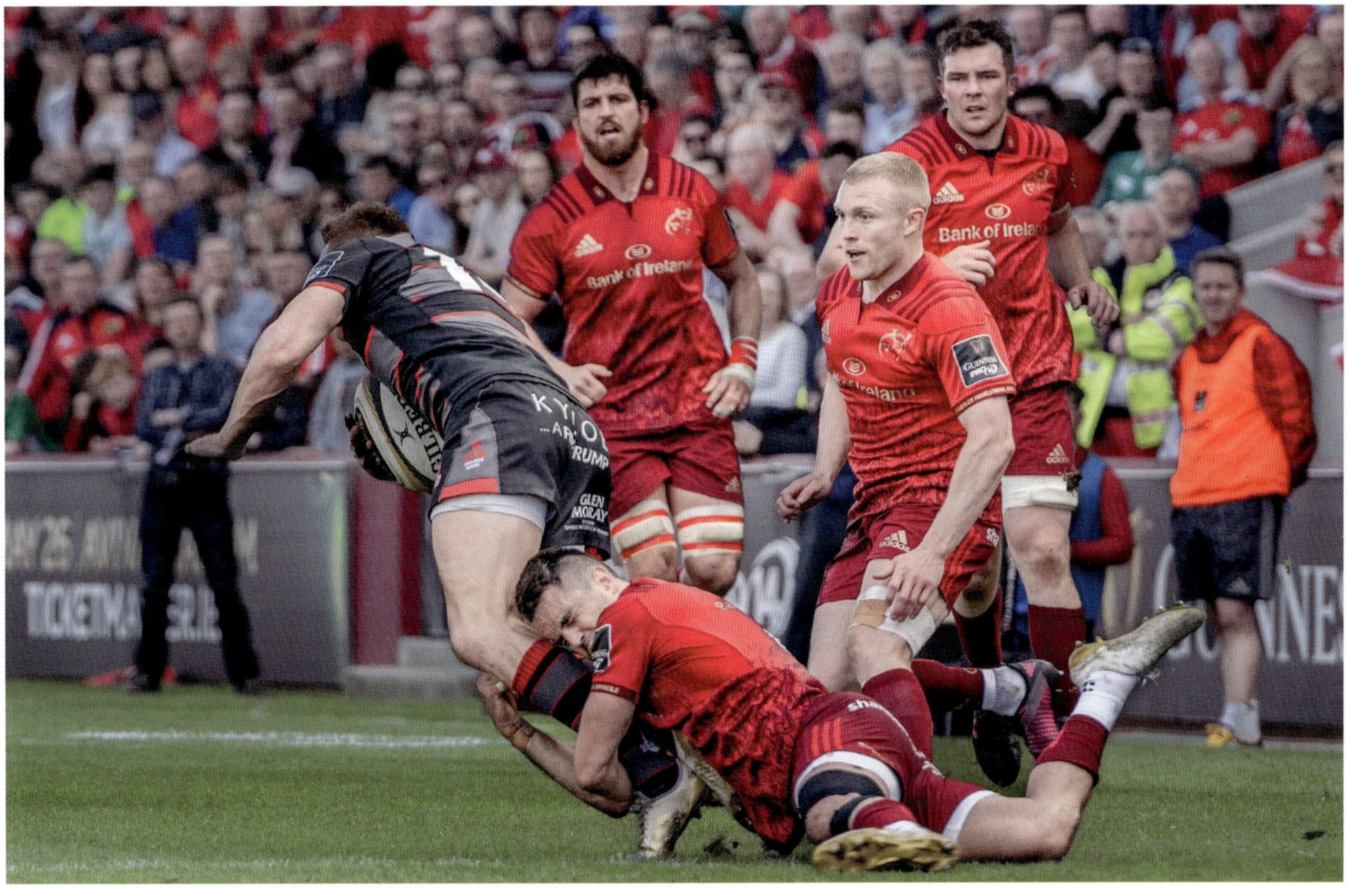

Above: In the URC quarter-final against Edinburgh, Conor Murray makes a superb tackle, with (l–r) Jean Kleyn, Keith Earls and Peter O'Mahony in support.

Bottom: Celebrating Keith Earls' try. (L–r): Rhys Marshall, the try-scorer, James Cronin and James Hart. The 20-16 win sees Munster advance to the semi-final, where they face Leinster in the RDS, and lose agonisingly, 16-15.

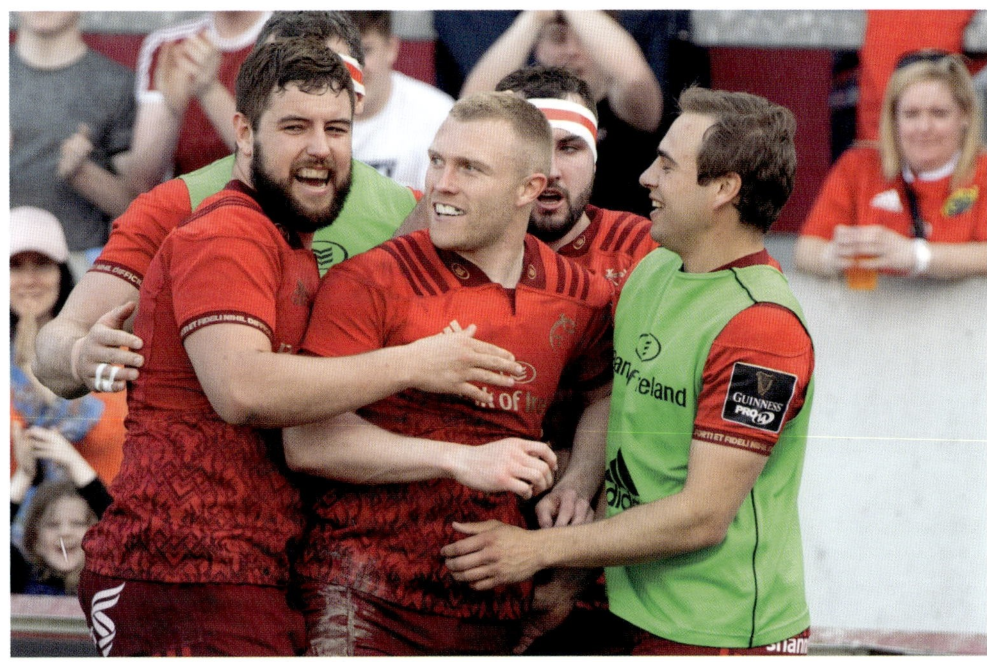

2018–2019

Tadhg Beirne joined the province, and there were first appearances for Diarmuid Barron, Arno Botha, Joey Carbery (ex-Leinster), Craig Casey, cousins Gavin Coombes and Liam Coombes, Shane Daly, Mike Haley, Alby Mathewson and Alex McHenry. Simon Zebo moved to Racing 92. Also to leave were: Robin Copeland, Stephen Fitzgerald, Gerbrandt Grobler, Mike Sherry and Ian Keatley. Ronan O' Mahony was forced to retire through injury. Munster reached semi-finals in both the Champions Cup (where they faced Saracens) and the Guinness Pro14 (where they met Leinster). It was Johann van Graan's first full season as head coach. Joey Carbery was top points scorer with 154 points and Andrew Conway and Keith Earls were joint top try-scorers with eight tries each.

Pro14

The Pro14 season started with a home 38-0 victory over Cheetahs on 1 September 2018, with Arno Botha, Joey Carbery, Mike Haley, Gavin Coombes and Shane Daly all making their competitive debuts for Munster. The six try-scorers against Cheetahs were Rory Scannell, Dave Kilcoyne, Tommy O'Donnell, JJ Hanrahan, Dave O'Callaghan and man of the match Darren Sweetnam, with Hanrahan adding four conversions.

Tadhg Beirne made his debut for Munster in the away game against Glasgow Warriors on 7 September. Always formidable on home soil, Warriors were victorious by 25-10. In Irish Independent Park on 14 September, Ospreys were felled 49-13. Munster's season see-sawed, with a loss to hosts Cardiff Blues, 37-13, on 21 September before a 64-7 home victory against Ulster, a record win for Munster in the Pro14. Try-scorers were Dan Goggin (two), Tommy O'Donnell (two), Peter O'Mahony, Joey Carbery, Sammy Arnold, Keith Earls and Alex Wootton. Carbery converted five out of six, and added a penalty; Ian Keatley converted three out of three. Munster lost to Leinster, then beat Glasgow Warriors, Cheetahs, Zebre and Edinburgh, before losing to Ulster. They revenged themselves on Leinster, winning 26-17 in Thomond Park on 29 December, and won their next four matches (against Connacht, Dragons, Southern

Kings and Ospreys). Scarlets broke their run on 2 March 2019, but the province returned to winning ways against Zebre, Cardiff Blues, Benetton and Connacht to finish second in Conference 2. They won all of their home pool games – six at Thomond Park and four in Irish Independent Park – and the quarter final against Benetton, 15-13, in Limerick.

Unfortunately, the old nemesis Leinster got the upper hand in the semi-final at the RDS on 18 May 2019, winning 24-9. Munster had the best defensive record in the Pro14, conceding only 44 tries. Thirteen Munster players also represented Ireland during the season: Sammy Arnold, Tadhg Beirne, Joey Carbery, Andrew Conway, Keith Earls, Mike Haley, Conor Murray, Tommy O'Donnell, Peter O'Mahony, John Ryan, Niall Scannell, CJ Stander and Darren Sweetnam.

EUROPEAN CHAMPIONS CUP

Munster were drawn to play against Exeter Chiefs, Gloucester and Castres in this season's European Cup. In round one, Munster drew 10-10 with Exeter Chiefs on 13 October at Sandy Park, with a try scored by CJ Stander, converted by Joey Carbery, who also scored a penalty. Exeter were most hospitable hosts and provided a hundred free chicken curries for Munster supporters. Tadhg Beirne was awarded man of the match in his first European match. There were also first starts in Europe for Neil Cronin as scrum half, Goggin, Haley and Carbery. The following week, on 20 October, Munster played Gloucester at Thomond Park, cruising to a 36-22 win after the visitors earned a red card at 29 minutes. Munster's try-scorers were Haley, Rhys Marshall, Carbery, Arnold and Conway. Carbery, in a man-of-the-match performance, also kicked four conversions and a penalty.

Next came Castres in the double December fixture. Rory Scannell, CJ Stander and JJ Hanrahan crossed for tries and JJ scored fifteen points from conversions and penalties in the home 30-5 win on 9 December. However, they lost away the following week, 13-12, with Carbery scoring all of Munster's points from penalties.

Munster defeated Gloucester at Kingsholm by 41-15 on 11 January 2019 with tries from Carbery (two), Rory Scannell, Earls and Conway. Carbery scored sixteen points with the boot. Round 6 saw Munster defeat Exeter Chiefs, 9-7, on 19 January in front of a full house at Thomond Park to advance to a record eighteenth Champions Cup quarter-final. Carbery scored all of Munster's points from penalties.

Munster defeated Edinburgh at Murrayfield 17-13 on 30 March to reach the semi-final. Earls scored two tries, converted by Carbery and Tyler Bleyendaal, who also scored a penalty. However, Saracens ended Munster's European dream with a 32-16 win at the Ricoh Arena on 20 April. Darren Sweetnam got Munster's only try, converted by JJ Hanrahan. Bleyendaal added two out of two penalty attempts, and Conor Murray added a third. It was no consolation that Saracens would defeat Leinster in the final.

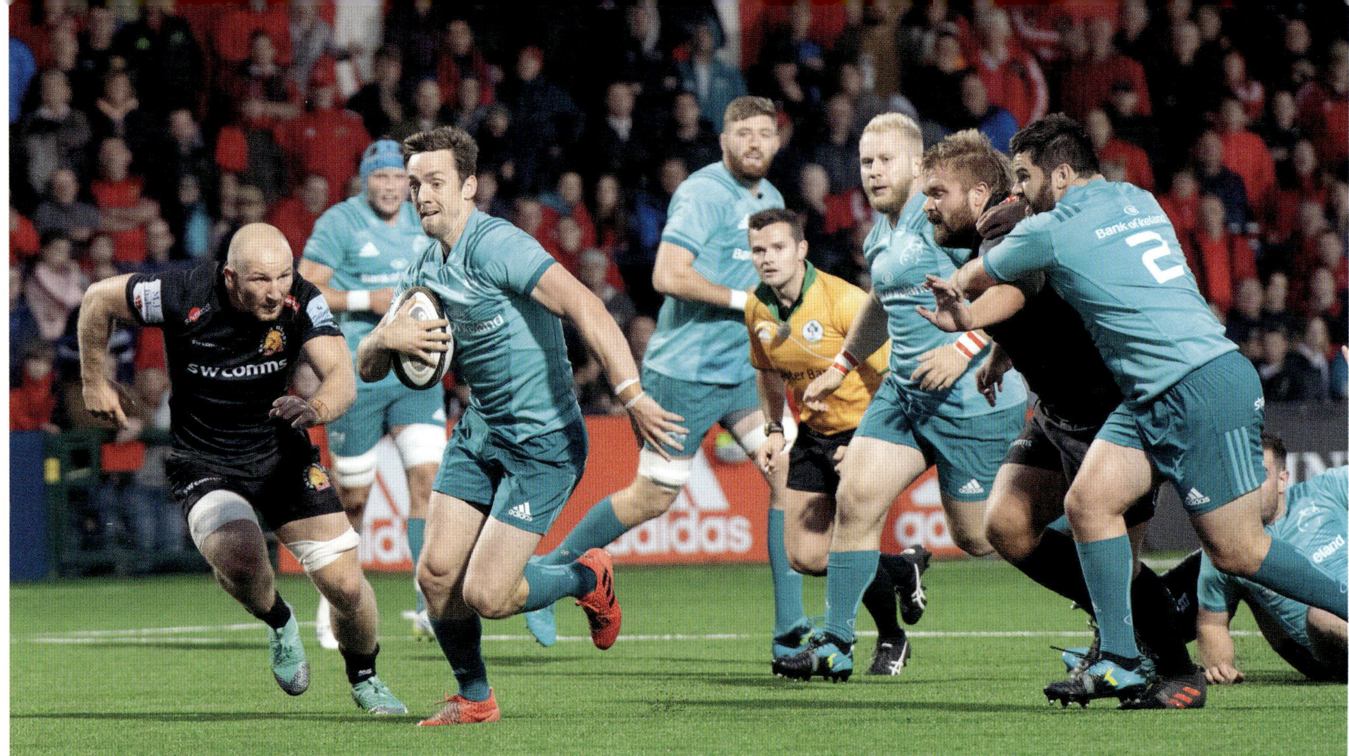

24 August 2018

Darren Sweetnam makes an outstanding break against Exeter Chiefs in a pre-season friendly at Irish Independent Park. Disappointingly for the home fans, however, Exeter put twelve unanswered points on the board before half-time. The second half is scoreless.

1 September 2018

Stephen Archer in action against Cheetahs in the opening round of the Pro14, a match that Munster win 38-0.

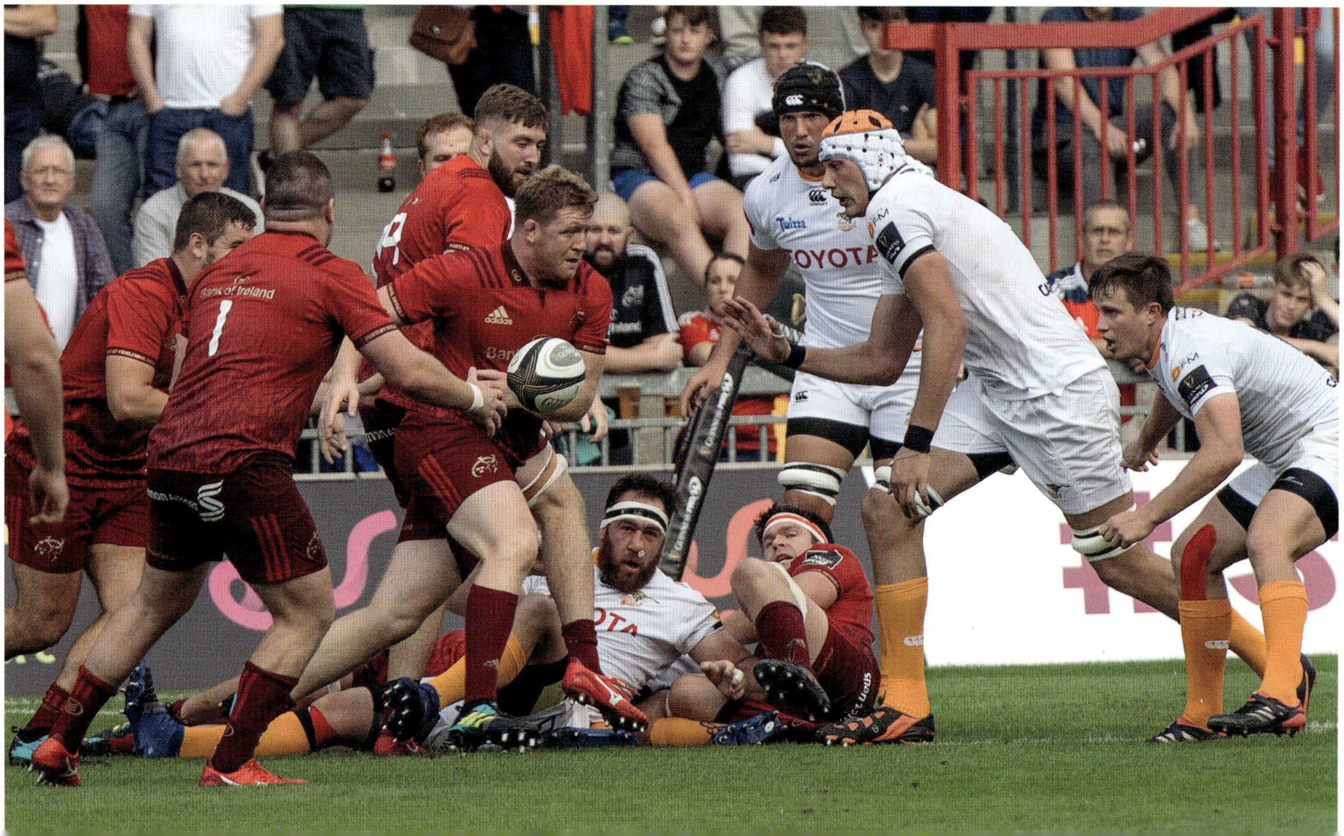

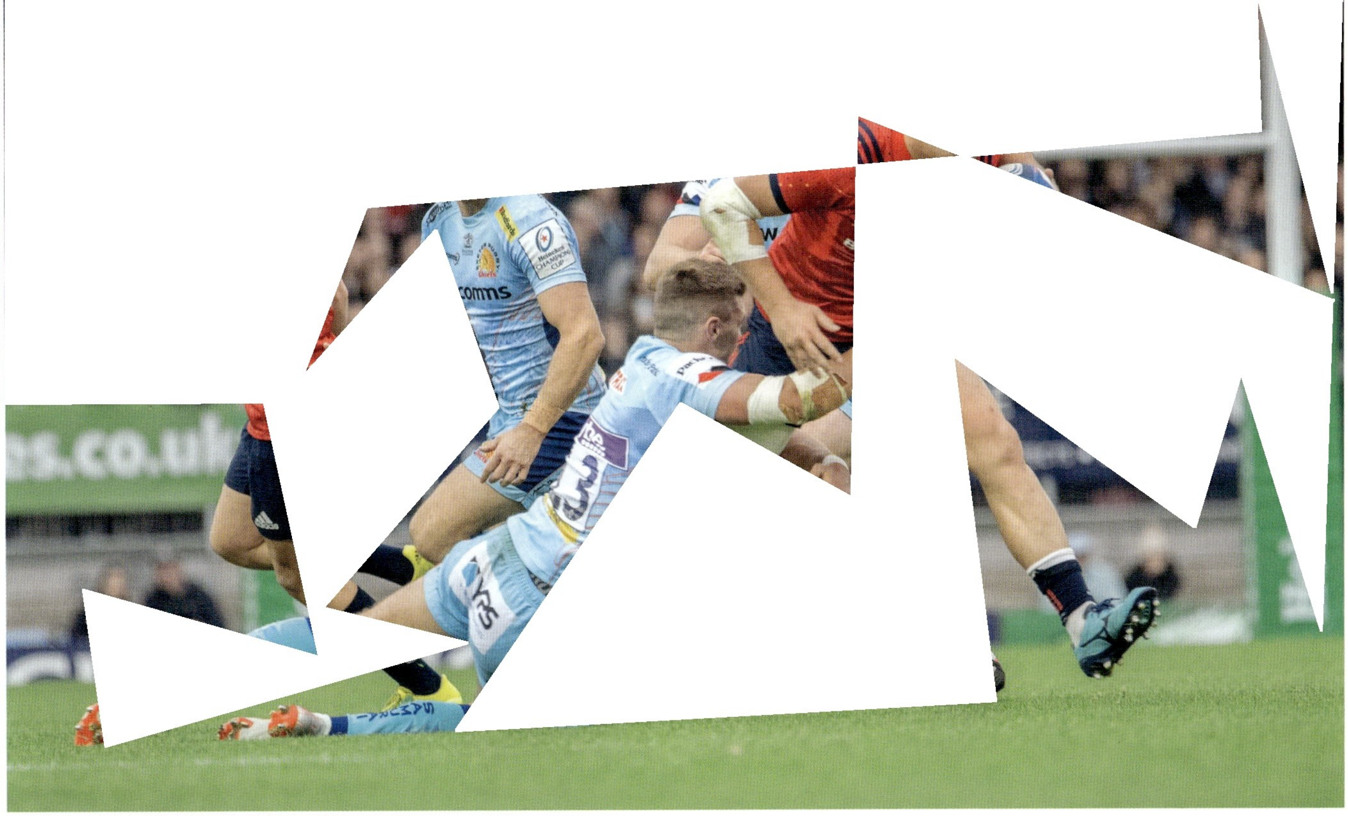

13 October 2018

Dan Goggin is hauled down by Exeter Chiefs in a 10-10 draw at Sandy Park.

20 October 2018

Kevin O'Byrne shows his strength in Munster's 36-22 home victory over Gloucester.

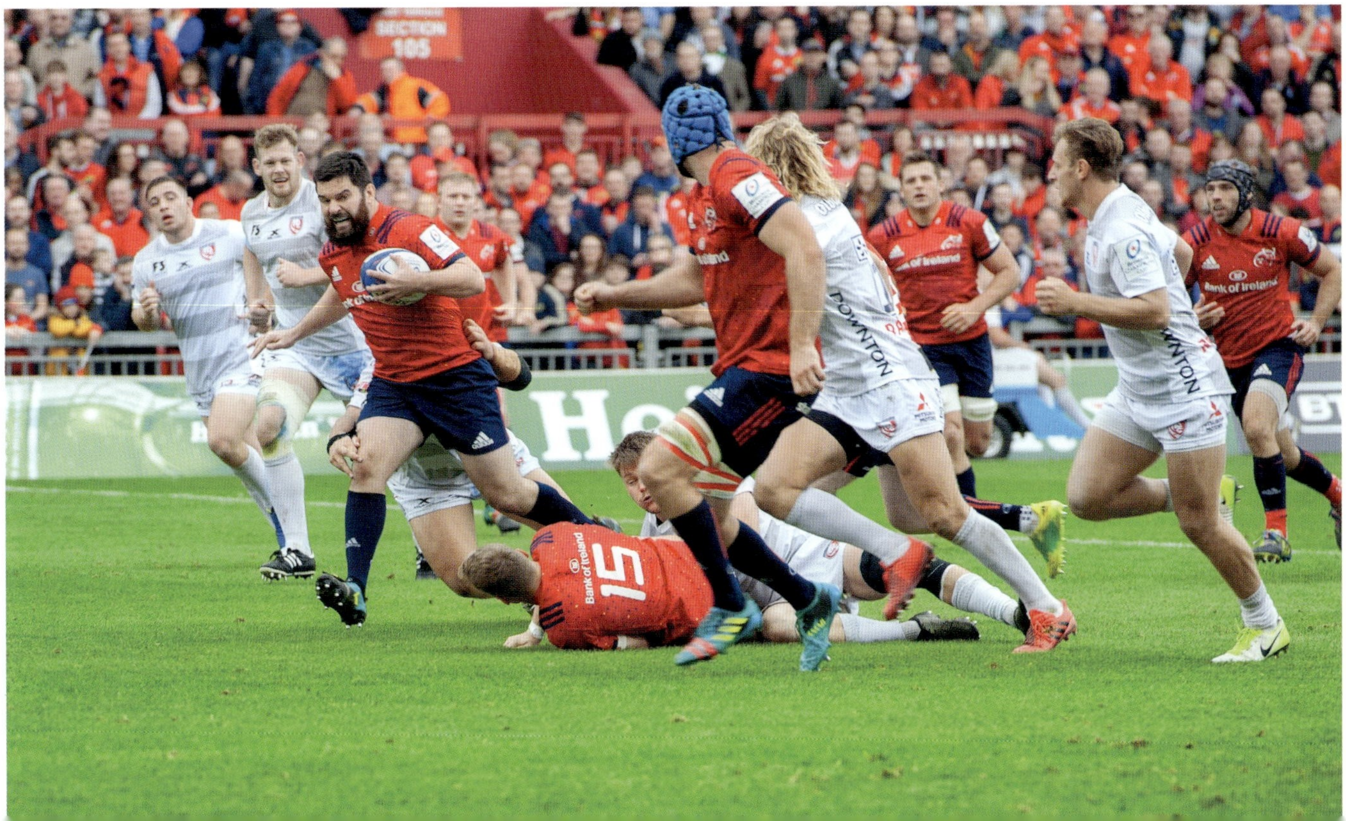

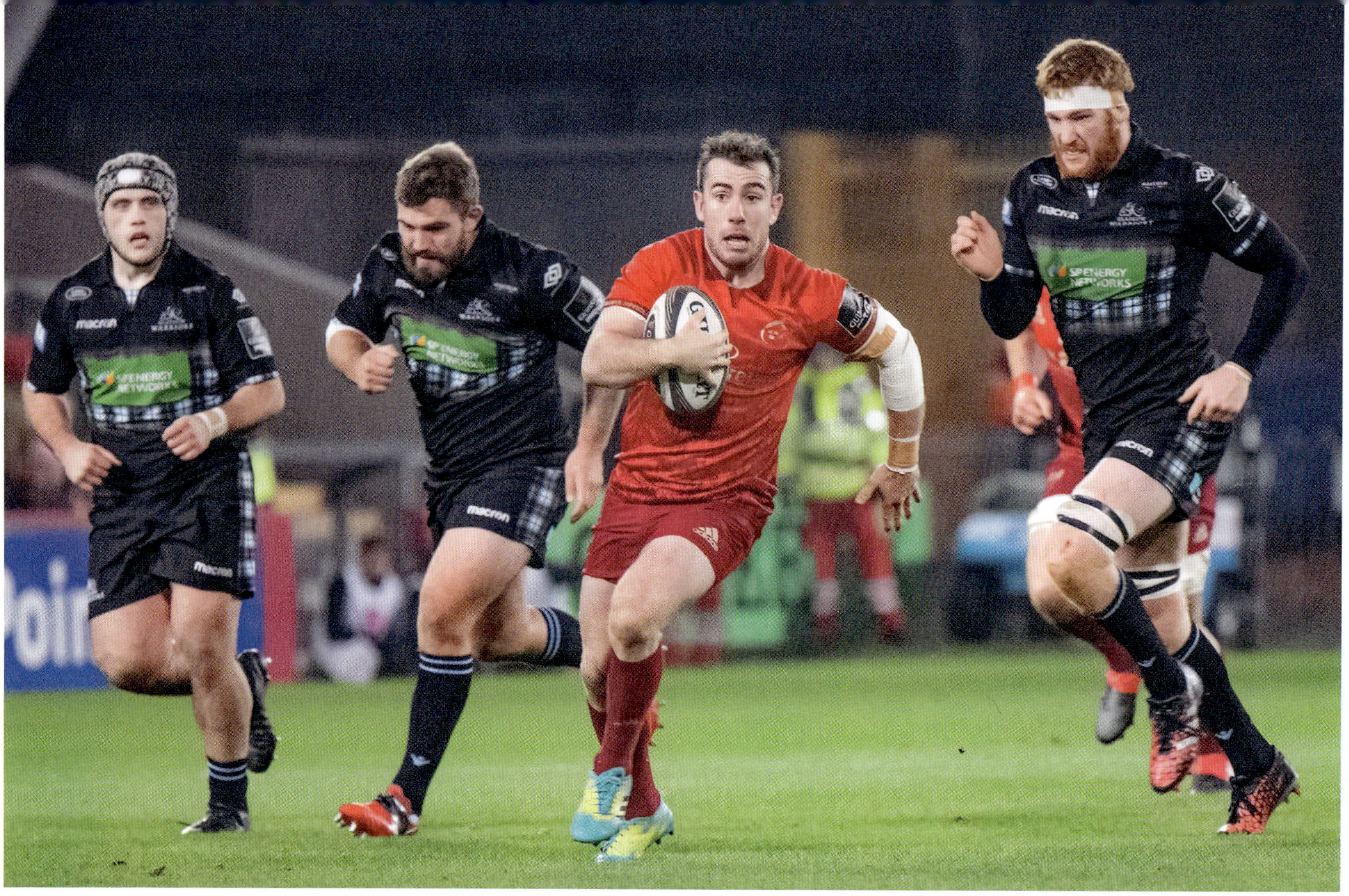

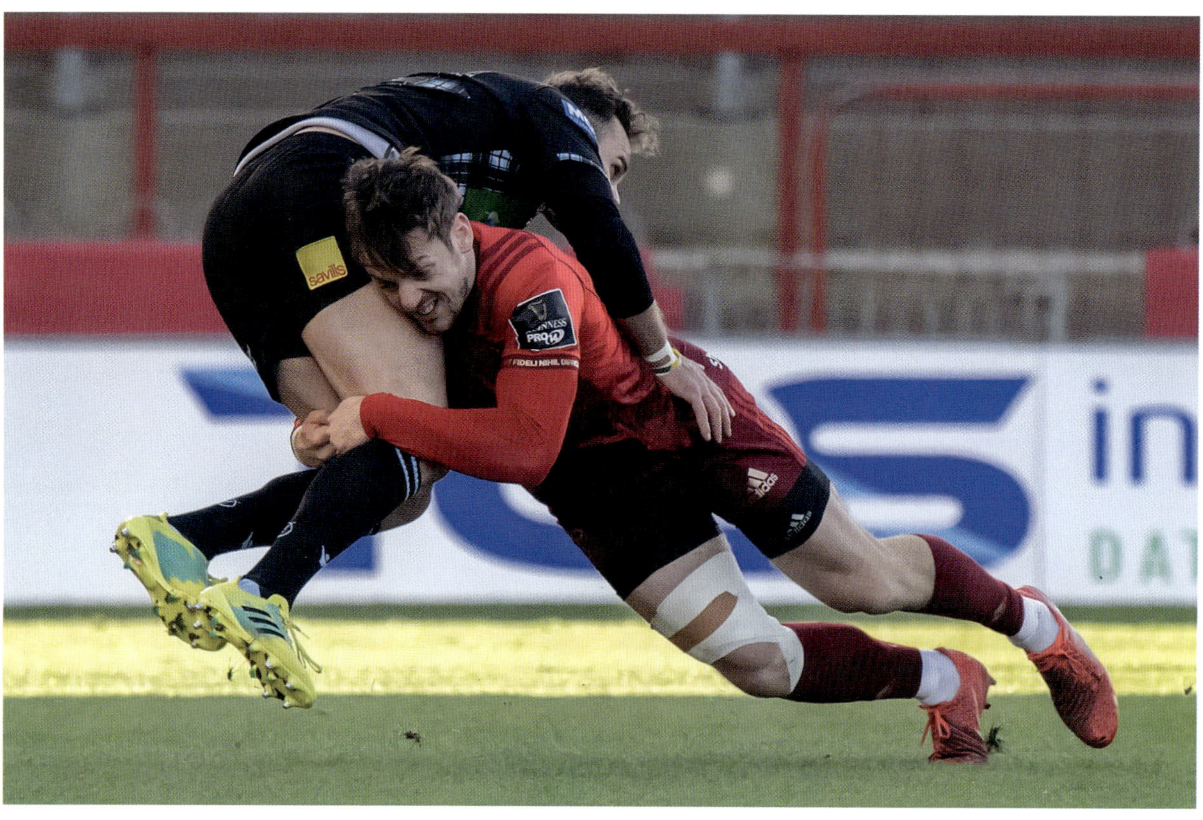

Opposite top: JJ Hanrahan shows Glasgow Warriors a clean pair of heels. Munster steal the win with a long-range penalty by Rory Scannell in the dying seconds to bring the score to 25-24.

Opposite bottom: Darren Sweetnam makes a crunch tackle on a Glasgow Warriors attacker.

9 December 2018

Below: Keith Earls takes off against Castres, supported by (l–r) Niall Scannell and Conor Murray. The half-time score was 6-0, leaving it all to play for. Munster plugged away to make the full-time score 30-5.

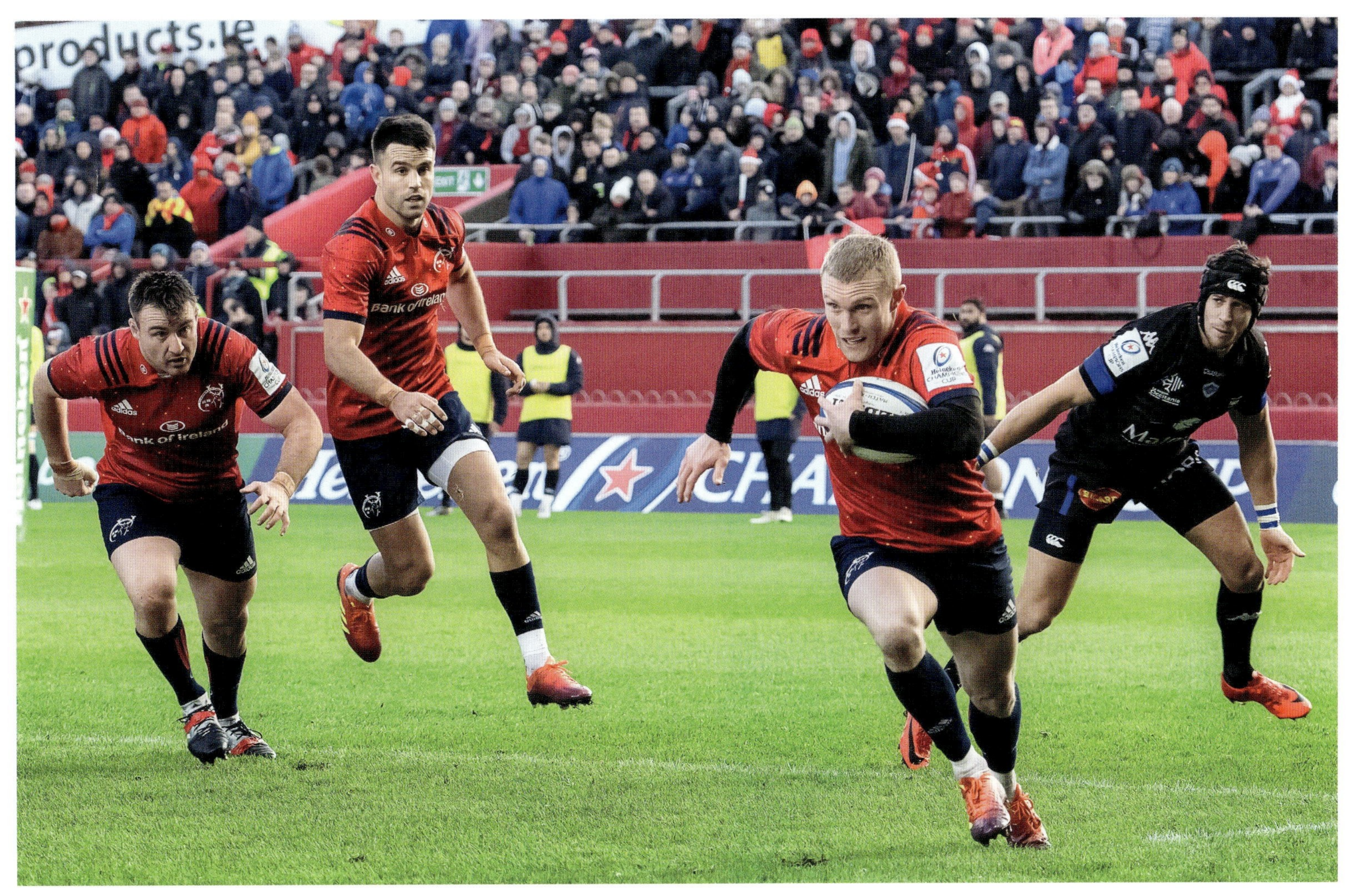

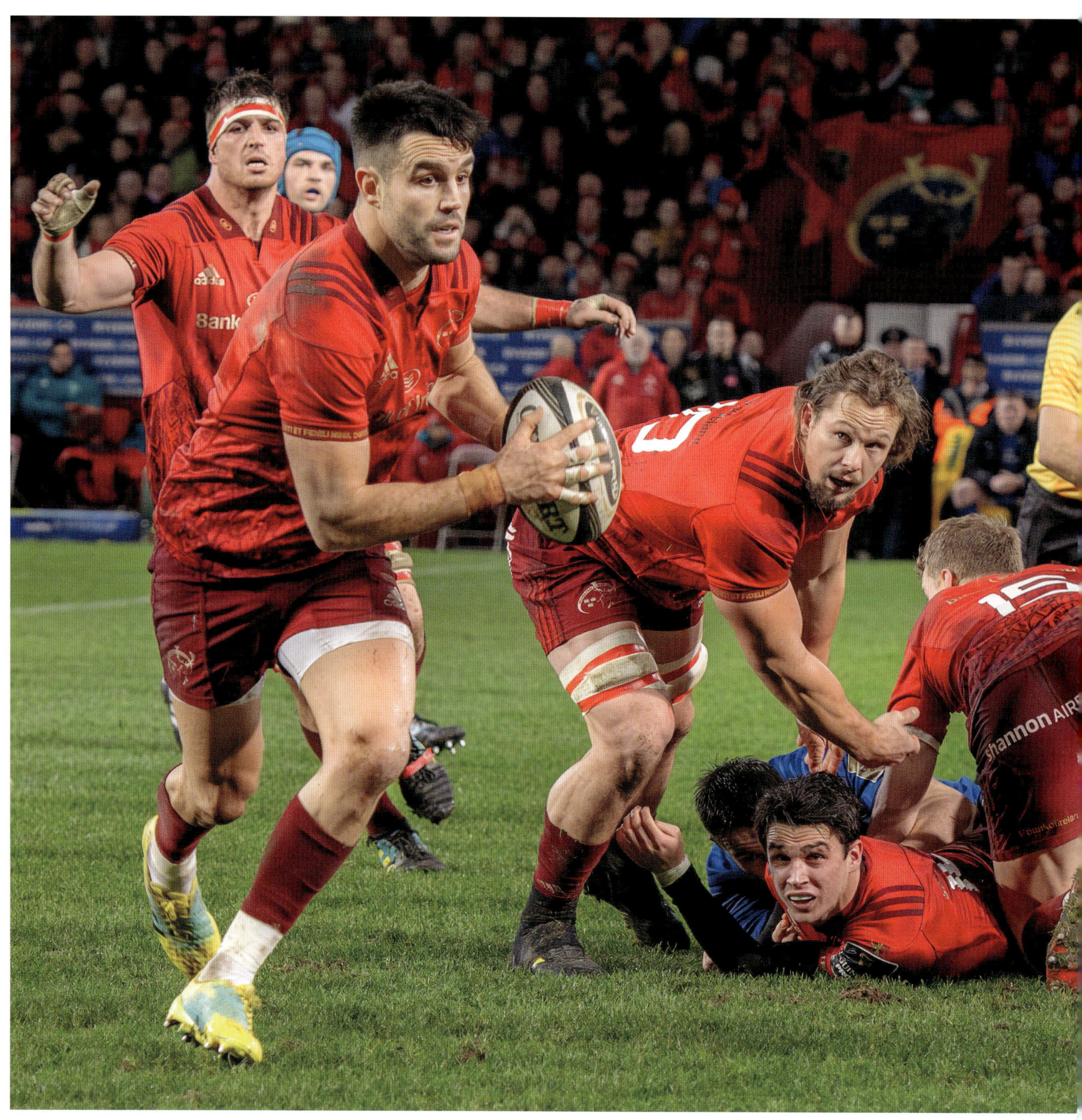

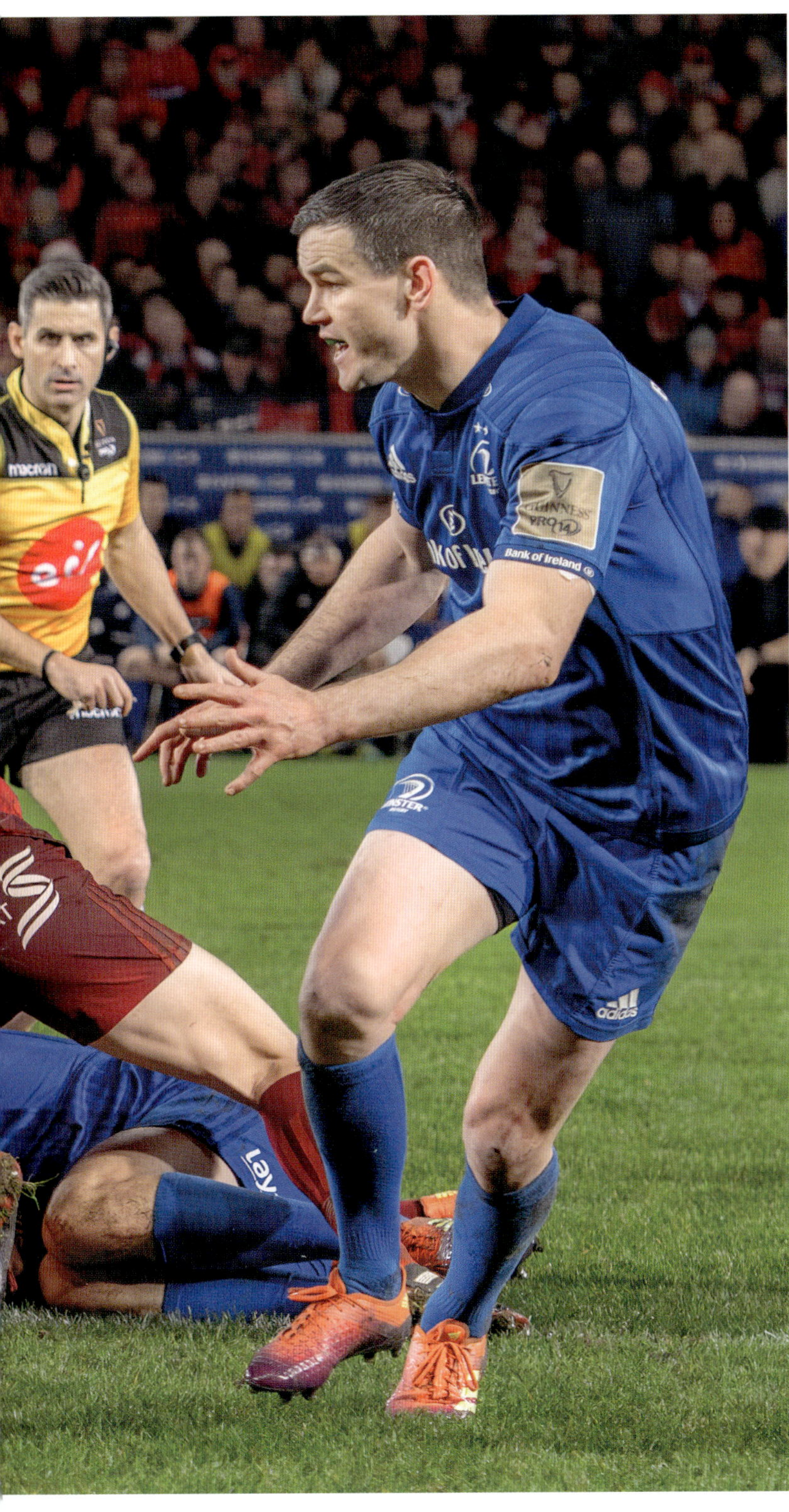

Conor Murray makes a break against Leinster's Johnny Sexton. Munster seal the win, 26-17, to maintain their unbeaten home record in 2018.

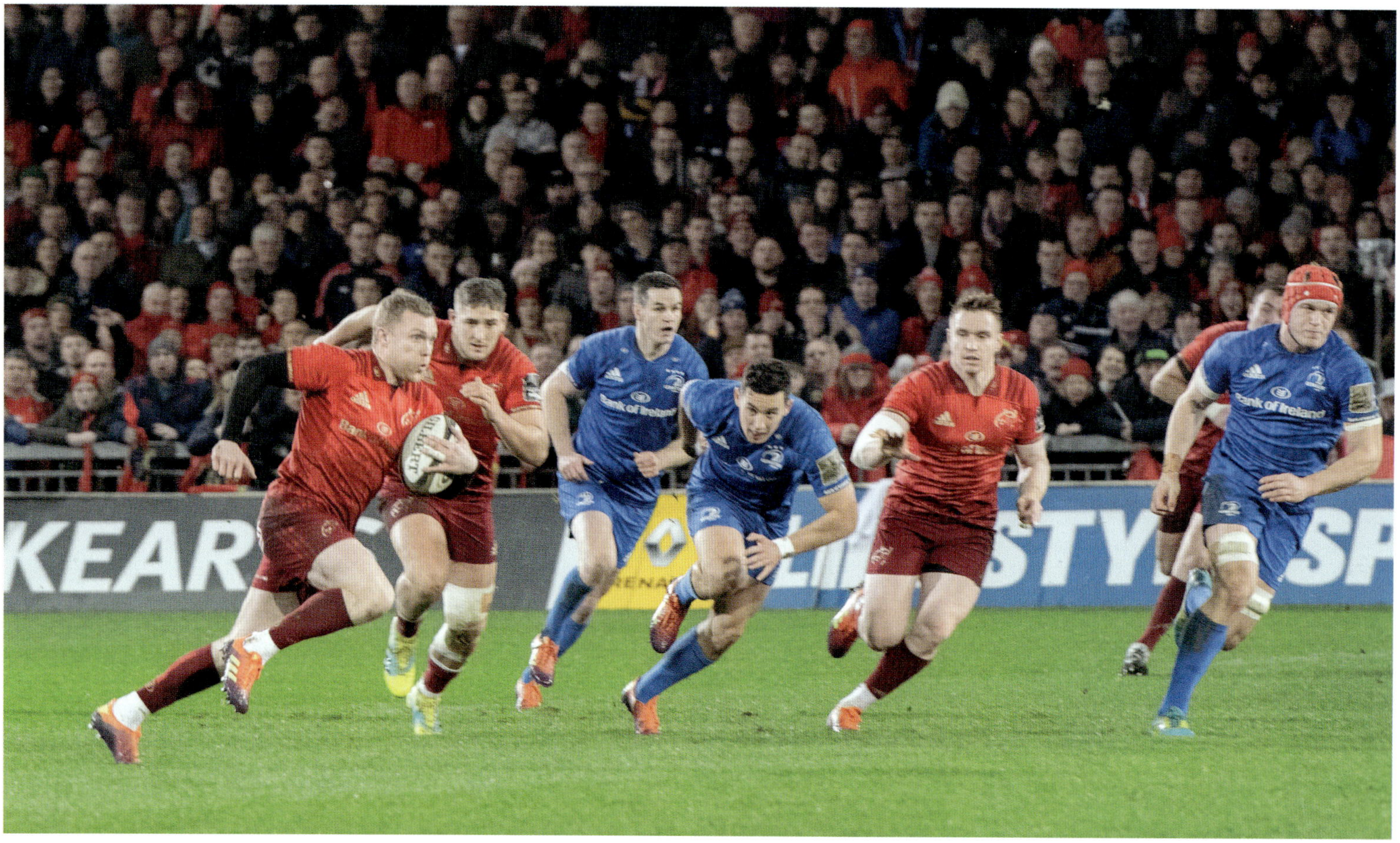

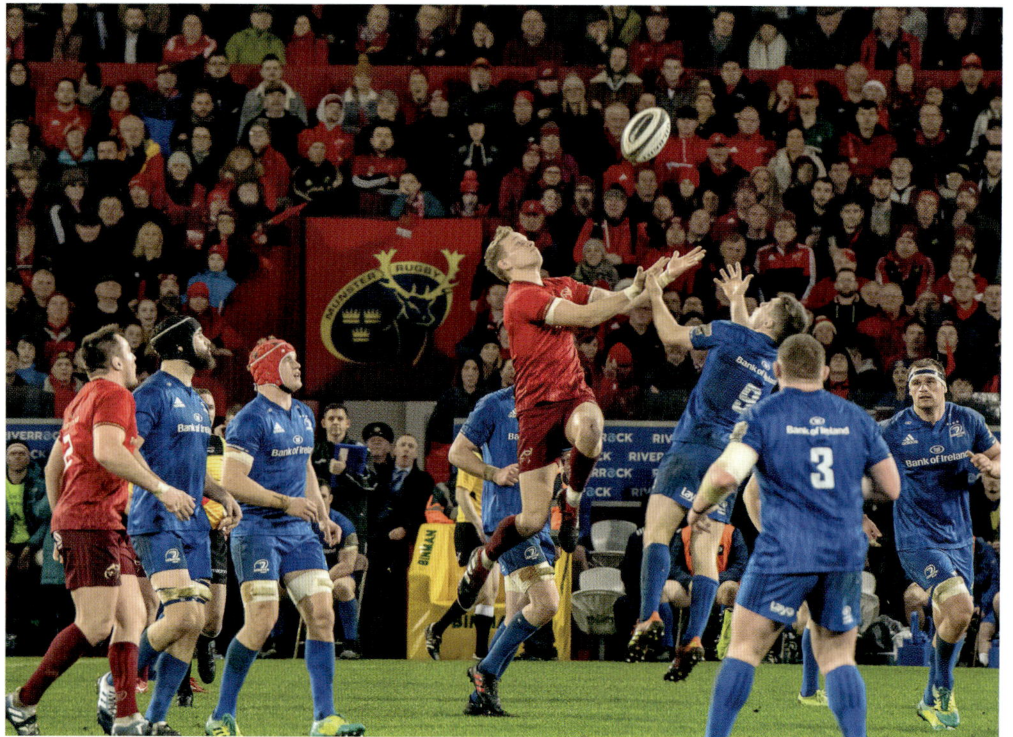

29 December 2018

Top: Keith Earls sprints for the line against Leinster.

Bottom: Mike Haley is a safe pair of hands under the high ball.

23 March 2019

Opposite top: John Ryan fends off a Zebre tackler, supported by Tyler Bleyendaal. Munster enjoy a 31–12 home win.

27 April 2019

Opposite bottom: Jean Kleyn in the blue light, winning the line-out against Connacht in Munster's 27–14 home win.

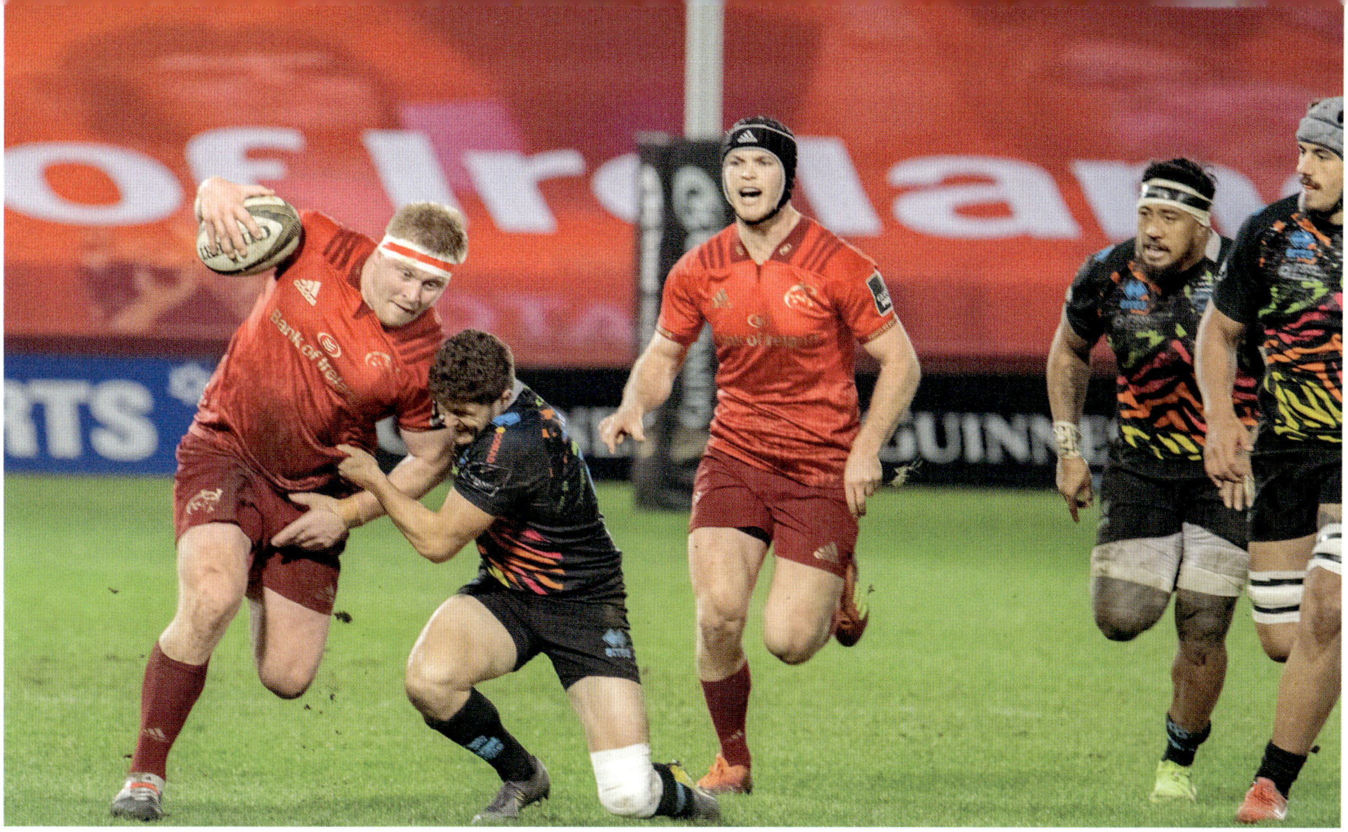

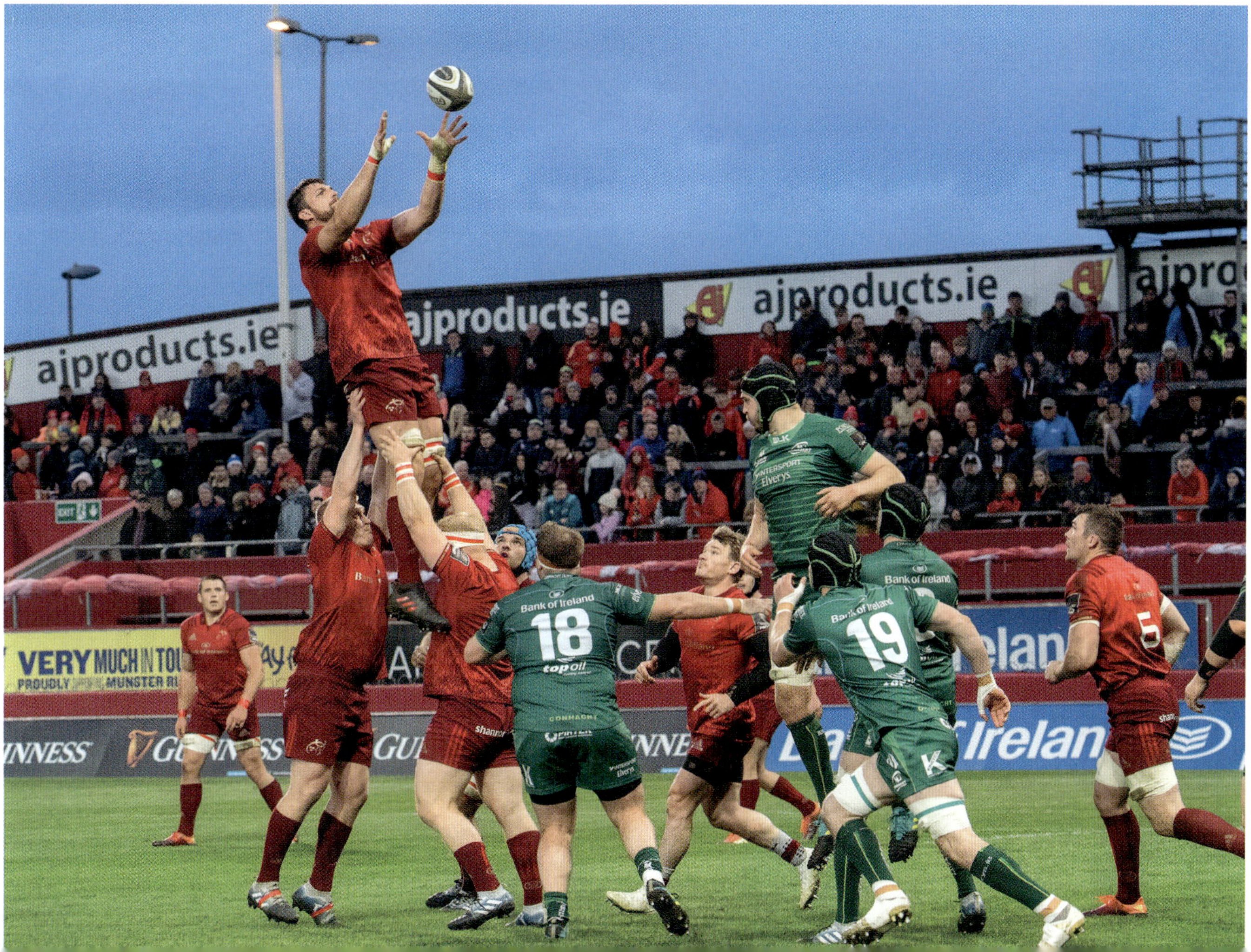

Bank of Ireland
ajproducts.ie
ajproducts.ie
Bank of Ireland
VERY MUCH IN TOU
PROUDLY MUNSTER R
18
top oil
19
GUINNESS
Ireland

2019–2020

PRO14   **POOL WINS: 10; POOL LOSSES: 5; ELIMINATED: SEMI-FINAL**

EUROPEAN CHAMPIONS CUP **POOL WINS: 3; POOL LOSSES: 2; POOL DRAWS: 1; DID NOT PROGRESS FURTHER**

Graham Rowntree joined Munster as forwards coach, replacing Jerry Flannery who left when his contract expired in June 2019. Felix Jones (backs coach) also left. Stephen Larkham joined as senior coach. Doug Howlett, Munster's head of commercial and marketing since 2017, returned to New Zealand. Also leaving the province were Stephen Fitzgerald, James Hart, Bill Johnston, Dave O'Callaghan, Duncan Williams and Jaco Taute. Taute, a three-times Springboks centre, had joined Munster in 2016 on a four-month contract as a replacement for the injured Francis Saili, and his contract had been extended. Tyler Bleyendaal and Mike Sherry retired. Promotions from the academy included Craig Casey, Gavin Coombes and Shane Daly.

PRO14

Munster were drawn in Conference B. Their first game was played against Dragons in Thomond Park on 28 September 2019, which Munster won 39-9. Try-scorers were Arno Botha, Jack O'Donoghue, Shane Daly, Tyler Bleyendaal and Diarmuid Barron. JJ Hanrahan kicked fourteen points. Nick McCarthy, Keynan Knox and Jack O'Sullivan all made their debuts. Shane Daly was man of the match and hooker Kevin O'Byrne earned his 50th cap.

Next was an away match against Southern Kings on 5 October, which Munster won 31-20, with tries from Mike Haley, Alby Mathewson, Fineen Wycherley and Botha. JJ Hanrahan converted all four tries and scored a penalty. Another away game, against Cheetahs, followed on 11 October, which the home team won decisively 40-16. Munster played Ospreys in Cork on 25 October, winning 28-12, with tries from James Cronin, Rhys Marshall, man of the match Haley and Botha. Munster won away against Cardiff on 2 November, 33-23, with tries by Chris Cloete, Mathewson (two) and Calvin Nash. JJ Hanrahan scored the remainder of the points from the tee.

A 22-16 win over Ulster at Thomond Park followed on 9 November. CJ Stander, Rory Scannell and Andrew Conway were the try-scorers. Stephen Archer won his 200th cap for Munster on 29 November in

Cork against Edinburgh. Academy player Ben Healy made his Munster debut at out-half, scoring eleven points in the 18-16 defeat to the Scots. Munster had a good away win against Connacht, 19-14, on 21 December. Jack O'Donoghue was the try-scorer. The post-Christmas fixture against Leinster in Limerick resulted in a 6-13 loss. More misery followed on 3 January 2020 in Belfast, Ulster winning 38-17.

Munster's 68-3 win against Southern Kings on 14 February in Cork was a record score and a record margin of victory for the province in the competition, while the ten tries scored also set a new Munster record. Academy player John Hodnett marked his debut by scoring a try and earning the man-of-the-match award. Botha scored a hat trick of tries, with tries also from Nash, O'Donoghue, Neil Cronin, Daly and Dan Goggin. Hanrahan converted six out of six, and Healy a further three.

Round 12 saw Munster win away to Zebre on 21 February, 28-0. Nash, Hanrahan, Rory Scannell and Darren Sweetnam crossed for tries, all of which Hanrahan converted. The form continued with a 29-10 victory over Scarlets at Thomond Park on 29 February. Jack O'Sullivan, Billy Holland and Gavin Coombes (two) scored tries.

The Pro14 was suspended indefinitely on 12 March 2020 in response to the coronavirus pandemic. Tyler Bleyendaal was forced to retire from rugby owing to a serious neck injury. The league resumed in August. Munster lost 27-25 to hosts Leinster on 22 August, in a close encounter in Aviva Stadium. Munster beat Connacht, again in the Aviva, on 30 August with a decisive 49-12 win. The try-scorers were Cloete, a penalty try, Jeremy Loughman, Tadhg Beirne, Conway (two) and Cronin. In the semi-final on 4 September at the Aviva, Leinster got the better of Munster 13-3, thus ending the southern province's interest in the competition.

European Champions Cup

In the opening rounds, Munster beat Ospreys 32-13 at Liberty Stadium on 16 November, with tries from Loughman, Earls, Conway and Cronin and twelve points off the tee from Bleyendaal, before drawing 21-21 at home against Racing 92 on 23 November. (In October 2020, Conway's try was named Try of the Year at the Irish Rugby Player awards.) The Racing side included former Munster players Donnacha Ryan and Simon Zebo.

Back-to-back games against Saracens followed: Munster won 10-3 at home on a wet and windy night on 7 December 2019, with the Saracens picking up a losing bonus point. In the return fixture in Allianz Park on 14 December, Munster lost 15-6. Round 5 was played in Paris against Racing 92 on 12 January 2020, Craig Casey making his European debut at scrum half. Three late tries saw the home team win 39-22, unfortunately ending Munster's participation in the competition, even though their last game against Ospreys had yet to be played.

Munster duly beat Ospreys at Thomond Park on 19 January in their final game, 33-6, with Casey scoring his first try for Munster. The match had added poignancy for Munster, as their long-serving CEO Garrett Fitzgerald, who had retired the previous June, died earlier that day.

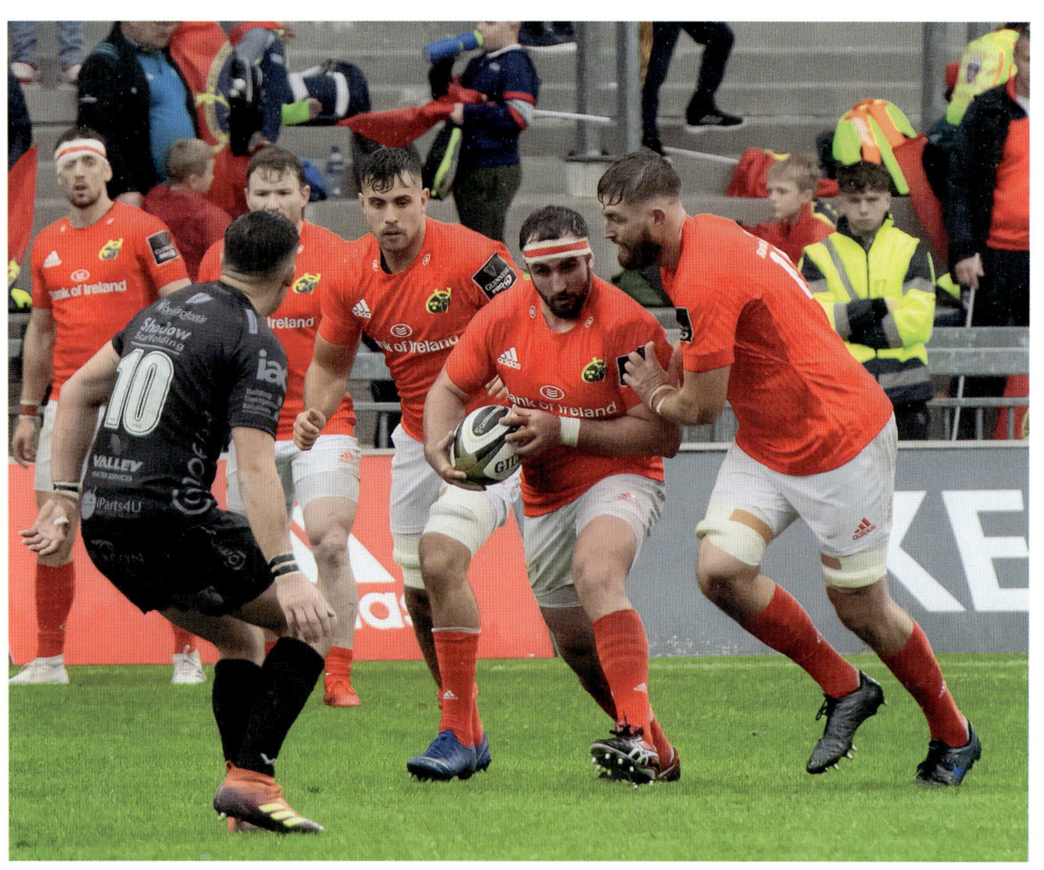

28 September 2019
Left: James Cronin carries against Dragons, backed up by (l–r) Darren Sweetnam, Chris Cloete, Jack O'Sullivan and Darren O'Shea. In sodden conditions, Munster clinically slay the Dragons in this opening match of the Pro14 season. The final score is 39-9.

9 November 2019
Below: Alby Mathewson gets the back line moving in this home match against Ulster, watched by teammate CJ Stander and referee Frank Murphy. Munster secure the win, 22-16, thanks to a superb try by Andrew Conway at the 65th minute.

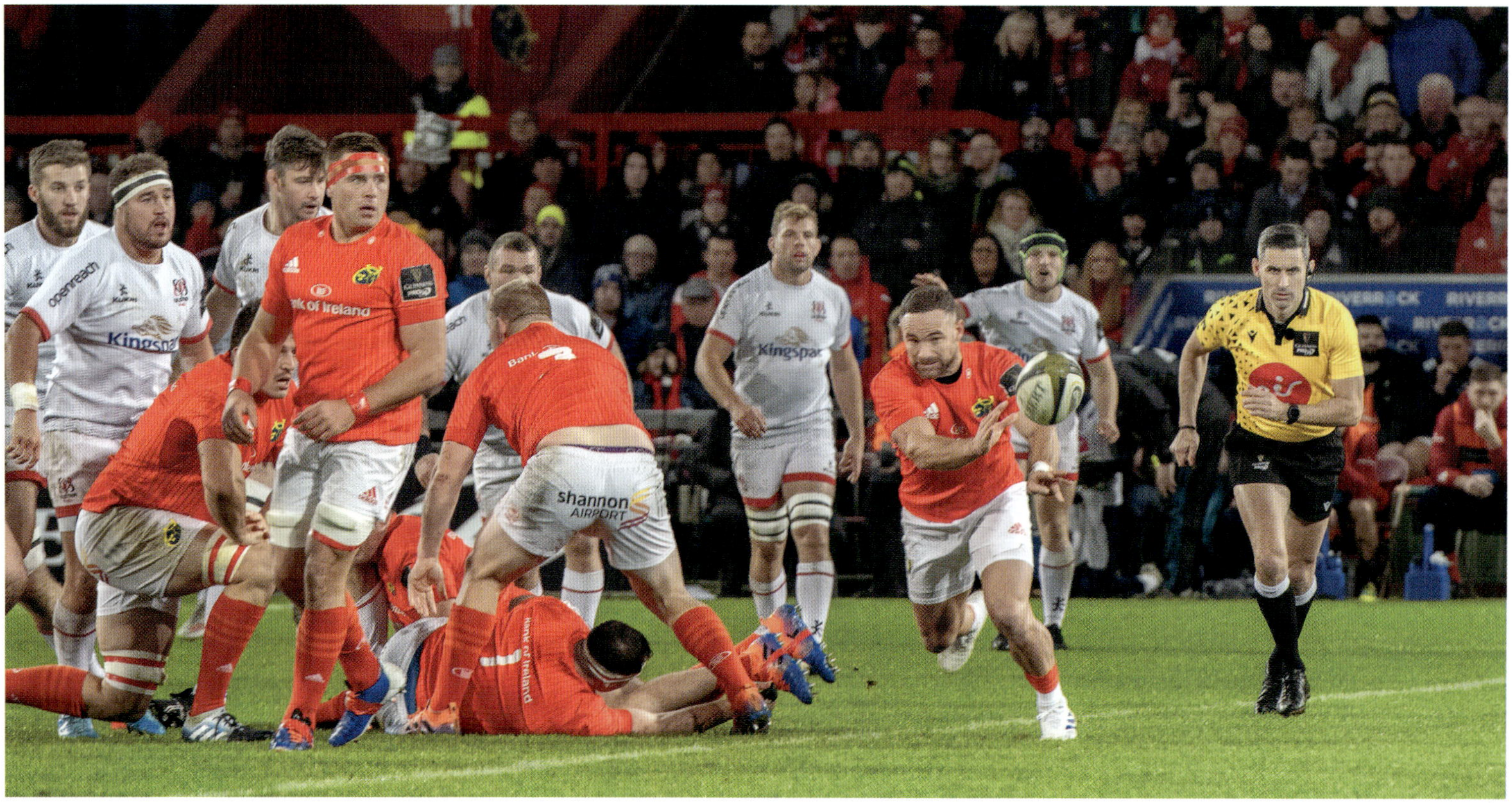

9 November 2019

Top: Man of the match Rory Scannell passes to Chris Farrell.

Bottom: (L–r) Tyler Bleyendaal and Alby Mathewson hold up the Ulster attack.

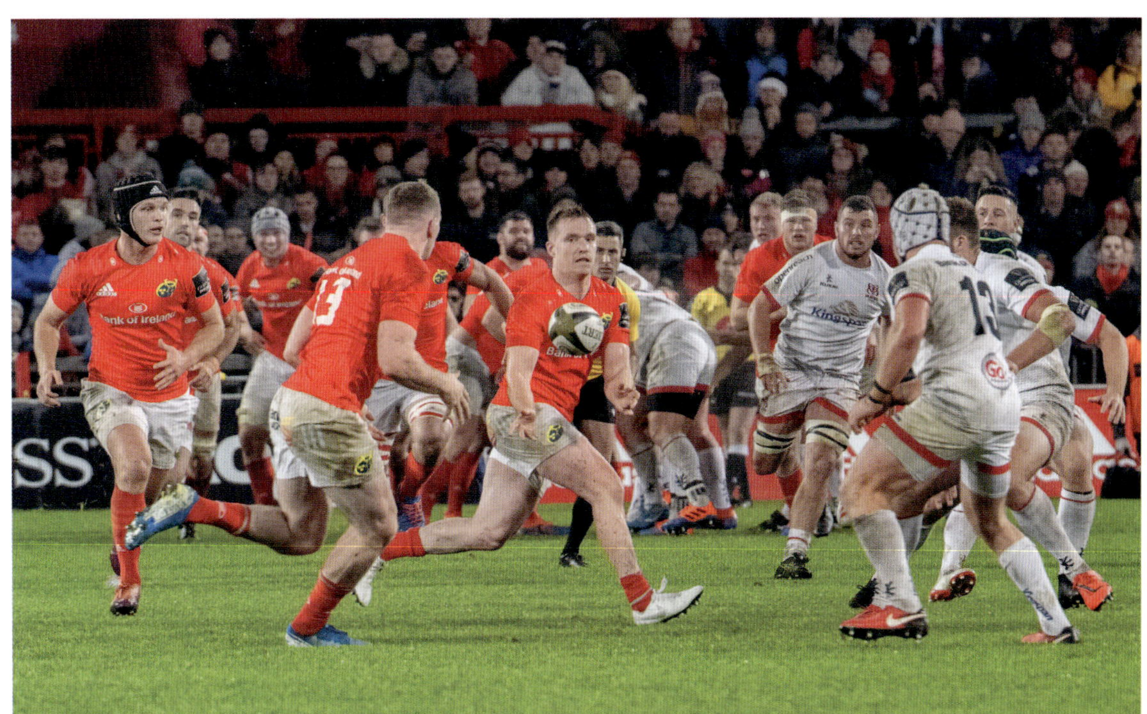

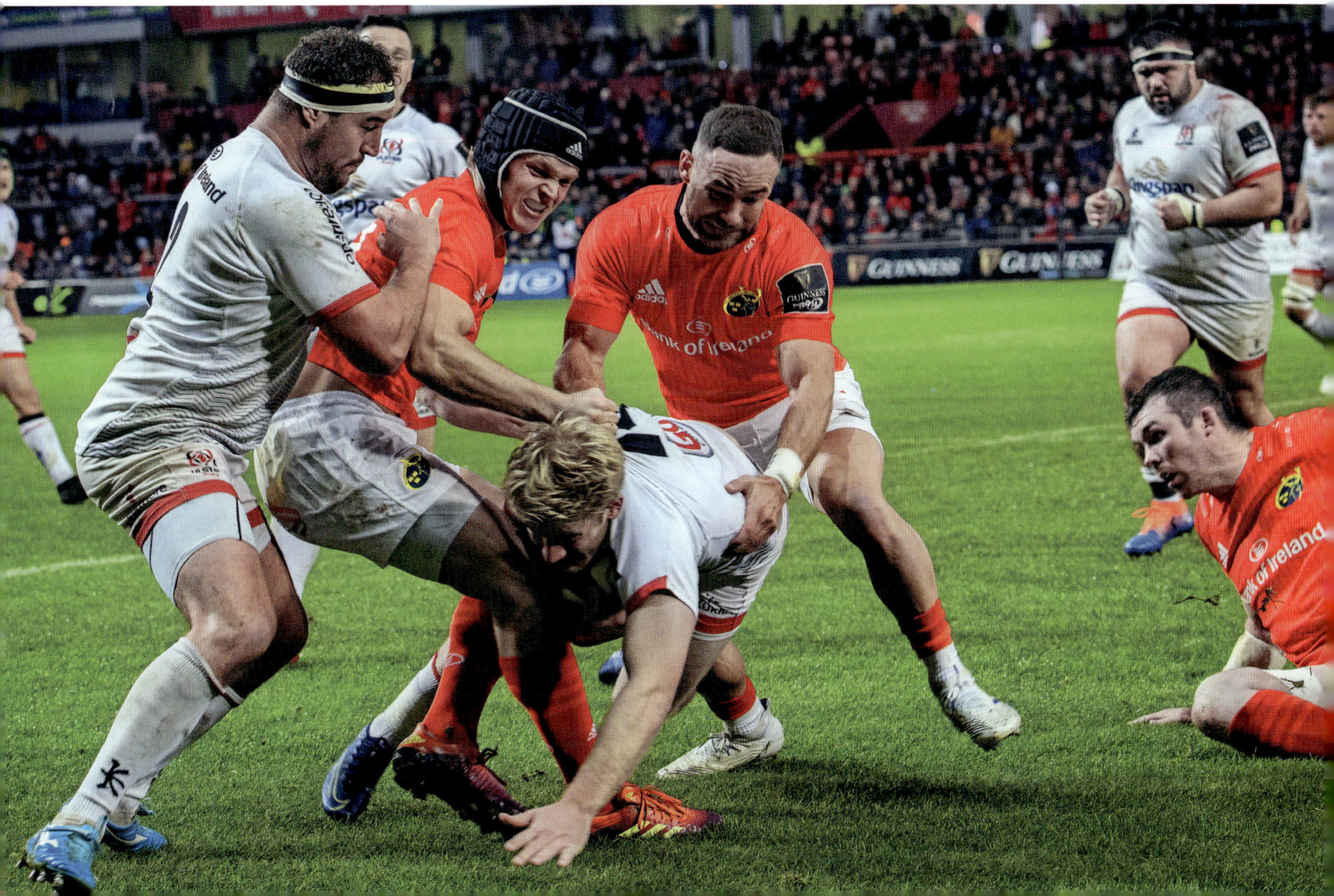

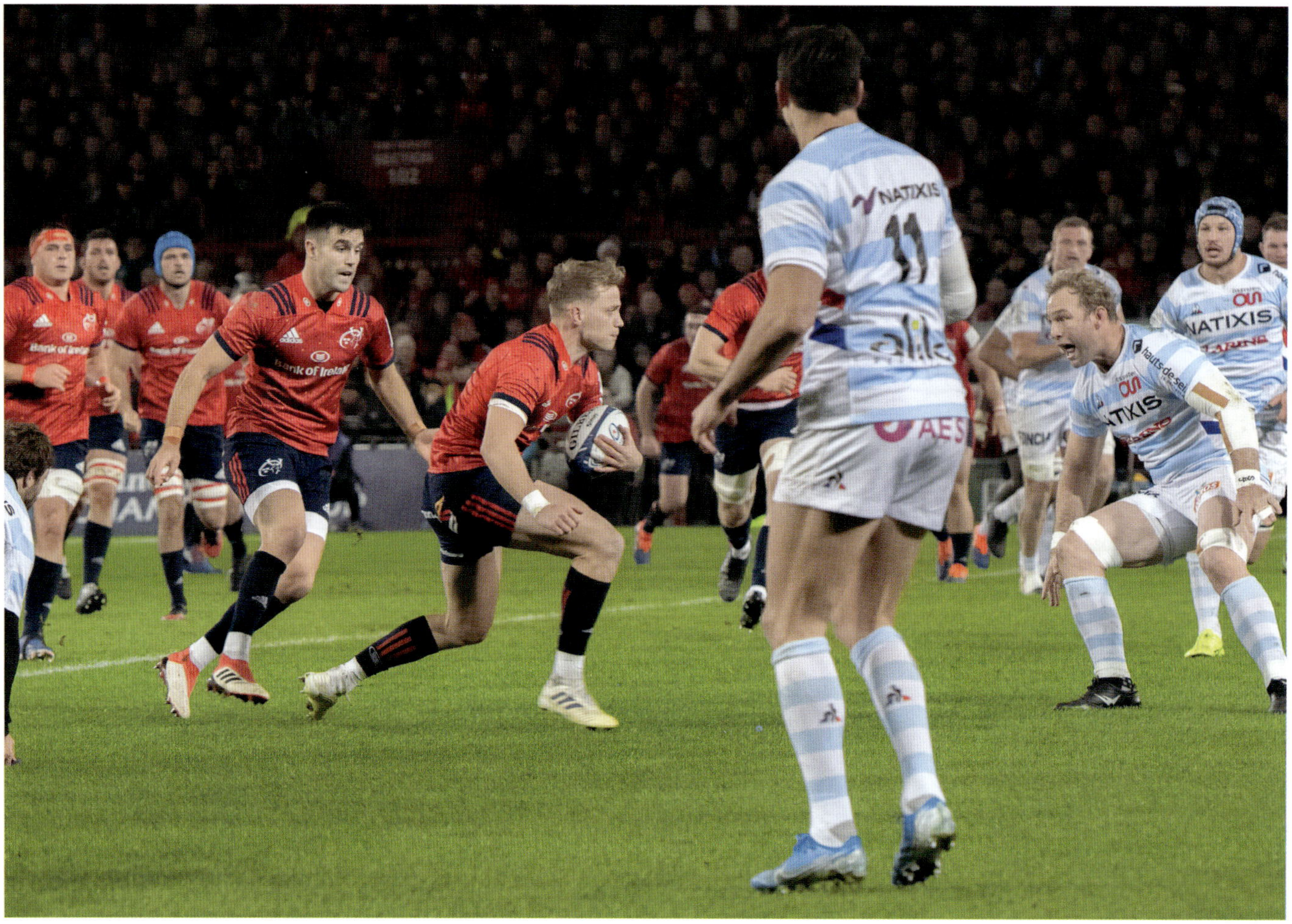

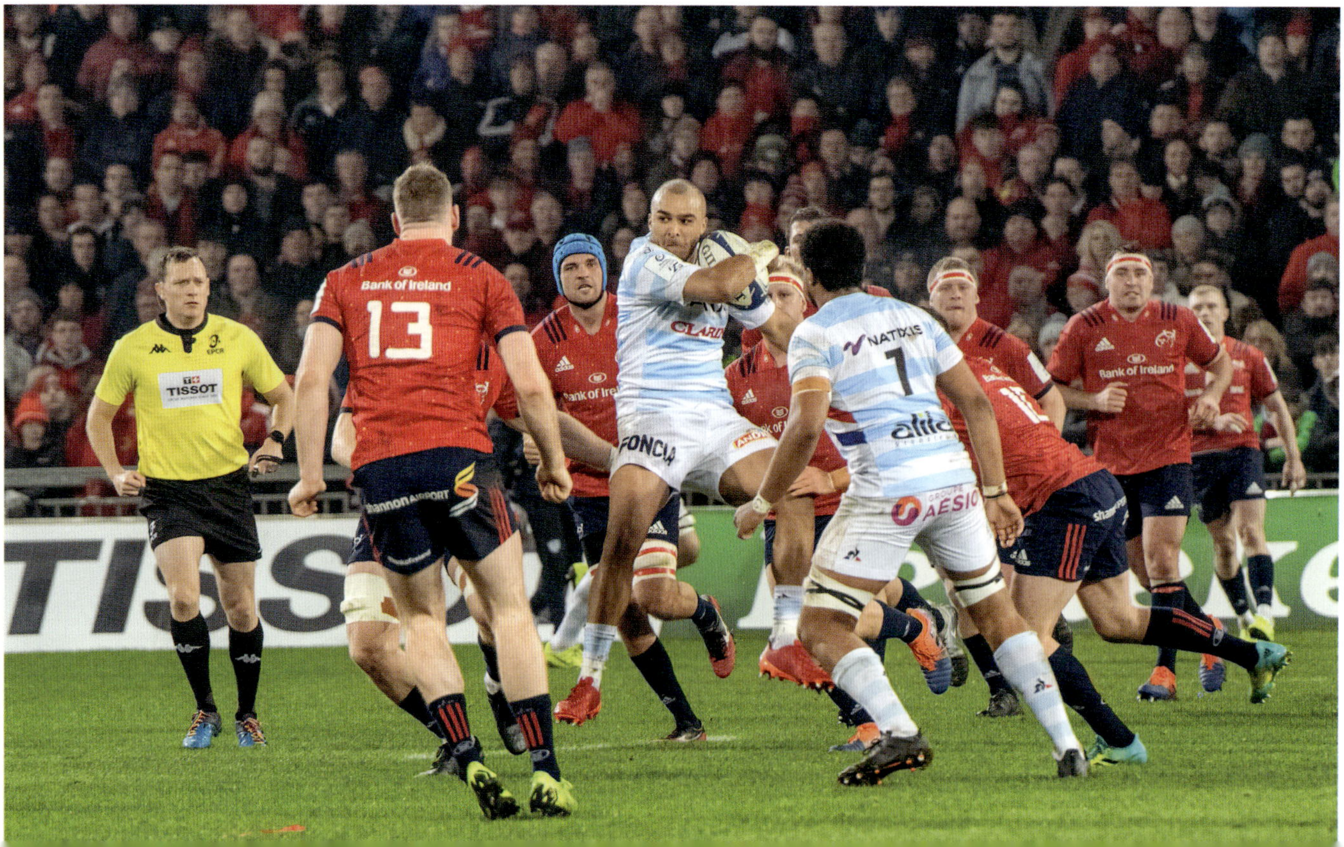

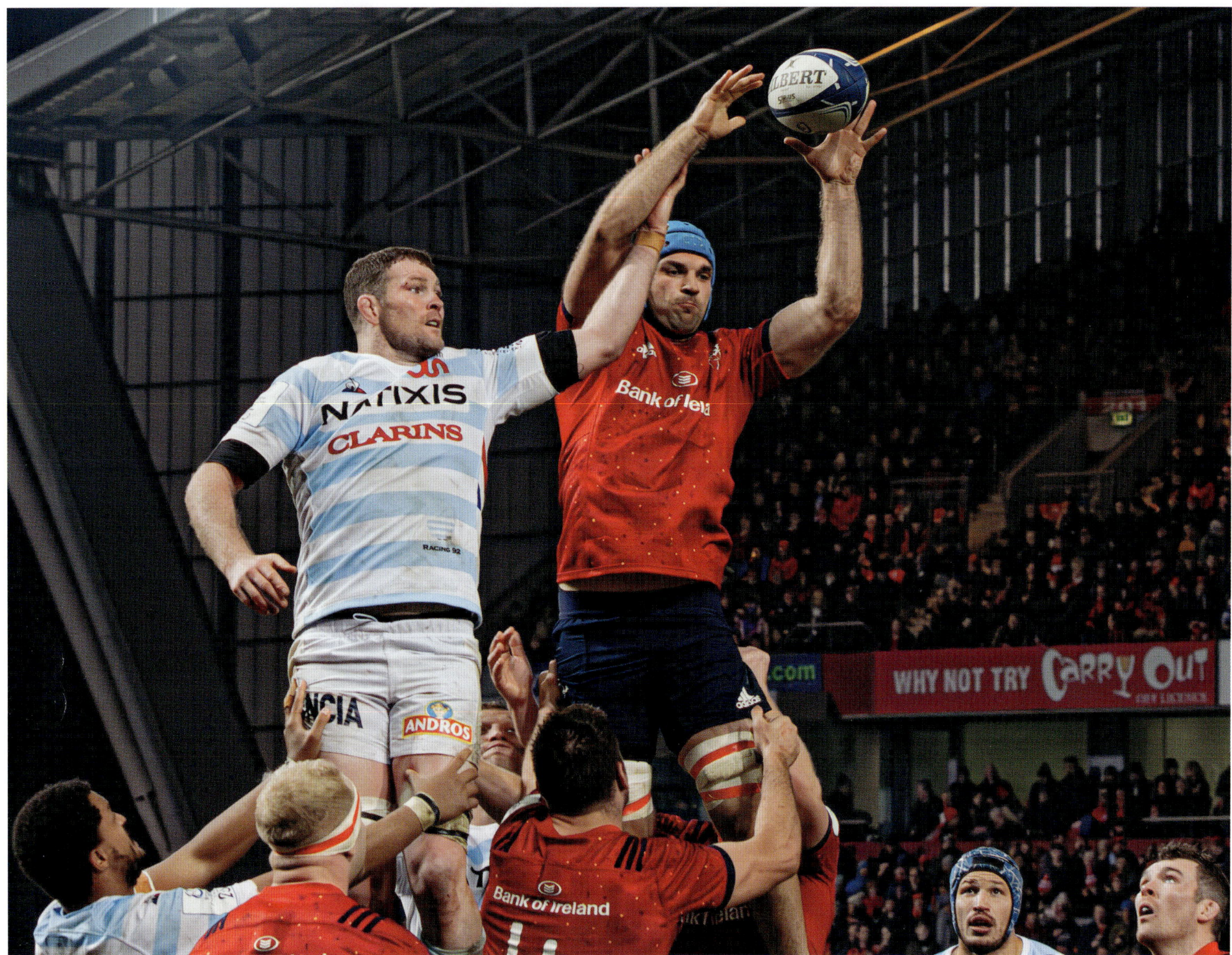

23 November 2019

Opposite top: Man of the match Mike Haley, flanked by Conor Murray, in action in a thrilling 21-21 draw against Racing 92. Munster's unbeaten home run, begun in December 2017, remained intact after Andrew Conway's 74th-minute try brought the sides level.

Opposite bottom: Simon Zebo – playing for Racing 92 – is surrounded by red shirts.

Above: Tadhg Beirne beats Donnacha Ryan, now also in the Racing colours, in the line-out.

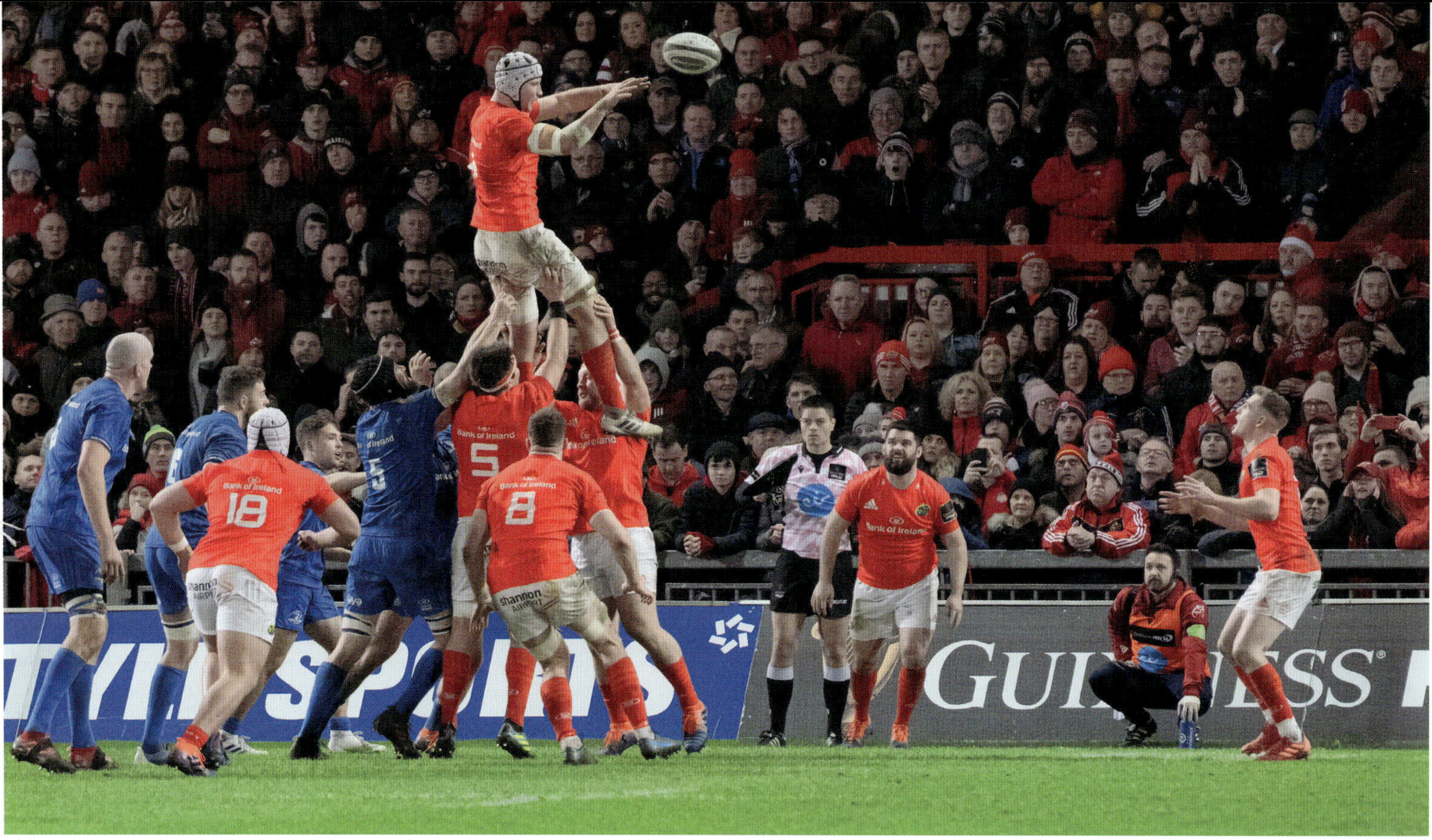
Bank of Ireland
18
5
8

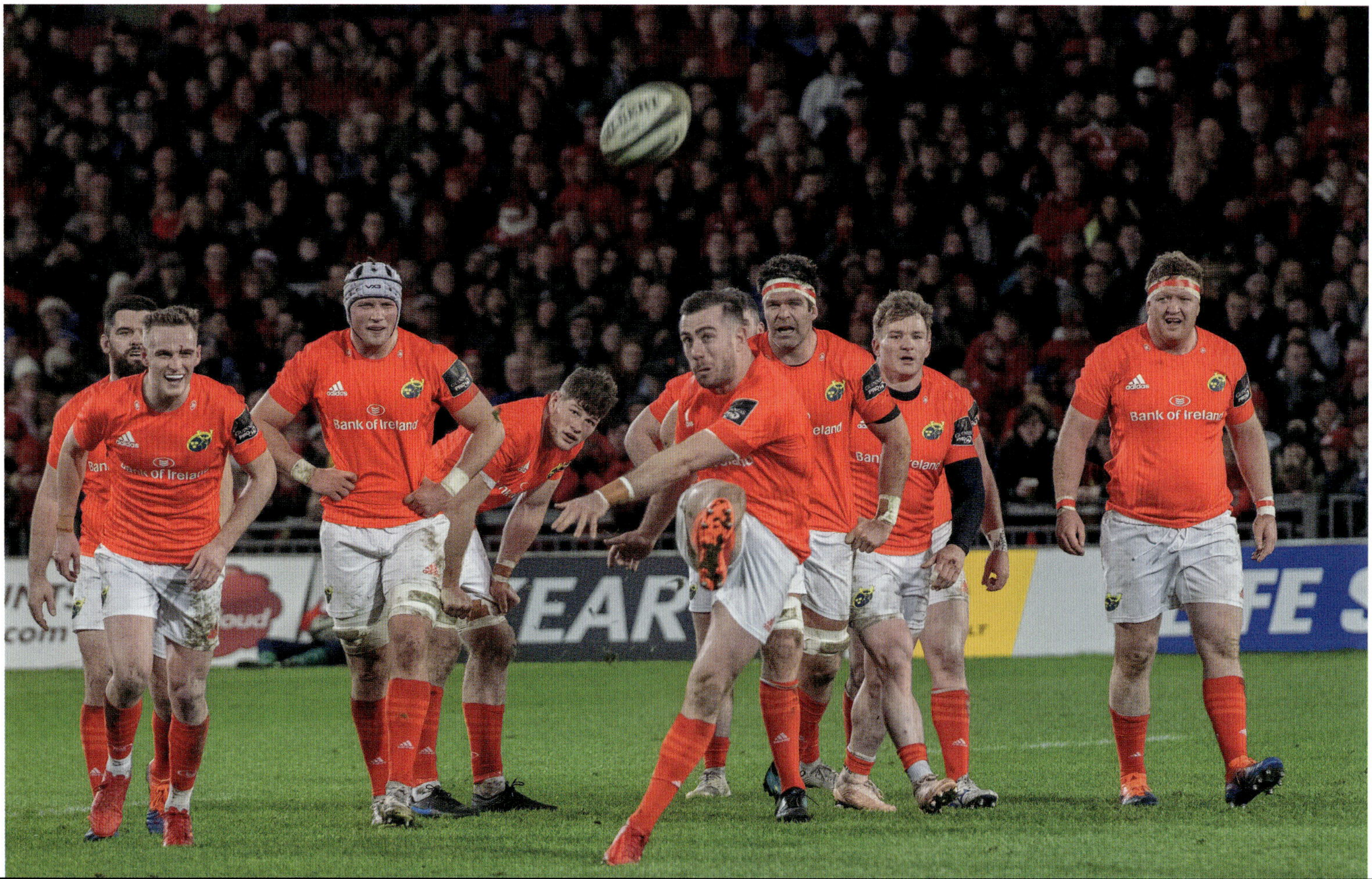
Bank of Ireland

28 December 2019

Opposite top: Fineen Wycherley takes to the air for a line-out against Leinster. The 13-6 loss is Munster's first home defeat in two years.

Opposite bottom: JJ Hanrahan kicks for touch on a gusty day in the annual derby against Leinster.

19 January 2020

Top: Jack O'Donoghue makes a strong run against Ospreys in Thomond Park. Despite a vigorous start by the visitors, the home team pinned Ospreys' wings and didn't let them score again. Munster won 33-6 in a game that saw the European debuts of Calvin Nash and, off the bench, Ben Healy and Jack O'Sullivan. Conor Murray was awarded man of the match.

30 August 2020

Right: The Pro14 resumed in August and played out in front of empty stands. Munster beat Connacht 49-12 in Aviva Stadium.

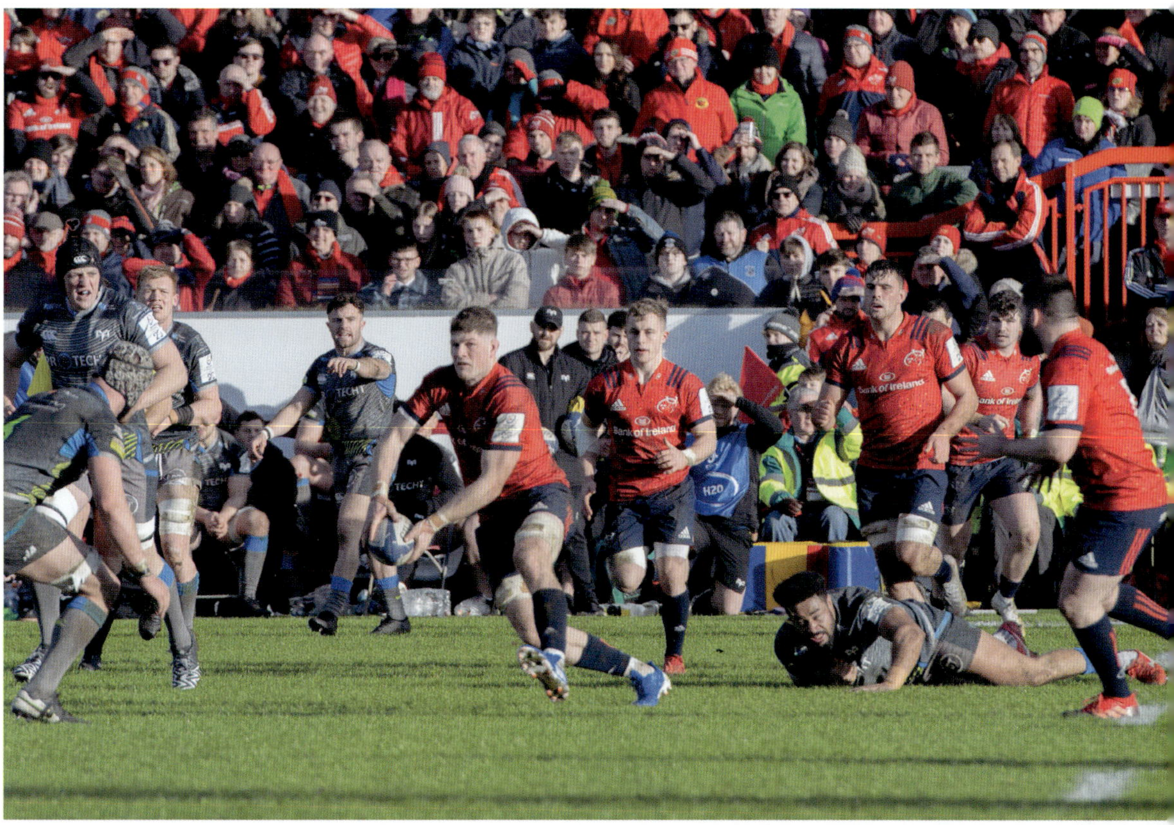

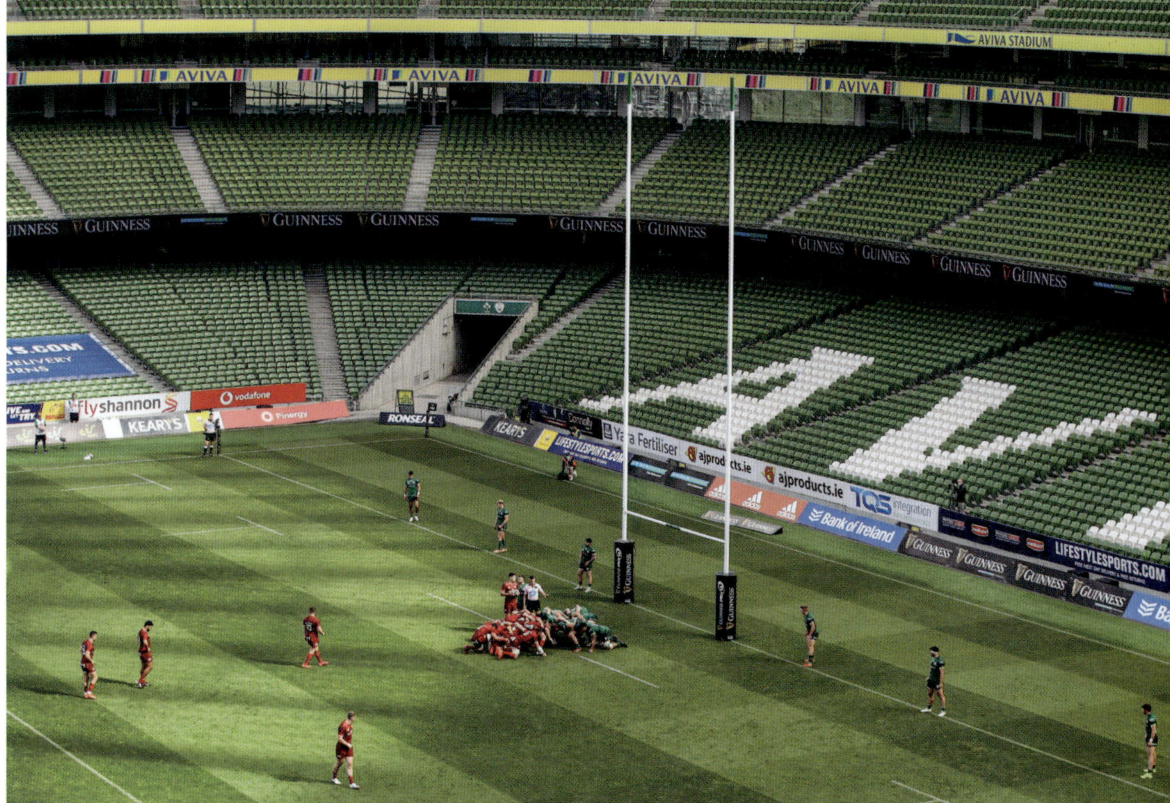

2020-2021

The Munster squad was boosted with the arrival of two of South Africa's 2019 Rugby World Cup winners, centre Damian de Allende and the six-foot-ten-inch lock RG Snyman. Other additions were Roman Salanoa and Matt Gallagher. Promotions from the academy included Diarmuid Barron and Liam Coombes. Arno Botha left for Bulls, while Sammy Arnold and Alex Wootton moved to Connacht.

Pro14

Munster were drawn in Conference B with Benetton, Cardiff Blues, Connacht, Edinburgh, Scarlets and Southern Kings (who had to withdraw, owing to Covid restrictions). It was announced in December 2020 that the Pro14 season would conclude after sixteen rounds, with winners of each conference advancing straight to the final.

Munster got off to a flier, winning the first seven matches and ending the year unbeaten. First to fall were Scarlets on 3 October in Parc y Scarlets. Tries from Jack O'Donoghue, Chris Farrell and Kevin O'Byrne, all converted by JJ Hanrahan and Ben Healy, who also added penalties, kept pace with Scarlets Leigh Halfpenny, who kicked nine penalties. The sides were level as the clocked ticked into red and Munster were down to fourteen men. A magnificent 50-metre penalty in the 81st minute from Ben Healy earned Munster a 30-27 win.

Munster's first defeat came on 3 January 2021, away to Ulster with a 10-15 loss. Another away game, against Connacht on 9 January, resulted in a 16-10 win for the visitors. The Leinster fixture, rescheduled because of Covid, was played at Thomond Park on 23 January, the men in blue winning 13-10. Then came a run of six wins: against Benetton (away), Edinburgh (away), Cardiff Blues, Connacht, Scarlets and Benetton at home. Munster's 20-17 win against Connacht in round 14 saw them qualify for the Grand Final, as they had an unassailable twelve-point lead at the top of Conference B with two rounds remaining.

They faced old rivals Leinster at the RDS, on 27 March. Munster's only points came from Joey Carbery's boot and they lost 16-6 as Leinster claimed a record fourth Pro14 in a row. More agony!

Rainbow Cup

Owing to Covid restrictions, the two Pro14 South African teams could not travel internationally. The Rainbow Cup was played between the twelve European clubs, while the Rainbow Cup SA was played between four South African clubs (the Bulls, Lions, Sharks and Stormers), with a play-off between the respective victors to decide the overall winner.

Munster's Pro14 Rainbow Cup commenced with a 27-3 away win against Leinster on 24 April. Next came a six-try 38-10 home win against Ulster on 7 May 2021. The try-scorers were Rory Scannell (two), Conor Murray, Mike Haley, Hanrahan and Andrew Conway, with Hanrahan converting four of the five. However, Connacht were surprise 24-20 winners at Thomond Park on 14 May. Munster beat Cardiff Blues on 28 May in Limerick, 31-27, in CJ Stander and Tommy O'Donnell's last match in the red jersey. A 54-11 win followed, away against Zebre on 11 June, in Billy Holland's final game for Munster. In spite of these two bonus-point victories, the unbeaten Benetton side topped the table. They faced Bulls in the final and won, 35-8.

European Champions Cup

In response to Covid, a new format was implemented: the top eight eligible teams from the Pro14, the Premiership (top ten English clubs) and Top 14 (France) competed in a 24-team tournament divided into two pools of twelve games, each team playing two home games and two away. Covid played havoc, and rounds 3 and 4 were cancelled.

Munster's campaign began with a 21-7 home win against Harlequins (coached by Jerry Flannery) on 13 December 2020. Gavin Coombes marked his Munster debut with a try. Damian de Allende and Josh Wycherley also made their European debuts. Next were Clermont Auvergne, on 20 December at the Stade Marcel-Michelin. Munster came from behind at half-time to win 39-31. Try-scorers were Haley, man of the match Stander and O'Byrne; Hanrahan was immaculate from the tee, converting all three tries and slotting six out of six penalties.

The Champions Cup was temporarily suspended in early January 2021 because of Covid, and resumed in April with the top eight teams from each pool at the time of suspension progressing to round 16. Munster had home advantage, thanks to their victories against Harlequins and Clermont. Pitted against Toulouse on 3 April, a pulsating first half, with two tries from Keith Earls and two penalties from Carbery, saw Munster lead 16-9 at half-time. Then Matthis Lebel followed with a try for Toulouse, converted by Roman Ntamack. Gavin Coombes got over from close range, converted by Carbery, only for Toulouse to level the score five minutes later. Hanrahan slotted a penalty to put Munster ahead again, but outstanding Toulouse scrum half Antoine Dupont scored two late tries and, despite an 80th-minute try from Coombes, converted by Craig Casey, Toulouse won 40-33, becoming only the second French team to win a European match at Thomond Park.

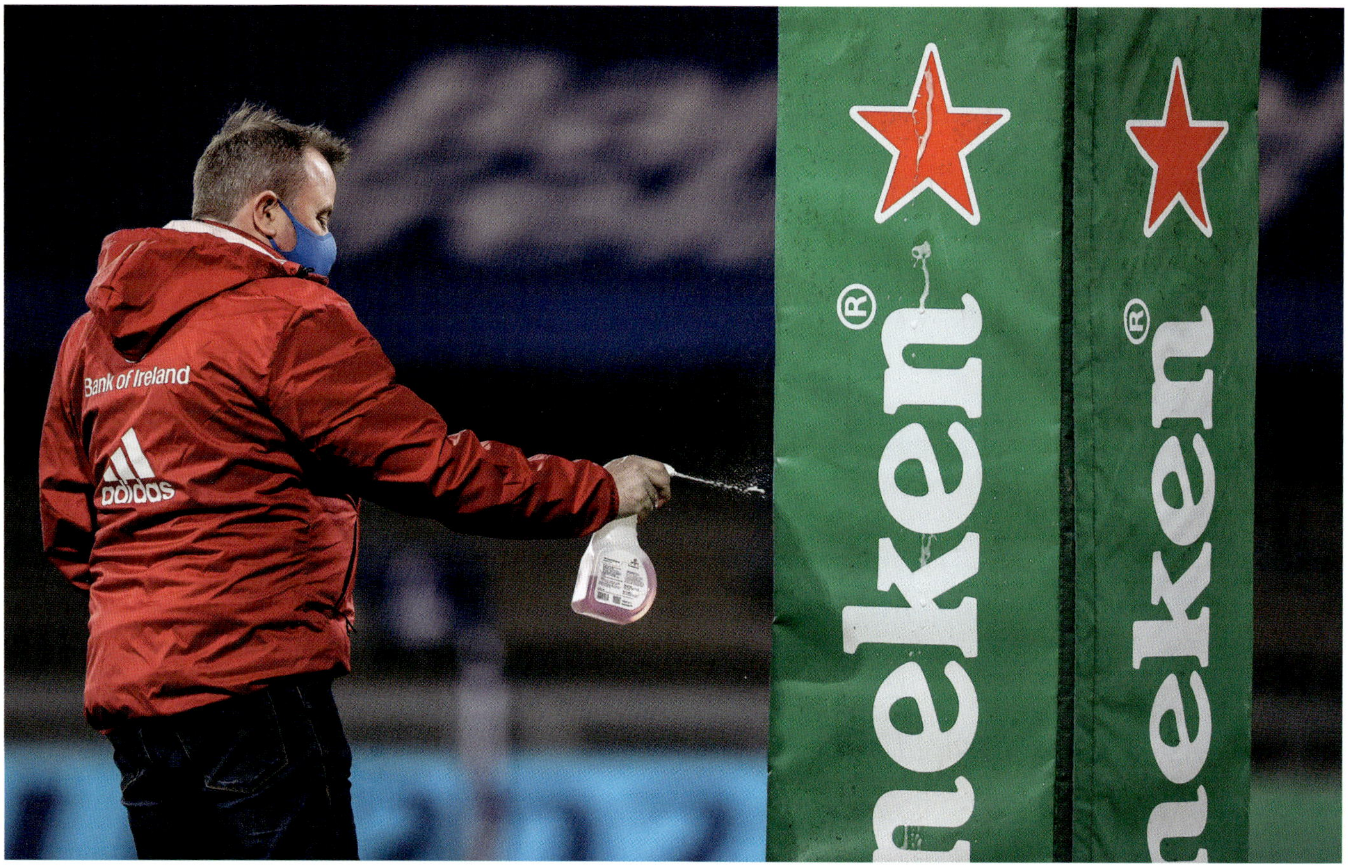

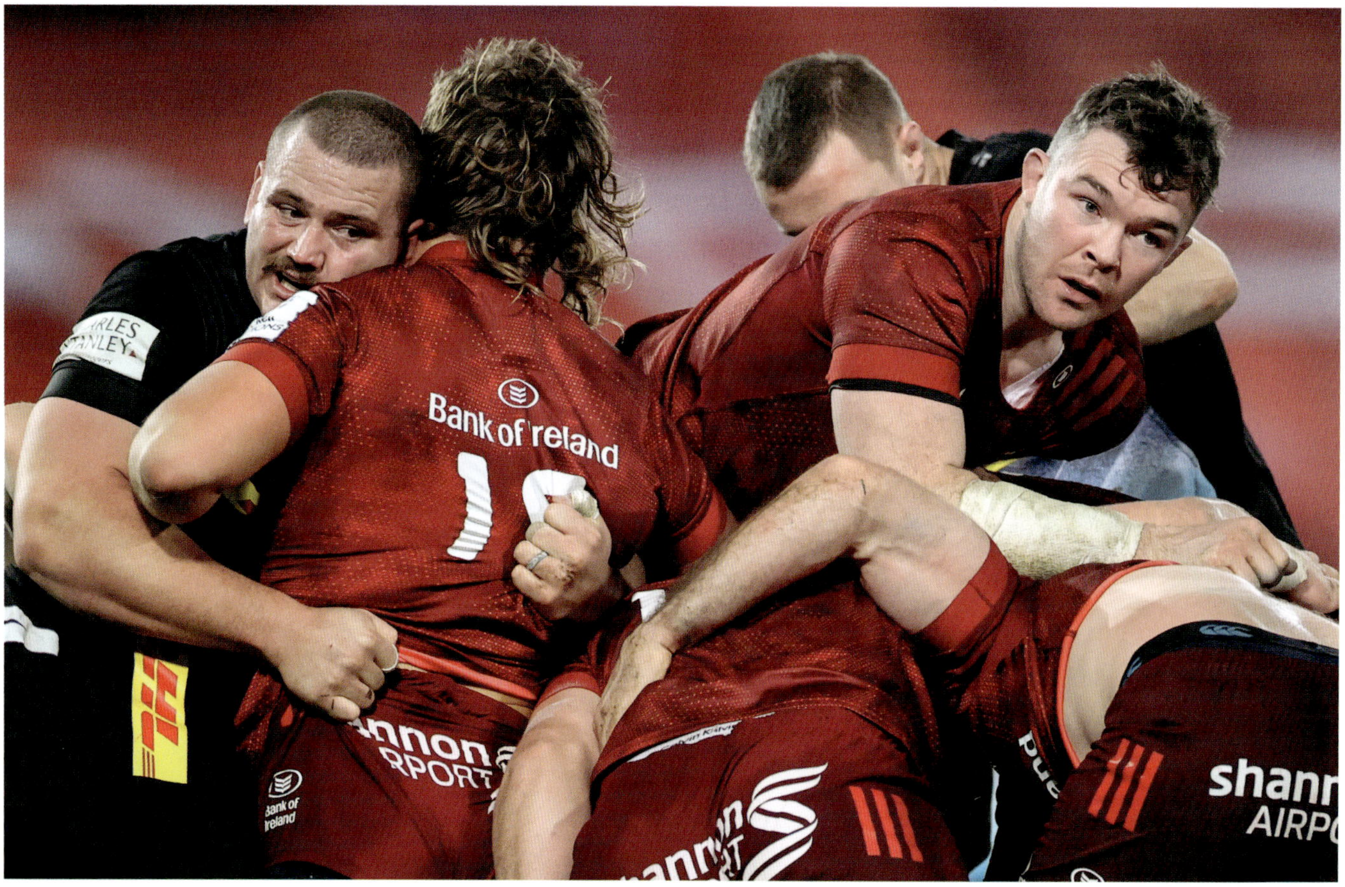

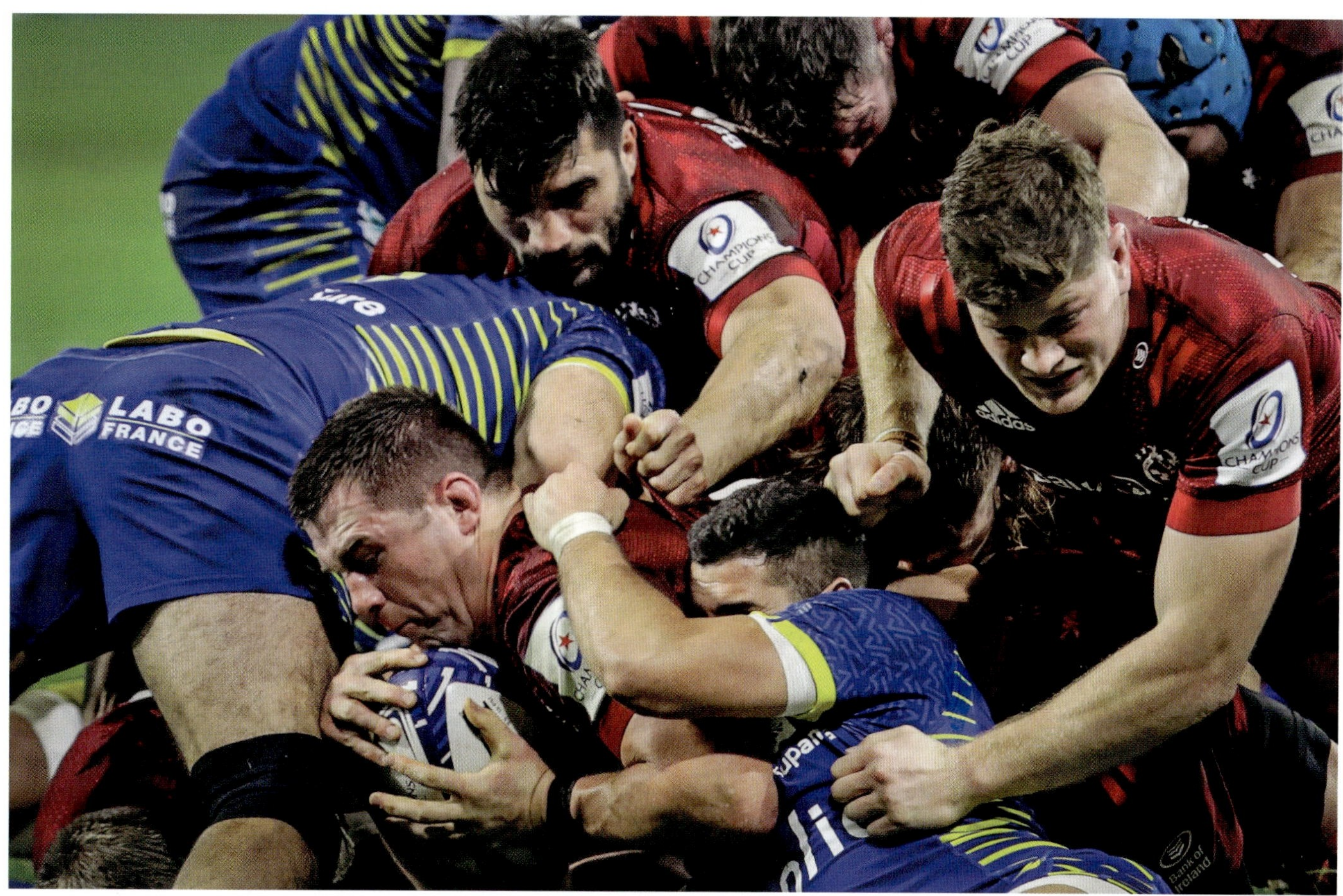

13 December 2020

Opposite top: A staff member sanitises the post pads.

Opposite bottom: Peter O'Mahony in a maul against Harlequins in Thomond Park in Munster's 21-7 victory.

19 December 2020

Above: CJ Stander scores the second of Munster's three tries against Clermont in Stade Marcel-Michelin. Munster win 39-31.

Following pages: In an initiative to make the stadium seem less empty, Munster fans' photos adorn the seats in Thomond Park.

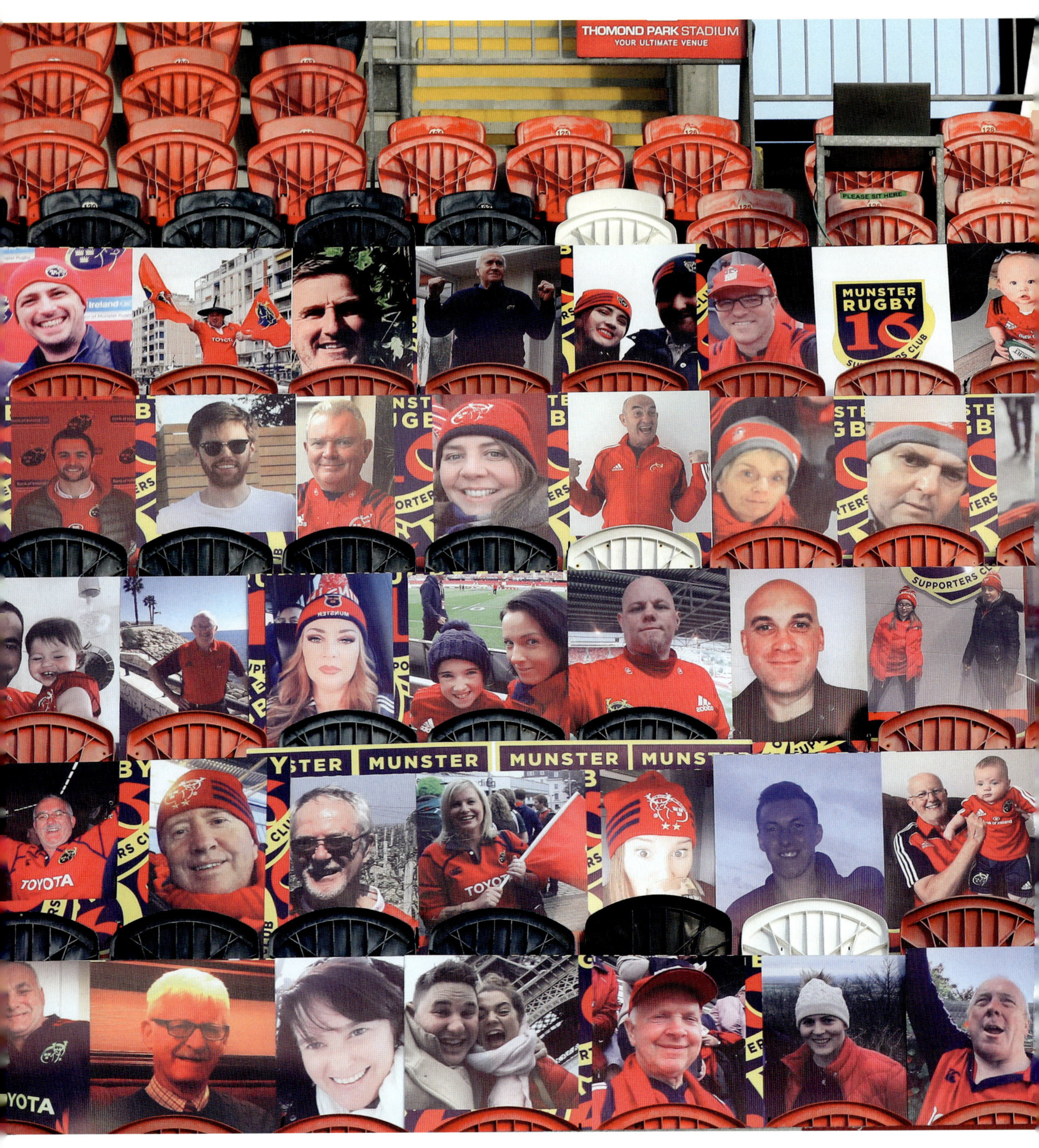
THOMOND PARK STADIUM
YOUR ULTIMATE VENUE
PLEASE SIT HERE
MUNSTER RUGBY
SUPPORTERS CLUB
MUNSTER
TOYOTA

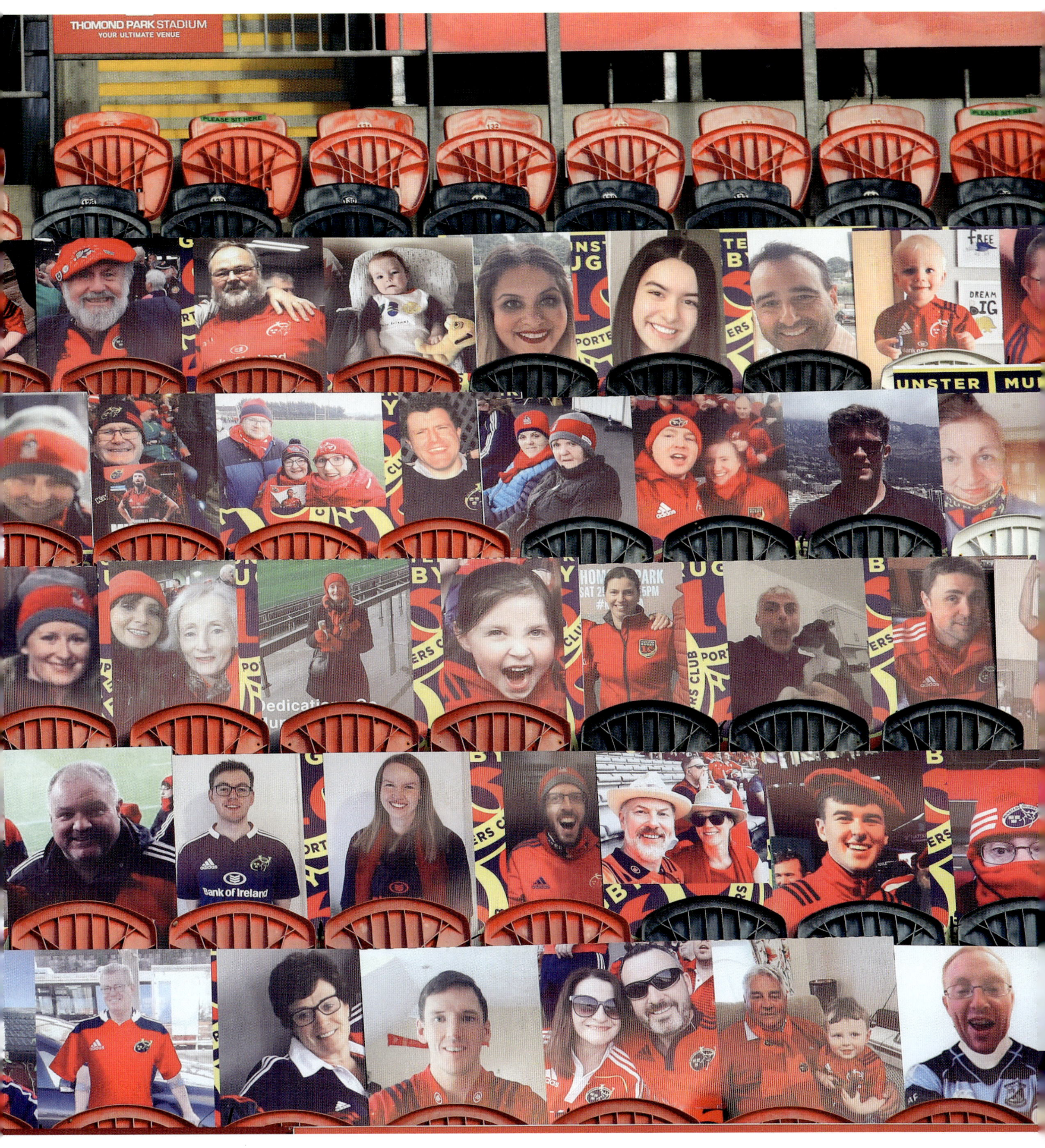

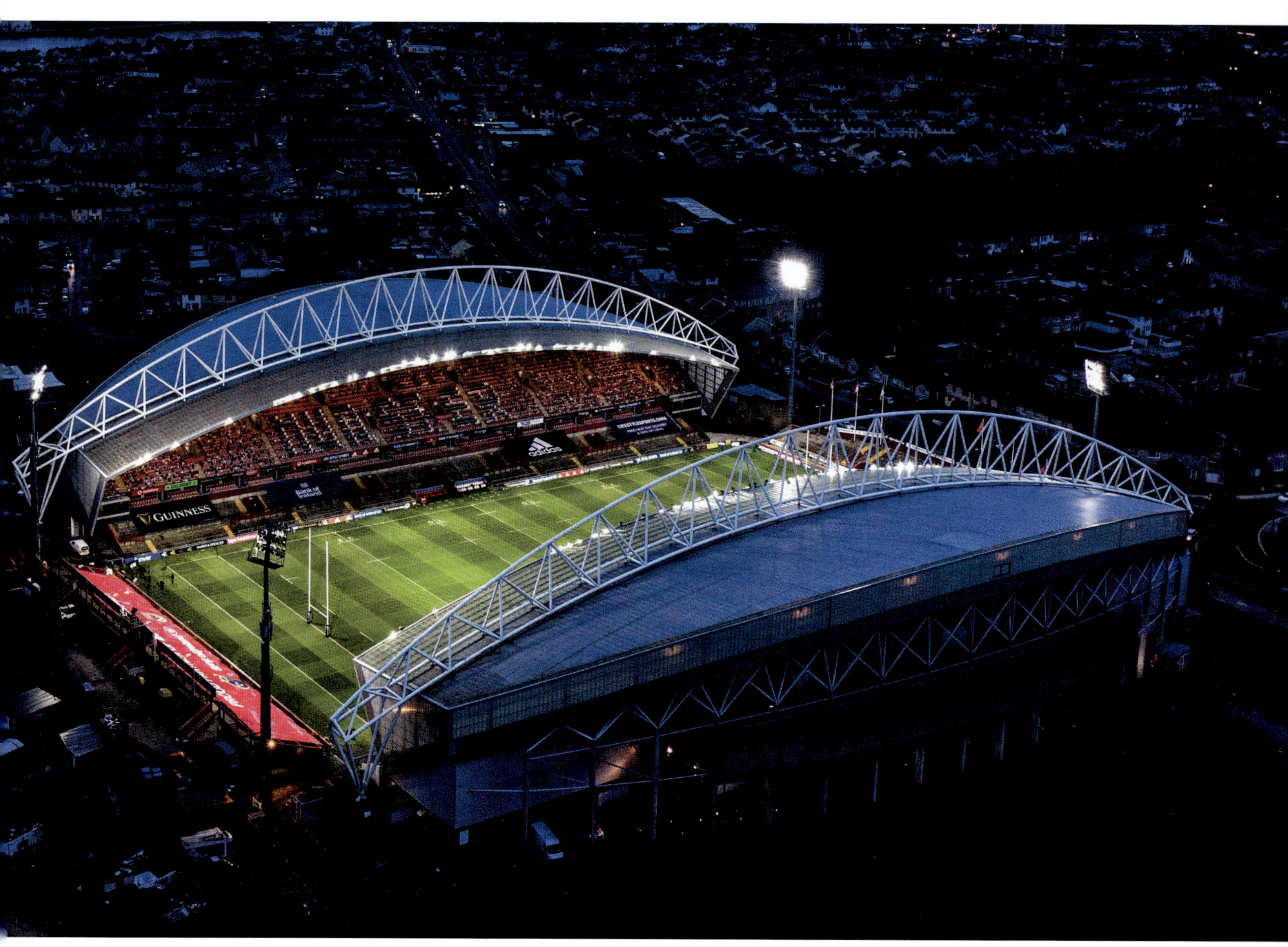

23 January 2021

Above: The unthinkable: Thomond Park devoid of fans. Munster play Leinster in a rescheduled Pro14 match.

Opposite: Steam rises from the scrum on a cold night in Thomond. The visitors edge the win 13-10.

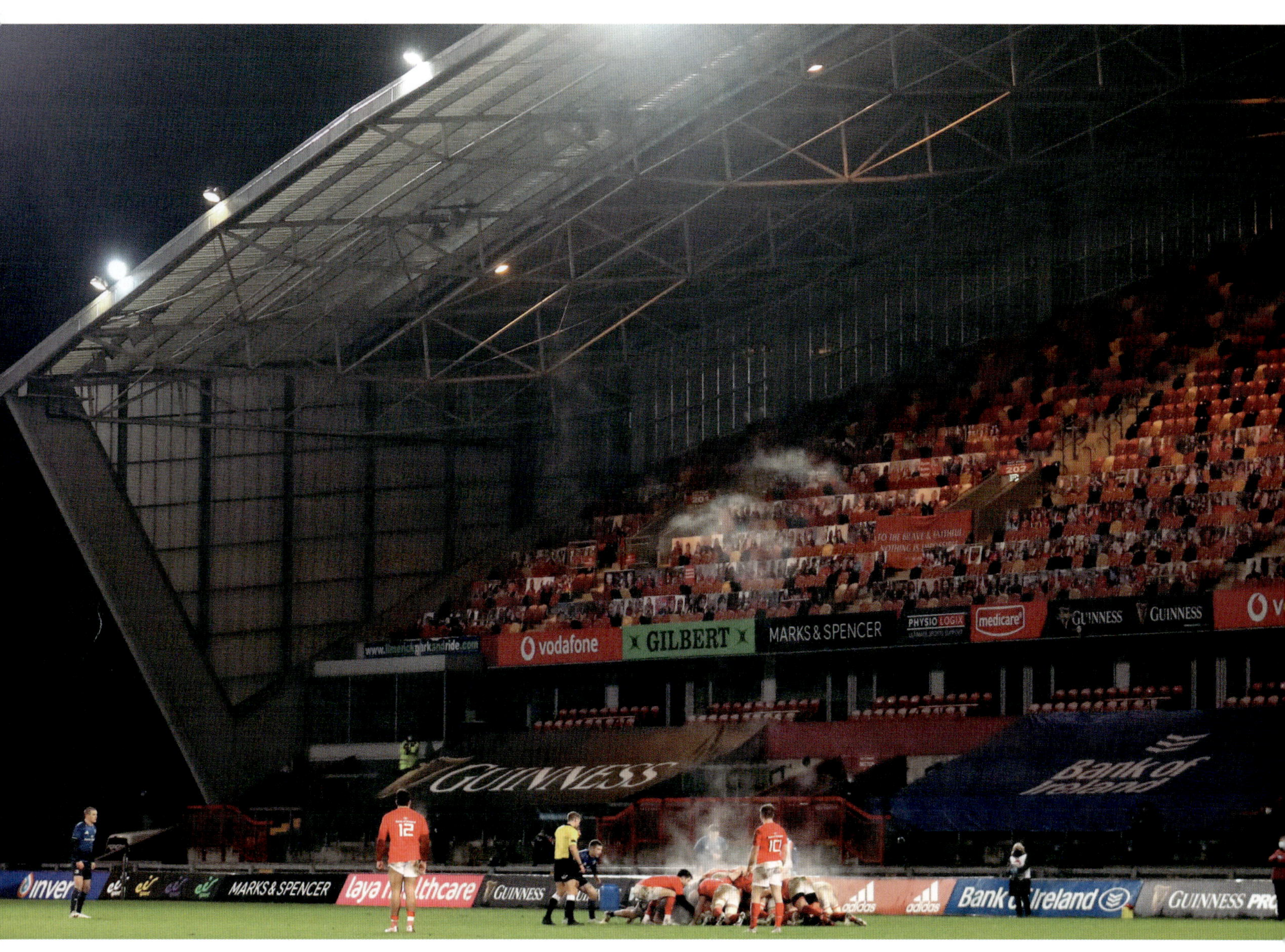

2021-2022

URC   **Pool wins: 11; Pool losses: 7; Eliminated: quarter-final**

European Champions Cup   **Pool wins: 5; Pool losses: 2; Pool Draws: 1 ; Eliminated: quarter-final**

Johann van Graan announced his retirement as head coach in December 2021, but stayed for the rest of the season. Several notable names would also leave the province this season: JJ Hanrahan left for Clermont; Alex Wootton's loan move to Connacht became permanent. Scrum half Nick McCarthy returned to Leinster and hooker Rhys Marshall to New Zealand, while James Cronin moved to Biarritz. Simon Zebo returned after three seasons at Racing 92, while nine academy players were promoted to the senior squad: Tom Ahern, Jack Crowley, Jack Daly, Jake Flannery, James French, Sean French, Ben Healy, John Hodnett and Josh Wycherley. Former assistant coach Ian Costello was appointed academy manager, and Caroline Currid joined the backroom team part-time.

URC

The Pro14 was rebranded as the United Rugby Championship (URC), following the introduction of the four South African Super Rugby teams – the Bulls, Lions, Sharks and Stormers. Clubs were formed into regional pools, which saw Munster paired with Leinster, Ulster and Connacht. The highest-ranked team from each pool qualified for the Champions Cup, with a further four spots going to the next four highest-ranked teams in the single league table who had not already qualified from their pool.

Munster opened the campaign with a bonus-point 42-17 win against the Sharks at Thomond Park on 25 September 2021. Simon Zebo scored a brace of tries, extending his club record to 62. Gavin Coombes also scored two tries; Chris Cloete and man of the match Craig Casey crossed for one each. Joey Carbery and Ben Healy scored twelve points from the tee between them. This match saw fans return to the ground for the first time since February 2020. Wins followed against Stormers (34-18), away against Scarlets (43-13) and back in Thomond Park against Connacht (20-18), then an 18-10 defeat to Ospreys in Swansea. Covid struck while Munster were in South Africa for rounds 6 and 7, and their matches against the Bulls and Lions were postponed. Fourteen players and staff tested positive and had to stay in South Africa while the rest returned home, entering ten days of mandatory self-isolation. The annual post-Christmas derby against Leinster was also postponed.

The new year began with a narrow defeat, 10-8, to hosts Connacht on 1 January, an 18-13 win against visitors Ulster on 8 January and a 34-17 away win against Zebre on 29 January. Jack Crowley opened the scoring with a penalty, followed by tries from Jack O'Donoghue, Dan Goggin, brothers Fineen and Josh Wycherley and Diarmuid Barron. Jake Flannery added three conversions. On 11 February, hosts Glasgow ground out a narrow win, 13-11. Back on home soil a week later, Munster beat Edinburgh 34-20, with a hat trick of tries from Simon Zebo and one from Fineen Wycherley. Healy converted all four and added two penalties. On 5 March, visitors Dragons were overwhelmed by the hosts, 64-3. Back in South Africa, Munster lost both to Bulls (29-24) and Lions (23-21) on 12 and 19 March respectively. In Cork, they beat Benetton 51-22 on 25 March. They lost to Leinster, 34-19, on 2 April in Thomond Park, but beat hosts Ulster 24-17 on 22 April and visitors Cardiff (42-21) on 29 April. A 35-25 defeat away to Leinster on 21 May 2022 meant that Munster finished sixth in the league overall. They then headed to Belfast to play a quarter-final match against Ulster on 3 June, but lost 36-17 to bring the season to another disappointing close.

EUROPEAN CHAMPIONS CUP

Munster's opening fixture in Coventry against Wasps on 12 December featured twelve debutants, as the team was Covid-stricken, but the province pulled off one of their greatest away victories, defeating the hosts 35-14. Castres came to Thomond Park for the next game on 18 December, which Munster won 19-13. Jack O'Donoghue scored a second-half try and out-half Ben Healy scored fourteen points from the tee. In the reverse fixture against Castres on 14 January 2022, Munster ground out a 16-13 away win, with a try from Gavin Coombes. Jack Crowley, making his European debut, converted and slotted three penalties, securing a place in the knock-out stage for Munster.

In Thomond Park on 23 January, Munster had an outstanding 45-7 win against Wasps, with tries from Conor Murray, Zebo (two), O'Donoghue, Jeremy Loughman and Rory Scannell. Zebo became Munster's leading try-scorer in the European Cup and the leading Irish try-scorer in the competition overall.

In Sandy Park on 9 April, Exeter Chiefs won 13-8, in spite of strong defence from Munster. Aggregate scores counted, so Munster needed to overturn a five-point deficit in the return leg a week later. Joey Carbery struck first with a penalty for Munster before Exeter scored an unconverted try. Carbery struck again to give Munster a 13-5 half-time lead. Exeter slotted a penalty in the second half before Carbery replied with two more. Then centre Damian de Allende scored a 74th-minute try, converted by Carbery, to secure the win 26-10 for Munster.

Munster started well against Toulouse in the quarter-final with Alex Kendellen scoring early and Carbery converting. Almost immediately, Romain Ntamack hit back with a try, converted by Thomas Ramos to level the scores. And so it continued. After 80 minutes, the score was 24-24. Extra time of two 10-minute halves didn't end the stalement, and a penalty shoot-out ensued. In the cruellest fashion, Munster lost 4-2 and Toulouse advanced to the semi-final, crushing Munster's hopes for the second successive year.

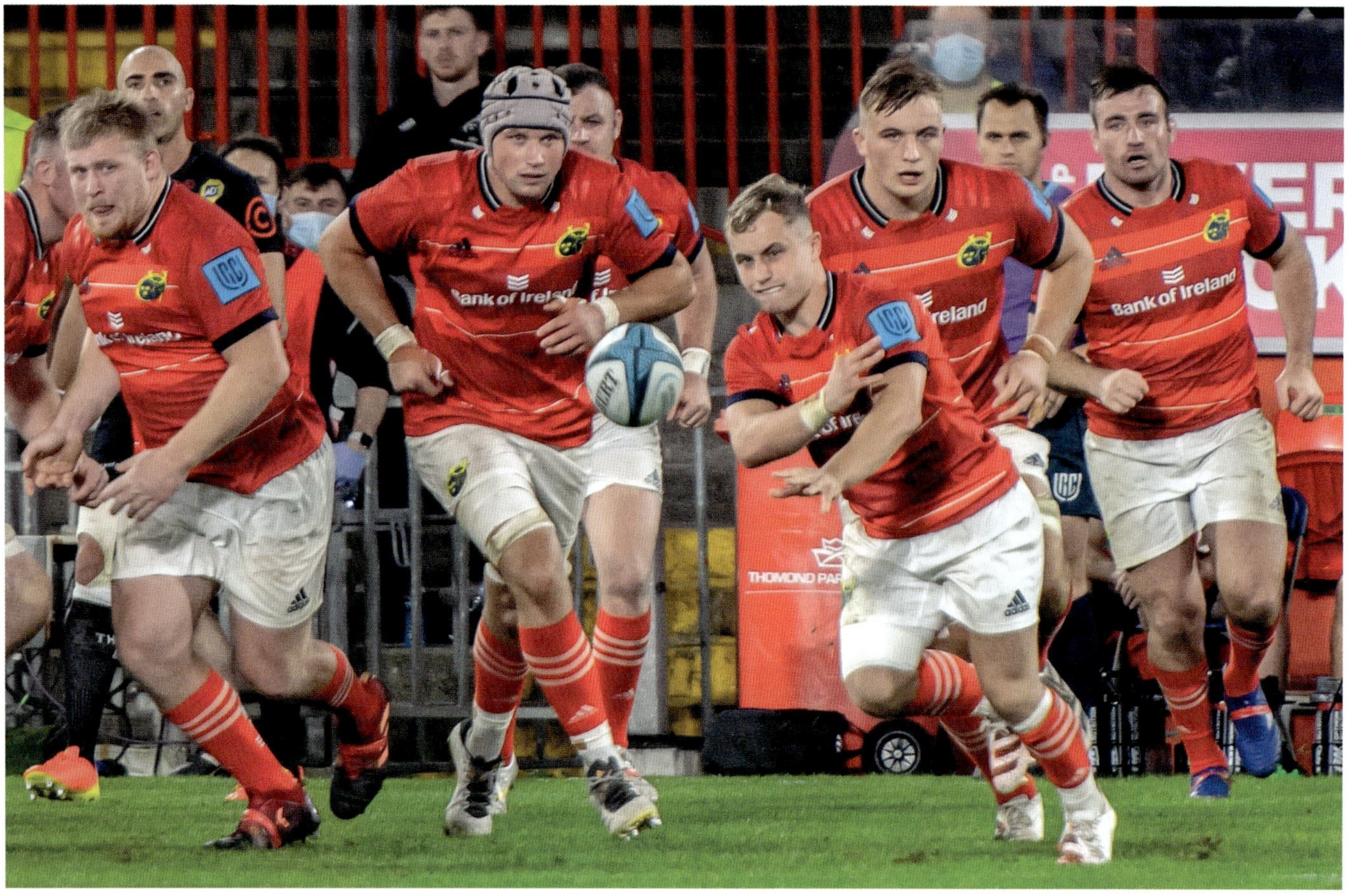

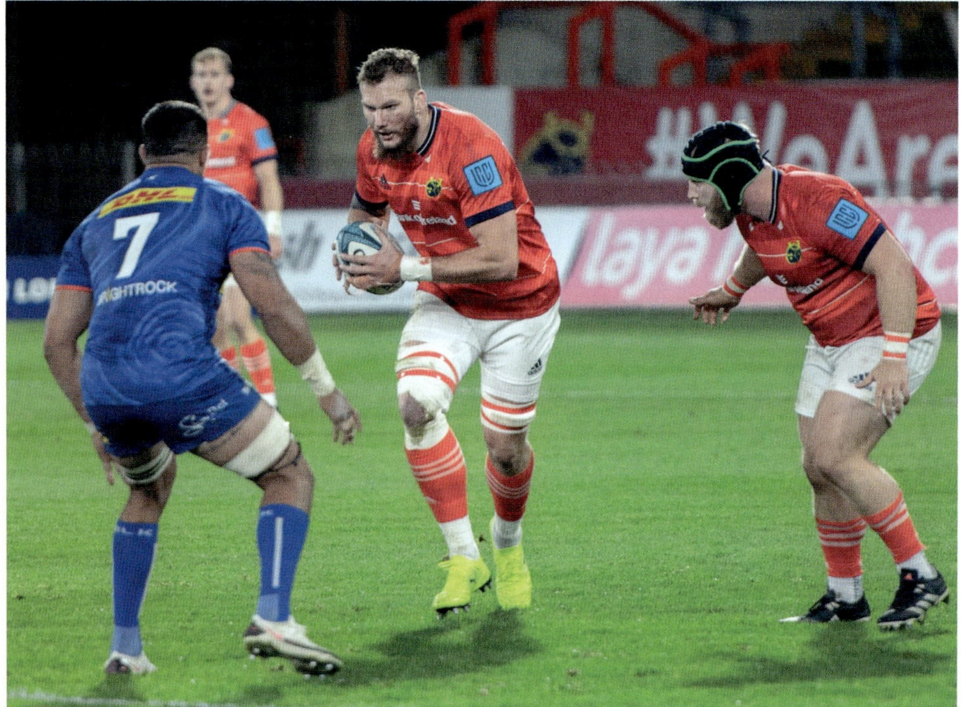

25 September 2021

Above: Craig Casey passes the ball, flanked by (l–r) John Ryan, Fineen Wycherley, Gavin Coombes and Niall Scannell. Munster get the season off to a cracking start with a 42–17 victory over Sharks.

2 October 2021

Left: RG Snyman supported by Jeremy Loughman in Munster's 34–18 victory over Stormers in Thomond Park.

Opposite: Jean Kleyn beats Stormers' Gerbrandt Grobler for a line-out ball. Grobler made eleven appearances for Munster in 2017–2018.

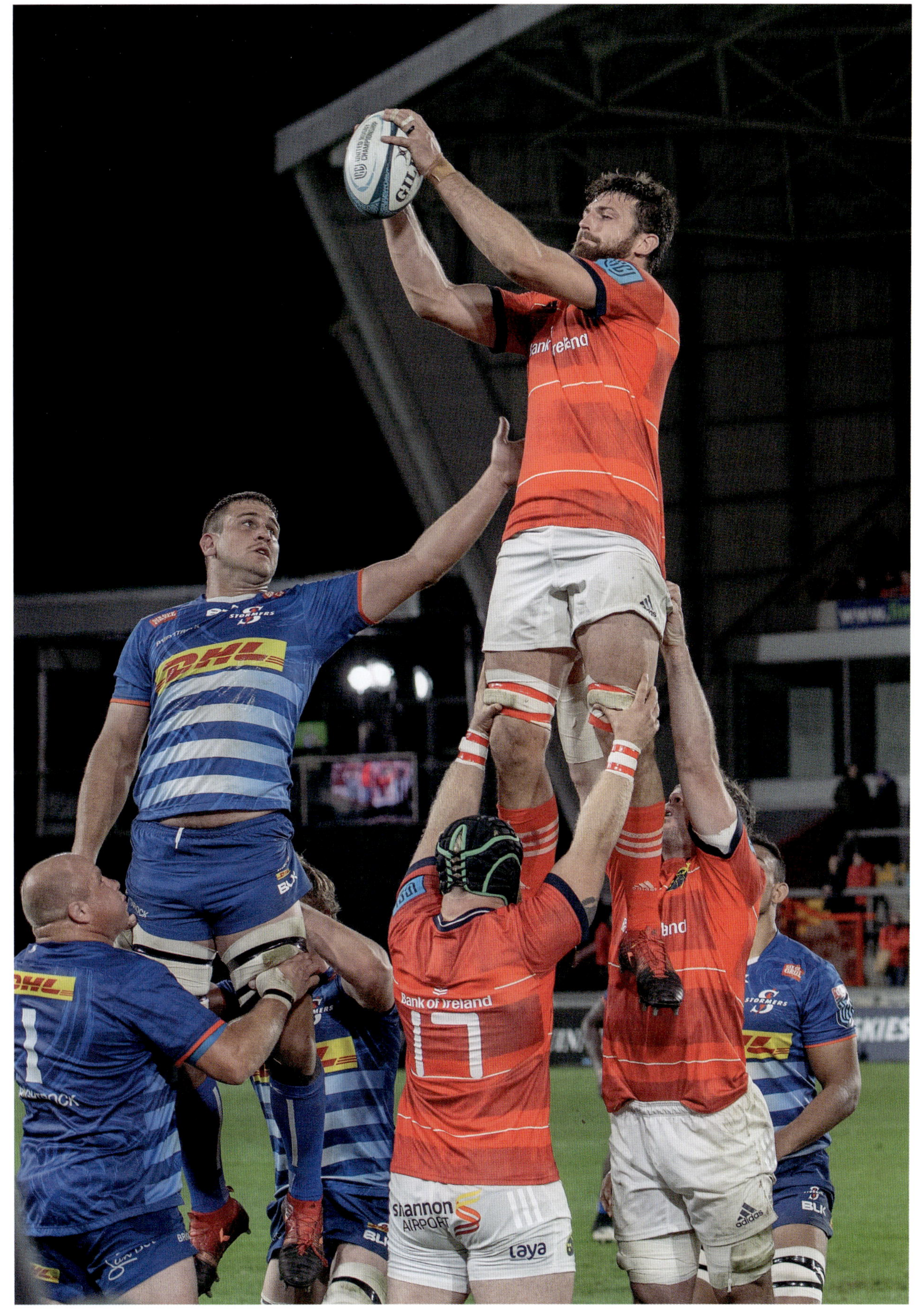

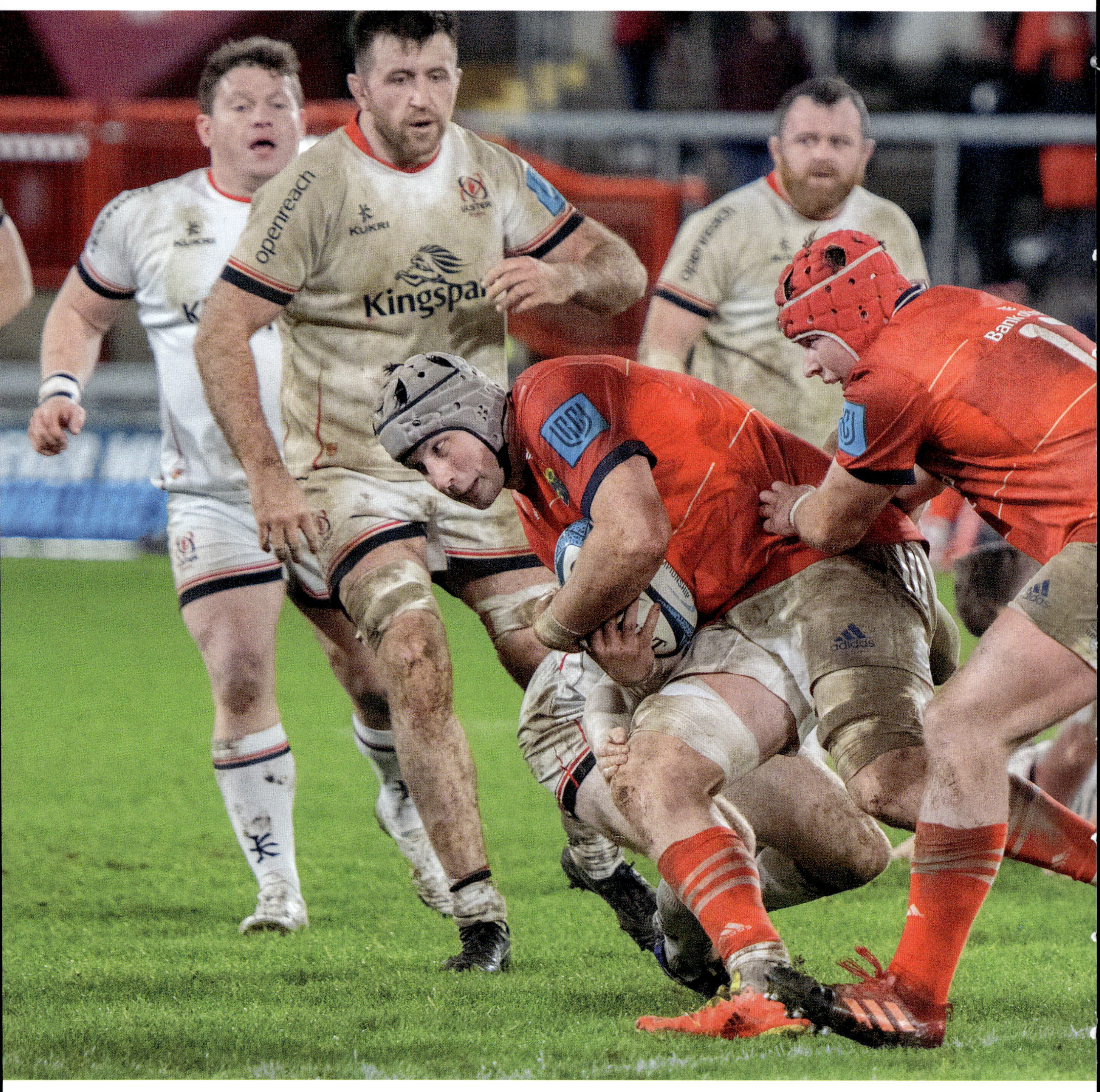

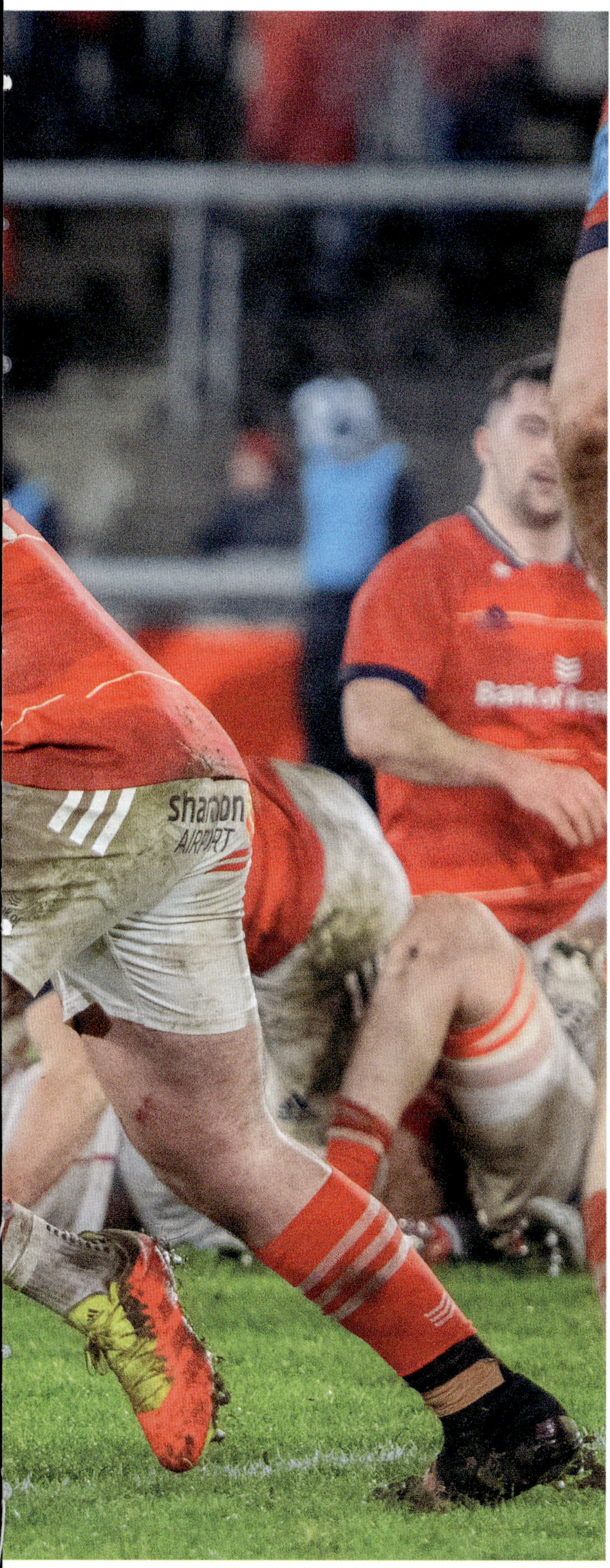

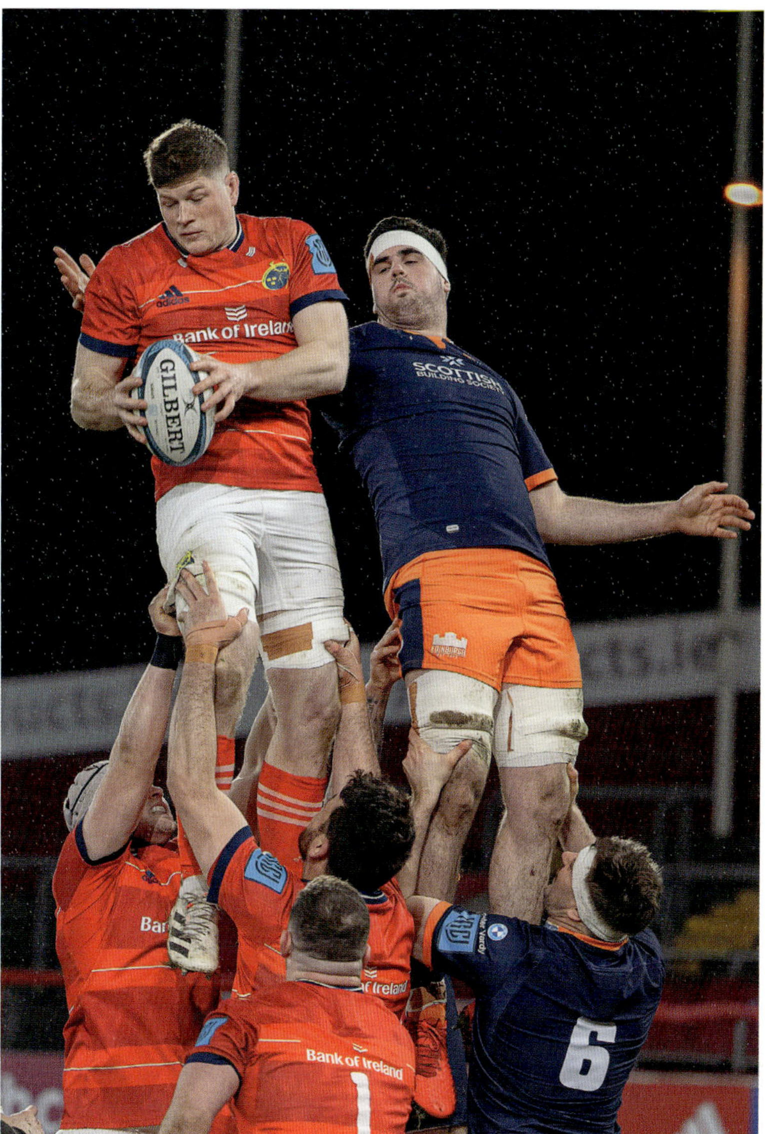

8 January 2022

Opposite: Wycherley brothers (l–r) Fineen and Josh in action against Ulster. Tries from Mike Haley and Alex Kendellen (his first for Munster) helped the home team to an 18-13 victory, in spite of being down to fourteen men when Simon Zebo was red-carded after fifteen minutes. Tadhg Beirne was named player of the match, in his first outing as Munster captain.

18 February 2022

Above: Jack O'Donoghue wins a line-out against Edinburgh.

Ben Healy kicks for touch with this penalty, watched by (l–r) Stephen Archer, Fineen Wycherley, Chris Cloete, Jean Kleyn, Dave Kilcoyne and Gavin Coombes. On a cold and gusty night in Limerick, Munster secured a bonus-point win (34-20) against Edinburgh, helped by a hat trick of tries from Simon Zebo. Dave Kilcoyne earned his 200th cap for Munster.

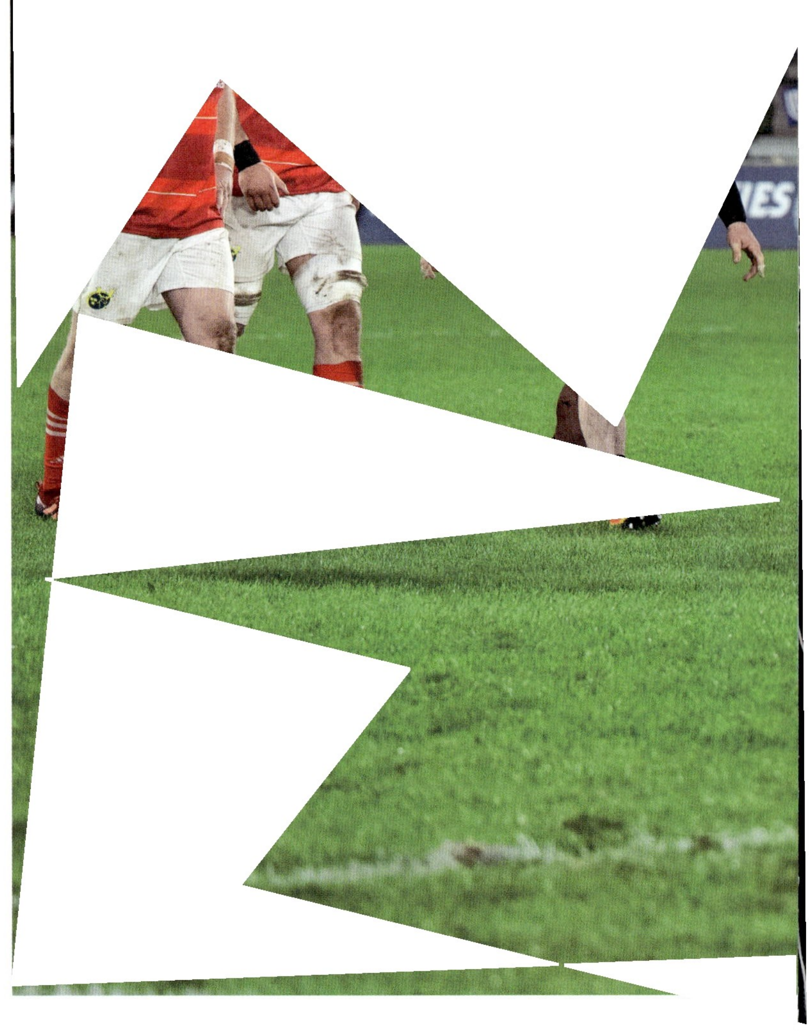

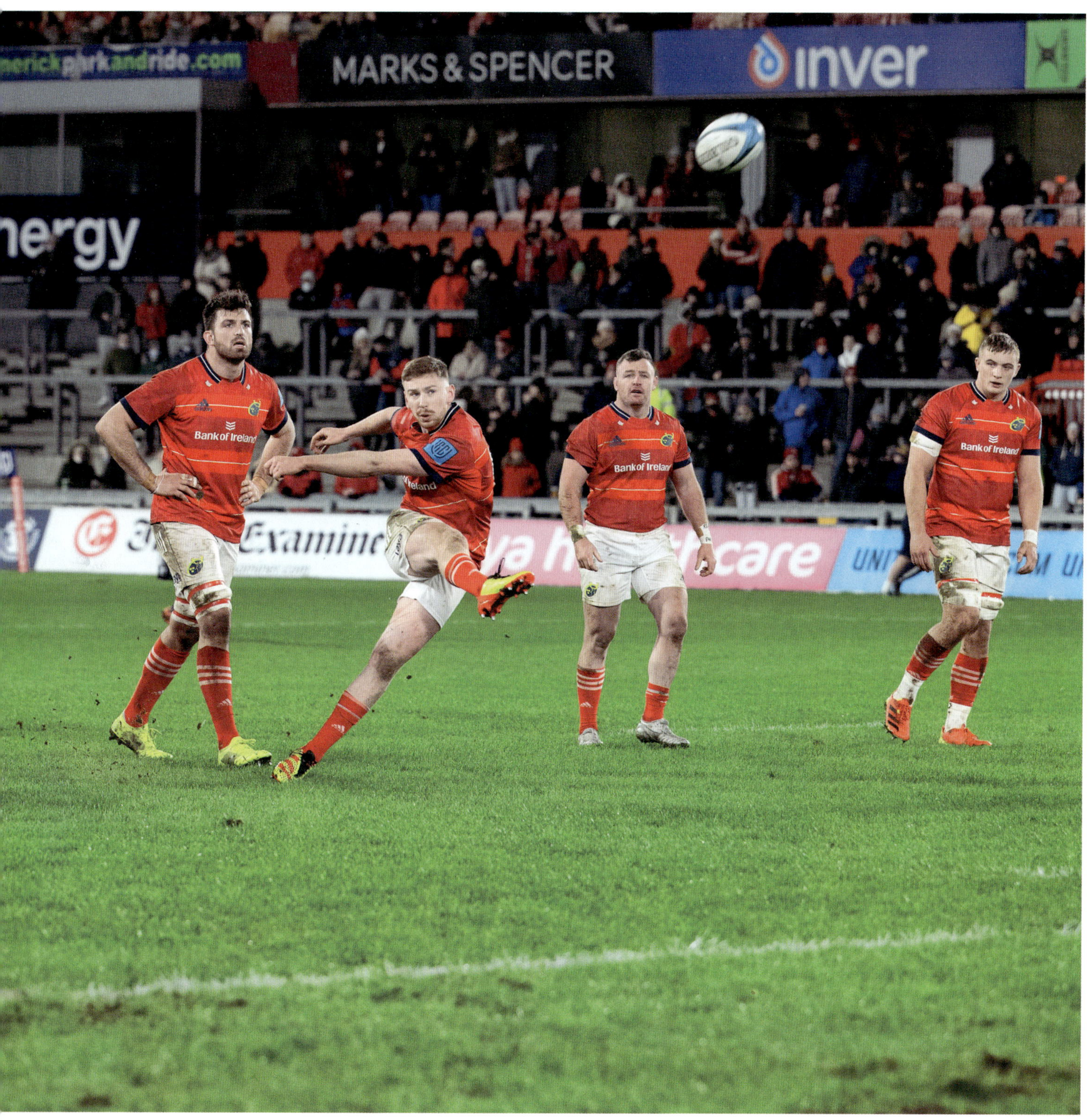

erick park and ride.com
MARKS & SPENCER
INVER
nergy
Bank of Ireland
Bank of Ireland
Bank of Ireland
Examine
care
UNI

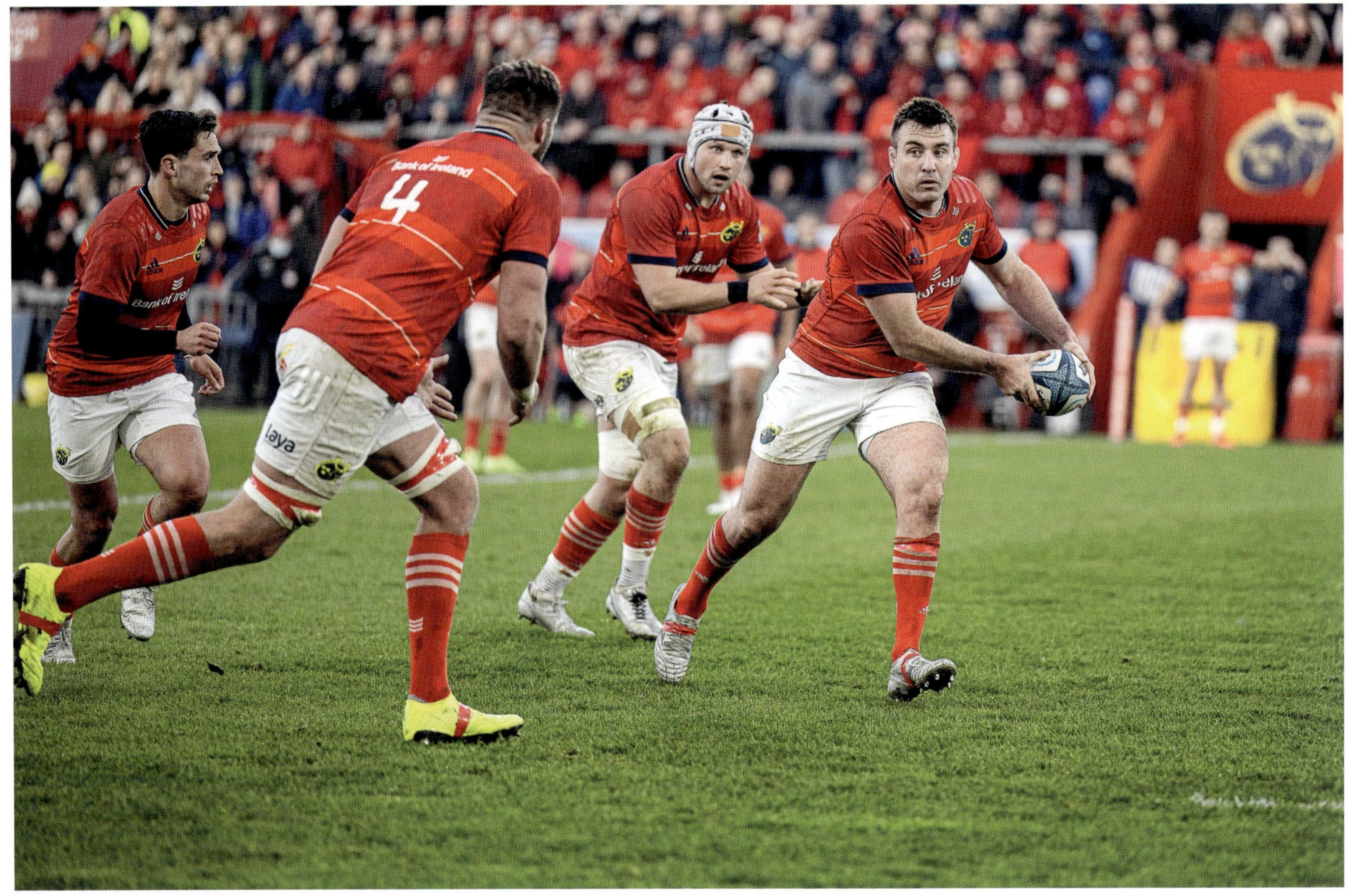

2 April 2020

Above: Niall Scannell starts the attack against Leinster. In spite of a try by Damian de Allende and fourteen points from the boot of Joey Carbery, Munster lose 34-19.

16 April 2020

Opposite top: Mike Haley plays scrum half against Exeter Chiefs in the Champions Cup. Munster win resoundingly, 26-10.

Opposite bottom: Jean Kleyn and Chris Farrell celebrate the victory over Exeter Chiefs.

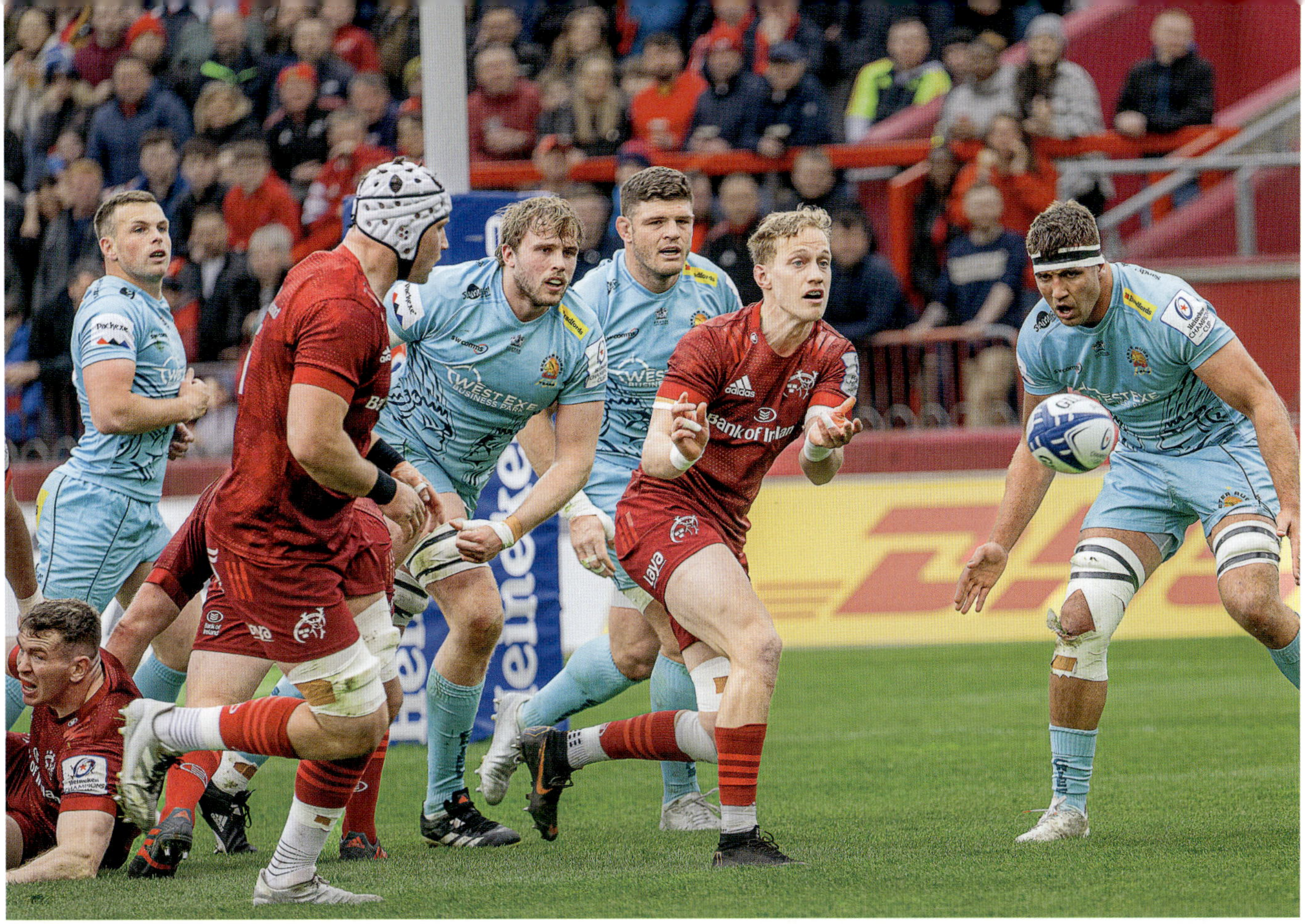

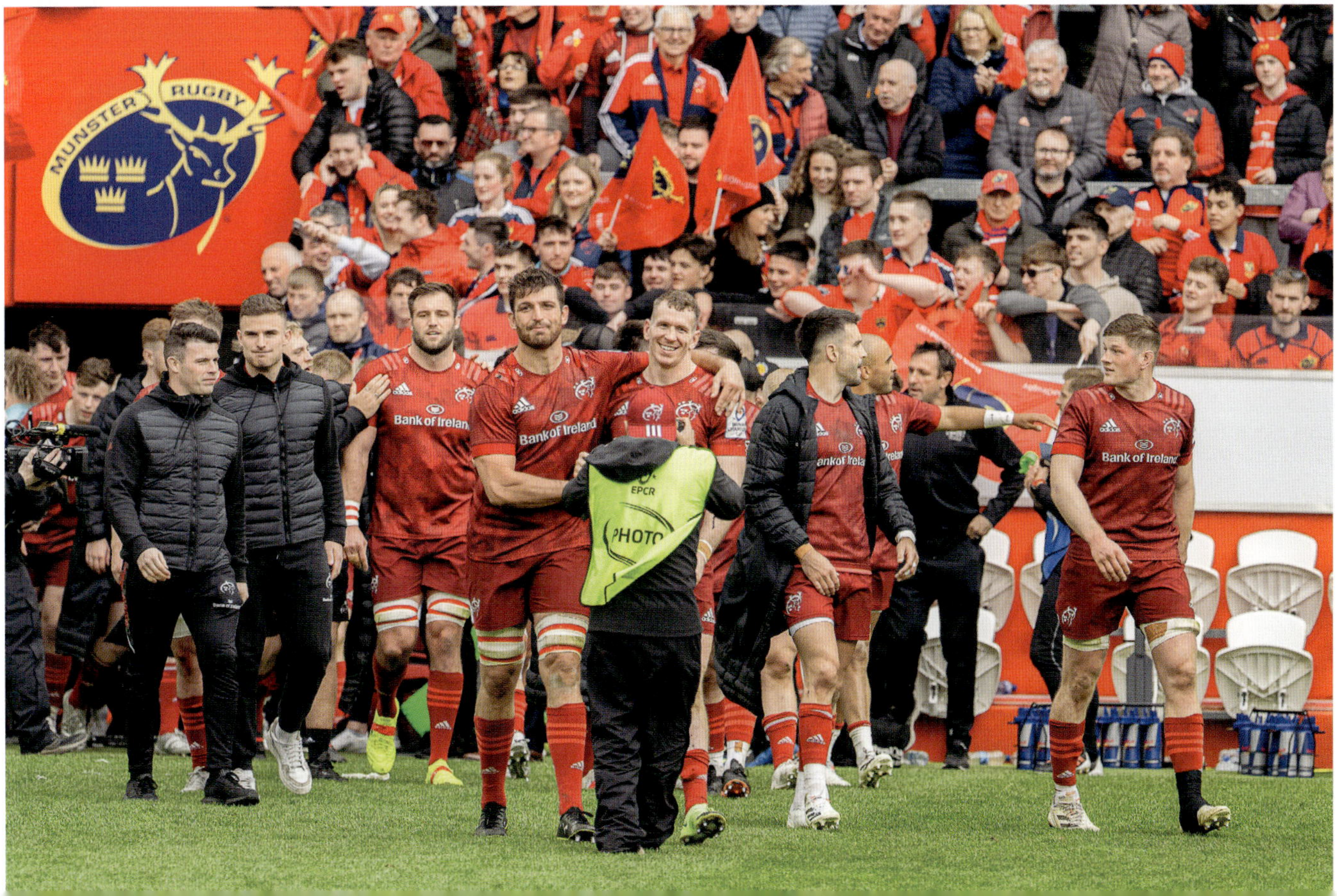
MUNSTER RUGBY
Bank of Ireland
EPCR
PHOTO

2022–2023

URC   **Pool wins: 10; Pool losses: 7; Pool draws: 1; Final: won**
European Champions Cup   **Pool wins: 2; Pool losses: 2; Eliminated: round of 16**

This season saw forwards coach Graham Rowntree appointed head coach. Former scrum half Mike Prendergast joined as attack coach and Andi Kyriacou was promoted to forwards coach, with Denis Leahy returning to the province as defence coach. Former players Brendan O'Connor and Tommy O'Donnell joined as elite player development officers and Matt Brown as pathway development coach.

The big signing for the year was Malakai Fekitoa, who was part of New Zealand's 2015 Rugby World Cup-winning team. Scott Buckley, Paddy Kelly, Alex Kendellen, Eoin O'Connor and scrum half Paddy Patterson were promoted from the academy. Antoine Frisch also signed up. Names leaving the squad included Chris Cloete, Damian de Allende, Chris Farrell, James French, Sean French, Matt Gallagher, Dan Goggin, Jason Jenkins, Alex McHenry, Declan Moore, Kevin O'Byrne and John Ryan. New arrivals to the academy included Evan O'Connell, Ruadhán Quinn, Jack Oliver and Kieran Ryan.

URC

Graham Rowntree's squad stuttered and stumbled through the early games, losing away twice in succession: 20-13 to Cardiff Blues on 17 September 2022 and 23-17 to Dragons a week later. At Musgrave Park on 1 October, a scrappy 21-5 win over lowly Zebre was achieved. This was followed by another away loss, to Connacht on 7 October, by 20-11. At home on 15 October, Munster defeated the Bulls by 31-17. Then came the match against Leinster on 22 October at the Aviva, which the hosts won 27-13. Round 7, played against Ulster at Thomond Park on 29 October, ended in a narrow win for the visitors, 15-14.

A transformation then occurred, with Munster hitting a winning streak. A bonus-point 24-17 win against Connacht in Thomond Park on 26 November was followed by a 38-17 away victory against Edinburgh on 2 December. Carbery converted all five tries, including one of his own, and added a penalty. Leinster came to Thomond Park on 26 December and beat the hosts 20-19 in a closely fought match.

An excellent 15-14 away win over Ulster at the Kingspan Stadium was next on 1 January 2023, with

Paddy Patterson getting his first try for Munster. He would score again in the next four matches, including against Lions at Musgrave Park, in a 33-3 bonus-point win for the hosts, and away to Benetton on 28 January 2023, in another bonus-point victory for Munster, 40-30 the final score. On 17 February in Thomond Park, Munster crushed Ospreys 58-3 with an emphatic nine-try haul, Gavin Coombes with a hat trick. The other try-scorers were Malakai Fekitoa, Antoine Frisch, Carbery, Patterson, Zebo and Shane Daly. Munster went on the rampage against Scarlets at Musgrave Park on 3 March, with a a 49-42 win. To their credit, Scarlets scored six tries, which must have been of some concern to the Munster coaching team.

The wheels came off temporarily when Glasgow won in the round 16 match played at Thomond Park on 25 March on a scoreline of 38-26. Munster travelled to South Africa for rounds 17 and 18 with a large contingent of supporters. At DHL Stadium in Cape Town on 15 April, Munster had a bonus-point 26-24 victory over Stormers with a brace of tries from Diarmuid Barron and one each from Shane Daly and Coombes. The following week, in Durban, on the night Andrew Conway earned his 200th cap for Munster, a 22-22 draw against Sharks led to the tough prospect of facing Glasgow Warriors away in the quarter-final on 6 May. However, tries from Malakai Fekitoa and Antoine Frisch, both converted by Jack Crowley, saw Munster win 14-5 at Scotstoun.

Could it get any harder than facing Leinster in Aviva Stadium for the semi-final? The men in blue were leading 15-13 in the 77th minute when man of the match Jack Crowley landed a drop goal, which he celebrated with ROG-style wag of the finger.

Munster now had to travel to Cape Town for the final against Stormers, on 27 May. Would the Stormers be ready for the Red Army this time? In a close encounter in front of 56,100 supporters at the DHL Stadium, Manie Libbok gave the home team an early lead with a try in the fifth minute, which he also converted. Munster struck back with a Diarmuid Barron try four minutes later and Calvin Nash's try pushed the visitors further ahead in the second quarter. Early in the second half, Stormers went ahead again, 14-12, with a try by Deon Fourie, which Libbok converted. The next 24 minutes were scoreless until, in the 74th minute, John Hodnett crossed the whitewash for a try, converted by Crowley, to give a 19-14 victory. Hodnett was awarded man of the match. The twelve-year drought was over, and Munster finally had silverware again. The returning heroes were given a euphoric homecoming by ecstatic supporters at Thomond Park.

EUROPEAN CHAMPIONS CUP

French club Toulouse came to Thomond Park on 11 December 2022. In foggy conditions, Munster took the lead with an early try from Carbery, which he also converted. In spite of a yellow card for Antoine Dupont in the final minutes, Toulouse won 18-13.

A huge defensive effort was required against Northampton Saints away on 18 December. Gavin Coombes opened the scoring early, converted by Carbery. Saints hit back with two penalties, but Coombes crossed for his second try before half-time, again converted by Carbery. In spite of three Munster yellow cards in the second half, they secured the victory 17-6. In the reverse fixture on 14 January 2023 at Thomond Park, Munster stormed ahead with two tries by Coombes and one by Jack O'Donoghue, all converted by Carbery, who added a penalty. O'Donoghue was red-carded in the second quarter, but Munster clung on for a 24-0 half-time lead. Saints capitalised on the man advantage, scoring twenty unanswered points in the second half, before Jack Crowley scored a penalty, and Munster scraped the win 27-23.

On 22 January in Stade Ernest-Wallon, Toulouse raced into an 11-0 lead before Hodnett scored an unconverted try in the 30th minute. A penalty from Carbery closed the gap to 11-8 at half-time. A superb team try early in the second half gave Munster a slender 13-11 lead. However, three penalties from Toulouse full-back Melvyn Jaminet secured a 20-16 win for the home team. Munster reached the last sixteen to face to Sharks on 1 April in Hollywoodbets Kings Park. Tries from Shane Daly, Dave Kilcoyne, Diarmuid Barron, Mike Haley and Fineen Wycherley, all of which Crowley converted, were not enough: Munster fell, 50-35.

Below: Jeremy Loughman scores Munster's third try of the night against the Bulls in Munster's 31-17 home victory.
Opposite top: Joey Carbery passes to Jack Crowley against the Bulls. Carbery had a perfect night, converting all four tries and adding a penalty.
Opposite bottom: Tom Ahern breaks the first tackle against the Bulls and is faced by two more defenders.

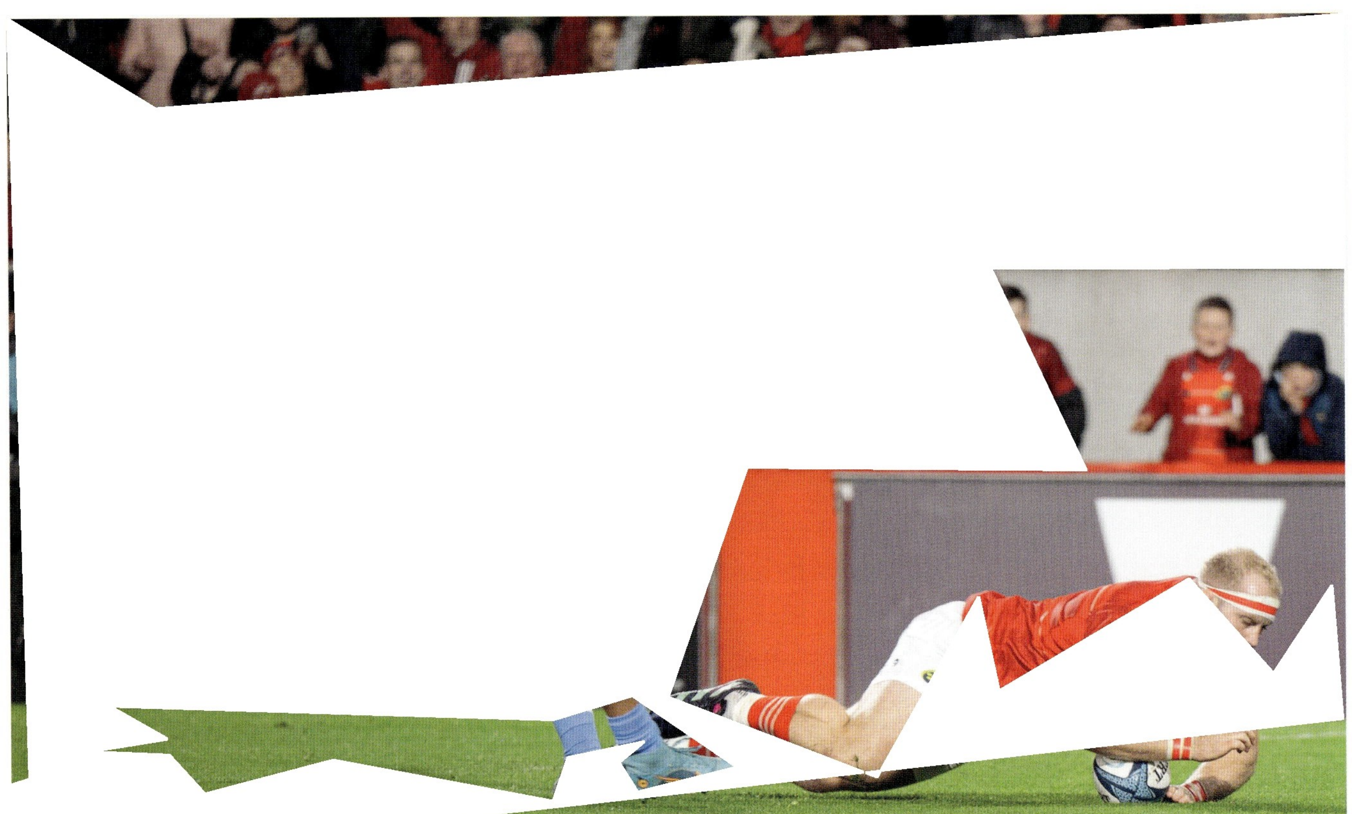

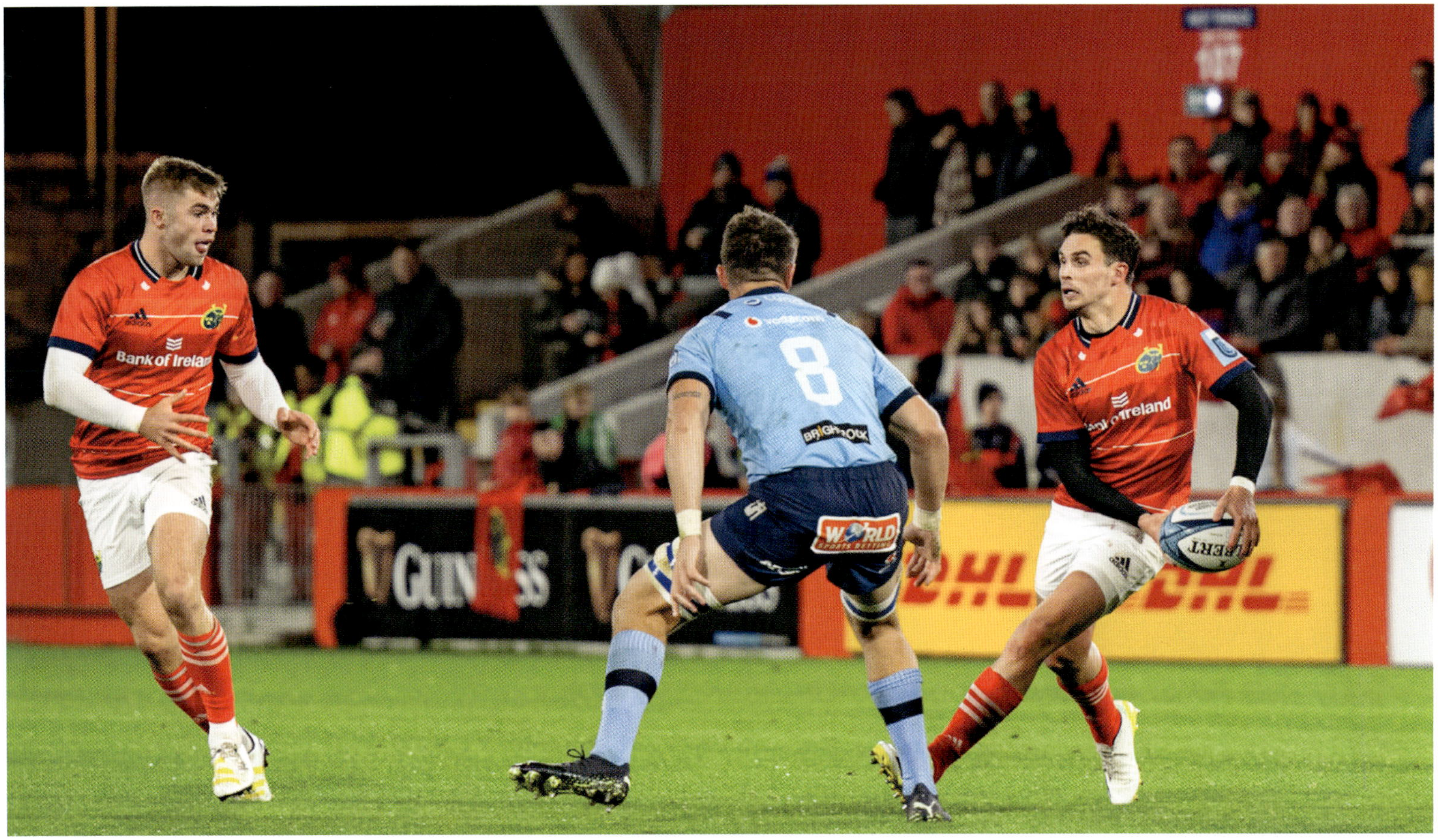
Bank of Ireland
8
BRIGHTROCK

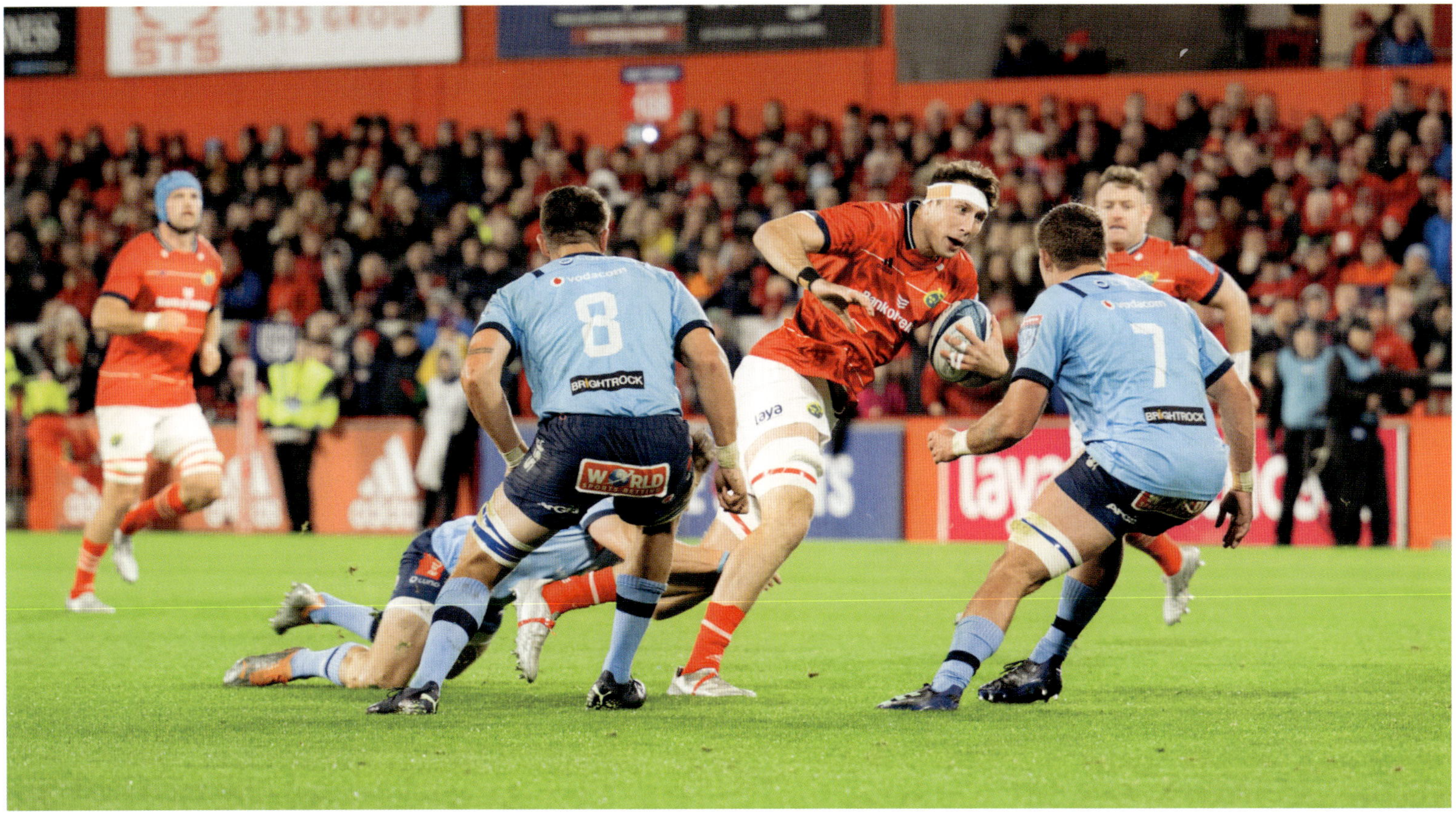
STS
STS GROUP
8
BRIGHTROCK
7
laya

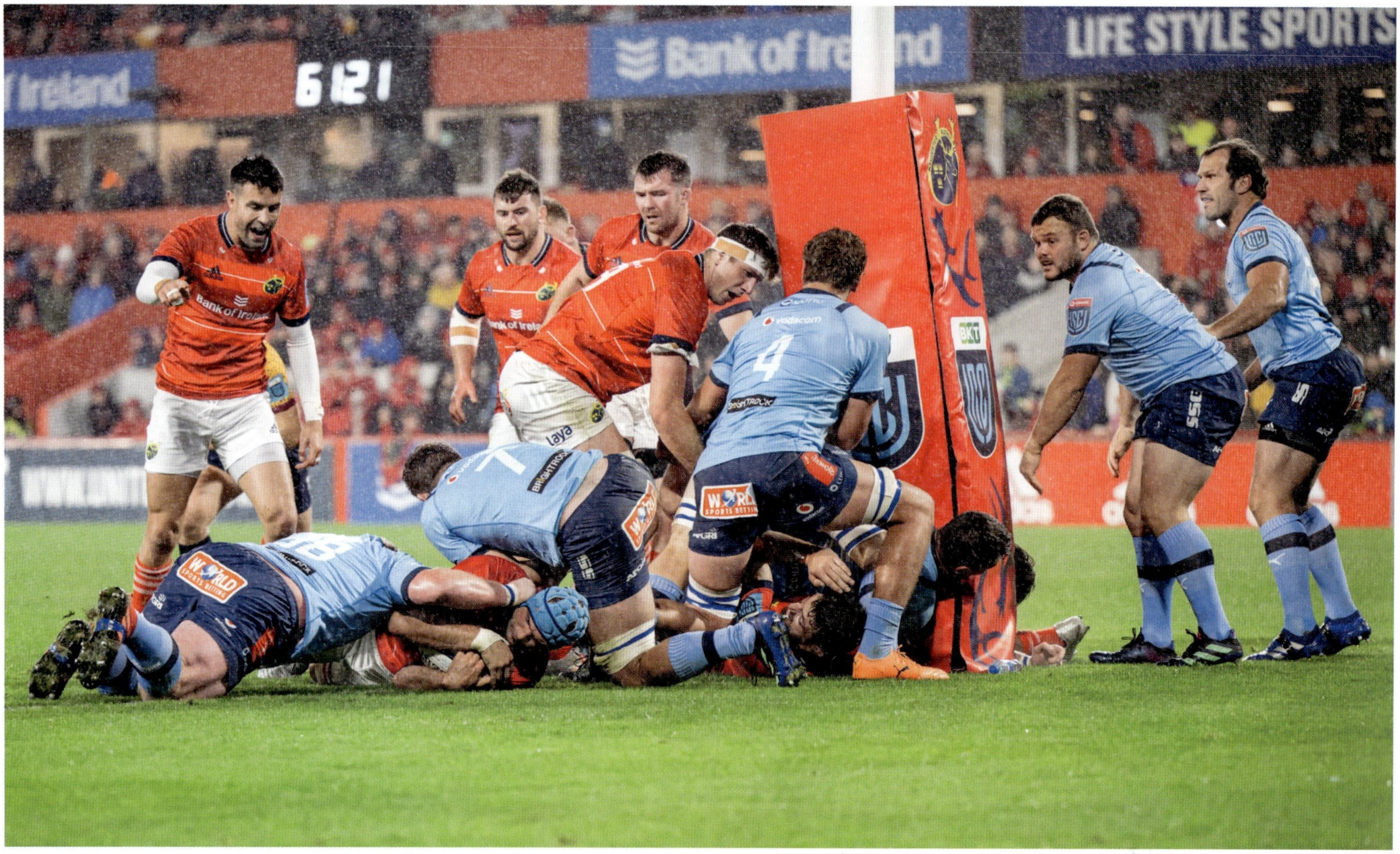

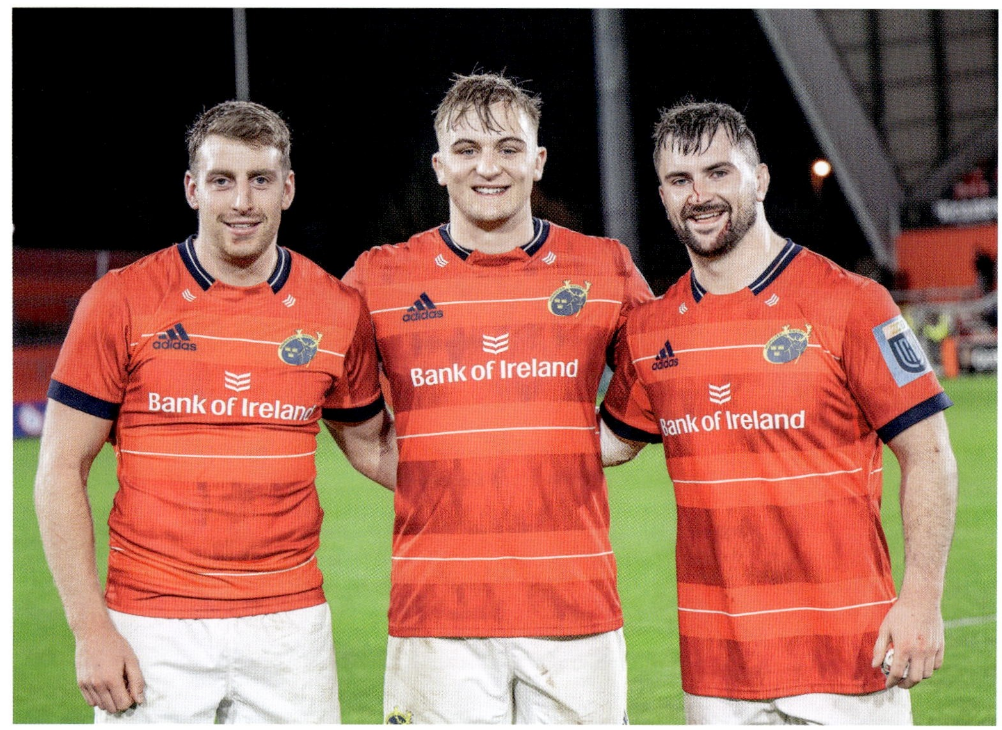

15 October 2022

Top: A try for Tadhg Beirne after a sweet behind-his-back pass from Conor Murray brings Munster the bonus point as the rain pours down.

Bottom: Celebrating the win: (l–r) cousins Liam Coombes and Gavin Coombes with Jack Hodnett after the Bulls match.

Top: Malakai Fekitoa battles for the ball against Ulster in a match that Munster lose agonisingly by a point, their first home defeat of the season.

Bottom: Left wing Patrick Campbell attempts to break the tackle of Ulster's Ben Moxham.

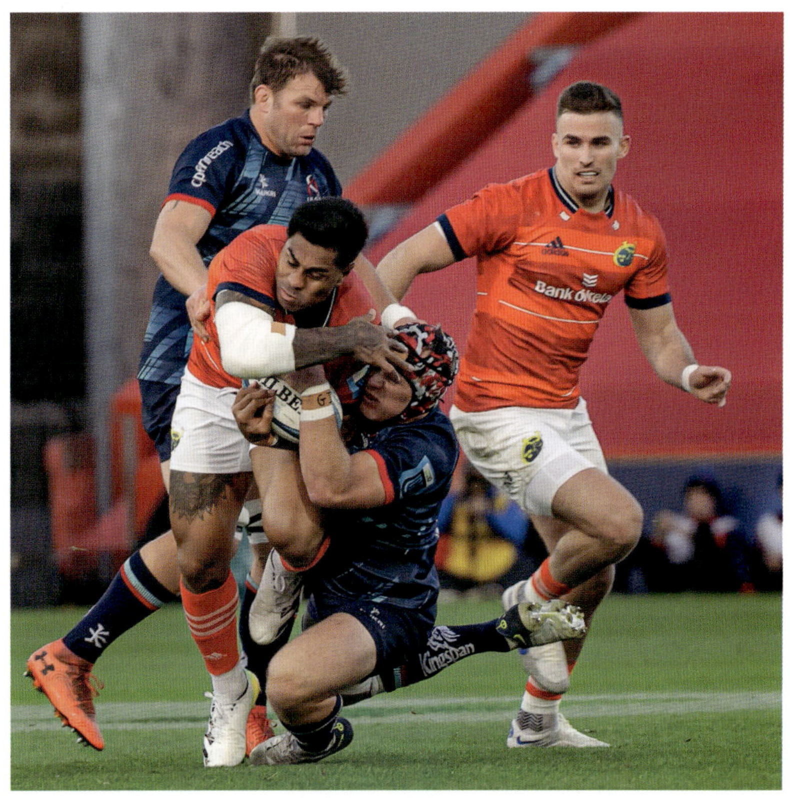

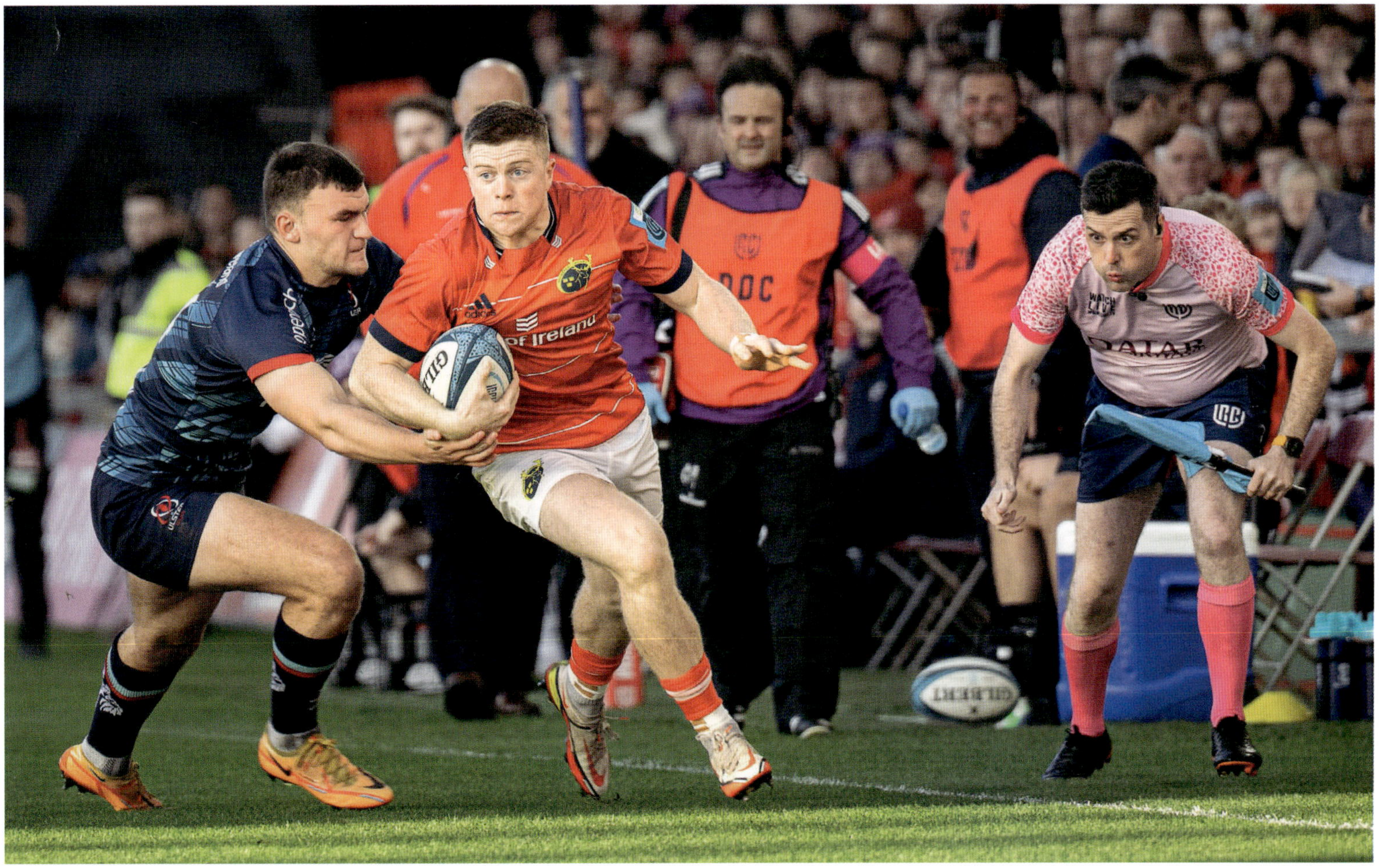

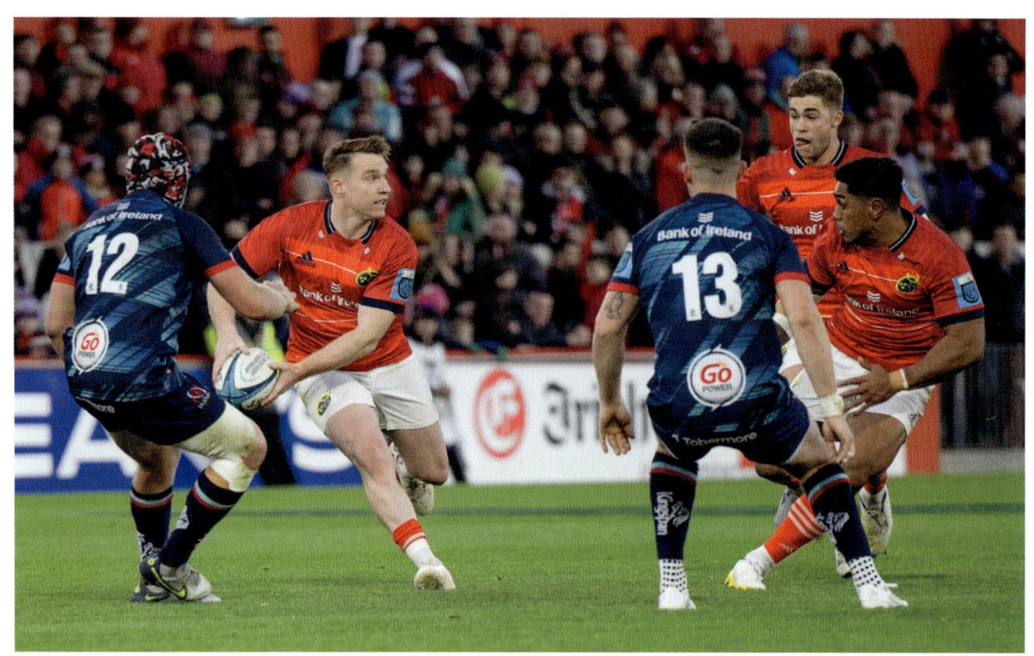

29 October 2022

Top: Rory Scannell prepares to pass to Malakai Fekitoa, with Jack Crowley in support. (L–r): Ulster's Luke Marshall and James Hume prepare to pounce.

Bottom: Diarmuid Barron finds a gap between Ulster's Sam Carter (far left) and James Hume (far right) with Jack Crowley in support.

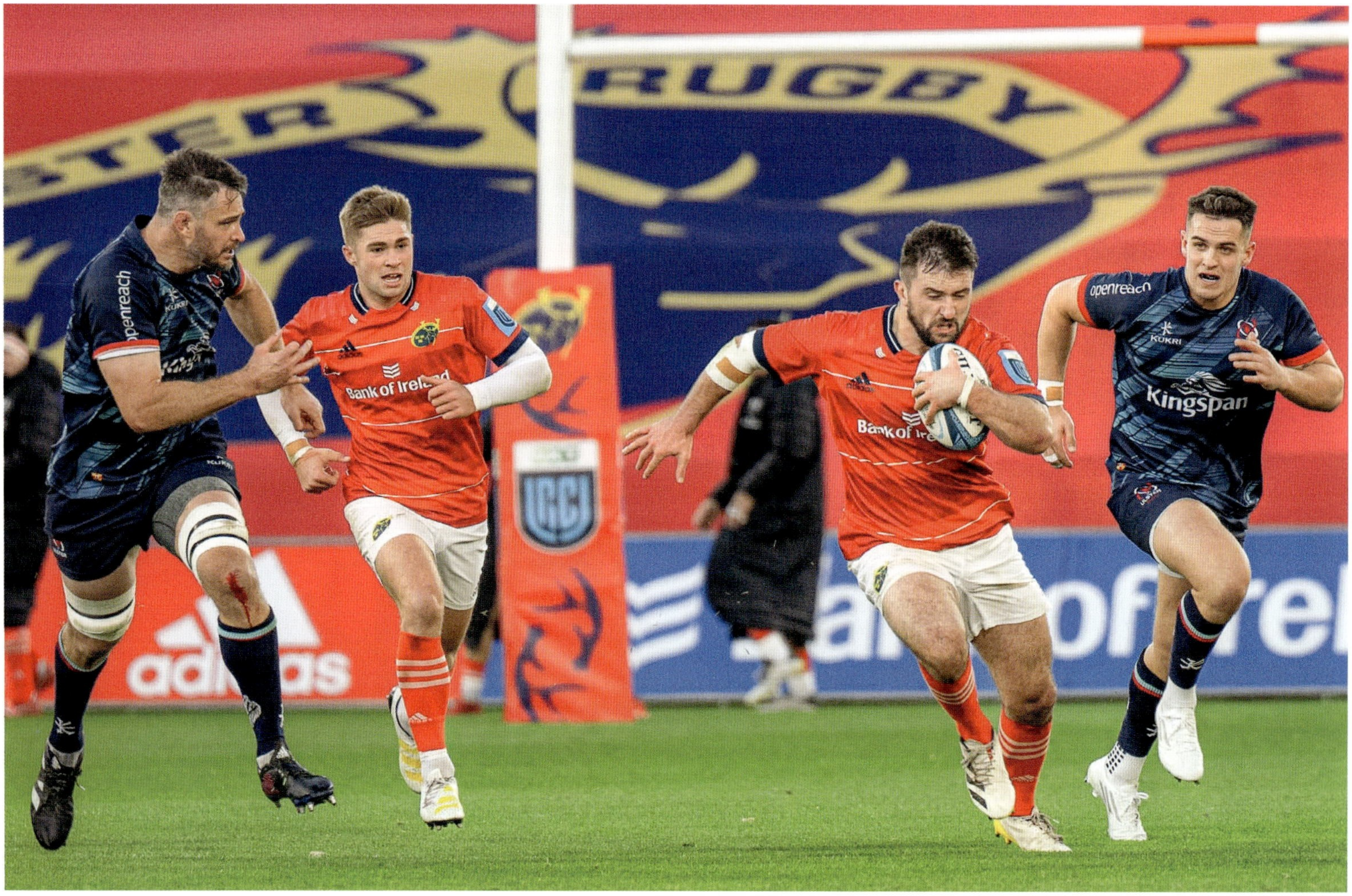

Right: John Ryan and Finlay Bealham exchange goodwill after Munster's 24-17 win over Connacht.

Below: Joey Carbery tackles in the fog against Toulouse, who go on to defeat the home team 18-13. Munster at least earn a losing bonus point.

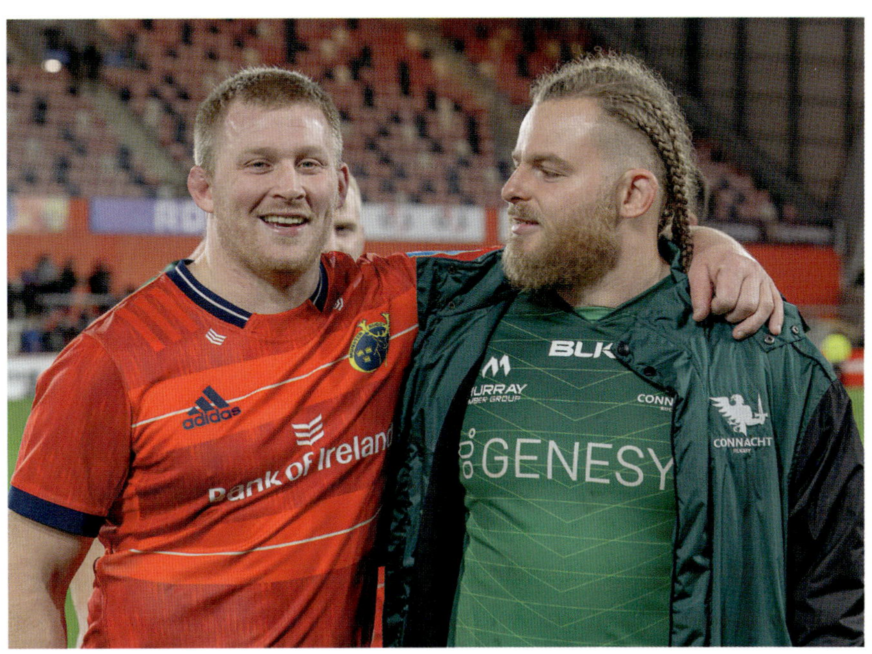

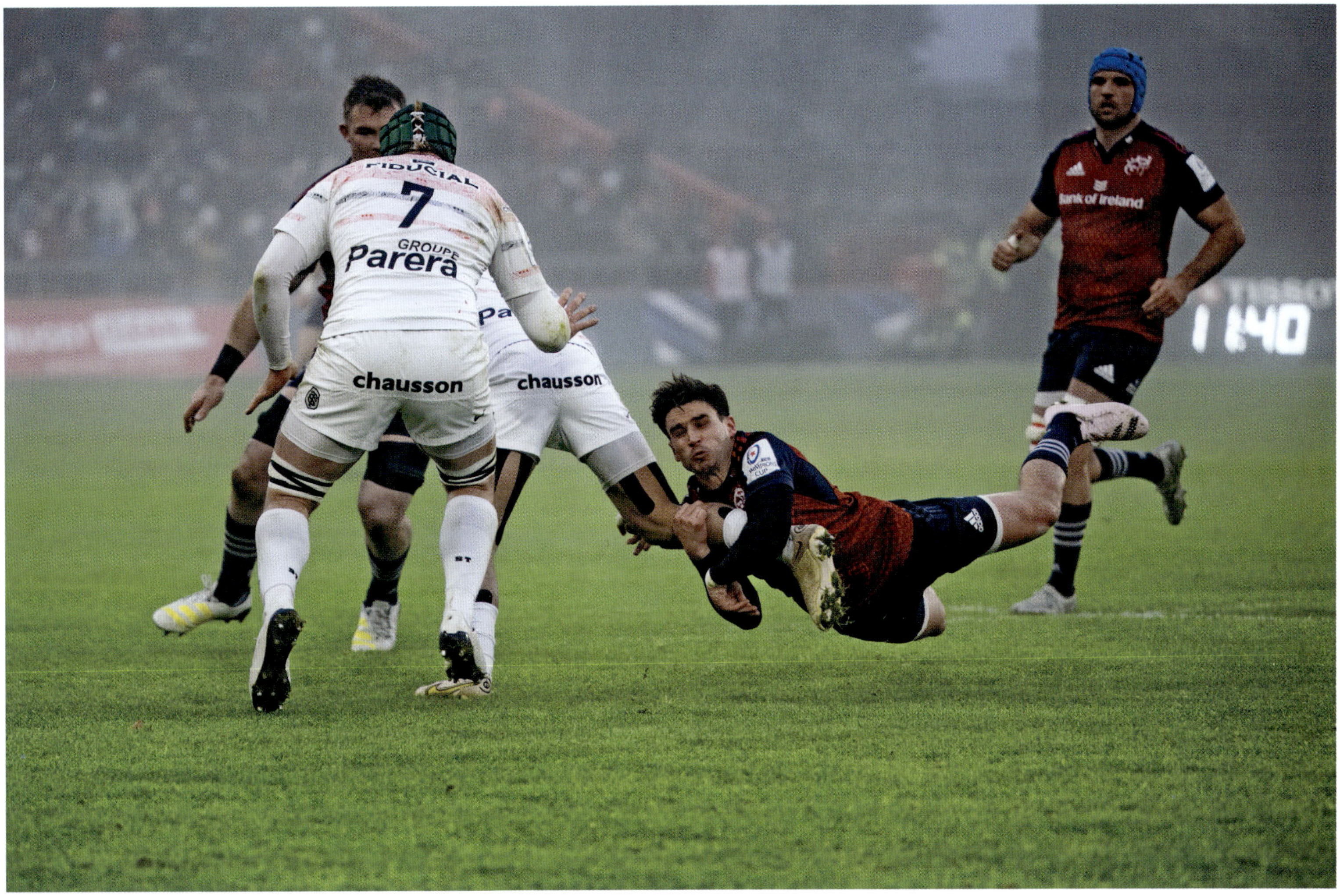

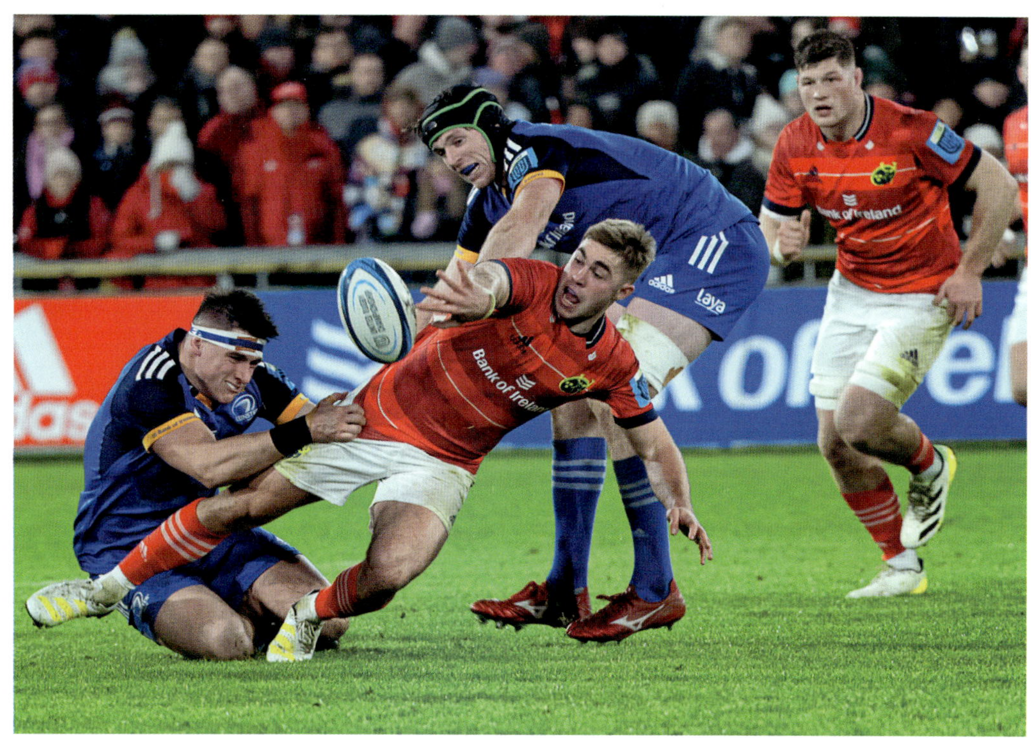

26 December 2022

Left: Watched by Jack O'Donoghue (far right), Jack Crowley passes the ball despite the best efforts of Leinster's formidable hooker Dan Sheehan and Ryan Baird (with skullcap). In spite of leading 14–6 early in the second half, Munster lose by a point in front of a capacity crowd of 25,600.

Below: Shane Daly gathers the high ball.

Opposite top: Referee Chris Busby looks on as the scrum sets. The steam reflects the chill of the night and the heat of the action.

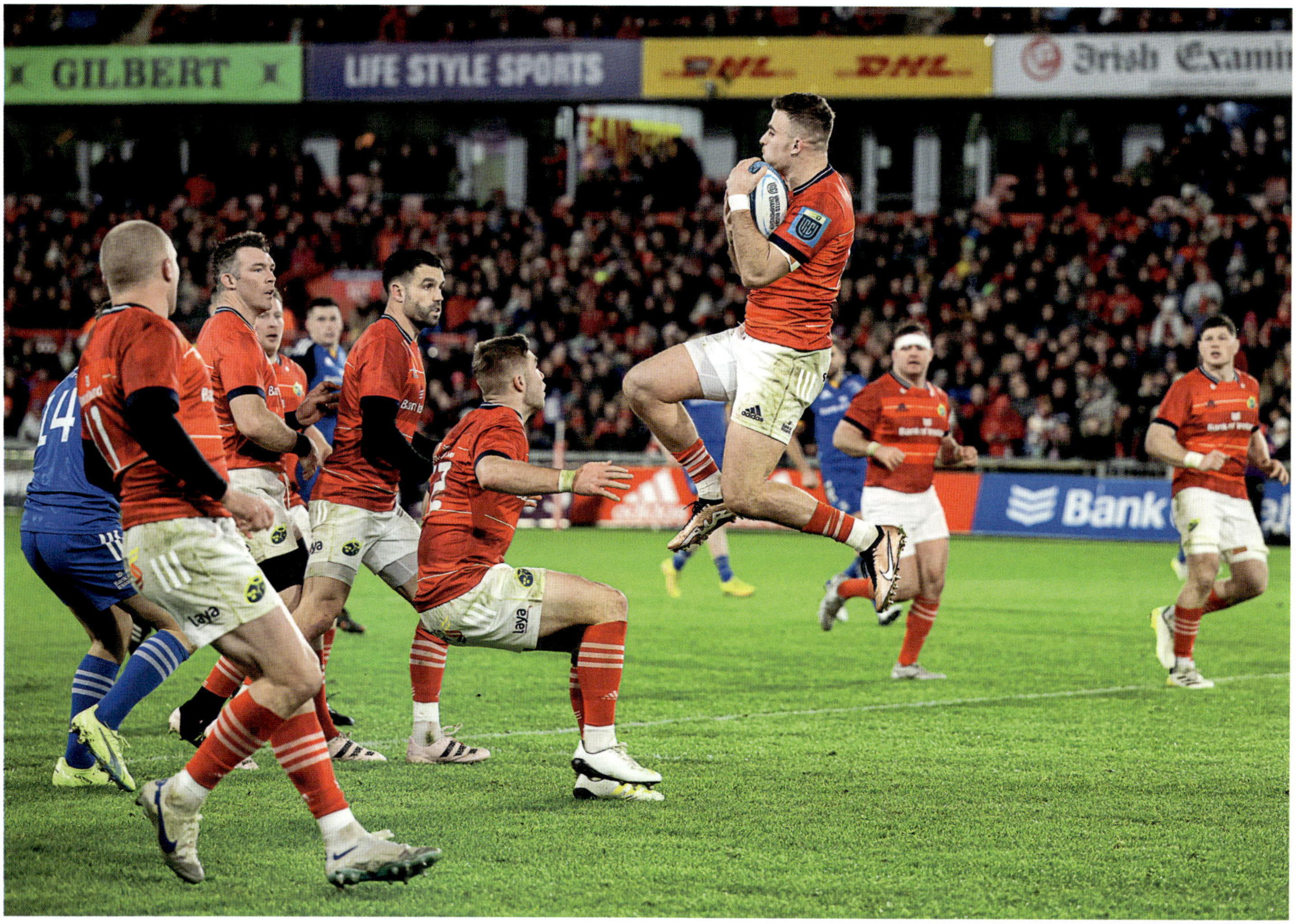

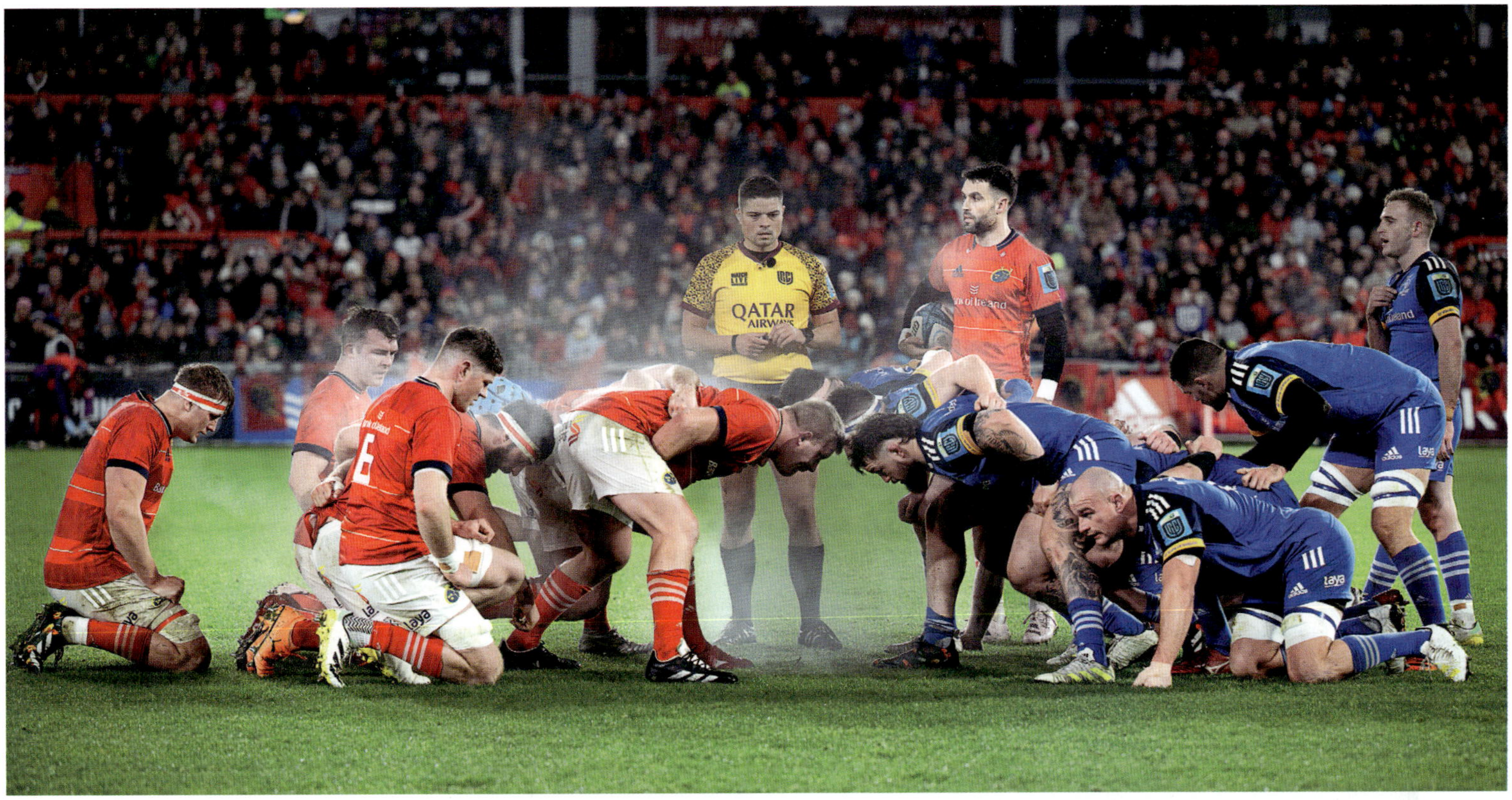

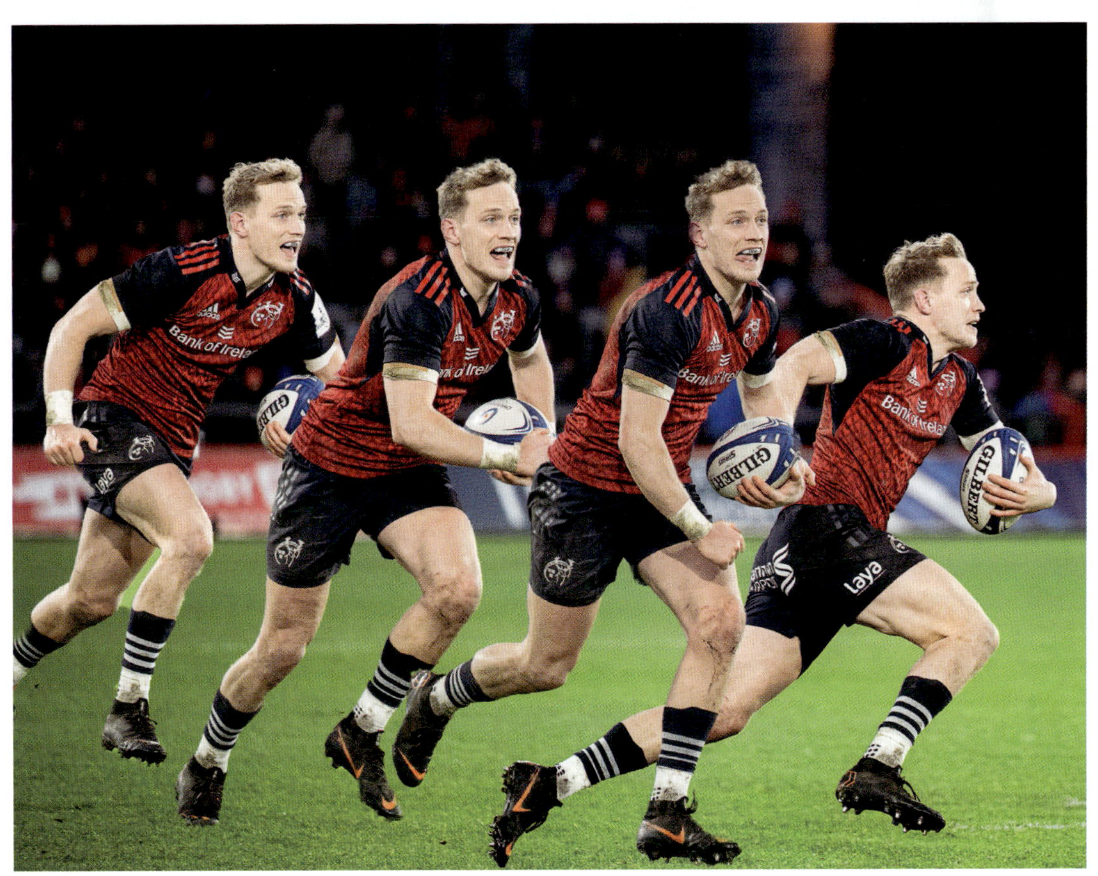

14 January 2023

Mike Haley in action against Northampton Saints. In spite of being down to fourteen men, Munster led by 24 unanswered points at half-time. Saints piled on the pressure in the second half and came to within four points, but a penalty in the 75th minute, ably taken by Jack Crowley, saw the home team win 27–23.

(Photo edited by Denis Ryan)

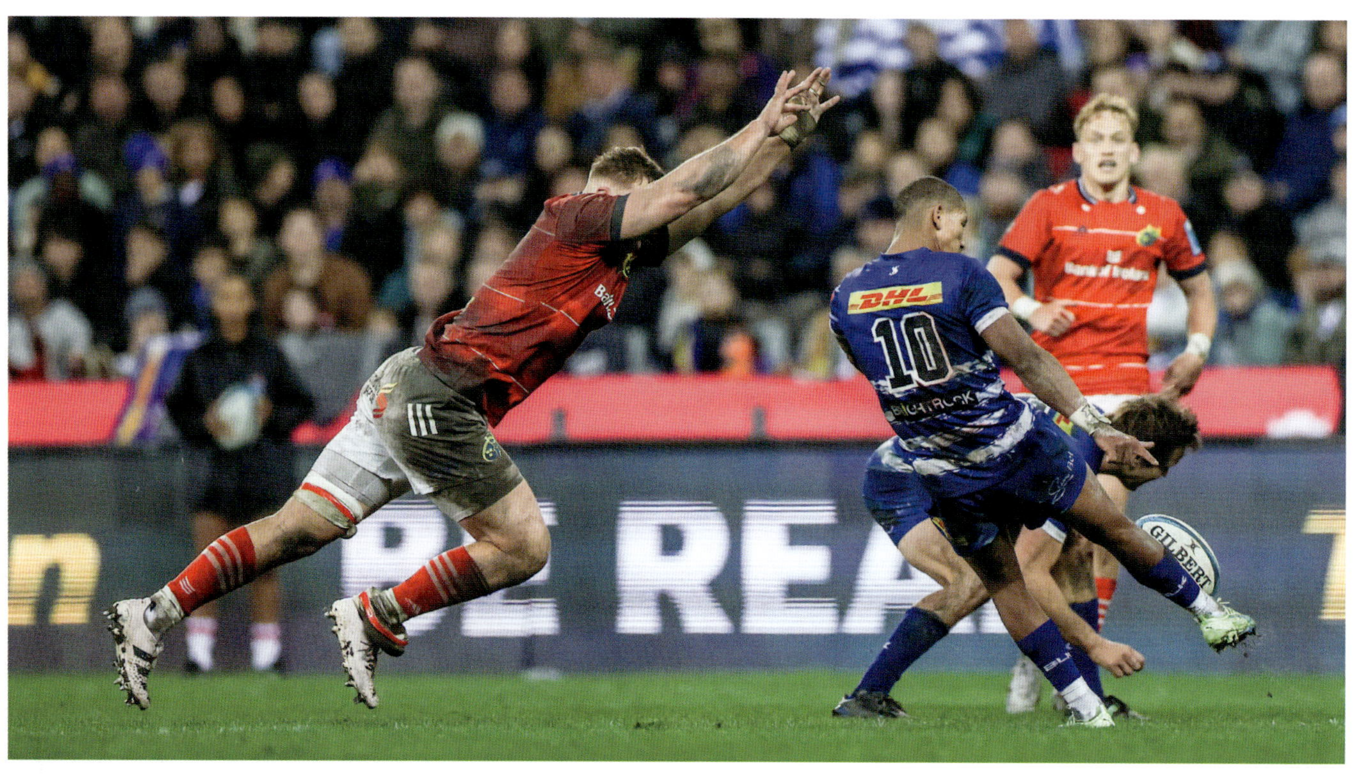

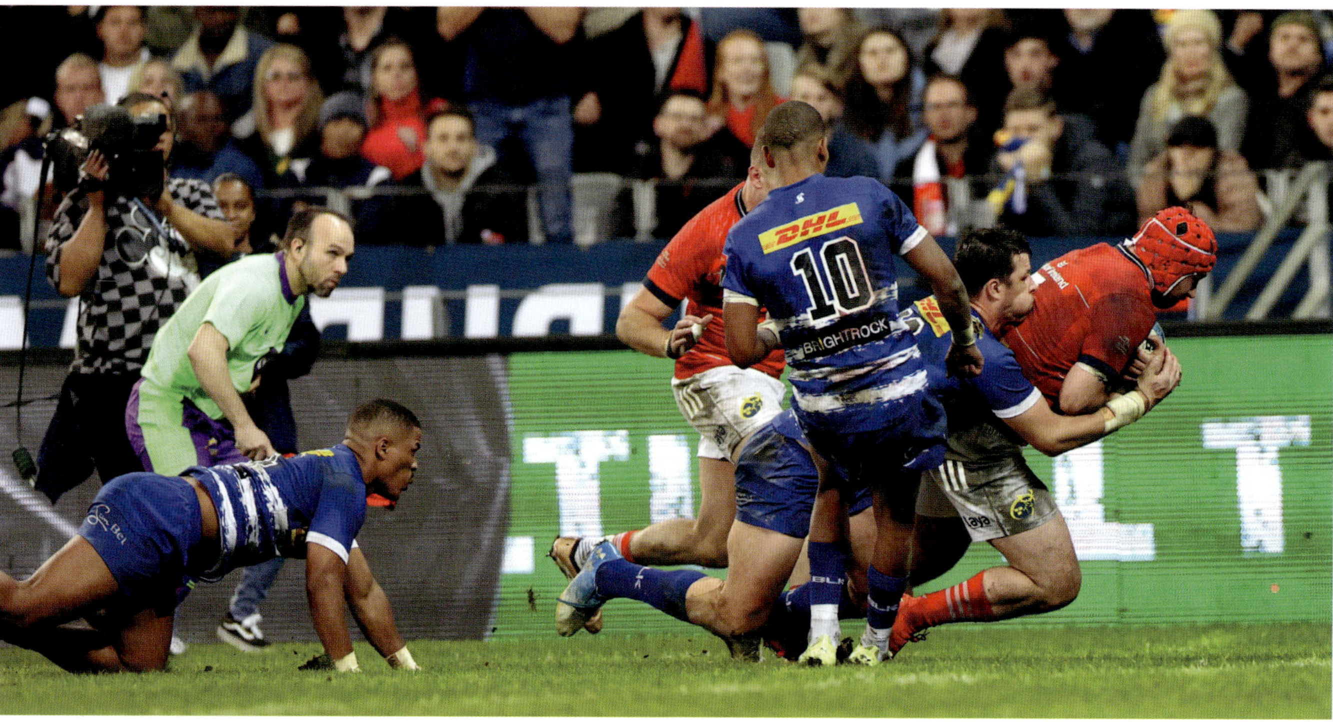

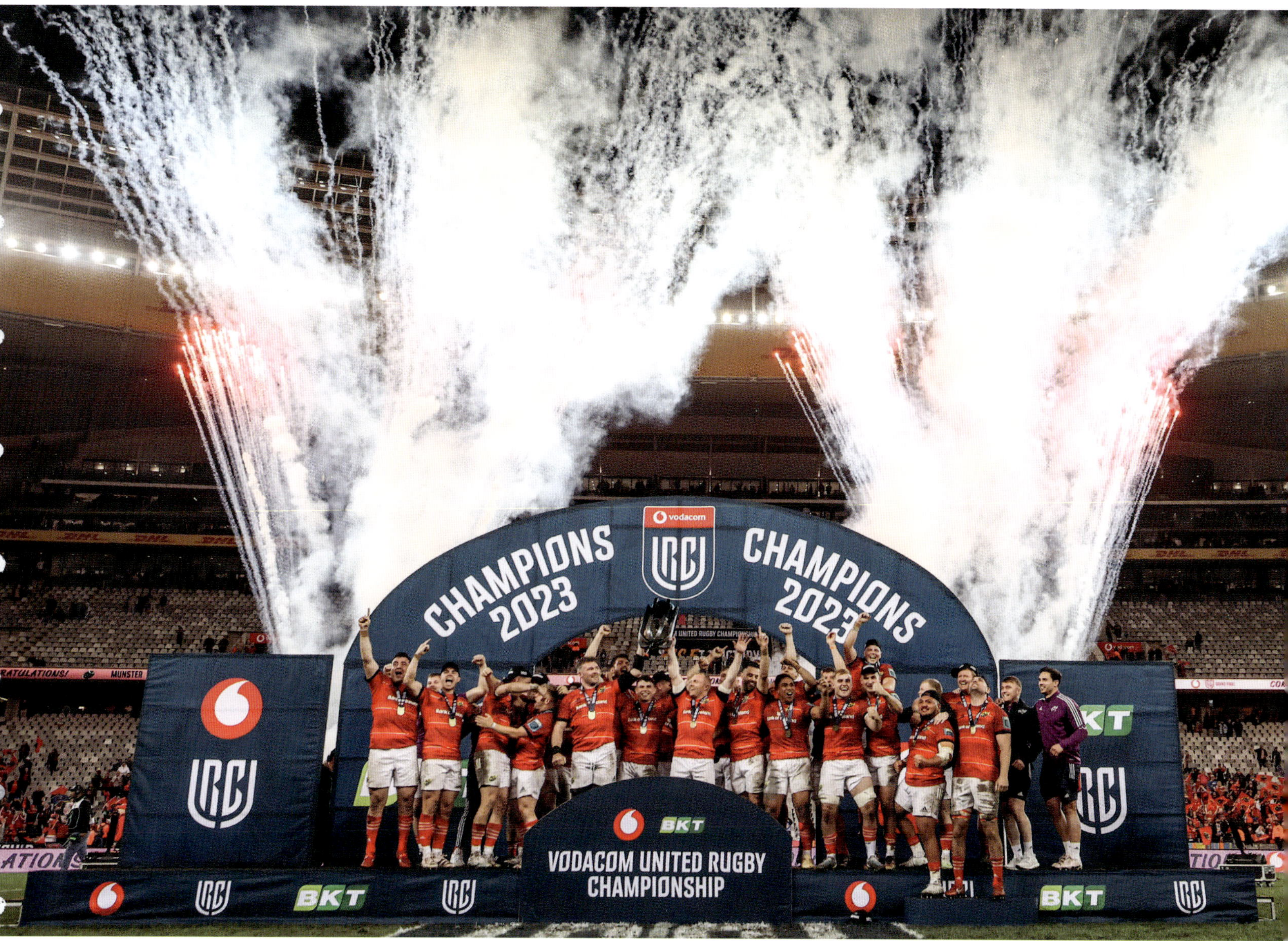

27 May 2023

Opposite top: Gavin Coombes blocks Manie Libbok of DHL Stormers.

Opposite bottom: John Hodnett's 74th-minute try steals the win and sends Munster fans into ecstasy. A thrilling passage of play saw the ball pass from Craig Casey to Jack Crowley to Mike Haley, who made a superb pass to Shane Daly. Daly made a short pass on the inside to Hodnett, who surged over for the try.

Above: Proud URC Champions 2023.

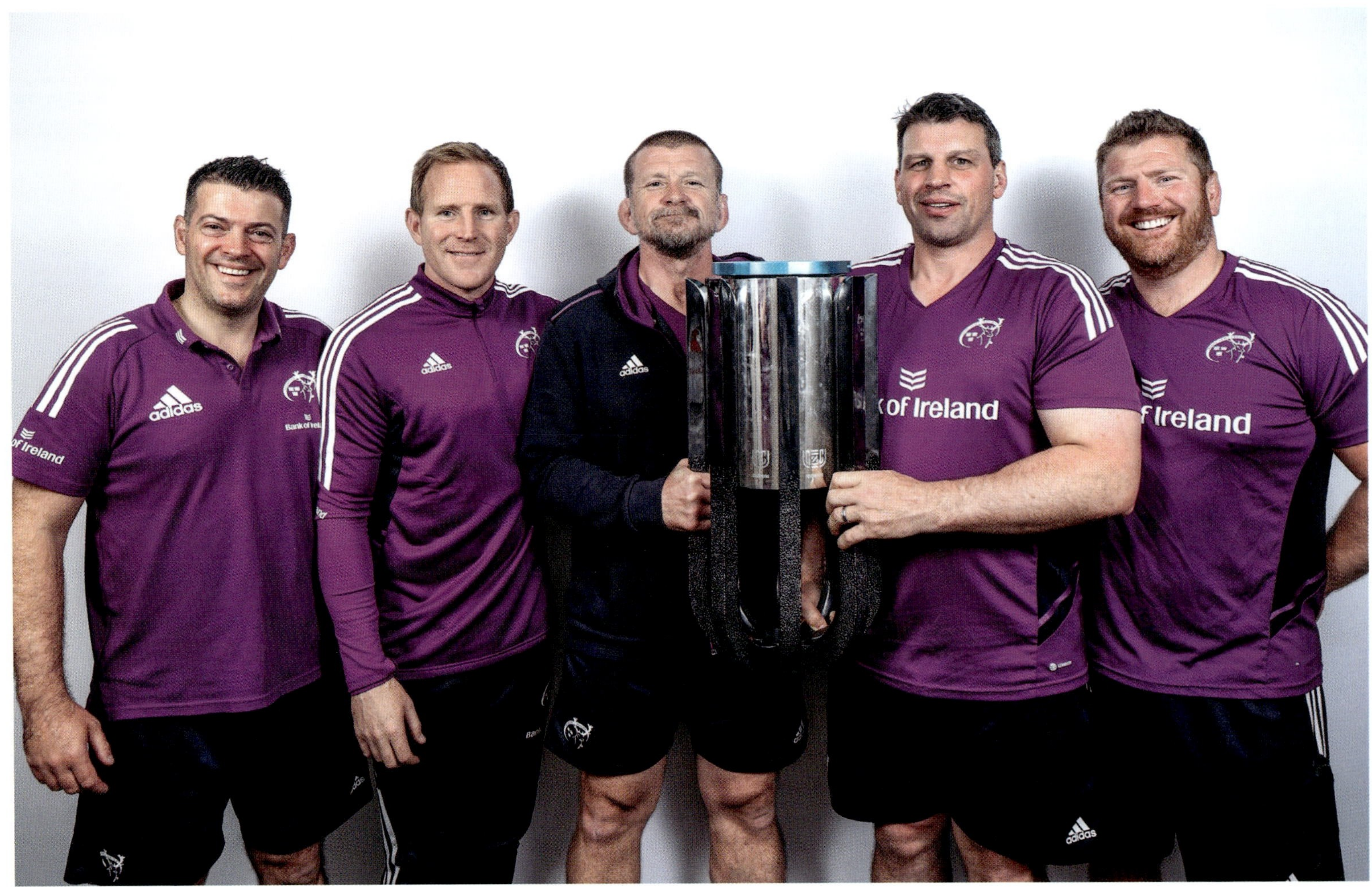

27 May 2023

Victorious Munster coaches holding the URC trophy. (L–r): George Murray, Mike Prendergast, Graham Rowntree, Denis Leamy and Andi Kyriacou.

29 May 2023

Opposite top: Jack O'Donoghue raises the trophy as URC Champions Munster celebrate back at Thomond Park.

Opposite bottom: URC Champions (l–r) Calvin Nash, Keith Earls and Dave Kilcoyne.

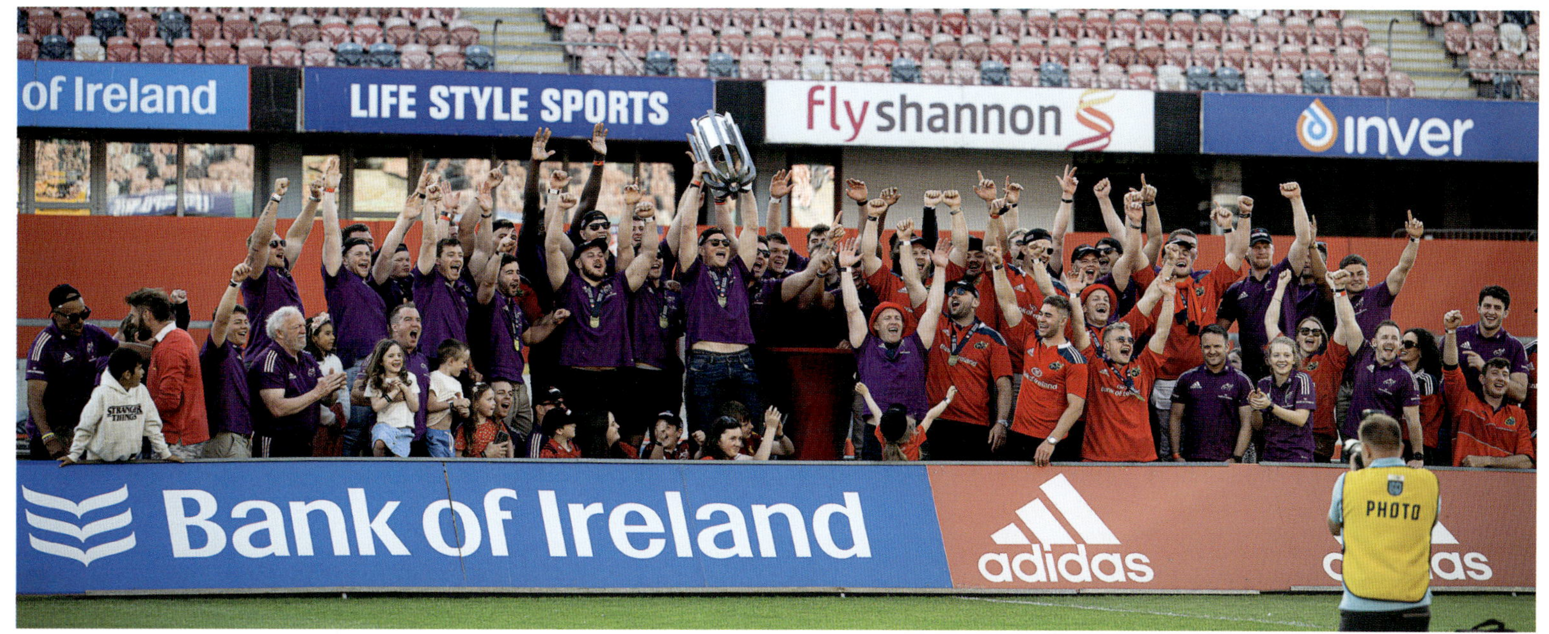

of Ireland
LIFE STYLE SPORTS
fly shannon
inver
Bank of Ireland
adidas
PHOTO

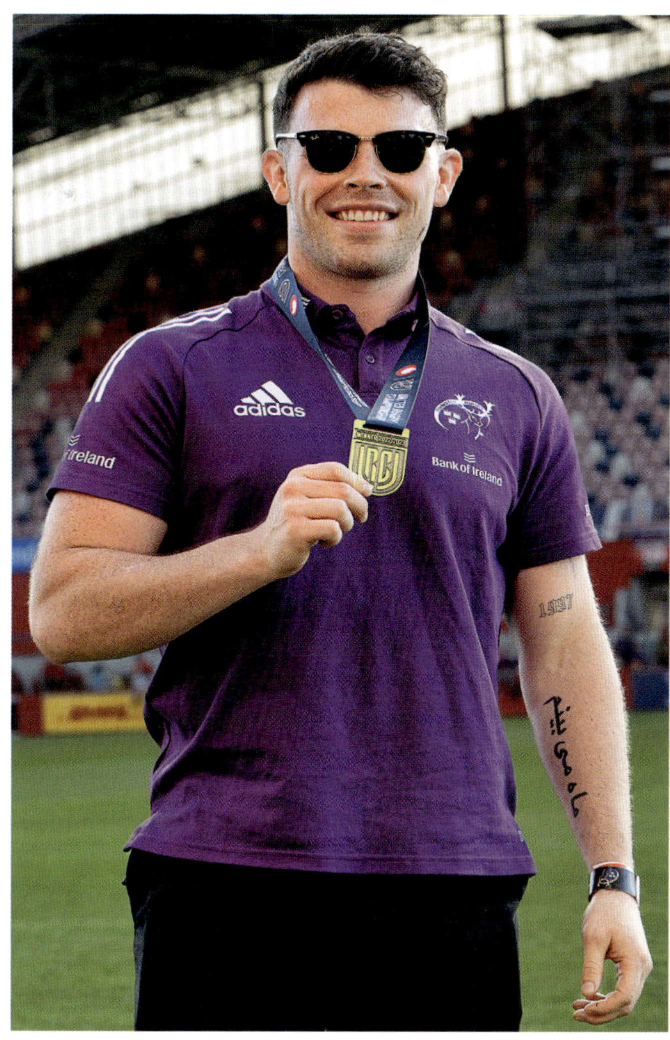

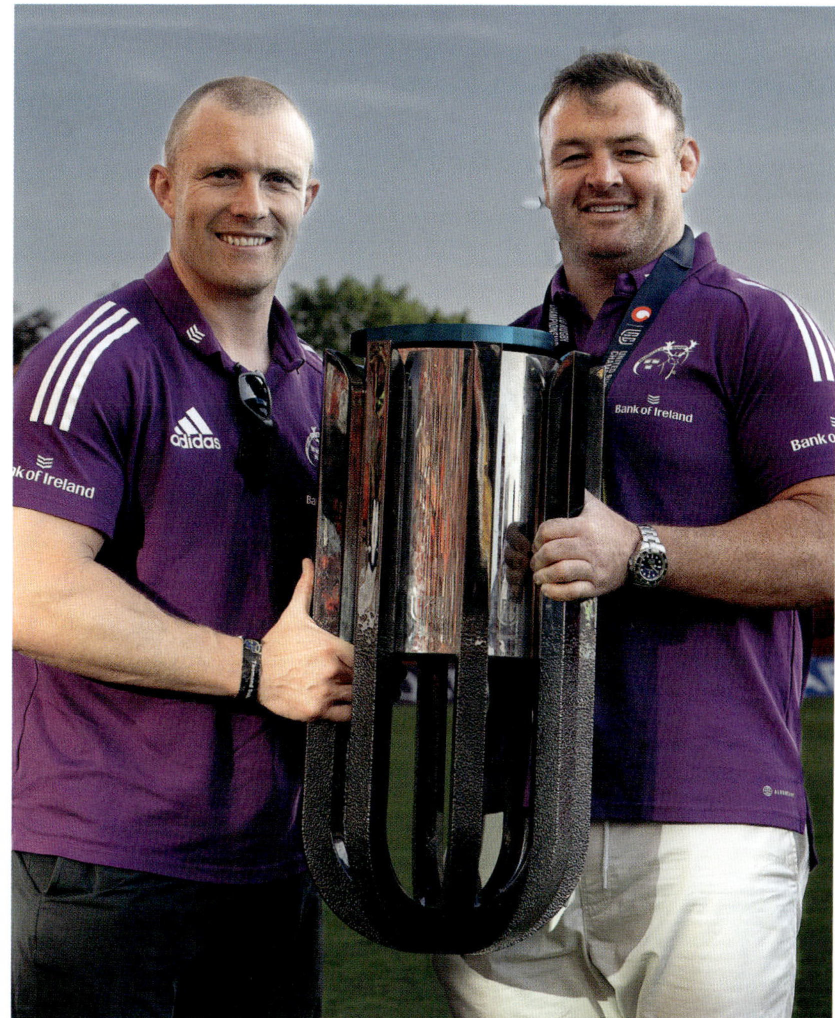

2023–2024

URC   **POOL WINS: 13; POOL LOSSES: 4; POOL DRAWS: 1; ELIMINATED: SEMI-FINAL**
EUROPEAN CHAMPIONS CUP   **POOL WINS: 1; POOL LOSSES: 2; POOL DRAWS: 1; ELIMINATED: ROUND OF 16**

Graham Rowntree's second season as head coach saw Patrick Campbell and Cian Hurley make the step up from the academy. Prop John Ryan rejoined Munster and new signings included Alex Nankivell and Sean O'Brien. Brian Gleeson, Shay McCarthy and Ben O'Connor were among those joining year one of the academy. Lock Paddy Kelly and prop Liam O'Connor were forced to retire, as was Andrew Conway in November owing to a serious knee injury. The great Keith Earls ended his illustrious sixteen years with Munster following the 2023 Rugby World Cup.

Greig Oliver, an elite player development officer with Munster's academy since 2011, tragically died in a paragliding accident in Cape Town on 3 July 2023. Greig was following his son Jack, who was playing with the Ireland under-20s team in the 2023 World Rugby U20 Championship.

Munster played the Barbarians for the first time in a pre-season friendly at Thomond Park on 30 September, winning an engaging try-fest 52-35. In later friendlies, Munster defeated Crusaders 21-19 in front of 40,885 supporters at Páirc Uí Chaoimh and beat Harlequins 43-35 at Twickenham Stoop.

URC

Munster suffered an inordinate number of injuries during the season, which weakened the team for long periods, including: Patrick Campbell, Peter O'Mahony, Jean Kleyn, Jack Daly, Liam Coombes, Niall Scannell, RG Snyman, Joey Carbery, Roman Salanoa, Mike Haley, Edwin Edogbo and Dave Kilcoyne.

The season started on 21 October with a 34-21 win over Sharks at Thomond Park. At Stadio Comunale di Monigo against Benetton on 29 October, Munster struggled until the 79th minute, when Tom Ahern dotted down, and Joey Carbery converted, to salvage a 13-13 draw. Against Dragons at Musgrave Park on 4 November, Munster secured a bonus-point 45-14 win. The scoreboard ticked over steadily with tries from Rory Scannell on the thirteenth minute, Gavin Coombes on the seventeenth and Calvin Nash on the 21st. Tom Ahern and Craig Casey scored in the second half and Nash crossed the whitewash for a second time. The tries were all converted, by Tony Butler (four) and Jack Crowley (one).

Munster's first defeat came at Kingspan Stadium on 10 November, which Ulster won 21-14. Stormers – no doubt hunting for revenge for the URC final – gave Munster a close game at Thomond Park on 18 November, but the home team won 10-3 courtesy of a try from Edwin Edogbo, with Jack Crowley adding the conversion and a penalty. At Aviva Stadium on 25 November, old rivals Leinster won 21-16.

Glasgow Warriors came to Musgrave Park on 1 December. Munster had a decisive 40-29 win. Tries came from Edogbo, Ahern, Diarmuid Barron, Alex Nankivell and John Hodnett, with Crowley having a perfect night, converting all five. Next up were Leinster in Thomond Park on a rainy night on 26 December, which the visitors won 9-3. Connacht proved too strong for Munster on 1 January 2024 at the Galway Sportsgrounds, the hosts winning 22-9.

Away to Scarlets on 16 February, Munster had an emphatic 42-7 victory. Coombes (with two), Jack O'Sullivan, Ahern, Sean O'Brien and Shay McCarthy were the try-scorers, with Jack Crowley converting all six. This win started Munster on a run of ten winning matches: Zebre Parma fell at Musgrave Park on 1 March, 45-29; Ospreys lost in Swansea 27-17 on 22 March; Cardiff fought bravely in Thomond Park on 30 March, but went down 20-15 to the hosts. In South Africa, Munster beat Bulls 27-22 on 20 April and tamed the Lions 33-13 a week later. Back at Thomond Park on 11 May, Munster defeated Connacht 47-12 in a seven-try haul, With tries from Snyman, Nash, Nankivell, Conor Murray, Carbery, Ahern and Daly, with Crowley and Carbery converting three apiece. On 17 May, Munster had a close 29-26 win against Edinburgh at the DAM Health Stadium. Next, on 1 June, Munster defeated Ulster 29-24 at Thomond Park in a close match.

The quarter-final was at Thomond Park against Ospreys on 7 June. Munster had a comprehensive 23-7 win, Simon Zebo scoring in the first minute. Glasgow Warriors came to Thomond Park for the semi-final in front of 20,000 fans on 15 June. Munster were very flat on the day and went down 17-10 to the visitors. Thus, the run of ten victories in a row ended in disappointing circumstances.

European Champions Cup

The first match, on 9 December 2023 against Bayonne at Thomond Park, ended in a 17-17 draw. Next, it was away to Exeter Chiefs on 17 December. Although Munster scored four tries through Nash, Ahern, Antoine Frisch and Daly, with Crowley converting two, there was no Christmas present: the Chiefs won 32-24.

Munster travelled to Toulon on 13 January 2024 and defied the odds to win at this difficult venue by 29-18. Nankivell, Zebo, Ahern and Nash all scored and Crowley converted twice.

Back to Thomond Park for round 4 on 20 January: Northampton Saints came from behind to win 26-23. Munster met Saints again in the last sixteen on 7 April at Franklin's Gardens. O'Brien and Haley scored first-half tries, which Crowley converted, but the hosts proved too strong, and the 24-14 loss ended Munster's campaign.

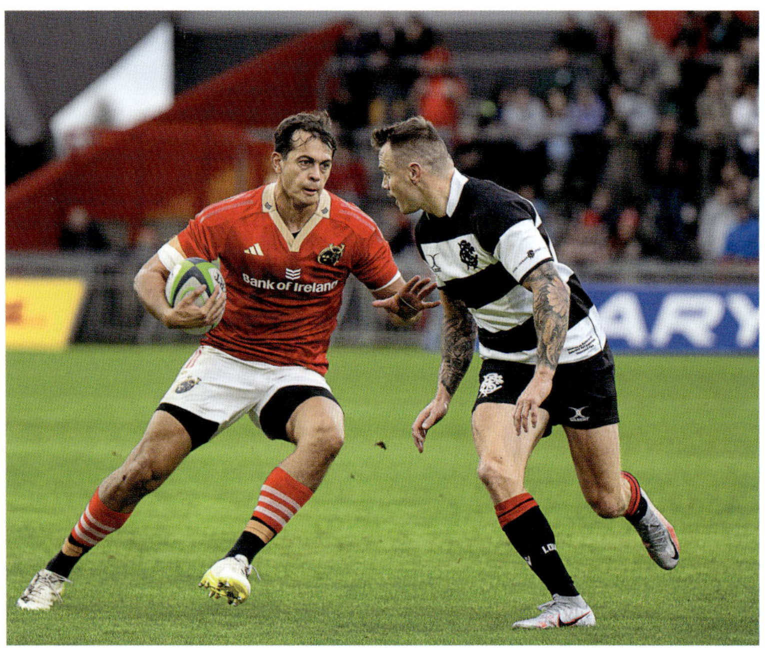

Top: Antoine Frisch in action in a pre-season friendly against the Barbarians. The tries came thick and fast, with Munster winning 52-35.

Bottom: Joey Carbery in determined form.

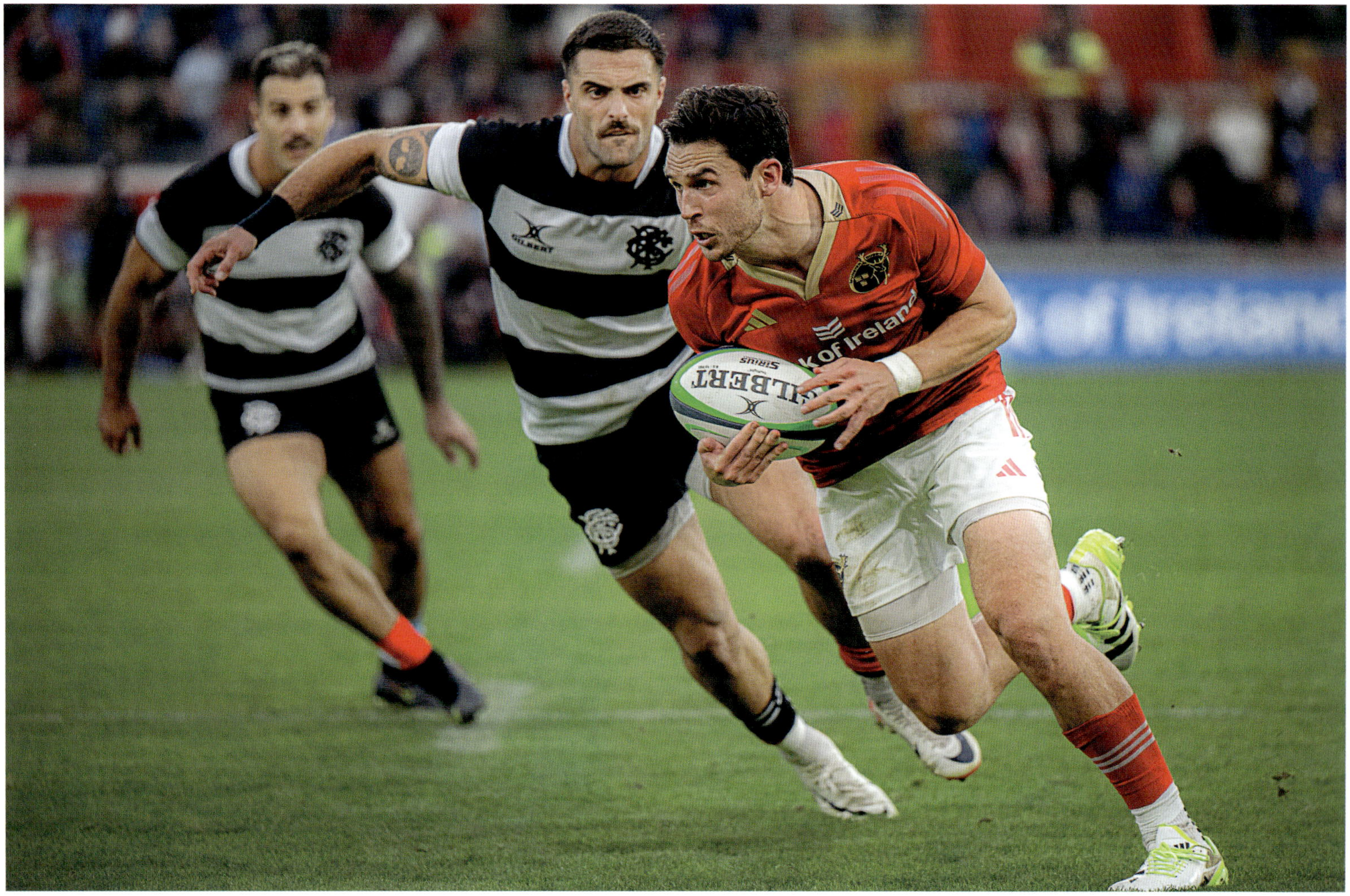

21 October 2023

Edwin Edogbo claims
the line-out against
Hollywoodbets Sharks.
Munster open the URC
season with a 34-21
bonus-point win over
the visitors.

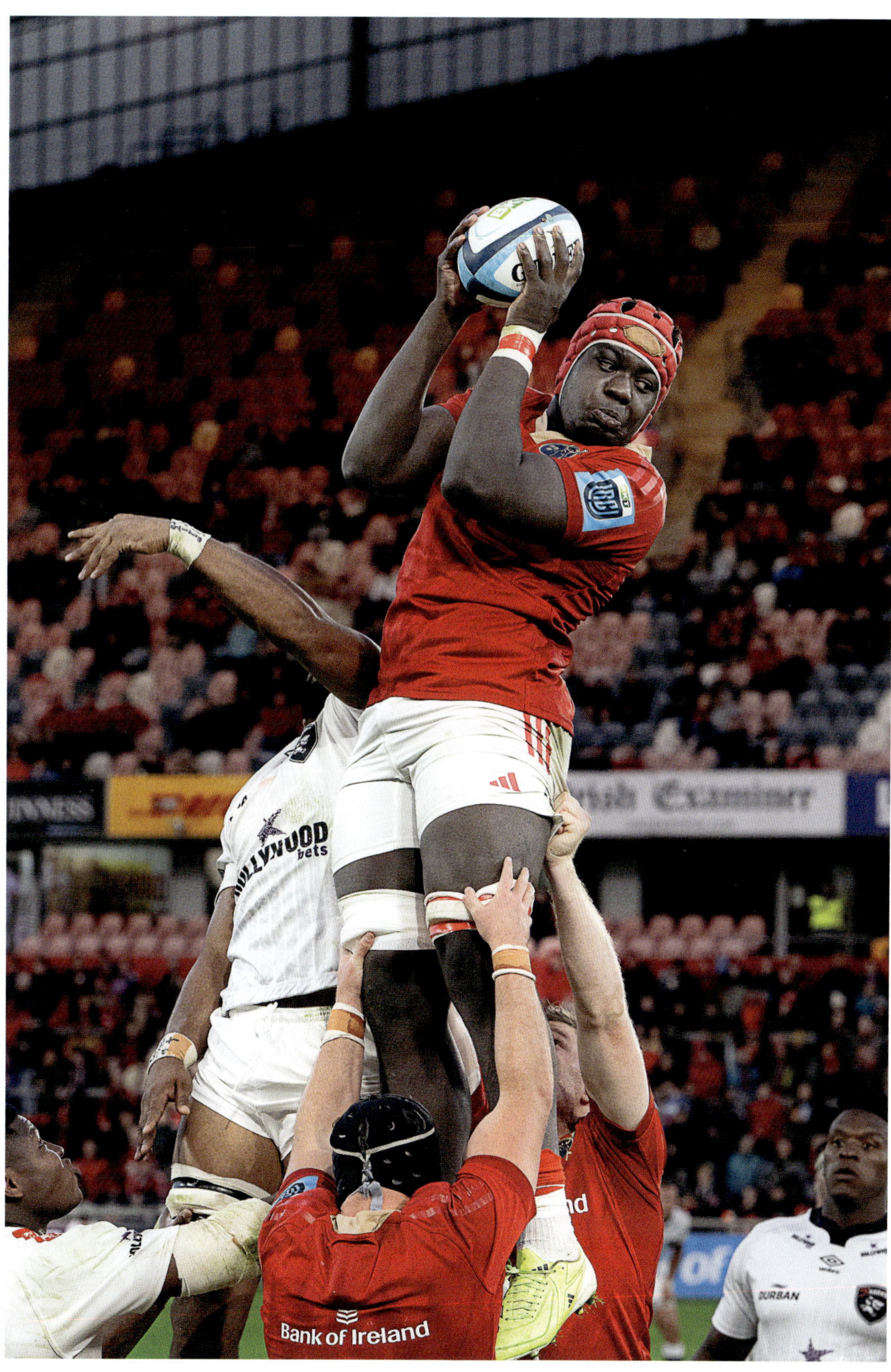

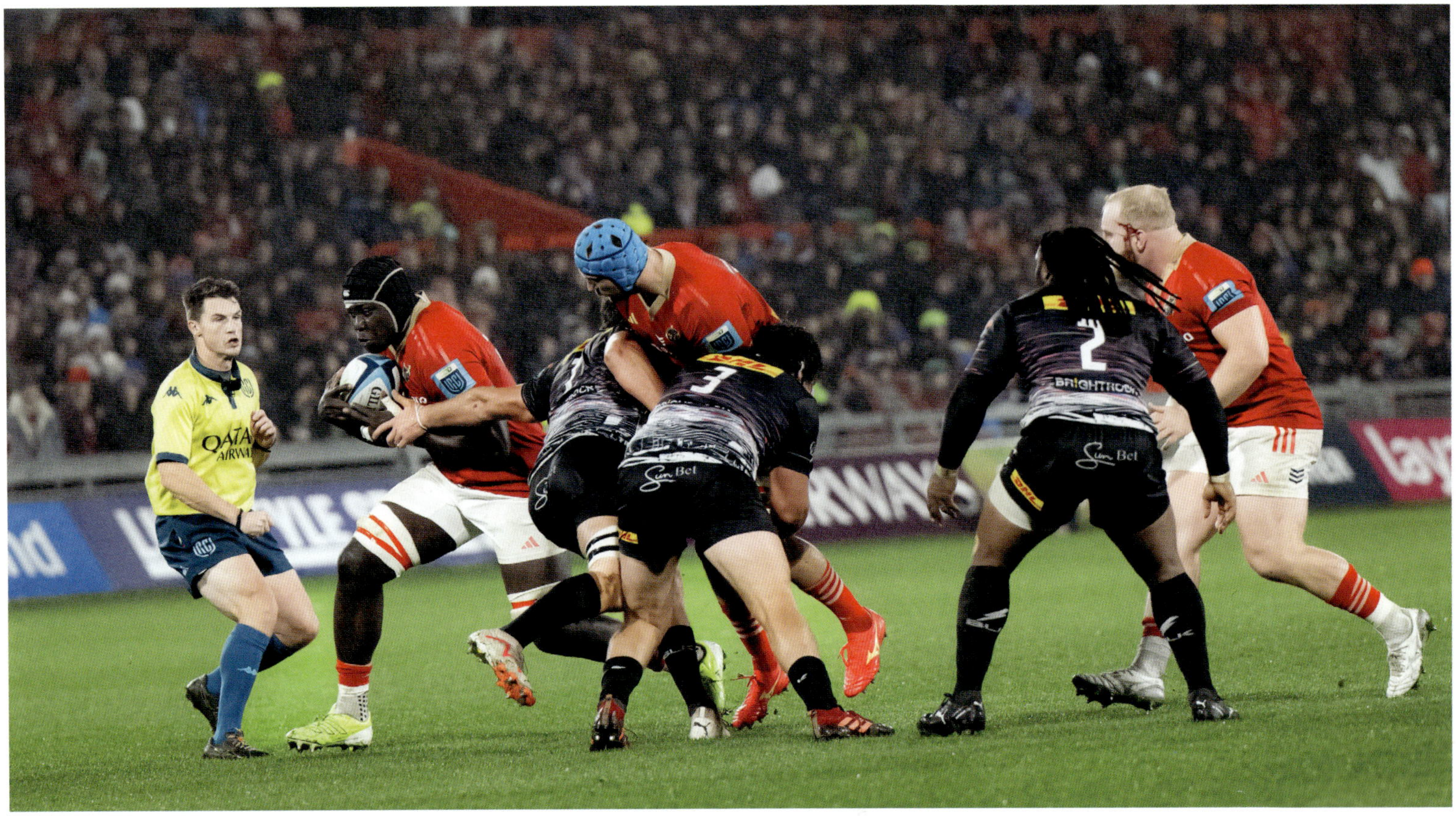

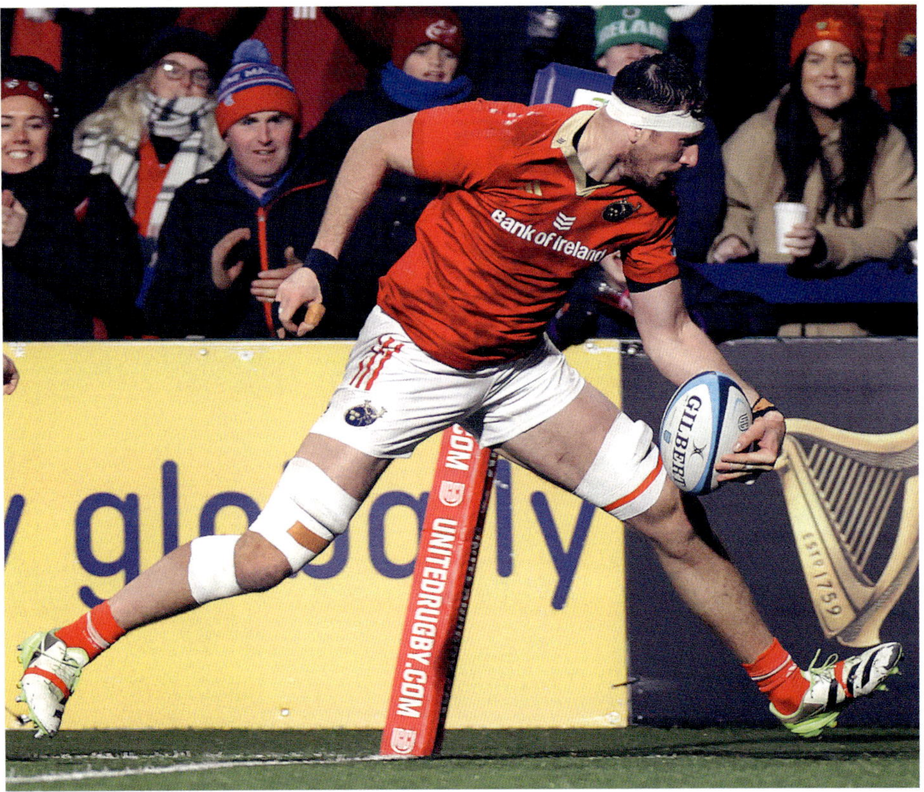

Above: Edwin Edogbo finds the gap against Stormers, supported by Tadhg Beirne and Jeremy Loughman. Munster win 10-3.

1 December 2023

Left: Tom Ahern scores his second try in Munster's barnstorming 40-29 victory over Glasgow Warriors.

13 January 2024

Opposite: Against Toulon in Stade Mayol, Munster's 29-18 victory was their sole Champions Cup win this season. Man of the match Jack Crowley kicks a conversion.

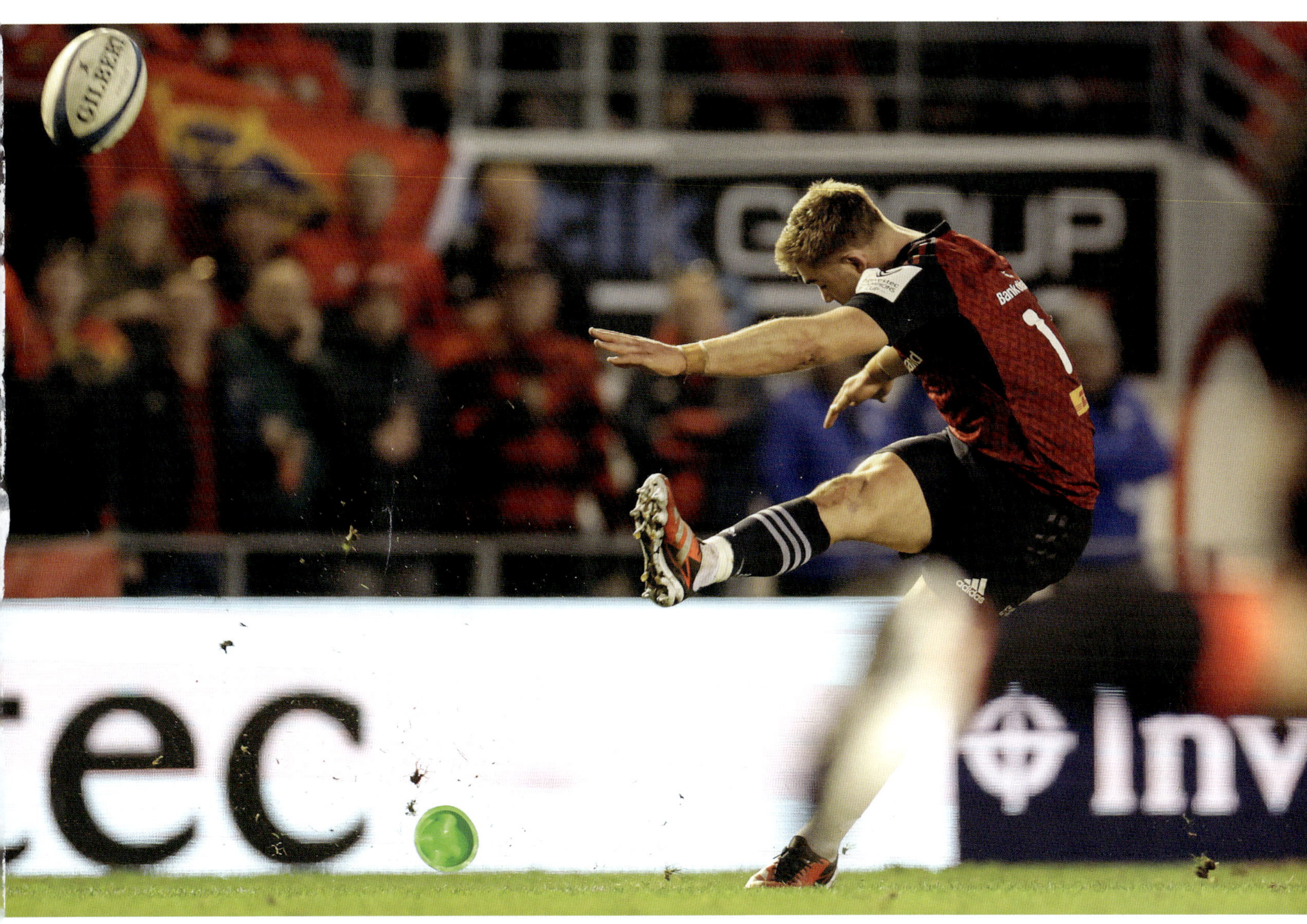

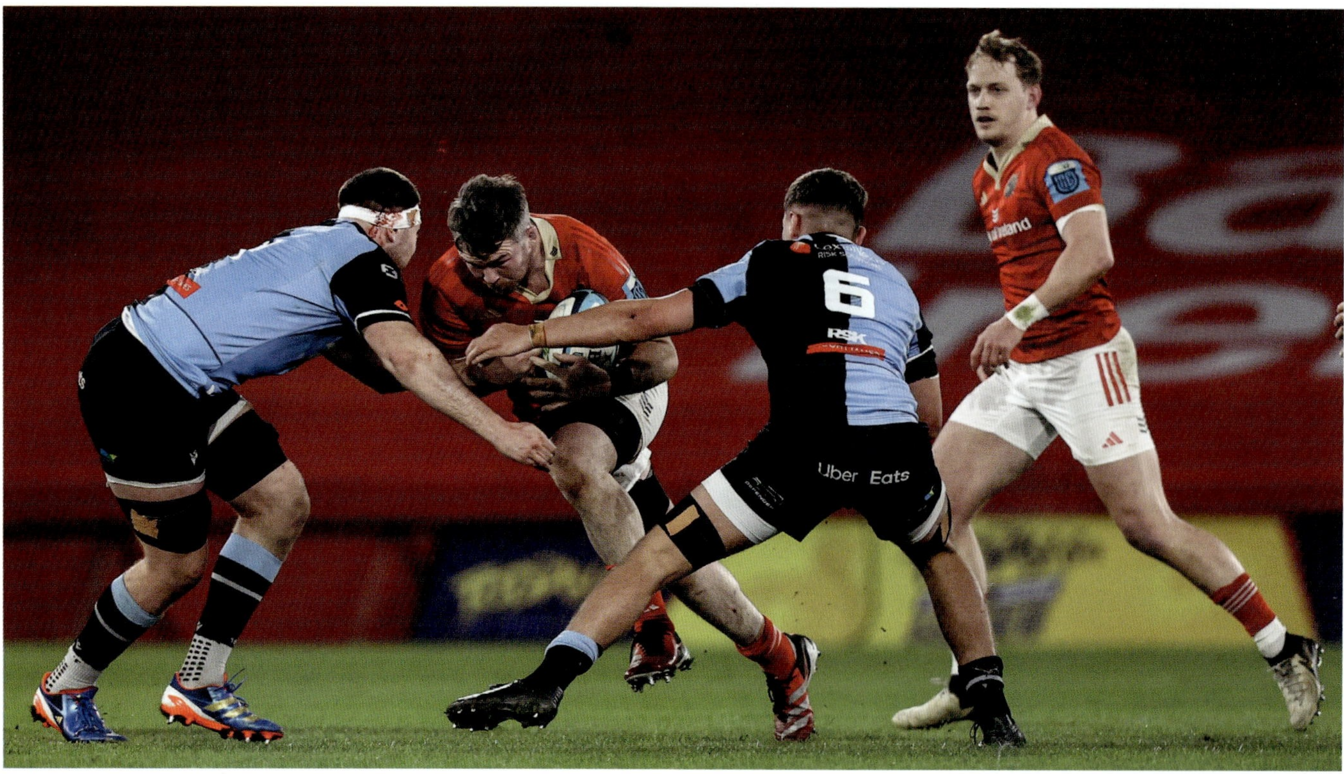

30 March 2024

Above: Peter O'Mahony comes up against Ben Donnell and Alex Mann of Cardiff in Munster's 20-15 home win.

20 April 2024

Opposite top: Shane Daly is tackled, with Antoine Frisch and John Hodnett in support, in Munster's 27-22 victory over hosts Bulls in Loftus Versfeld Stadium in South Africa.

11 May 2024

Opposite bottom: Calvin Nash scores an outstanding try against Connacht, Munster's second of seven. Captained by Tadhg Beirne, Munster win 47-12. Player of the match was Alex Nankivell.

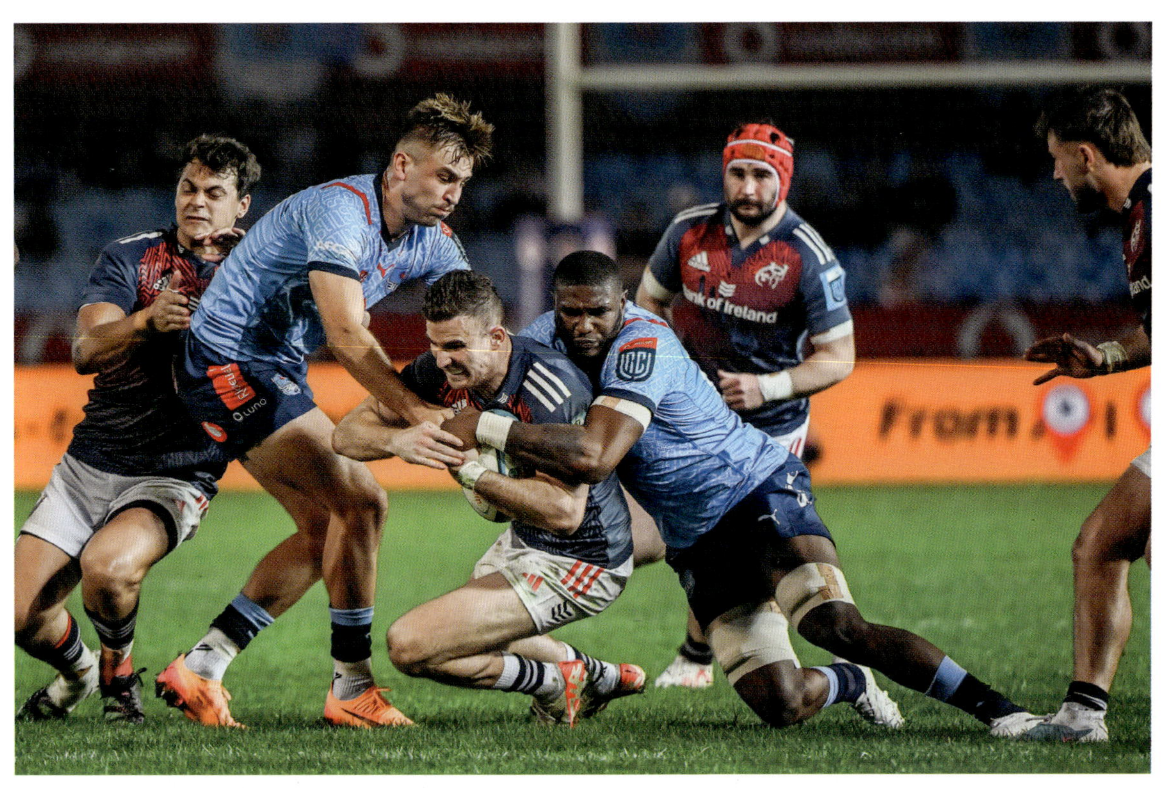

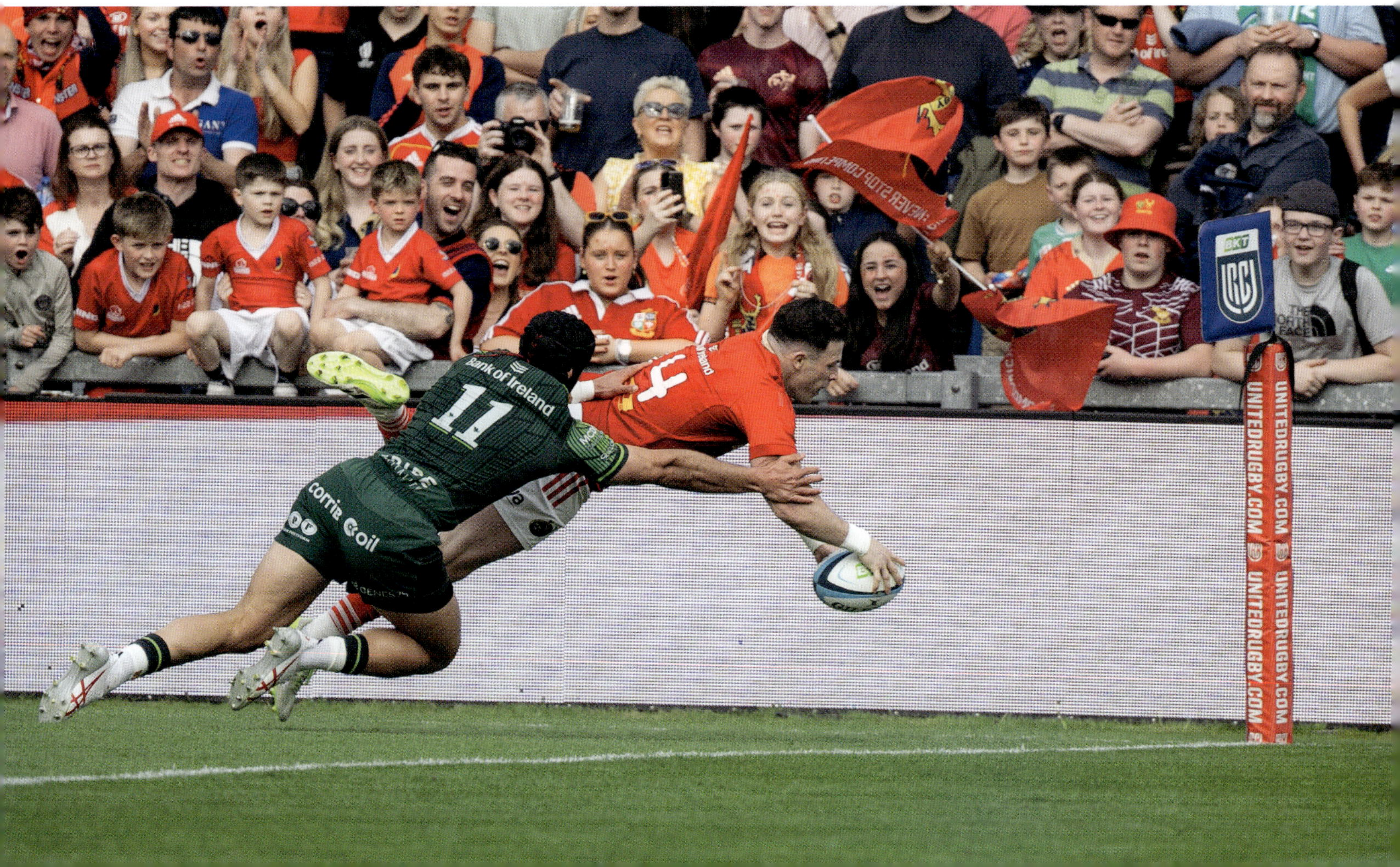

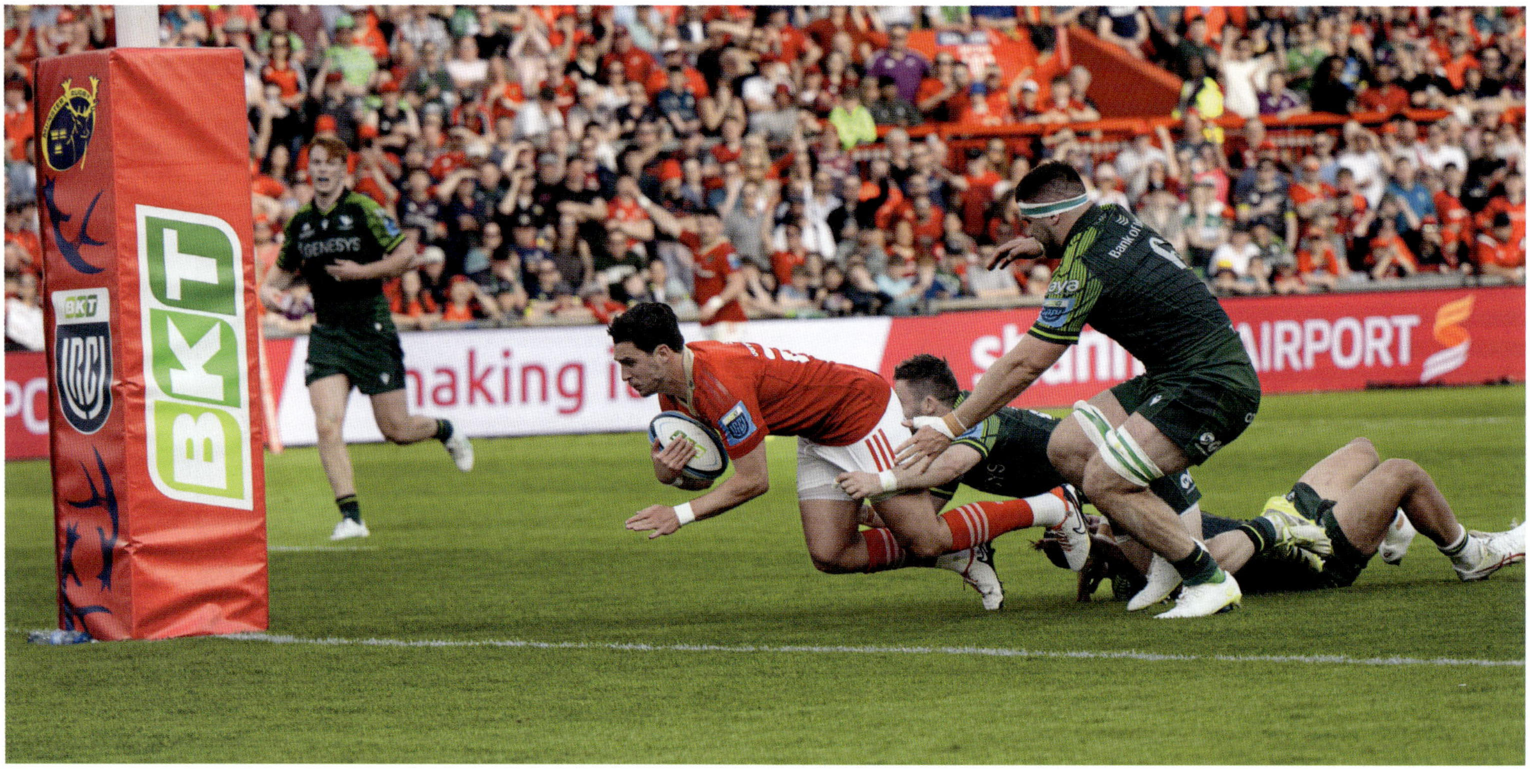
BKT
GENESYS
aking i
AIRPORT

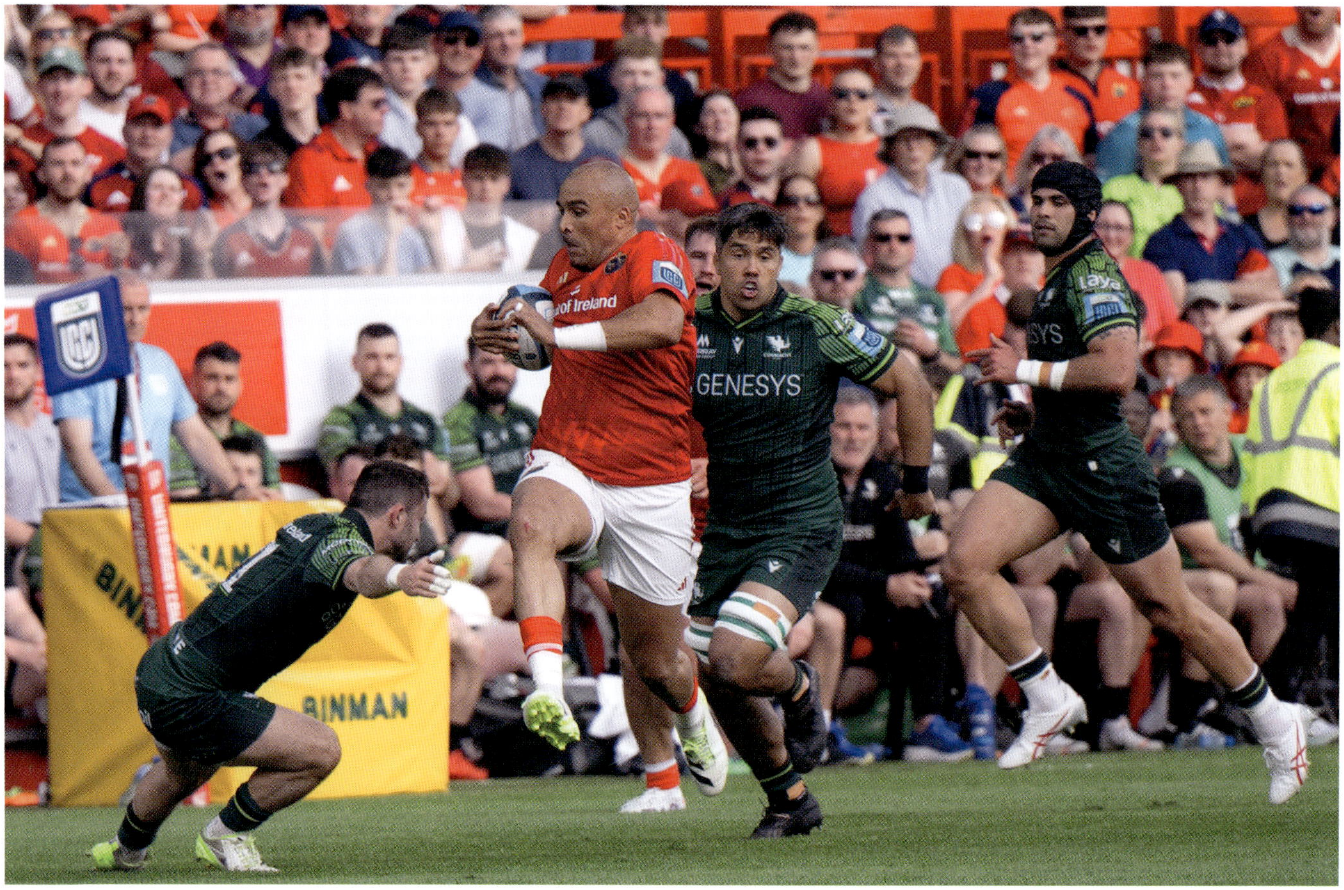
of Ireland
GENESYS
BINMAN

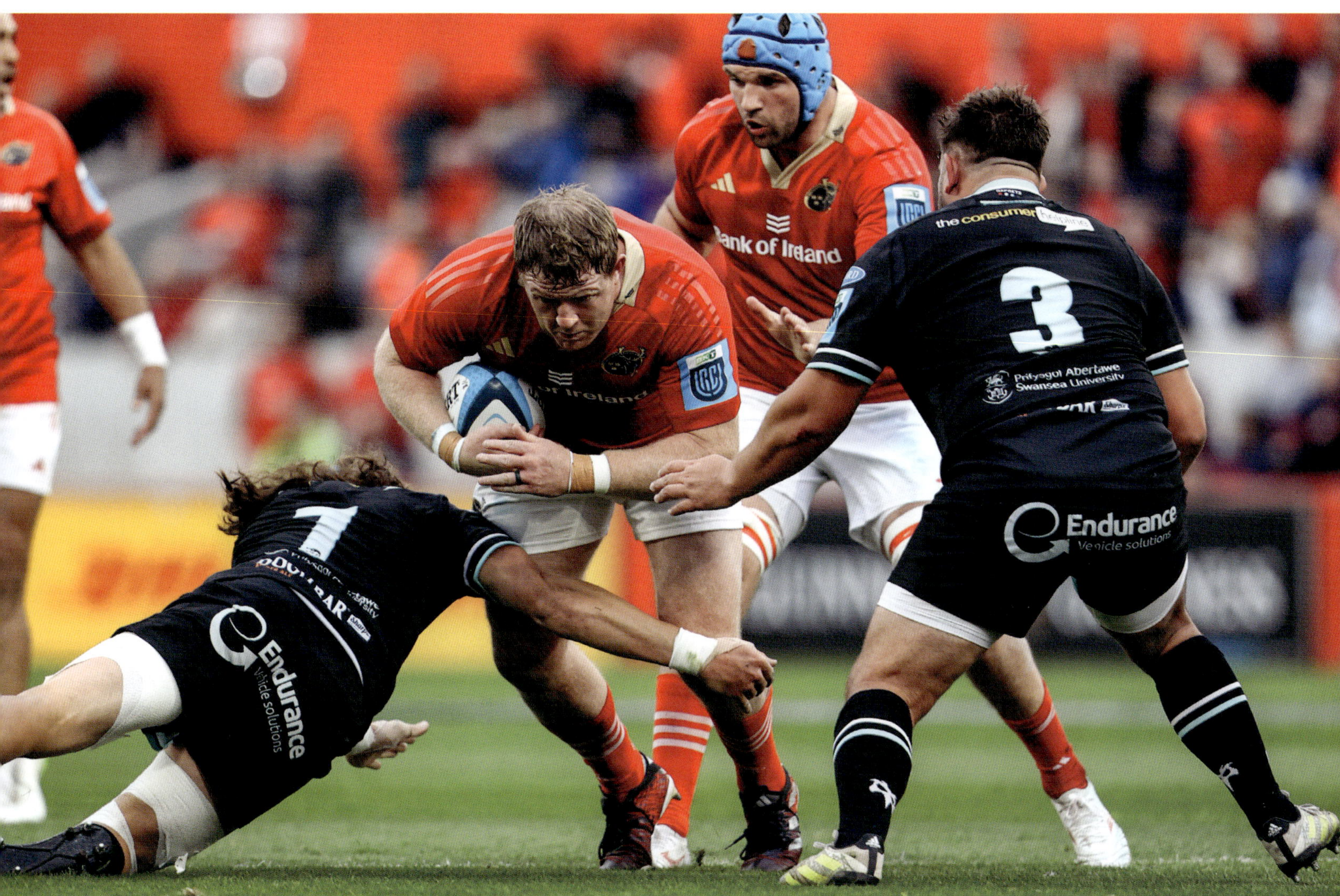

11 May 2024

Opposite top: Joey Carbery about to score against Connacht.

Opposite bottom: Simon Zebo makes a strong break.

7 June 2024

Above: Stephen Archer is tackled by Justin Tipuric and Tom Botha of
Ospreys in Munster's 23–7 URC quarter-final victory.

2024-2025

The season saw huge change, with retirements of Munster stalwarts Conor Murray and Rory Scannell (from the province), and Stephen Archer, Dave Kilcoyne and Peter O'Mahony (from rugby). Also leaving the province were Joey Carbery, RG Snyman, Antoine Frisch, Keynan Knox and Neil Cronin. Graham Rowntree departed in October 2024. Munster played a friendly on 2 November 2024 against an All Blacks XV coached by Clayton McMillan, later appointed Munster head coach for 2025–2026. The New Zealand side won 38-24 in an entertaining match in front of a packed house.

URC

In the opening match against Connacht at Thomond Park on 21 September 2024, ten tries were shared in a free-flowing match with both defences exposed at times. Munster won 35-33. Away to Zebre on 28 September, a sloppy display from the visitors saw Zebre beat them for the first time in 21 attempts, by 42-33. On 5 October in Virgin Media Park, Munster defeated Ospreys 23-0. In a match played in terrible conditions, Peter O'Mahony, Mike Haley and Oli Jager went off injured.

On 12 October at Croke Park, Leinster scored three tries by the fifteenth minute, which virtually killed off the game, and they won 26-12. Two games in South Africa followed: Stormers beat Munster 34-19 in Cape Town on 19 October. The Munster line-out saw only a 57 per cent success rate and the scrum was repeatedly overpowered. On 26 October, Sharks, fielding almost a dozen Springboks, overcame the visitors 41-24 in Durban. Calvin Nash showed international class for Munster. Emirates Lions were the next opponents, at Thomond Park on 30 November, and Munster had an invaluable 17-10 win in a tough encounter. Munster travelled to Kingspan Stadium on 20 December. An outstanding display by Tom Farrell, who scored a hat-trick of tries, helped Munster beat Ulster 22-19 in a match that could have gone either way. Leinster came to Thomond Park on 27 December, and an injury-hit Munster, missing twenty squad members, fell 28-7.

An outstanding first-half performance from Munster saw them defeat Dragons at Rodney Parade 38-19 on 25 January 2025. Scarlets were next to Thomond Park on 15 February, where Munster won 29-8, their tenth win in a row against Welsh opposition. Munster then lost to Edinburgh by 34-28 at Virgin Media Park on 28 February. In Scotstoun on 21 March, Munster narrowly lost, 28-25, to Glasgow Warriors.

In McHale Park in Castlebar, Munster played Connacht in front of a record crowd of 27,580 on 29 March. Jack Crowley and Craig Casey oozed class and controlled the game, Munster winning by 30-24.

Vodacom Bulls got the better of Munster by 16-13 points at Thomond Park on 19 April, the province's first defeat to a South African team at Thomond Park. Massive line-out issues and confusion by the officials cost Munster dearly. At Cardiff Arms Park on 25 April, Munster lost 26-21. On 9 May, Munster beat visitors Ulster, 38-20, in what was Peter O'Mahony, Stephen Archer and Conor Murray's last match in Thomond Park.

The shoot-out between Munster and Benetton took place in Cork on 16 May, the prize a guaranteed European Champions Cup spot for the victor next season. Munster trailed 14-10 at the interval, but upped their intensity in the second half. Man of the match Casey took over kicking duties when Crowley went off injured. It was another emotional night as O'Mahony, Murray and Archer bade farewell to the Virgin Media Park in front of an enthusiastic crowd. Munster won 30-21. Munster faced Sharks in the quarter-finals on 31 May in Durban. Murray slotted a long-range penalty in the 77th minute to level the sides. After twenty minutes' extra time without a score, the game went to a penalty shoot-out, which Munster lost agonisingly by one score.

INVESTEC CHAMPIONS CUP

On 7 December 2024, Thomond Park witnessed an outstanding team performance, spearheaded by Peter O'Mahony, with tries from player of the match Thaakir Abrahams, Shane Daly, Alex Nankivell, Tom Farrell and Gavin Coombes. Jack Crowley converted four of the five in the 33-7 win against Stade Français. Next, Munster played away against Castres Olympique on 13 December. An error-strewn game saw Munster concede seventeen penalties. Six players went off injured: Dian Bleuler, Dave Kilcoyne, Diarmuid Barron, O'Mahony, Abrahams and Craig Casey, who was also ruled out of the Six Nations. Munster lost 16-14.

On 11 January 2025, in Thomond Park, Saracens led 6-3 at half-time, but a rampant five-minute spell in the second half saw tries from Bleuler and John Hodnett. Crowley converted both for Munster to win 17-12. Away to Northampton Saints on 18 January, a brace of tries each from Calvin Nash and Diarmuid Kilgallen, with Crowley converting three and adding two penalties, was not enough: Saints won 34-32. Away to Ronan O'Gara's La Rochelle on 5 April for the round of 16, in front of 3,000 travelling Munster supporters, Munster had one of their greatest away European victories. Captain Tadhg Beirne was immense. Try-scorers were Casey, Coombes and Andrew Smith. Crowley converted two and added a penalty, but it took his sublime 40-metre drop goal in the 68th minute to ensure victory, 25-24.

On 12 April, Munster faced Bordeaux Bègles at Stade Chaban-Delmas for the quarter-final. Travelling two weeks in a row took its toll. With a misfiring line-out, Munster bowed out 47-29.

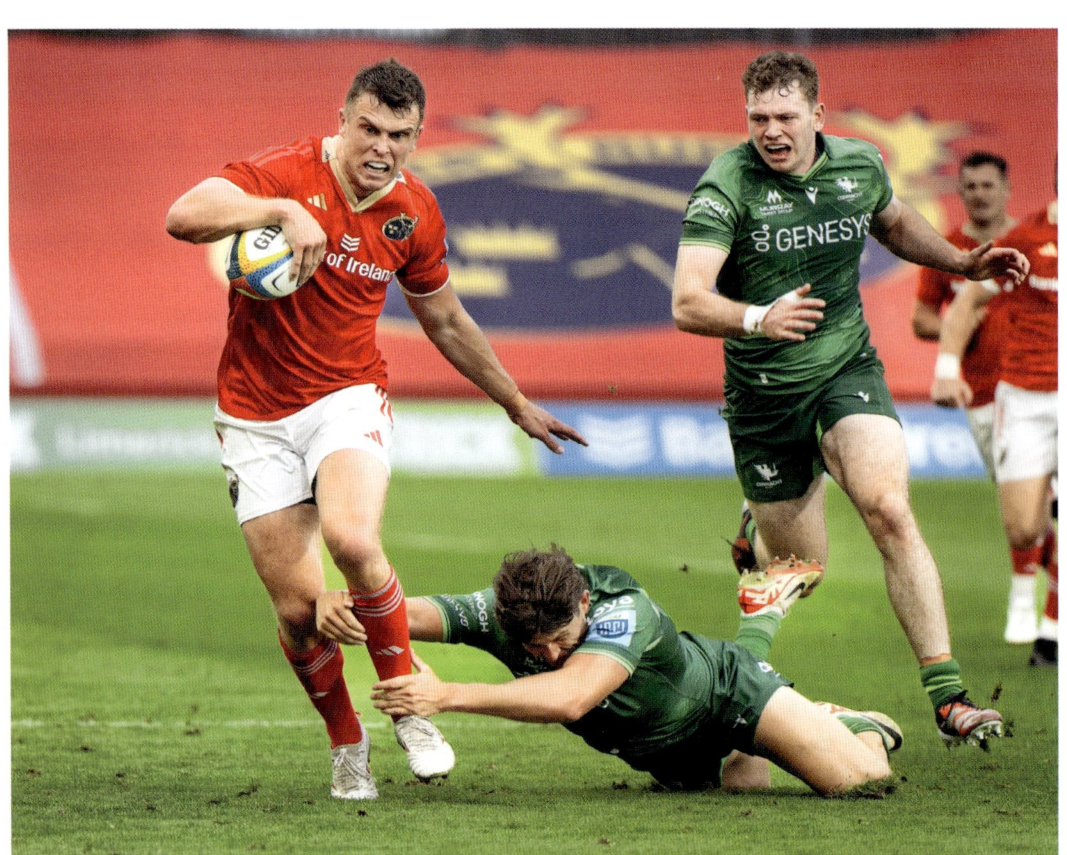

21 September 2024

Left: Tom Farrell slips a Connacht tackle at Thomond Park in Munster's 35–33 win.

19 Ocotber 2024

Below: Eoghan Clarke scores against Stormers in the DHL Stadium in Cape Town.

30 November 2024

Opposite top: Jack O'Donoghue in his man-of-the-match performance in Munster's 17–10 victory against Emirates Lions.

Opposite bottom: Alex Nankivell passes to Thaakir Abrahams, who scored his first try for the province in this game against Emirates Lions.

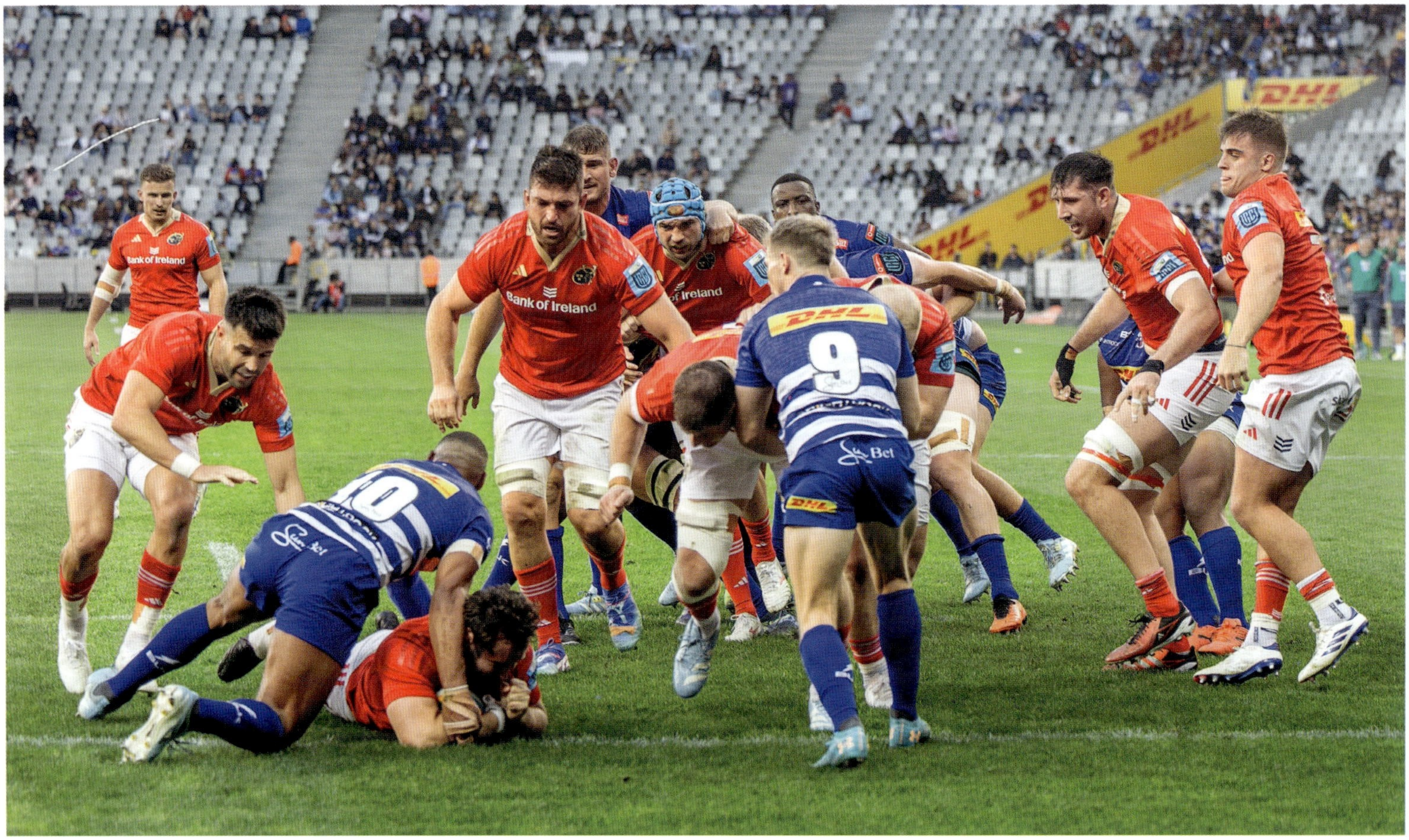

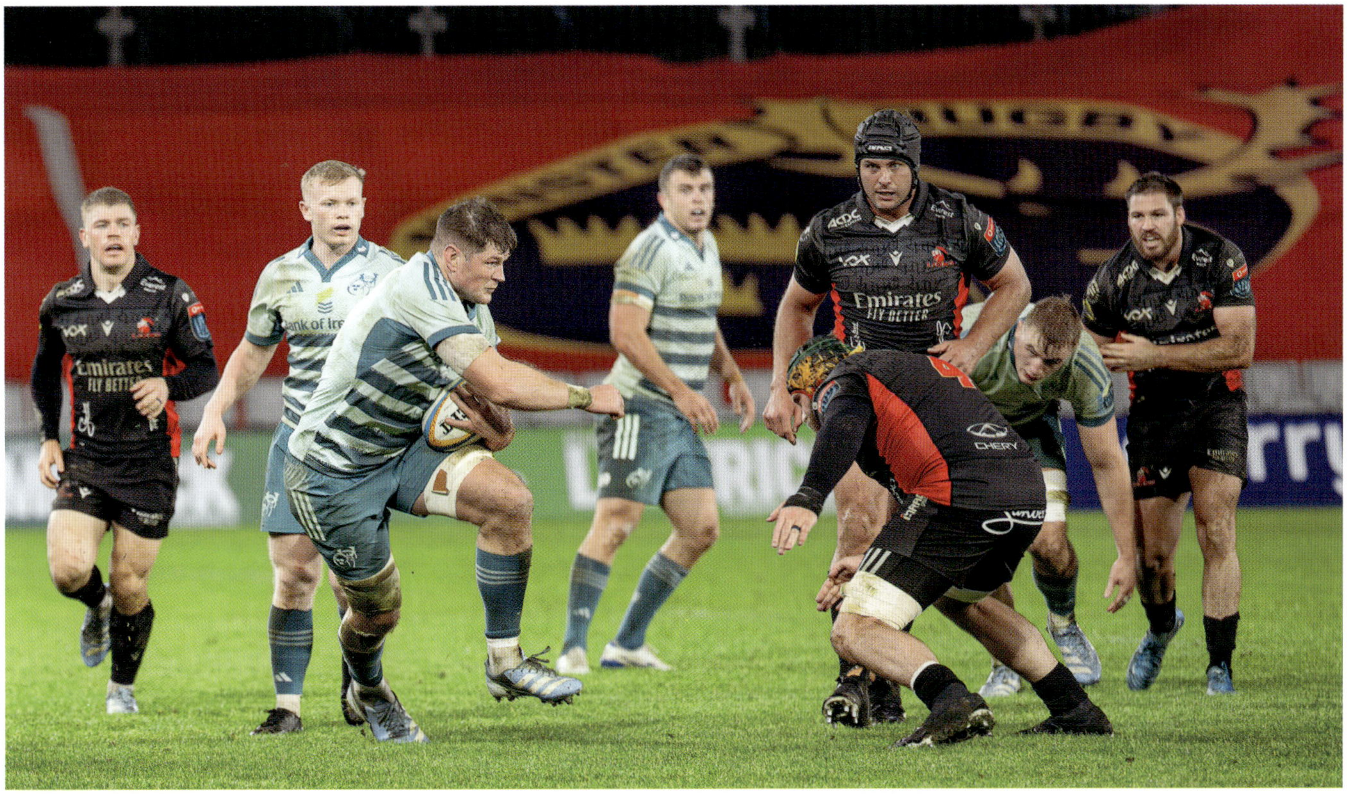

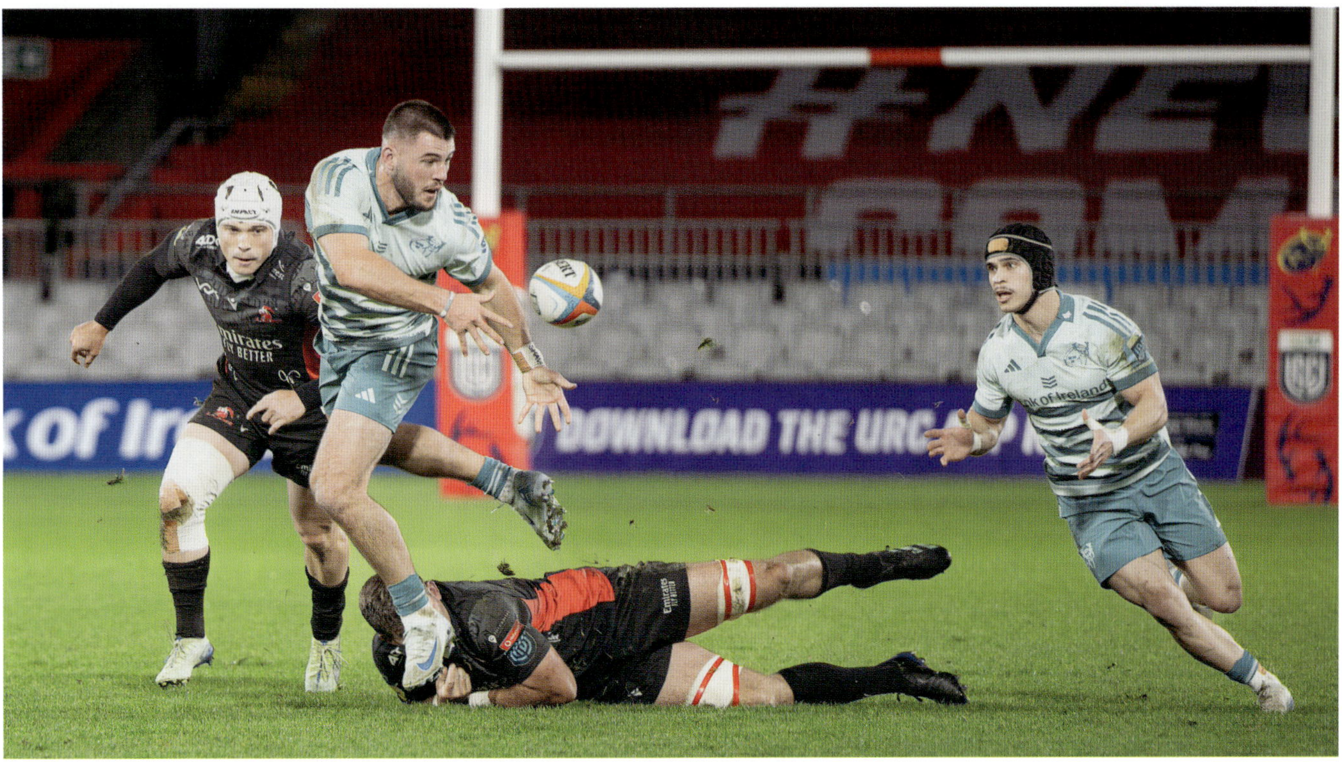

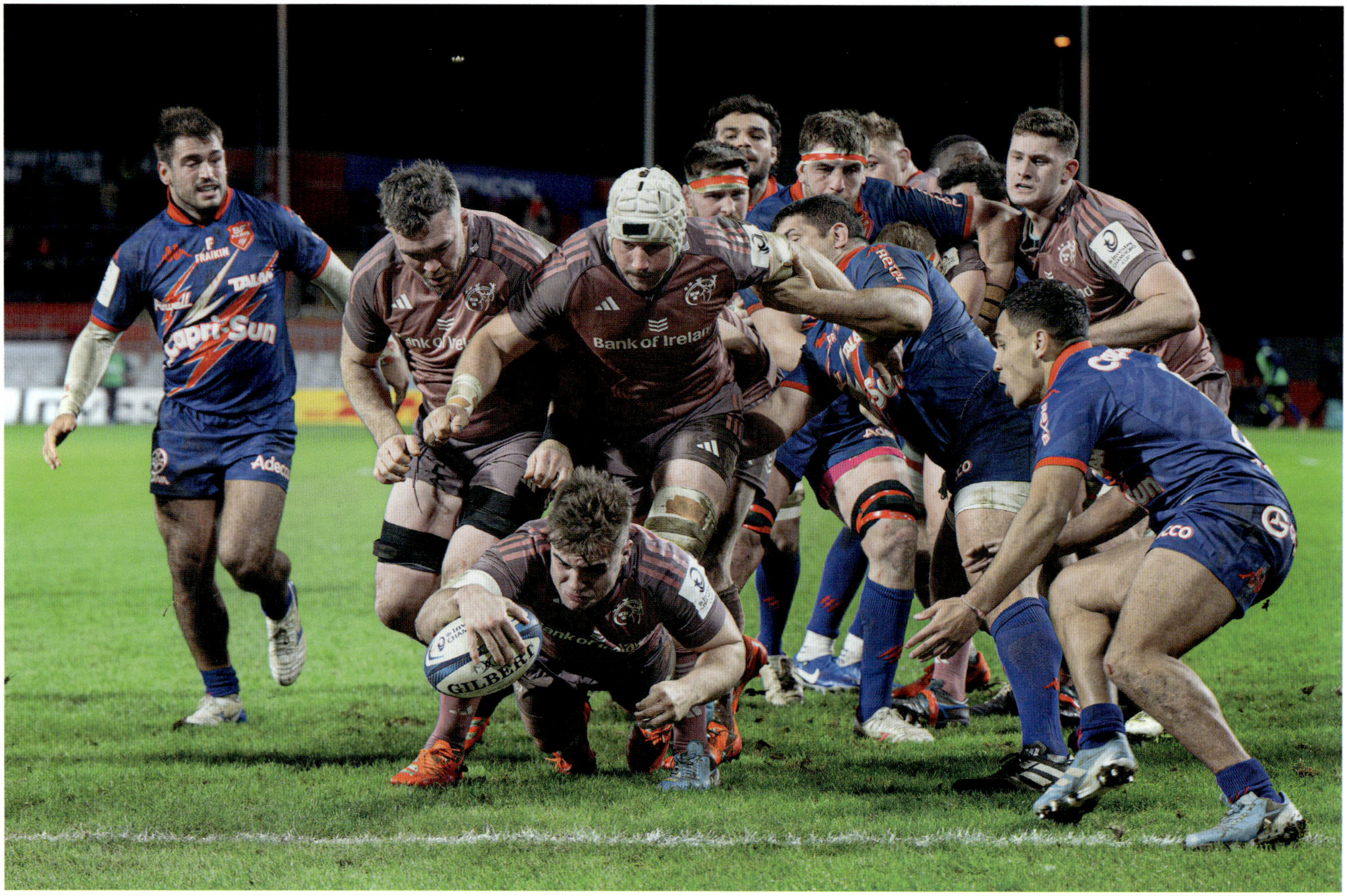

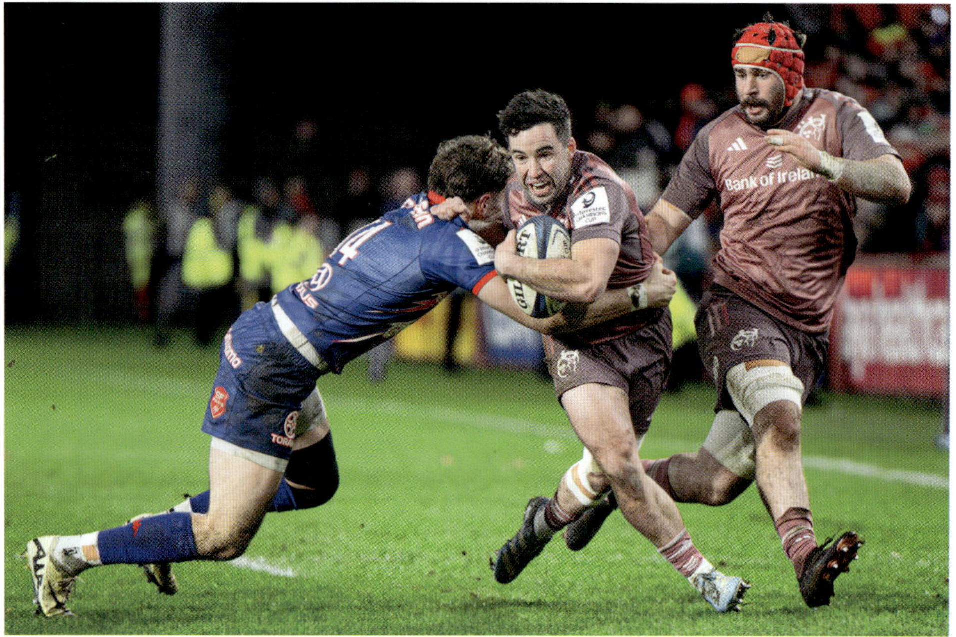

Above: Alex Kendellen scores an outstanding try against Stade Français. Munster dug deep, to the delight of the home crowd, to win 33-7.

Left: Paddy Patterson on the attack, ably backed up by John Hodnett.

Opposite top: John Hodnett on his way to score against Saracens in Munster's 17-12 win.

Opposite bottom: Man of the match Tadhg Beirne showing his pace and speed against Sarries, with Diarmuid Barron in support.

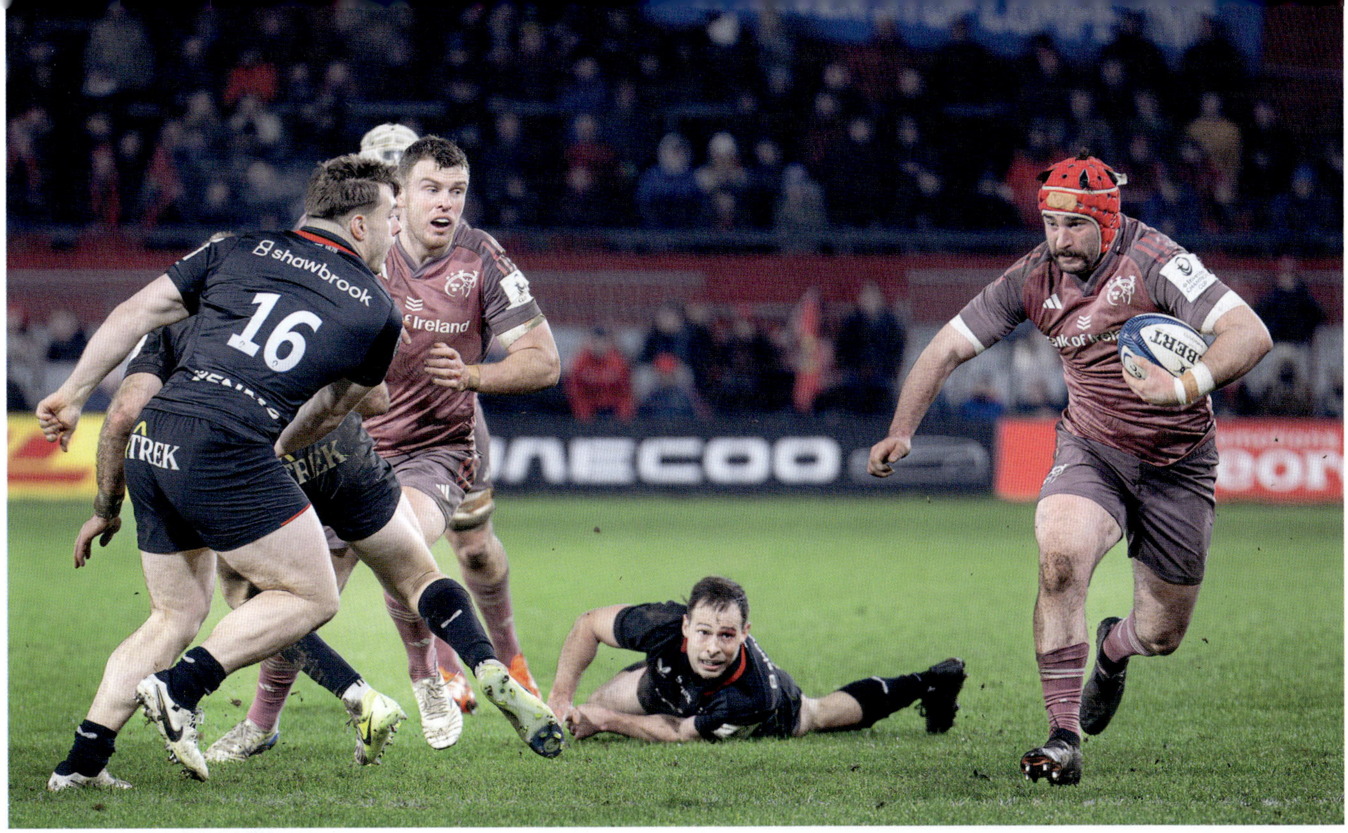
shawbrook
16
TREK
Ireland

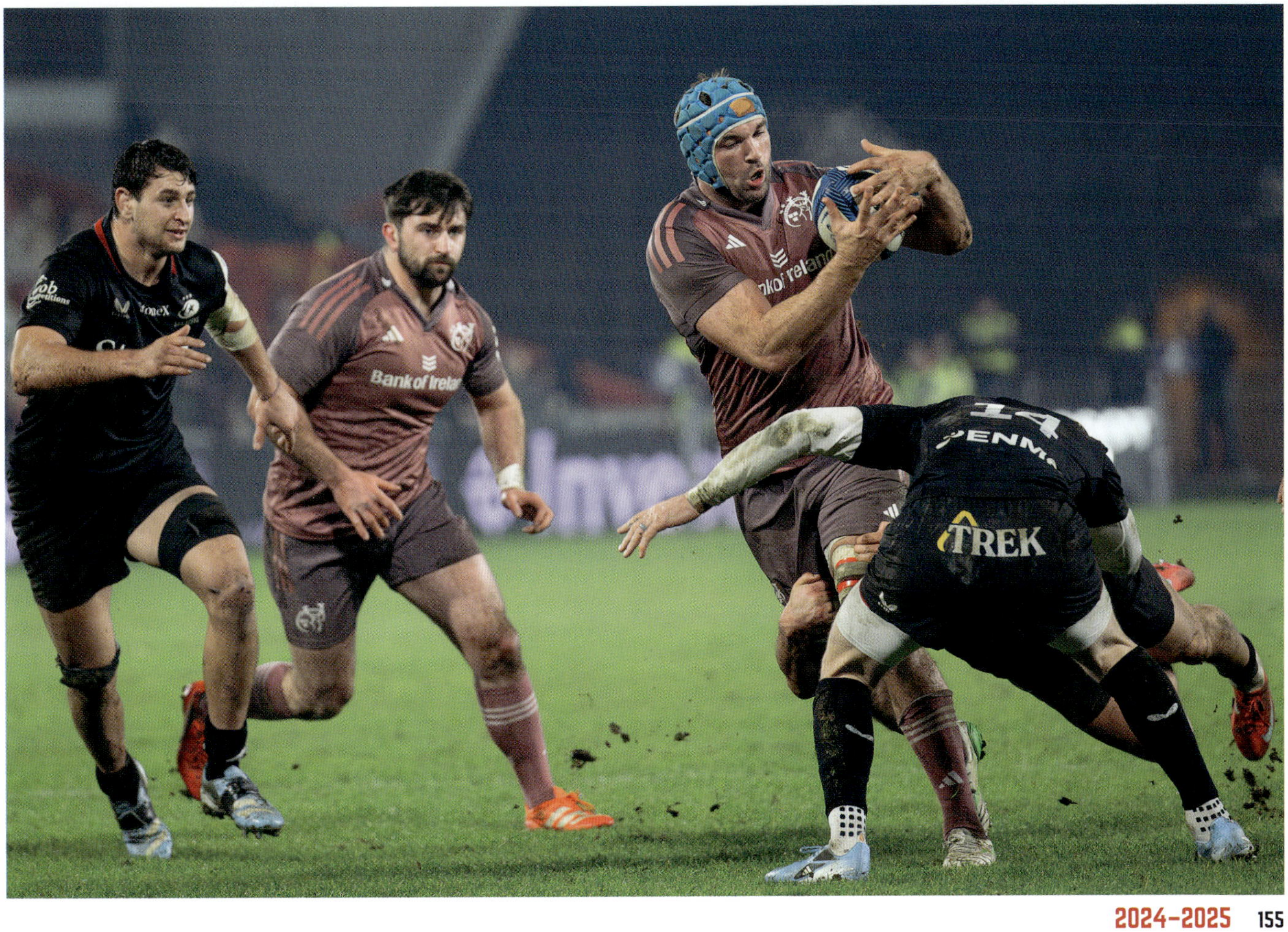
Bank of Ireland
TREK

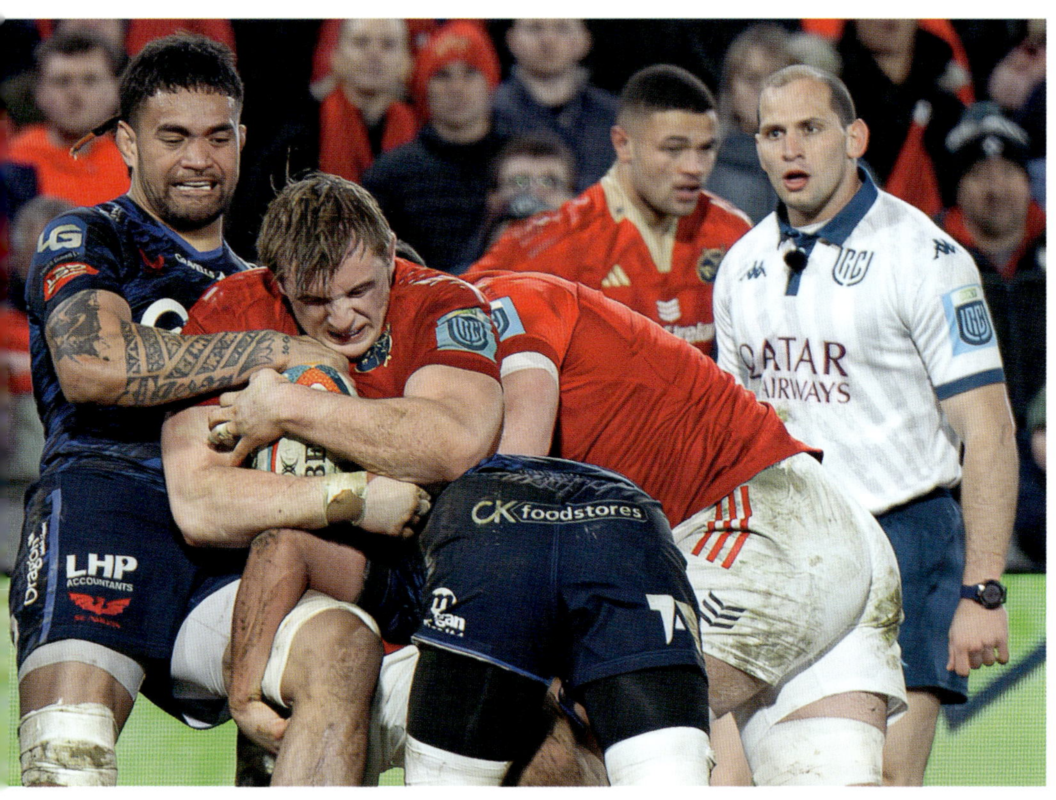

15 February 2025

Left: Gavin Coombes proves hard to stop, despite the Scarlets' best efforts. Munster go on to win 29-8.

Below: Tom Ahern makes one of his typical wing breaks.

5 April 2025

Opposite top left: Munster's Craig Casey celebrates scoring a try in the barnstorming 25-24 win against La Rochelle.

19 April 2025

Opposite top right: Tom Ahern wins the aerial battle against the Bulls in Thomond Park.

Opposite bottom: No way through for Diarmuid Kilgallen as he is tackled by David Kriel of the Bulls. The visitors win 16-13.

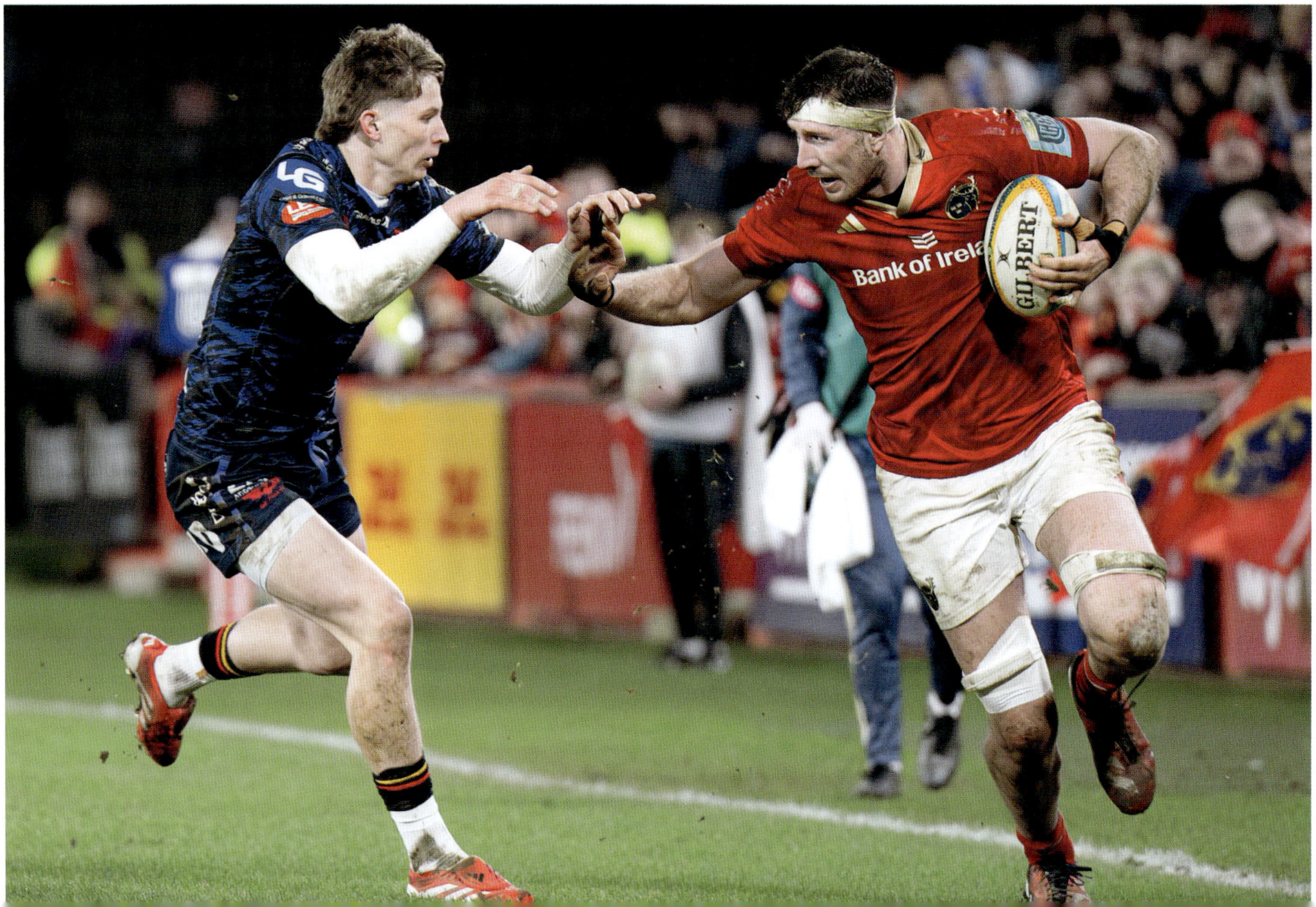

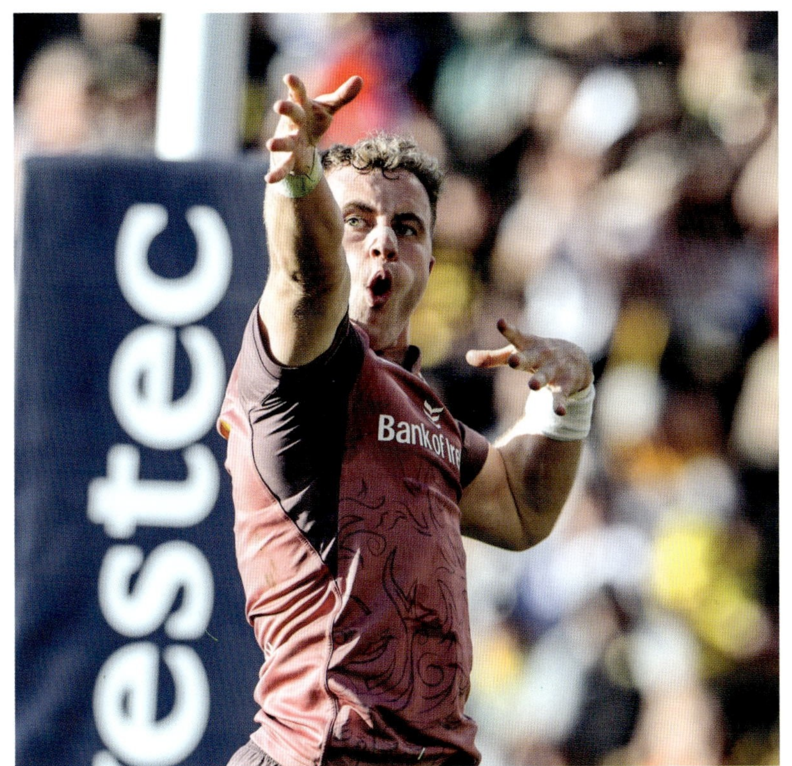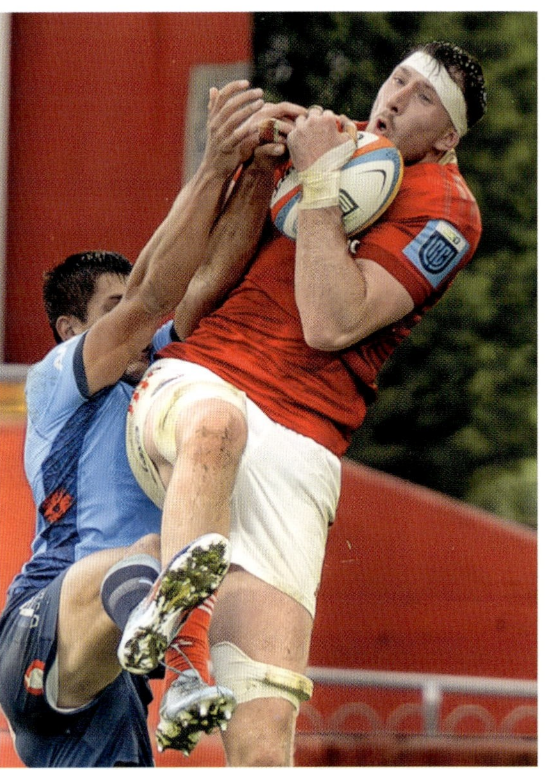

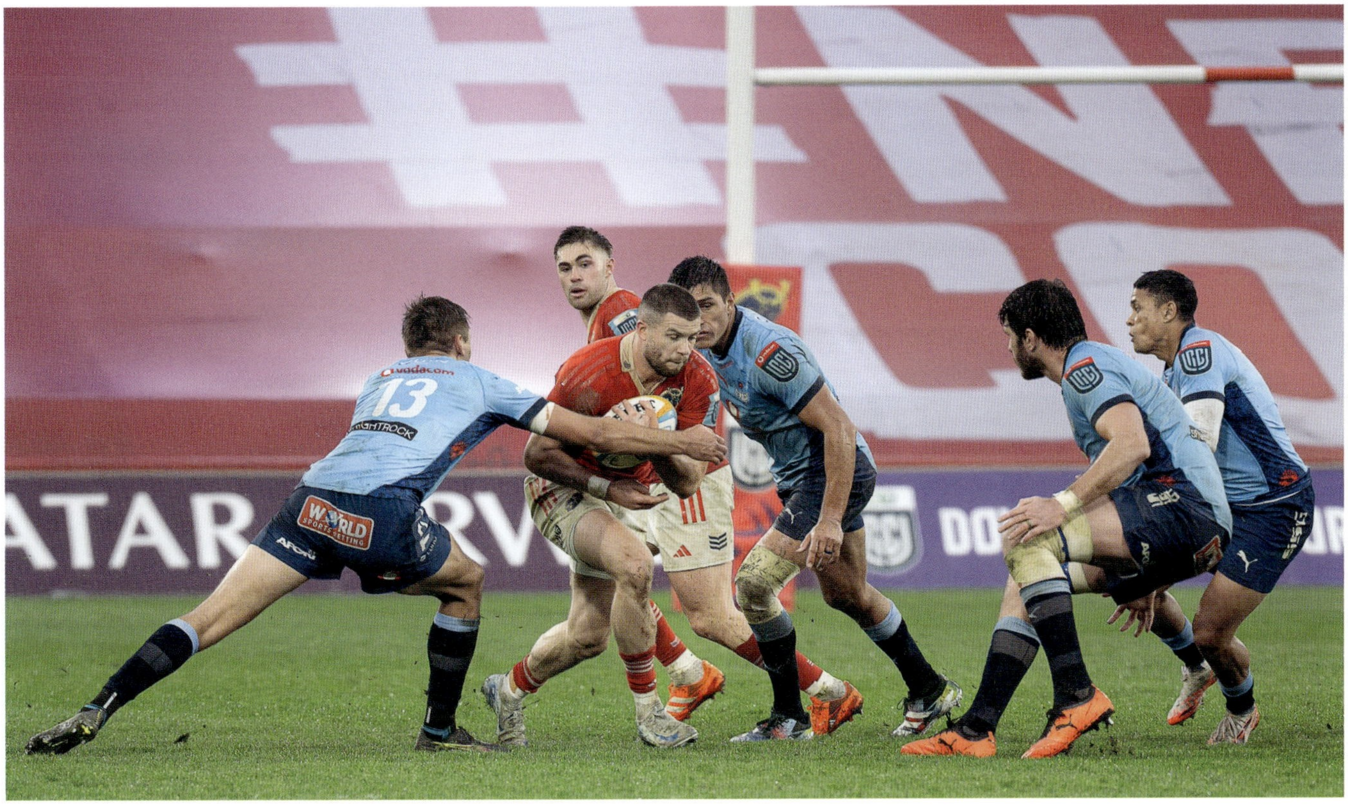

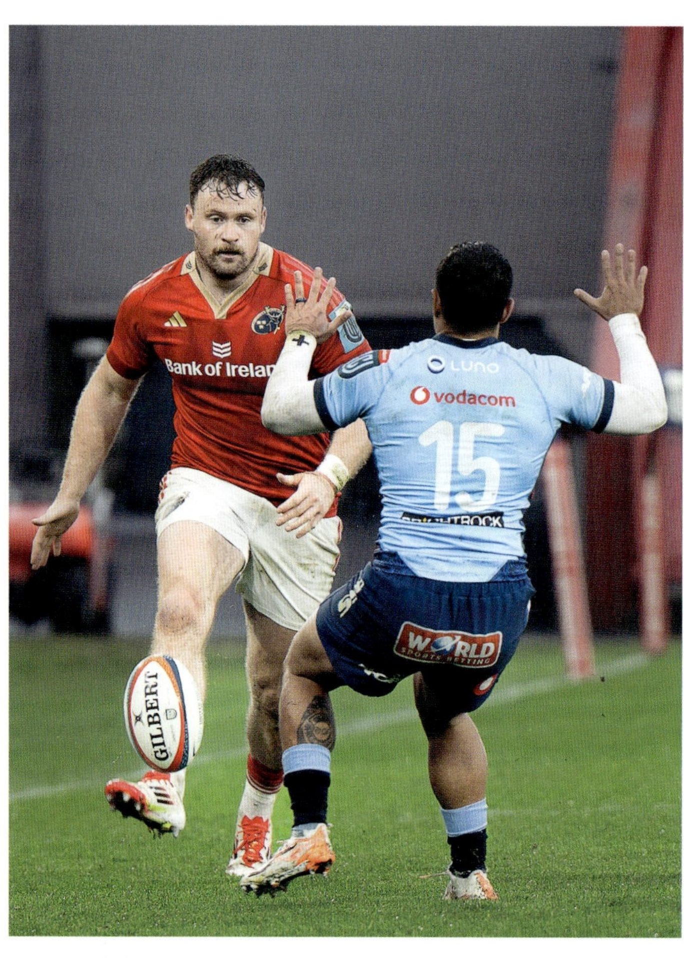

19 April 2025

Left: Sean O'Brien chips past Bulls full-back Devon Williams. Sadly, this match would be the first defeat at home for Munster by a South African team.

9 May 2025

Bottom: Diarmuid Kilgallen breaks Iain Henderson's tackle attempt, with Calvin Nash in support, in Munster's 38–20 win over Ulster at Thomond Park.

16 May 2025

Opposite top: Peter O'Mahony in action against Benetton at Virgin Media Park. With (l–r) Jack Crowley and Gavin Coombes in support. O'Mahony's outstanding break led to a try scored by Lee Barron. Munster won 30–21.

31 May 2025

Opposite bottom: The Sharks' Eben Etzebeth and Munster's Craig Casey duke it out in the URC quarter-final in Durban, which ended in heartbreak for Munster.

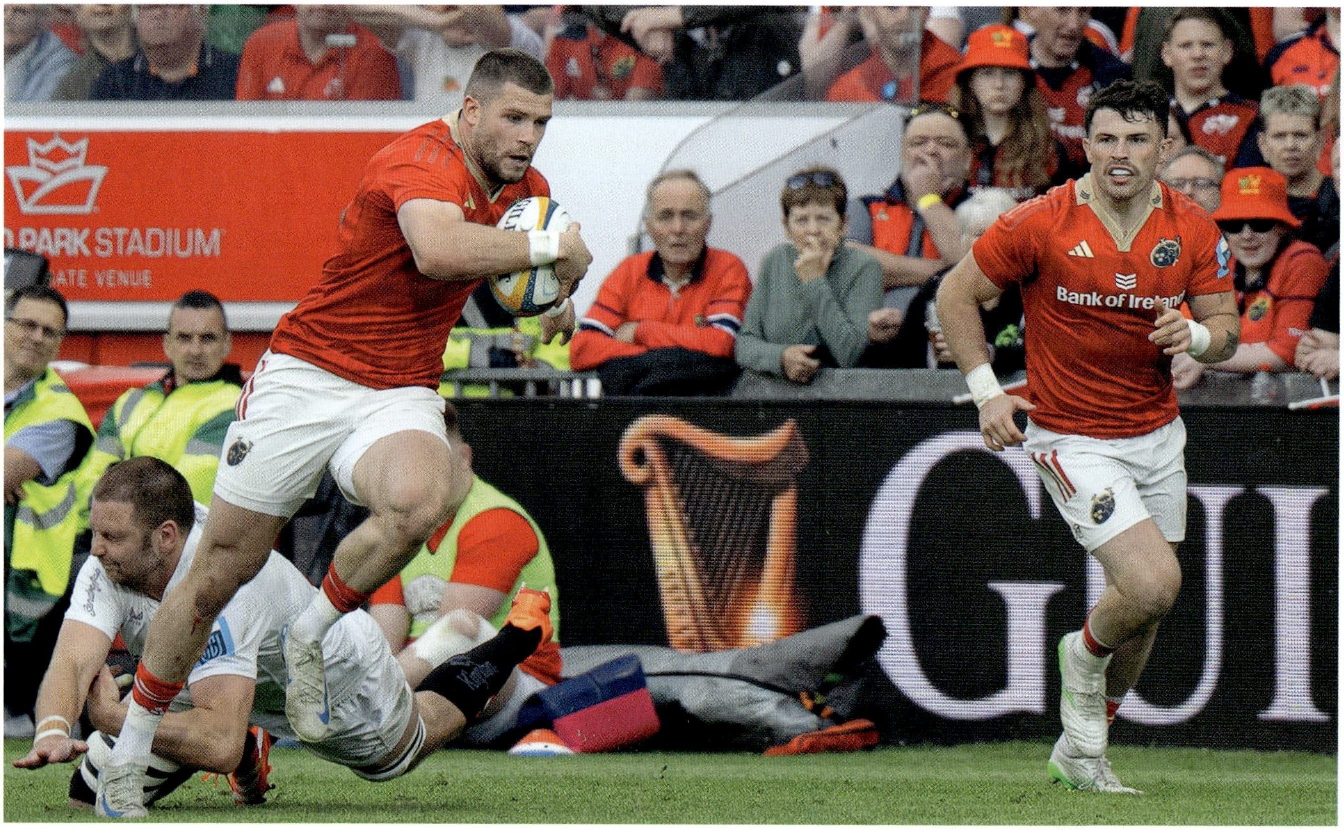

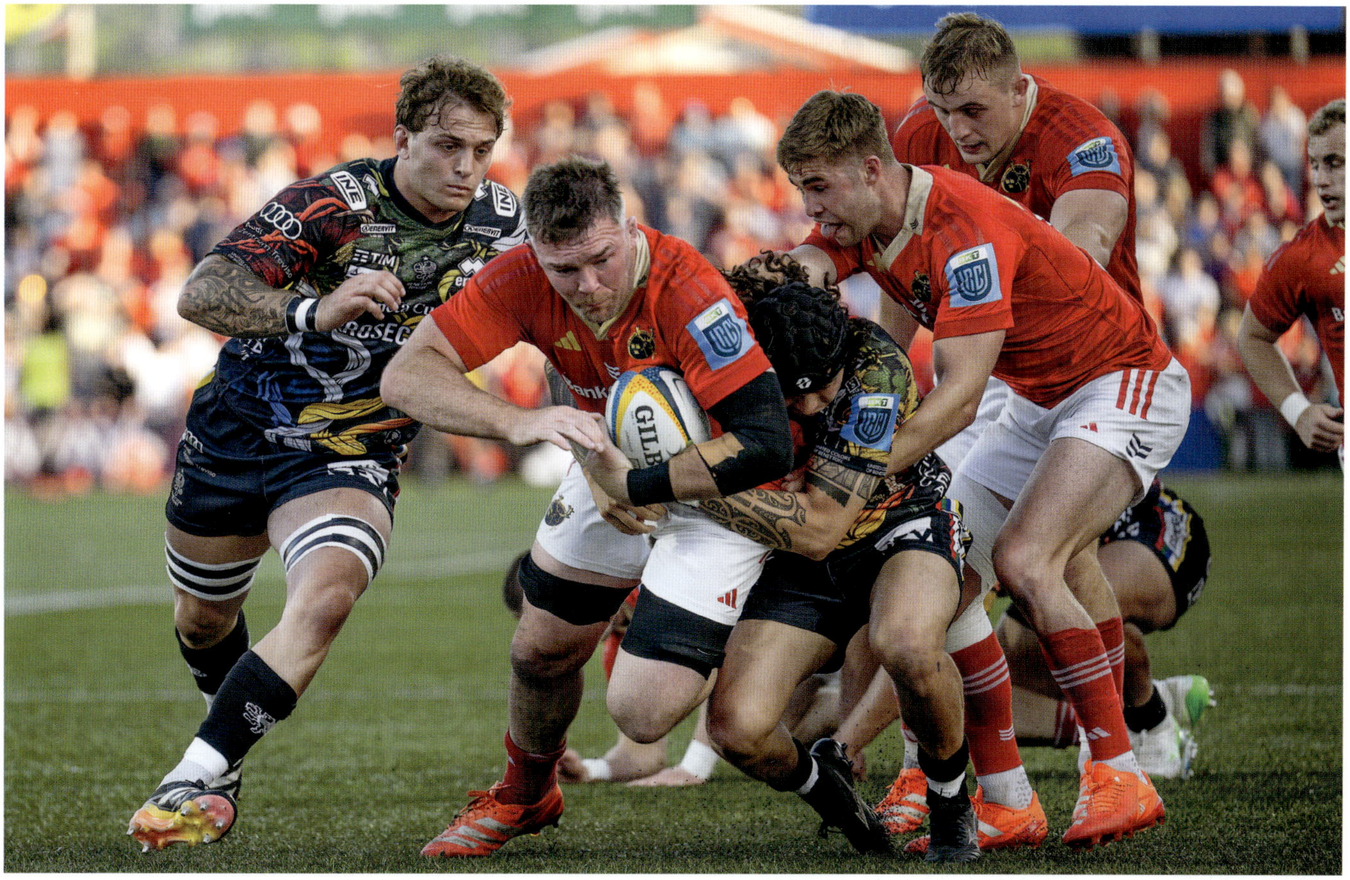
GILB

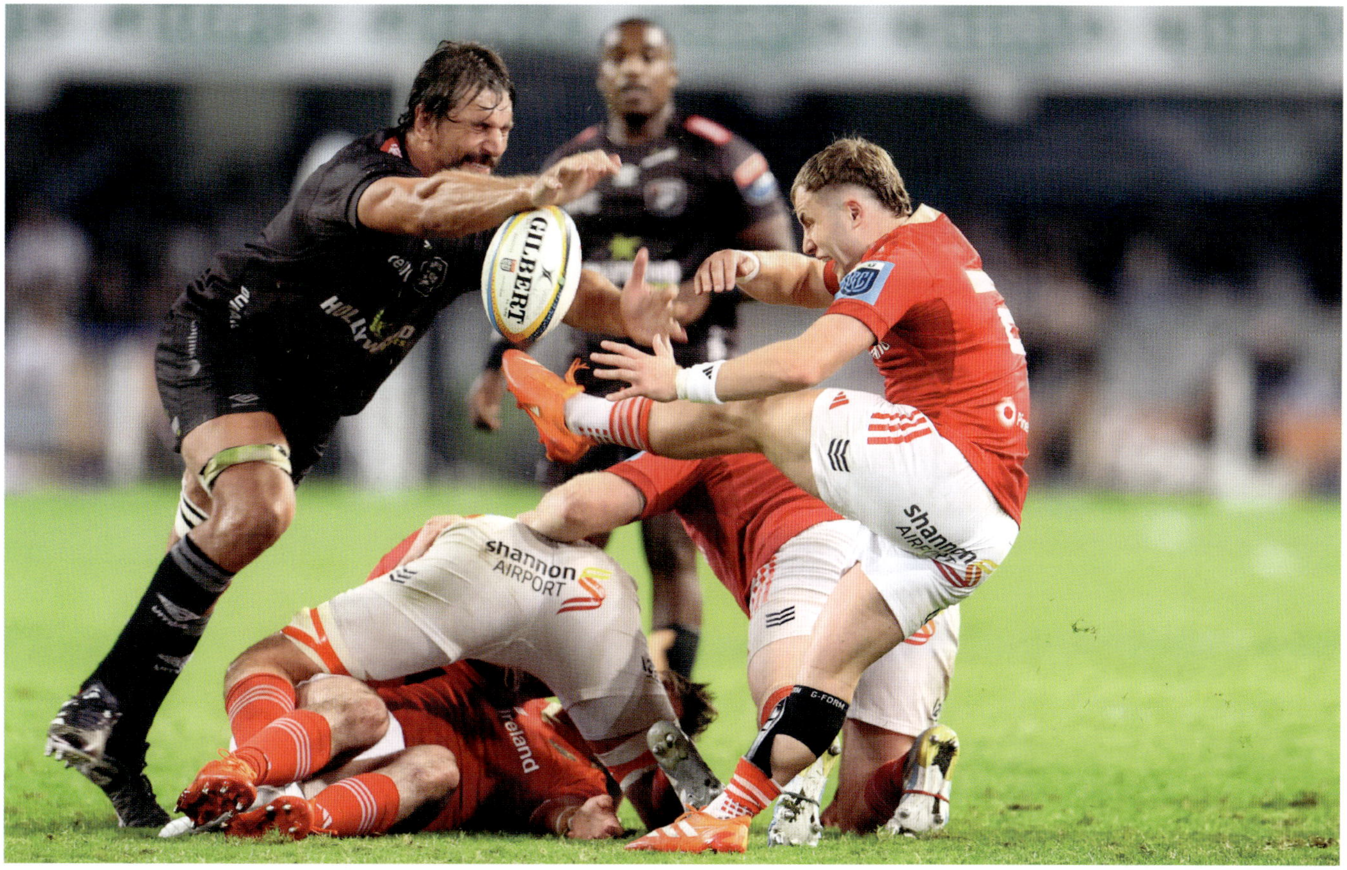
GILBERT
shannon
AIRPORT

To the memory of Paul Darbyshire, Garrett Fitzgerald, Pat Geraghty, Anthony Foley, Jerry Holland, Greig Oliver and Michelle Payne

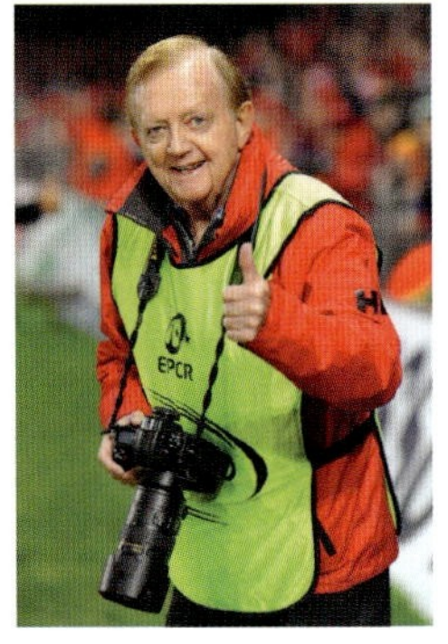

IVAN O'RIORDAN has been photographing Munster Rugby since 2008, when he stepped back from a career in management and marketing. A proud member of Munster Rugby Supporters Club, he has followed his team around Ireland and to France, the UK and South Africa. Through his photographs, he has raised over €17,000 for Munster charities.

Ivan is a keen amateur photographer and a member of Limerick Camera Club. His photos have appeared in *N-Photo* and *Digital Camera* magazines, in the *Limerick Leader* and *Limerick Post*. A former President of Limerick Lions Club, he holds an MBA from Trinity College Dublin. He lives in Limerick with his wife, Annemarie.

First published 2025 by The O'Brien Press Ltd,
12 Terenure Road East, Rathgar, Dublin 6, D06 HD27, Ireland.
Tel: +353 1 4923333; e-mail: books@obrien.ie; Website: obrien.ie
The O'Brien Press is a member of Publishing Ireland.

ISBN: 978-1-78849-593-6

8 7 6 5 4 3 2 1
29 28 27 26 25

Printed by EDELVIVES, Spain.

The paper in this book is produced using pulp from managed forests.

To the best of our knowledge, this book complies in full with the requirements of the General Product Safety Regulation (GPSR). For further information and help with any safety queries, please contact us at productsafety@obrien.ie.

Published in

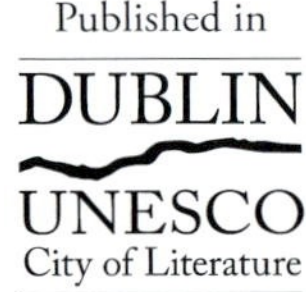

DUBLIN
UNESCO
City of Literature

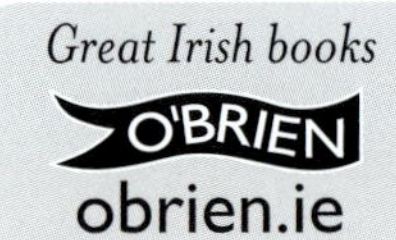